Delirious Consumption

Border Hispanisms
Jon Beasley-Murray, Alberto Moreiras,
and Gareth Williams, series editors

SERGIO
DELGADO
MOYA

Delirious Consumption

Aesthetics and Consumer Capitalism in Mexico and Brazil

University of Texas Press
Austin

Printed in the United States of America
First edition, 2017

♾ The paper used in this book meets the minimum requirements of ANSI/NISO Z39.48-1992 (R1997) (Permanence of Paper).

Library of Congress Cataloging-in-Publication Data

Names: Delgado Moya, Sergio, author.
Title: Delirious consumption : aesthetics and consumer capitalism in Mexico and Brazil / Sergio Delgado Moya.
Other titles: Border Hispanisms.
Description: First edition. | Austin : University of Texas Press, 2017. | Series: Border Hispanisms | Includes bibliographical references and index.
Identifiers: LCCN 2017010837| ISBN 978-1-4773-1434-0 (cloth : alk. paper) | ISBN 978-1-4773-1435-7 (pbk. : alk. paper) | ISBN 978-1-4773-1436-4 (library e-book) | ISBN 978-1-4773-1437-1 (nonlibrary e-book)
Subjects: LCSH: Avant-garde (Aesthetics)—Mexico—20th century. | Avant-garde (Aesthetics)—Brazil—20th century. | Art and literature—Mexico—20th century. | Art and literature—Brazil—20th century. | Consumption (Economics) in art.
Classification: LCC BH301.A94 D45 2017 | DDC 111/.850972—dc23
LC record available at https://lccn.loc.gov/2017010837

doi:10.7560/314340

Para Estela y para Ángel, para Angélica,
René y Wendy, por tanto amor

SOMEONE DIVIDES MANKIND INTO BUYERS AND SELLERS AND FORGETS THAT BUYERS ARE SELLERS TOO. IF I REMIND HIM OF THIS IS HIS GRAMMAR CHANGED??

LUDWIG WITTGENSTEIN, *CULTURE AND VALUE*

Contents

Acknowledgments ix

Introduction: Aesthetics in the Age of Consumer Culture—Some Terms 1

ONE Attention and Distraction: The Billboard as Mural Form 44

TWO Fascination; or, Enlightenment in the Age of Neon Light 83

THREE Poetry, Replication, Late Capitalism: Octavio Paz as Concrete Poet 119

FOUR Lygia Clark, at Home with Objects 153

Conclusion 193

Notes 195

Bibliography 251

Index 269

Acknowledgments

Friends, family, and colleagues have given me invaluable support in the years leading up to the publication of this book. Luis Moreno-Caballud, Jeffrey Lawrence, Dylon Robbins, Rachel Galvin, Dora Zhang, Laura Gandolfi, Enea Zaramella, Ana Sabau, and Ingrid Robyn all provided brilliant and joyous dialogue during the early stages of this project. Special gratitude goes to Cecilia Palmeiro and to Luis Othoniel Rosa (a.k.a. roommate), hermanxs del alma. Your friendship, knowledge, and extraordinary kindness sustain me, lovingly. Kassaundra Gutierrez-Thompson and Héctor Corral have been unwavering in their love and support at every stage of this project. In São Paulo, Grazielly Basso, caçula, made me feel right at home. Patricia Méndez Obregón opened the doors of her home to me during my first research trip to Mexico City, and I remain grateful for my time there and for our friendship. From afar, my siblings René and Wendy have been models of hard work and diligence. Their light and love are shining examples that have nourished me in ways I can't thank them enough for. At home in Tijuana, on the phone everywhere, in person in most every city where I've set up shop over the past decade, my sister Angélica, mi héroa, has been there for me: lovingly, joyfully, generously. For three decades plus of encouragement, for a lifetime of sisterly love, for the model of humanity she has always been to me, I thank her.

José Rabasa and Jesús R. Velasco patiently guided me to the scholarly path, as did, most especially, Natalia Brizuela. Her brightness, her guiding wisdom, her unwavering kindness, and the friendship that unites us have shaped the better part of my academic career. Gracias, de corazón. Jussara Menezes Quadros, Antonio Monegal, Marina Brownlee, Ángel Loureiro, Claudio Brodsky, Rubén Gallo, Michael Wood, Devin Fore, Germán Labrador, Pedro Meira-Monteiro, Bruno Carvalho, and Rachel Price all contributed generously to the foundations on which this work is based. At Princeton and again at Harvard, Karen Jackson-Weaver has been tremendous in her support and untiring in her advocacy. Gabriela Nouzeilles's attentive, incisive commentary and her extraordinary ability to bring forth the most critical aspects of intellectual work got this project off the ground. Much of what is good about this book owes its merit to her exceptional prowess as a scholar and mentor. Gracias mil, siempre.

The earliest phase of this investigation began in Mexico City at the Sala de Arte Público Siqueiros, where Mónica Montes Flores received me warmly, guided me expertly, and gave the archival part of this research the best start it could have had. Conversations with Itala Schmelz and Irene Herner made that early research all the more productive. Generous support from the David Rockefeller Center for Latin American Studies at Harvard and the William F. Milton Fund made possible long research stays in Brazil and in Mexico. In São Paulo, a research grant generously provided by the Instituto de Estudos Brasileiros at the Universidade de São Paulo made possible a term as visiting researcher at USP.

At Harvard, Diana Sorensen's brilliant vision for an expanded place for the arts in higher education provided the framework for exhibitions and courses related to this research. Marcela Ramos, my brilliant collaborator, was instrumental in organizing cultural programming born of this book. In Brazil, the staff of the DRCLAS Regional Office in São Paulo shared their office with me and made my research there all the more productive. Special thanks to Jason Dyett for the expert local guidance and the friendliest of company. Elisabete Marin Ribas at IEB USP guided me to the most relevant sources for my work. Augusto de Campos has been tremendously generous since my years in graduate school. This book began as an effort to better understand his extraordinary legacy as poet, and I thank him for the support he's given me in every facet of this project. In Rio de Janeiro, the staff at O Mundo de Lygia Clark, Sonia Menezes and Fabiane Moraes in particular, provided generous support and expert advice. In Los Angeles, the staff at the Getty Research Institute acceded gracefully to my insistence on seeing all their holdings on Siqueiros. While working at the Getty Institute, my dearest friend Paul Luelmo welcomed me at his home in LA.

Opportunities to share findings related to this book have been fundamental. Thank you, Amanda Anderson, David Russell, Patrick Mullen, Adela Pineda, Florencia Garramuño, Gonzalo Aguilar, Timothy Hampton, Miryam Sas, Natalia Brizuela, Sebastián Vidal, Gerardo Pulido, Ana Paula Cavalcanti Simioni, Robert Kaufman, Graciela Montaldo, Jesús R. Velasco, Carlos J. Alonso, Estelle Tarica, Candace Slater, Ignacio Navarrete, Dora Zhang, Judith Butler, Ivonne del Valle, Daylet Dominguez, Alexandra Saum-Pascual, Francine Masiello, and Frances Hagopian, for the invigorating dialogue. Doris Sommer, Esther Gabara, David Russell, Luis Othoniel Rosa, and Ingrid Robyn read drafts, and I'm grateful for their generosity and constructive criticism. Natalie Ramirez, my research assistant, copyedited the manuscript and provided invaluable support.

At Harvard, the sources of brilliance and inspiration have been plenty. Students with whom I've had the pleasure of discussing materials herein analyzed, students of my seminar on consumer culture in Latin America, have improved this book tremendously with pointed questions and animated discussion. I'm grateful for the warmth and the encouragement of my colleagues Virginie Green, Diana Sorensen, Mary Gaylord, Doris Sommer, Sylvaine Guyot, Joe Blackmore, Luis Girón-Negrón, Francesco Ersparmer, Kathy Richman, Jeffrey Schnapp, Tom Conley, Alice Jardine, Tom Cummins, Christie McDonald, Clémence Jouët-Pastré, María Luisa Parra, and the late Nicolau Sevcenko. A graduate seminar and undergraduate class cotaught with José Rabasa provided a year's worth of opportunities to improve the corpus of this book. Most especially, I'm thankful for the friendship, the collaboration, and the brilliant conversation of Brad Epps during my first years at Harvard. Mariano Siskind, Lorgia García Peña, and Paola Ibarra have been tireless in their support and encouragement. I treasure their friendship and thank them for the time they spend making the place we work for a better place to live in.

This book would not have materialized without the support of the editors of the Border Hispanisms series at University of Texas Press: Jon Beasley-Murray, Alberto Moreiras, and Gareth Williams. They, along with the anonymous readers working for the press, provided extremely valuable feedback. I'm indebted to their remarkable intellectual generosity. The attentiveness and support of Kerry Webb and Angelica Lopez-Torres at University of Texas Press were fundamental in the last stages of publication of this book. Thank you. Sandra Spicher's copyediting and sharp eye for crucial revisions made this book so much better. Every error and mistake herein contained is no one's fault but my own.

With force and fearlessness, with dignity and a great deal of courage, my parents Estela y Ángel blazed forth the life that I live today. My deepest gratitude and greatest admiration are and always will be with them.

Lastly and firstly, I thank the Thiagos: Alberto Thiago and Thiago Alberto. Thank you for making a life with me, for grounding me and soaring with me, for all the fun and all the love, for the time we share and for the place we call home.

Delirious Consumption

Introduction

Aesthetics in the Age of Consumer Culture—Some Terms

"A power in the realm of *consciousness*"

How does something become "a power in the realm of *consciousness*"?[1] The expression comes from the early Marx of the *Economic and Philosophic Manuscripts of 1844*, and it refers to the rise of labor and production as fundamental principles for the organization of societies. In reference to the "enlightened political economy, which has discovered—within private property—*the subjective essence* of wealth," Marx states: "this *external, mindless objectivity* of wealth is done away with, with private property being incorporated in man himself and with man himself being recognised as its essence."[2] Two realities hitherto thought apart—the life of the mind and the world of objects—are shown by Marx in mutual determination. The world looks different when property and the productive forces that make the accumulation of property possible are seen in this light. Consciousness itself transforms through this insight—it moves into the world, becoming part of what it thought to be objectively distanced from it. And Marx insists on this point, hammering it home with references to the selfhood, the personhood, the subjective essence of private property.

A tradition of puritanism in scholarly discourse; a distinctly intellectualist contempt for the material conditions of everyday life; a woefully reductive understanding of the passive and the introjective (of the part that consumes, of the "accursed share" in Georges Bataille's formulation) as against the active and the productive: these things keep us from regarding consumption the way Marx regarded production. Not that anyone doubts the powers wielded by consumption. Marx himself points to an incipient theory of a "movement" between production and consumption.[3] We know consumer culture has colonized our bodies, our beliefs, and the institutions that shape our bodies and beliefs into more or less cohesive social structures. We know it has fundamentally changed the way the world appears to us.[4] We need a set of terms that can help us interpret a regime of the sensible shaped first by mass culture, then by the culture industry, and more recently by the transnational network of practices and institutions that sustain and are themselves sustained by consumption and the logic of the market.

This book sets out to elucidate a few such terms, terms aligned directly with questions of aesthetics—questions of how we perceive the world, how we place ourselves in it, and how we make sense of it by means of perception and emotion. The book works through four categories that capture important features of the social constitution of subjects and the mode of presentation of objects in the age of consumer culture: distraction, fascination, replication, and homemaking. These categories, I argue, condense—in ambiguous terms—both a sequence of regressions and a set of actual potentials. These categories recur with some frequency in critical writings on consumer culture and the culture industry. They encapsulate a set of structural mechanisms as well as a range of possible actions within the order determined by consumer capitalism. Crucially, they also shape works of literature and works of art produced in the three decades after World War II, a period when consumer society as we now know it expands and consolidates.

It is against the background of the large social, political, and economic changes that take place in this period—rapid urban growth; shifts in development policy[5]; explosive growth in communications and media; repurposing of war industries and technologies for civilian markets; import-substitution industrialization; expansion of domestic markets and the ascendance of the consumer as paradigm of social organization—it is against this background that a new wave of modernist aesthetics began to take shape in major cities throughout the Americas. This book brings together Mexican and Brazilian artists and writers active during this period, pairing each of the book's key terms with readings of works by David Alfaro Siqueiros, the Brazilian concrete poets, Octavio Paz, and Lygia Clark.[6] The artists and poets whose work is studied in this book embrace and resist the spirit of development and progress that defines the consumer moment in the history of late capitalism. I see in the work of these writers a provocative positioning vis-à-vis urban commodity capitalism, a constitutive ambiguity in the sense that José Bleger conferred to the term—ambiguity not as confusion but as "primitive undifferentiation"; not as indecision but as a stage prior to contradiction.[7] I want to emphasize what I take to be an ambivalent position in the work of these artists, an assured but adjustable stance against commodification, alienation, and the politics of domination and inequality that define consumer capitalism.[8] These poets and artists appeal to uselessness, nonutility, and noncommunication—the markers of difference of the aesthetic—while drawing on terms proper to a world of consumption and consumer culture.

The artworks and poems studied in this book set a tone for the study of consumption and commodity capitalism. They model an approach keenly attuned to imitation as an incisive, at times subversive response to capitalist modes of signification—what Michael Taussig calls "capitalist mimetics."[9] The reference to delirium in the book's title conveys the sense of derangement, of going out of order, that this book proposes as a contribution to the study of the rationalized processes subtending both production and consumption. Delirium is here understood as a form of daydreaming, as an open-eyed distraction from the waking order of market capitalism, and as an expansion of desire. Delirium, viewed against the background of a capitalist order, should not (at least not necessarily) be understood as an affirmation of, or a blind complicity with, market forces and commodity capitalism. This is how Hélio Oiticica, Lygia Clark's closest collaborator, conceived of his own practice of delirium and daydreaming, his *delirium ambulatorium*, a defiant embrace of both the purposeless errancy of vagabond walking and of the "silly things" peppering the urban landscape.[10]

Among political economists as among cultural critics, consumption can hardly be said to have risen to the level of prominence that labor and production have attained since Marx first placed these terms at the foreground of our conceptual repertoire. This says less about the power consumption exerts on us than it does about our willingness as scholars to come to terms with it, with consumption as power. Consumption *is* power: it is coercion and control, but it is also, sometimes, resistance. At times, inasmuch as it mediates our inner lives and the world that makes us, consumption may serve as a road to freedom; it may even look like a promise of happiness. Like fear and like desire, consumption lurks in the background of our actions and our thoughts, acknowledged with frequency but rarely engaged with the seriousness we adopt when we reflect on the productive forces that cross our lives. This is not to suggest that consumption has been neglected as a subject of study. On the contrary, since Karl Marx's *Manuscripts*, since the publication of Thorstein Veblen's *The Theory of the Leisure Class* in 1899, and in subsequent works by Walter Benjamin, Georges Bataille, Jean Baudrillard, Guy Debord, Michel de Certeau, Néstor García Canclini, George Yúdice, Michael Taussig, Daniel Miller, Juliet Schor, Steven B. Bunker, John Sinclair, Anna Cristina Pertierra, Arlene Dávila, Graciela Montaldo, and others, consumption has been studied as a fundamental aspect of modern culture. A common thread runs through most of these critical works, varied as they are in their disciplinary approaches. To different extents, these works touch on certain, often gendered connotations of consumption (passivity, submission, mindlessness) that tend to keep consumption at some distance from what is considered essential about social structures and structures of thought. This book works through these connotations guided by the four categories I submit as critical for understanding aesthetics in the age of consumer culture: distraction, fascination, replication, and homemaking.

Some Terms for an Aesthetics of Consumer Culture

Consumption functions in much the same way as private property and commodification do. These deeply imbricated threads of the social weave serve a crucial role as instruments of domination and as foils for emancipatory projects defined negatively in contrast to them. Considered jointly with private property and commodification, consumption opens up a series of questions that can and have been formulated in relation to private property and commodification. At what point did the market and consumption become naturalized as points of resistance for cultural practices and critiques of culture defined as contestatory? Under what conditions does consumption become a principal reference of artists, writers, activists, and intellectuals who construct their work from a position of resistance? How does one position oneself against what seems to be the paradigm of our times without acknowledging at least some complicity, at least some embedment? And how does our understanding of aesthetics, both as a discourse directly responsive to developments in the sphere of art and as the broader inquiry into the workings of sense perception, change vis-à-vis the growing importance of consumption and consumer culture?

A deliberate ambiguity characterizes the terms I propose as terms for an aesthetics of consumer culture. Each term can serve and has served to construct conflicting ways of interpreting consumer culture. Distraction is a case in point. Much like Siegfried Kracauer, Walter Benjamin makes an intriguing case for distraction as a form of social behavior opposed to bourgeois contemplation and rife with possibilities for transformation. In a letter dated March 1936, Theodor Adorno quickly rebukes Benjamin: "despite its shock-like seduction I do not find your theory of distraction convincing—if only for the simple reason that in a communist society work will be organized in such a way that people will no longer be so tired and so stultified that they need distraction."[11] Leaving aside for the moment Adorno's stark, perhaps unwarranted vision of work under the communist ideal, the disagreement between Adorno and Benjamin rests less on different interpretations of Marxist doctrine than on a crucial misunderstanding. When Benjamin writes "distraction," Adorno reads "entertainment," and entertainment is not what Benjamin has in mind when he writes about distraction, at least not in the essay on mechanical reproducibility.[12]

Dispersion gets closer to what Benjamin attempts to impress upon the reader when he makes the following distinction: "A person who concentrates before a work of art is absorbed by it; he enters into the work, just as, according to legend, a Chinese painter entered his completed painting while beholding it. By contrast, the distracted masses absorb the work of art into themselves. Their waves lap around it; they encompass it with their tide."[13] The language here is a language of dissolution: an image of liquid masses taking in the work of art, as if by engulfment. The sense of dispersion—dispersion of attention, dispersion of consciousness—implicit in this language is much stronger and much more complicated than the captivation, the holding of attention that entertainment entails. The equivocalness of the terms Benjamin chose is crucial to his account of distraction.

Later in his *Aesthetic Theory*, Adorno would arrive at a vision similar to Benjamin's. Grappling with the place of happiness in the experience of art ("What popular consciousness and a complaisant aesthetics regard as the taking pleasure in art, modeled on real enjoyment, probably does not exist"), fiercely skeptical of the role of joy ("Whoever concretely enjoys artworks is a philistine; he is convicted by expressions like 'a feast for the ears'"), and struggling mightily to account for pleasure in the aesthetic experience ("Yet if the last traces of pleasure were extirpated, the question of what artworks are for would be an embarrassment"), Adorno writes the following of the "traditional attitude to the work of art": "The relation to art was not that of its physical devouring; on the contrary, *the beholder disappeared into the material*."[14] This image of the viewer going into the artwork recurs elsewhere in Adorno's *Aesthetic Theory*, and its meaning remains more or less stable.[15] It captures an experience of art that remains powerfully, shockingly immediate, so much so as to make beholders "lose their footing."[16] But to what effect? What's the significance of the capacity of art to make beholders "lose their footing"? And what do we make of the fact that this and other effects that were traditionally attributed to the arts have been increasingly colonized by the culture industry and the business of consumer culture? What kind of subject is revealed in dispersion, distraction, fascination, replication, and homemaking? What kind of subjects, aesthetic and political, "lose their footing"?

The conceptual model of distraction at work in the writings of Benjamin—distraction as both false consciousness and as emancipation—has been expanded by more recent scholarship that draws on Foucauldian ideas of coercion and control to explain what Paul Virilio refers to as "the advent of the logistics of perception."[17] Virilio points to the parsing and routing of sense perception at work in technologies of vision to denounce what he calls "a eugenics of sight, a pre-emptive abortion of the diversity of mental images."[18] Virilio dates this subjection of perception to the beginning of the twentieth century and links it to the dissemination of "certain signs, representations and logotypes that were to proliferate over the next twenty, thirty, sixty years . . . the logical outcome," Virilio contends, "of a system of message-intensification which has, for several centuries, assigned a primordial role to the techniques of visual and oral communication."[19] Implicit in the last part of Virilio's argument is the growing appeal to bodily registers in printed language, the same registers engaged by "techniques of visual and oral communication." Jonathan Crary takes this point further by arguing that the very subjection of perception to mechanisms of control is underwritten by the rise of an embodied notion of sense perception.

In *Suspensions of Perception* (1999), where he sets out "to demonstrate how within modernity vision is only one layer of a body that could be captured, shaped, or controlled by a range of external techniques,"[20] Crary writes: "the relocation of perception (as well as processes and functions previously assumed to be 'mental') in the thickness of the body was a precondition for the instrumentalizing of human vision as a component of machinic arrangements."[21] Most interesting about this idea is the ambiguity with which it is rendered. For Crary, the embodied subject is "both the location of operations of power and the potential for resistance."[22] A question arises regarding the possibility that the repressive aspects of consumer society (aspects that, as Jean Baudrillard has argued, are analogous to those of the logic of productivity and its constitutive forces: abstraction, division, alienation, etc.) can be explored and suspended from within (for observation and diversion, for purposes other than productivity, or what Baudrillard calls consummativity). That is to say, they can be suspended from the very movement of consumption and consumer society, using and appealing to the techniques and forces driving consumer society, forces that are immanent to the system and that provide—because of their overt immanence, because they work at the surface—a way other than (although never completely out of) efficiency.

Fascination is one such force, together with its stand-ins: attraction, captivation, enthrallment, enchantment, and mesmerization, theorized in the build-up to the industrial revolution by Franz Anton Mesmer. Mesmer's enormously popular theses on human susceptibility to magnetic forces (forces operating beyond reason, emanating from objects) are but a moment in the continuum where the power of fascination belongs.[23] The power to mesmerize marks a rift in the persistent ideology of Enlightenment as modern science and reason. What Mesmer's writings on animal magnetism reveal is the extent to which enlightened society can be committed to reason all the while remaining subject to the powers of enchantment. The dialectic of reason and fascination appears in full force under the guise of the commodity both in its material charms, crossed as they are by a furious logic of utility and function, and in the forces of attraction radiating from the commodity world.

Even before they set out to contest commodity capitalism and the political regimes that sustain it, the Brazilian concrete poets broke through the spell of the culture industry by embracing fascination, incorporating it homeopathically. Imitation of neon light is what gives Brazilian concrete poetry its initial thrust in the poems Augusto de Campos wrote for *Poetamenos* (1953). Imitation (of newspapers, magazines, logos, and slogans) is also what sustains its lyric flight during the latter phase of its production, in the wake of military dictatorship and in a social and economic reality otherwise defined by underdevelopment and other such tools of colonial integration to a globalized whole. Brazilian concrete poetry's earnest conjugation of neon light and the lyric, of advertisements and—after its so-called *salto participante*—social critique, compels us to revise engrained, relatively unexamined views regarding the function of enchantment, attraction, and fascination in the greater social dynamic and in consumer culture in particular.

At certain moments in the writings of Adorno and Fredric Jameson, this revision seems worthy, even crucial. Both acknowledge the irresistible force of attraction operating at the heart of film, advertising, and the culture industry.[24] But Jameson moves swiftly past mesmerization to focus on what *really* matters, fascination's end result: manipulation. And

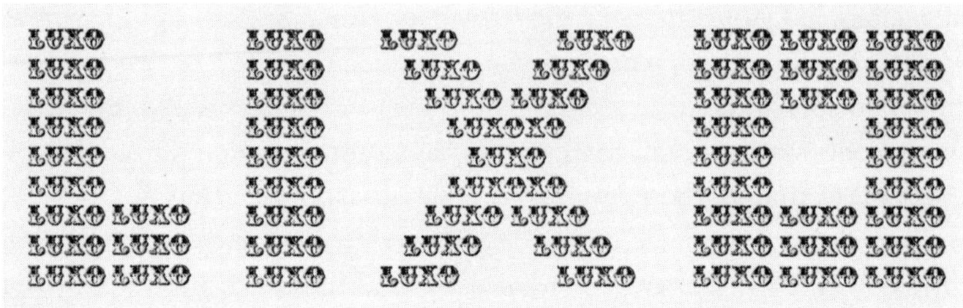

Figure 0.1. Augusto de Campos, "Luxo" (1965). © Augusto de Campos; courtesy, Augusto de Campos.

yet, Jameson writes, "even the most implacable theory of manipulation in mass culture . . . must somehow acknowledge the experiential moment in the mesmerization of the masses before the television set; if only then to dismiss it as the fix, addiction, false pleasure, or whatever."[25]

The Adorno of *Prisms* moves less swiftly past "the experiential moment in the mesmerization of the masses," dwelling on it at some length in his critique of Veblen's failure to account for the dialectics of production and consumption, of utility and waste, in the latter's writings on conspicuous consumption. "As the reflection of truth," Adorno writes, "appearances are dialectical; to reject all appearance is to fall completely under its sway, since truth is abandoned with the rubble without which it cannot appear."[26] This rubble without which truth does not appear takes many shapes; our failure to reduce these shapes to forms of the useful is what they share in common. Rubble, in Adorno's reading, endures, and it resists the logic of utility. Inasmuch as there remains in every concrete material circumstance, in moments of production as well as in moments of consumption, a residue of waste impervious to even the most furious displays of functionalism, rubble rises as a general aspect of social life and not as one of its compartments, as Veblen and others would have it. Not rubble but the pretension of absolute efficiency, not waste but transparency of purpose are revealed as what is deceptive, what stands in the way of truth. So much is revealed in one of Augusto de Campos's most seductive poems, *Luxo* (1965; fig. 0.1), a feast of font and ornament businesslike in its denouncement of luxury (waste as the building block of luxury, and luxury the more wretched for it). The poem is revelatory precisely to the extent that it exceeds this message, performing (typo)graphical squander when restrained accusation would have sufficed.

Fascination, much like luxury in Adorno's reading, mediates desire in a world dominated by the logic of commodity capitalism.[27] It takes the form of manipulation but is also, like distraction, a mode of deviation: deviation from utility, in the first instance. In Brazilian concrete poetry, fascination is what makes us deviate from what is useful in language, from its pretense of clear and transparent communication. Poetry has always been, in the first instance, excessive, and enchanting for that very reason: there is chant to it, song, *canto*. Concrete poetry vindicates the capacity of language to signify densely, concretely. It is excessive in its material making, exuberant in its sensorial dimensions. Color, visual form, and texture all play central roles in concrete poetry's ways of making sense, attracting readers in a way that mimics but isn't quite reducible to the logic of consumer capitalism. Lyric poetry and the language of consumer culture, conjugated as they are in concrete poetry, differ in substance and intent but not always in their approach to language as constitutive material.

Octavio Paz also proceeds ambivalently in his dealings with consumer culture. In typical aphoristic style, Paz writes that poetry has been modernity's antidote as well as its replica. This double stance vis-à-vis modernity finds its way to a series of visual poems Paz completed toward the end of the 1960s during the most experimental phase of his career. It was during this time that Paz incorporated into his poems forms and materials from mass and consumer culture. Replication and the multiple meanings of its Spanish translation (*réplica*: copy, response, aftershock) emerge as key features of the relationship between poetry and society in Paz's work. Replication is studied by Nicolas Bourriaud in *The Radicant* (2009), where he devotes a section to what he calls the aesthetics of the replica, identifying it as a key concept for our understanding of postmodern art and linking it to what he theorizes as a strategy for resisting the fetish aspect of the artwork. But while Bourriaud focuses on artists who copy or replicate the work of other artists, my focus will remain on the mimicking or reproduction of forms from consumer culture as practiced by Paz and as analyzed elsewhere in this book.

Homemaking, as I hope to demonstrate, is loaded with the same degree of ambivalence, the same contestatory power, and the same loaded contrariety of the other terms chosen as key concepts of this book. But its presence is elusive in most cultural criticism on mass and consumer culture. Home is the subject of some discussion in social studies on consumption. The space of the home is privileged by John Sinclair and Anna Cristina Pertierra, editors of *Consumer Culture in Latin America* (2012), which includes a section of essays titled "Domestic Practice" and is dedicated, in the editors' own words, to demonstrating "how across different

Latin American places and times, the material products of everyday life in and around the home form a primary site for the incorporation, innovation and maintenance of consumer practice."[28] The gendered figure of the housewife, however—both "quintessence of power in the modern world" and "global dictator," in the curious characterization by Daniel Miller[29]—remains overlooked and relatively understudied in the extant bibliography, perhaps because of unexamined overtones of passivity and coercion associated with the homemaker.

My reading of Lygia Clark's return to the space of the home in the last phase of her trajectory (the period coextensive with her work on the *Estruturação do self*) and of her decades-long research into what she calls relational objects will serve as grounds for a new look into the idea of homemaking. Precedent exists for the convergence of homemaking and experimental art: Dada artists familiar with the arts and crafts and prolific in the production of textiles and weaves, Bauhaus women and Bauhaus men, the many and fascinating inroads Soviet constructivists made into the world of domestic space. In a monograph on Bauhaus women, Ulrike Müller points out that the National Socialist myth of "*heimkultur*—'homemaking'—the bourgeois cliché of the modest housewife, who rules the home and never rests," was preceded in Germany by women artists who had "begun to rearrange things, to let light and air into the house, to look critically at lamps, furniture, dishes, all the furnishings, and all the rooms."[30] Sophie Taeuber, on her part, brought the Dada movement in Berlin a key critical inflection that was informed in large part by formal training in the arts and crafts.

Periodizing Consumption

Hemispheric geopolitics largely responsible for the cycles of growth and crisis in consumer societies of the Americas forms the basic context for the historical period that I grapple with—the three decades after the end of World War II. The arguments pursued over the course of this book address questions of aesthetics, politics, and consumption. To the extent that these arguments are posed against the background of events that took place in the 1950s, 1960s, and 1970s, the book stands as a timely revision of the narratives we tend to appeal to when understanding the political economy of Latin America after World War II, a period that is usually understood as defined by import-substitution industrialization. The point here is not to understress the role of import-substitution industrialization so much as it is to emphasize the importance of domestic market development as a fundamental element of this form of industrialization.

Consumption is the broader background this book assumes as context for the understanding of society and culture. To better trace the contours of a period in history defined principally by consumption, I draw on a few related terms (industry, technology, advertising) that serve as necessary points of reference in the construction of a rising but still relatively undertheorized object of research. Defining consumption as context for the understanding of society and culture presents an intrinsic challenge. Consumption seems to be—in practice and in theory—dispersed and diffused, at least in relation to the more centralized and more extensively researched activities subsumed under the category of production. Indeed, it seems like the demand for a precisely defined context of consumption is a demand more fitting to the notion of production, ballasted as it is with a more centralizing, better defined repertoire of figures (the work, the author, etc.).

Consumption as cultural paradigm[31] resonates with a number of recent studies by scholars interested in the Latin American region and in Mexico and Brazil in particular. For Steven B. Bunker, the "history of consumption is a cultural history of modernization at its most imperial."[32] Consumption makes for a rather strange form of imperial power, a queer form of empire. It is everywhere, acknowledged by everyone, yet its power is thought to be phony, superficial, ersatz. Consumption is powerful but it isn't the real site of power. It is too vacuous, too dispersed, too banal to be consequent. We have learned to see production as the true source of power, the field of forces where power is actually contested. A focus on consumption and consumer society allows for a new take on the history of modernization, one that displaces the state as the sole site of power. This is what Bunker reveals to us when he pictures "modernization as a phenomenon that arose from the bottom as much as it descended from above," when he sets out "to examine consumption as a measure of the popular and participatory nature of the Mexican modernizing process. . . . A history of consumption," Bunker concludes, "is, therefore, a history of everyday life."[33] Bunker argues that citizens of late nineteenth-century Mexico, anticipating a judgment nowadays all too naturalized, equated inclusion in the world of consumption with a sense of social development and well-being. "While historians," writes Bunker, "have been slow to recognize the centrality of consumption in the production of meaning in Porfirian society, Porfirians themselves made abundantly clear in their writings that nothing indicated individual and national progress better than changes in consumption and material culture."[34]

The period of experimentation that gave rise to 1920s avant-garde movements like Mexican muralism and Estridentismo in Mexico and the Semana de Arte Moderna in Brazil coincided with a marked growth of the economies of the region, a growth spurred in large part by the end of the First World War and, in the case of Mexico, by the end of the revolution of 1910–1920. Postwar conditions of growth for the economies of Latin America were also determining factors for the emergence of the literary, artistic, and cultural practices studied in this book.[35] The 1950s and 1960s in Mexico and Brazil are defined by fraught feelings of optimism and economic stability, a stability defended vigorously by the Mexican government in the mid-1950s.[36] In both countries, the idea of an economic "miracle" was widely disseminated during this period,[37] a "miracle" tethered largely to the promise of growth by way of import-substitution industrialization. An aura of prosperity, the rising importance of the consumer, and a "miraculous" leap toward development were crucial aspects of the political and economic outlook in Mexico and in Brazil in the decades after World War II.

During the war and in the decades after it, Mexico and Brazil—the first an immediate neighbor to the United States, a gateway to the rest of the continent; the second the largest nation in Latin America, with the potential to become the biggest economy in the region—became the subjects of interventionist policies that sought to implement a model of economic development friendly to the imperial interests of the United States. This, together with the sheer size of the Mexican and Brazilian culture industries, is what makes the comparative study of aesthetics and consumer culture in Mexico and Brazil so compelling. Both countries turned toward the United States, culturally and economically, earlier than other states in the region. And both became objects of sustained economic and political interest in the United States in the years leading up to World War II. Both Mexico and Brazil participated early in the expansion of what came to be known as the US brand of consumer democracy.[38] Sears, Roebuck and Company opened its first store in Mexico City on February 28, 1947,[39] a mere two years after the war ended, marking the beginning of what Julio Moreno characterizes, citing a *Harper's* magazine article published at the time, as a consumer revolution in Mexico.[40] The term captures the enormous weight, real and symbolic, of this major turn in the history of

Mexico, a perverse realization of the ideals of the Mexican Revolution of 1910–1920.

In Mexico, the growth or "miracle" that took place after the end of World War II was largely due to policies dating back to the administration of President Lázaro Cárdenas (1934–1940) and its development of the national economy through protectionist trade policies and the nationalization of natural resources, oil foremost among them. The economic growth experienced in Mexico in the 1950s and 1960s came with a series of public works championed by presidential administrations eager to maintain a façade of prosperity and progress even in the face of impending economic disaster. This series of major investments benefited, at least in principle, the popular segments of civil society.[41] Beginning with Conjunto Urbano Presidente Alemán (a massive housing project designed by Mario Pani), Mexico City saw its urban fabric transformed by a series of major infrastructural changes that included the transfer of the Universidad Autónoma de México—the largest higher education institution in the country—from its historic quarters in the city center to Ciudad Universitaria, a newly constructed and much-vaunted campus in the southern part of the Mexican capital. Large museums (the Museo Nacional de Antropología, the Museo de Arte Moderno), a new metro system, luxury and mass housing developments (Jardines del Pedregal, Ciudad Satélite, Conjunto Urbano Nonoalco-Tlatelolco), and the rise of Zona Rosa as a point of concentration for private and commercial galleries (emerging spaces of artistic and cultural brokerage and harbingers of the privatized and commercialized future of culture) were the major features of a Mexican capital transformed—culturally, infrastructurally, and recreationally—within the span of a few decades.[42]

Dissent from the developmentalist policies instituted in Mexico in the decades after World War II began to register almost as soon as these policies were enacted.[43] Dissent in culture also gained a voice in the 1950s, and it had a proper name: *la ruptura*. Octavio Paz coined the term in an essay on Rufino Tamayo,[44] where the poet reads the painter's expressionist, abstract style as a stark departure from the aesthetics of social realism and nationalist myth-making that the Mexican muralists had been defending for more than three decades. By 1968, with the publication of Juan García Ponce's *Nueve pintores mexicanos*, *la ruptura* acquired the spirit of a movement, a definitive generational break with the nationalist, figurative, social-realist art associated with Mexican muralism. What is intriguing, from my point of view, is the absence of clarity, the lack of definition at the origins of this break, at the heart of this rupture. Prescriptive notions of proper subject matter for art and literature (nationalist in a limited, mostly celebratory, sense) and a limited repertoire of styles sanctioned by the dominant segments of the visual arts (muralism and the so-called Mexican School) constitute the obvious targets of dissent for those who identified themselves with the *ruptura*. An opening—of institutional access, of aesthetic repertoires—was the driving force behind it. But in terms of the developmentalist policies that defined the period, artists and writers on both sides of the debate—artists for rupture and artists consecrated by the regime—found themselves defending positions critical of the government's push for development as often as they embraced forms and platforms closely aligned with consumption and market development. Paz is a case in point, as is José Luis Cuevas. In 1967, while staying on Madison Avenue in New York City, Cuevas imagines the possibility of reproducing one of his drawings in the billboards of Times Square. His vision materializes later that year, not in New York but in what was then the gallery-filled Zona Rosa neighborhood of Mexico City.[45]

As Werner Baer and Claudio Paiva note, the 1950s and 1960s were decades of high growth and modernization for the Brazilian economy.[46] During those years and until 1980, industry became the fastest growing sector of the Brazilian economy, "the main determinant of the economy's dynamism, triggering both the upturns and the downturns of the growth cycles."[47] The transformation of São Paulo into an industrial hub began to take place since at least the 1940s and largely, though not exclusively, as a response to the demands made by World War II on global industry. *Brazil at War*, a 1943 film produced and sponsored by Nelson Rockefeller's Office of the Coordinator of Inter-American Affairs (OCIAA), works hard to draw similarities and suggest political and ideological allegiances between the United States and Brazil. A 1944 film titled *São Paulo*, also produced and distributed by the OCIAA, puts the spotlight on the Paulista capital, "the fastest growing city in the Americas," a city thriving under an industrial boom. In the film, São Paulo's factories appear as enterprising suppliers for the Allied Forces, producing trucks, tires, dynamite, medical supplies, and shell casings, "each casing . . . earmarked for the Axis." "The war," the film's voice-over tells us, "has imposed heavy responsibilities on Brazilian industry. The Paulista has not been found wanting." In 1945, one year after the film was produced, World War II was over and industrial production, in Brazil as elsewhere, faced the task of repurposing factories no longer servicing the global armed conflict. A transnational industrial apparatus built for war provided the infrastructure necessary for the consumer-goods bonanza that defined the two decades following the war. A widespread, globalizing desire to live like the Americans, the winners of the war—an ardent wish to live out the American dream—was essential for the far-reaching transformation the world was about to begin.

Fast-paced economic growth in Brazil in the 1950s was spurred by the presidency of Juscelino Kubitschek (1956–1961) and his ambitious Programa de Metas, the crowning achievement of which was the construction of Brasília, a national capital built from scratch in the centrally located Brazilian *planoalto* and inaugurated in April 1960. From the 1940s onward and over the course of several presidencies, decisive government measures favoring development and industrialization[48] were implemented alongside private-sector efforts to consolidate the business of mass communication. With the massive infrastructural efforts to revamp Brazilian industry and its economy came what sociologist Nelson do Valle Silva calls a gradual "modernisation of values,"[49] a process that, while not concerted, was just as deliberate and no less fundamental to the modernization of Brazil. During and well after Kubitschek's term, and with the rise of the military dictatorship in 1964,[50] the transport and communications sectors experienced explosive levels of growth. Mass media consolidated under business magnates such as Assis Chateaubriand, who owned the magazine *O Cruzeiro*, a popular and influential publication with an average print run of five hundred thousand weekly copies in the 1950s and 1960s. In 1950, Chateaubriand established TV Tupi, the first television broadcasting station in Brazil and elsewhere in South America.[51] Chateaubriand's role in the development of modern mass media in Brazil goes well beyond the founding of *O Cruzeiro* and TV Tupi. In the first half of the twentieth century, Chateaubriand amassed the largest and strongest holding of communications outlets in Brazil, Diários Associados, which included newspapers and a news agency, a radio station, and an advertising agency. He secured large shares of advertising for his newspapers, revolutionizing the way newspapers were financed in his day. His role in the rise of Getúlio Vargas is well known, as are his own ventures into politics.[52] The years after World War II in Brazil mark the birth of what would eventually become one of the largest culture industries in the world, an industry robust enough to spawn TV Globo, which by the 1990s had become the fourth-largest television broadcasting company in the world (after US television companies CBS, NBC, and ABC).[53]

Advertising, a principal source of financing for mass media, played a crucial role in the growth of the communications sector, and this in turn sustained a growing belief in the modernization of Brazil. Radio and television, of course, do not bring about modernization on their own, but they do enact a process as transformative as any major upheaval in the national infrastructure. As Silva notes, "the importance of exposure to these means of communication rests in the fact that it creates a mechanism for positive feedback, with greater exposure leading to higher levels of absorption of 'modern' and consumerist values and attitudes, which in turn leads to a greater tendency to mobility and higher aspirations for consumption."[54] Of course, the social function of television in Mexico and in Brazil in the decades after World War II went beyond the general purposes of development and modernization. In these countries and in other countries of the region, mass media in general and television in particular played a more dismal role. The ability to screen—for mass audiences, in the intimacy of their living rooms—fantasies of optimism in the face of devastating crisis and unspeakable oppression is a crucial condition for the rise and the endurance of dictatorial regimes in the region.

Development and construction of cultural institutions in Brazil kept abreast with the general growth of industry and mass communications. The Museu de Arte Moderna (MAM) in Rio de Janeiro, founded in the 1940s, began its programming in earnest in the 1950s under the directorship of Niomar Moniz Sodré.[55] In 1948 Chateaubriand, the media magnate, helped inaugurate the MASP, to this day an emblem of the fine arts in the Paulista capital. Three years later in 1951, the first São Paulo Biennial opened its doors, supported largely by the efforts of the industrialist Francisco Matarazzo Sobrinho and his wife Yolanda Penteado. As Ferreira Gullar wrote in 1960, it was the São Paulo Biennial (specifically, the strong Swiss-German delegations present in the first three biennials) that first consolidated the language of abstraction and of concrete aesthetics present in Brazilian poetry and art movements from the 1950s.[56] Significantly for the comparative framework that this book offers, the São Paulo Biennial was also the first major presentation of Mexican muralism in Brazil. More than forty etchings by the muralists were featured in 1955, a highlight of the third biennial. Development of art institutions in Brazil in the middle of the twentieth century coincided with an increase in the formalization of its art criticism through the efforts of critics like Mário Pedrosa and Sérgio Milliet. It was upon his return from exile in 1945 that Pedrosa began to emerge as the foremost critic of art in Brazil. "Until this time," writes Glória Ferreira in a recently published English-language anthology of Pedrosa's writings, "it had been mostly poets who practiced—a generally impressionistic—criticism in newspapers and magazines."[57]

By 1955, the biennial moved to buildings designed by Oscar Niemeyer in the recently inaugurated Parque Ibirapuera. The construction of Parque Ibirapuera was comparable in breadth and impact to the construction of Ciudad Universitaria in Mexico City as well as other *ciudades universitarias* throughout Latin America in the late 1940s and early 1950s. All are examples of large-scale urbanization and art synthesis, with artists, architects, and urbanists aspiring to work in conjunction. In 1956 construction began on Brasília, the new federal capital of Brazil, crown jewel of the country's development aspirations of the mid-twentieth century. These and other modernization projects in Brazil have turned the country into a recurrent reference for utopian visions of modernity in the twentieth century. But as Aleca Le Blanc argues, the sheer number of large-scale building projects either active or completed in the 1950s made Brazil not a model of a modern nation but "a nation in the midst of a complicated transition and under actual construction,"[58] less a culmination than a beacon (a sign, a celebration, a warning) of modernity.

In Brazil and elsewhere, the 1950s were crucial for the growth and professionalization of design, marketing, and advertising.[59] The year 1950 marks the opening of the Escola Superior de Propaganda e Marketing, the first institution of higher education in Brazil dedicated to the academic study of marketing and advertising. It was founded, tellingly, under the institutional auspices of the MASP, the largest and most well-regarded institution of fine arts in Brazil. A year later in 1951 and again under the umbrella of the MASP, Pietro Maria and Lina Bo Bardi (the latter is the architect responsible for the iconic building that houses the MASP) opened the Instituto de Arte Contemporânea do Museu de Arte de São Paulo (IAC/MASP), part of a larger, diffused effort to professionalize design in Brazil. This was followed by the opening of a number of Brazilian design firms throughout the 1950s and 1960s, many led by artists associated with the concrete movement.

Design operates in the shifting middle ground between art and profit-driven enterprise. The tensest and most charged contradictions about the work of art in the age of consumer culture rest squarely at the heart of design as discipline. Design, together with advertising and marketing, consolidated as a major industry in the decades after World War II, in tandem with the growth of the private sector and the expansion of transnational corporations. In Brazil, perhaps more than anywhere else in Latin America, design was embraced by significant segments of culture and the economy, with artists, designers, and poets working as heads of marketing projects from logotype creation to brand identity to merchandising strategy and visual programming.[60]

Some Notes toward a Dialectics of Consumption

At the heart of this project rests a desire as well as a conviction. The desire is to explore forms of perception and forms of cognition that operate frequently, although not exclusively, in experiences associated with consumers and consumption, the same forms of cognition evoked by the categories privileged in this study as categories for an aesthetics of consumption. The conviction is that there is value to these forms of cognition, and that this value, while neither unknown nor understudied, deserves further exploration. This is the same conviction that animates García Canclini's study of the link between consumption and citizenship, *Consumers and Citizens* (2001; first published in Spanish in 1995). García Canclini's central hypothesis is that the transnational networks that sustain and are themselves sustained by consumption and consumerism provide alternative stages for imagining the figure of the citizen beyond the conceptual parameters of the nation-state. Consumption, García Canclini argues, is "good for thinking"—it sustains analysis and reflection beyond the "moral and intellectual disqualification" at work in prevailing discussions about consumption, ballasted, as they are, on "commonplaces regarding the omnipotence of the mass media, which presumably incite the masses to gorge themselves unthinkingly with commodities."[61]

García Canclini sets out to define the terms needed to recognize something like a logic in consumption, "the rationality—for producers and consumers—of an incessant expansion and renewal of consumption."[62] This rationality, García Canclini argues, is economic, but not exclusively macroeconomic. It rests in the myriad forms of adaptation and negotiation created by individuals in their capacity as consumers, as well as in the institutions that regulate production and consumption in free-market economies. Citing the work of Pierre Bourdieu, Arjun Appadurai, and Stuart Ewen, García Canclini appeals to "the logic that drives the appropriation of commodities as objects of distinction"; he appeals to other facets of consumption, "the *symbolic and aesthetic aspects of the rationality of consumption*."[63] Beyond distinction, García Canclini insists, the symbolic aspect of consumption is grounds for what he calls "the *integrative and communicative rationality of a society*."[64] This, García Canclini argues, is the unifying force that binds together transnational consumer communities, spaces of social division and integration that cut across the conventionally defined territories of identity formation. It is on the basis of a consumer reason or rationality that García Canclini can postulate the possibility of political associations that rest neither on the macro structures of the state nor on identitarian bonds of social attachment. Subtending the rise of this new understanding of citizenship and society—an understanding fundamentally embedded in transnational geographies and globalized consumer worlds—is a longer hemispheric history neatly summarized by Gareth Williams as a march "from the heyday of state-promoted national and regional ethnic identities—in Mexico, for example, from the construction of the corporatist Nation-State and its systematic incorporation of regional processes of population-fabrication—through to the postmodern crisis of the Nation-State and the dismantling of its previous projects of national socialization (a.k.a. the 'Mexican miracle')."[65]

García Canclini views consumption affirmatively, as a horizon toward which new forms of citizenship and social participation can be pitched in a moment marked by the dissolution of centralized, liberal nation-states. But Williams, like Francine Masiello in *The Art of Transition: Latin American Culture and Neoliberal Crisis* (2001), questions García Canclini's underlying assumption regarding the possibility that the terrain of social actions and operations staged by consumer capitalism can, in fact, as García Canclini argues, operate as a platform for political praxis. "The political, of course," Williams writes, "does not primarily consist in the composition and dynamic nor in the regulation of predominantly external corporate or transnational powers, which is ultimately how it appears in Canclini's treatise on peripheral consumption—fabrication and management. It could be argued that the political is the opening of a space that is inaugural, initial, and emergent as an action, a praxis of singularity itself (Nancy) or a means of establishing immediate tensions with the standardizing drives of the postnational world."[66] Williams is right to call into question the extent to which consumption and its attendant theater of social and political operations can sustain new formulations of the political. The principal gesture of García Canclini's formulation of the political vis-à-vis consumption, though, merits more reflection, to the extent that it can compel us to establish immanently the "immediate tensions with the standardizing drives of the postnational world"[67] that Williams calls for. In reference to a corpus of critical interventions aligned with García Canclini's, George Yúdice writes: "New interventions that challenge both right and [Todd] Gitlin-like left positions on multiculturalism and identity suggest that consumer capitalism has much to do with the ongoing redefinition of citizenship, a contradictory process that, though not a cause for celebration, is not to be lamented either."[68]

García Canclini ballasts his argument on the premise of a rationality proper to consumption, a rebuttal of the idea that consumption is driven by the manipulation of mindless wishes for consumer goods. This intellectual embrace of consumption fits into what Juliet B. Schor defines as a wave of studies published in the last quarter of the twentieth century, studies generally positioned against the more classic critiques of consumption that shaped discussions on consumer culture from the middle of the twentieth century onward (critiques by Thorstein Veblen, Theodor Adorno and Max Horkheimer, John Kenneth Galbraith, Jean Baudrillard, Herbert Marcuse, etc.). Schor refers to frameworks of interpretation such as that offered by Veblen as status models and notes that these models fell out of vogue and were subject to widespread dismissal and critique in more recent approaches to consumer culture—the kind of approaches that posit an active, informed viewer, the kind that advocate for, among other things, consumption as a site for identity construction. The recent wave of scholarship grouped together by Schor focuses on the interpretation of consumer behavior and consumer attitude, rather than on the more systemic critiques of the logic and the political economy of consumer society. The shift in focus, *grosso modo*, has rendered the figure of the consumer as a more active, rational, and informed subject, in opposition to the figure of a passive, coerced consumer that is often articulated in or assumed by the studies on consumption published toward the middle of the twentieth century. Schor argues for a qualified return to these earlier, systemic critiques of consumption, submitting that the latter turn toward the redemption of the figure of the consumer lacks critical perspective vis-à-vis consumption and consumer culture—the kind of perspective that, among other things, can shed light on the political and ethical consequences of the social dynamics that vector into and out of consumer culture.

Schor places her own analysis of consumption somewhere between the mid-twentieth-century structural critiques of consumer society and what she refers to as "micro-level, interpretive studies that are often depoliticized and lack a critical approach to the subject matter."[69] Intriguingly, she makes the point that the defense of consumer rationality and consumer agency (the kind of defense performed by critics like García Canclini) may not be entirely incompatible with the more structural, politically inflected critique of the culture industry (a term Schor reads as coextensive with consumer culture). Schor objects to what she describes as the "so-called totalized and functionalist vision without contradiction or possibility for resistance" ("the model cannot account for the fact that consumer resistance is always present in the marketplace") in Adorno and Horkheimer's writings on the culture industry.[70] Her larger point is to recognize the importance of the so-called agential interpretations of the figure of the consumer while attending to the critical acuity of earlier, structural analyses of consumer culture. "The point," Schor writes, "about the project of self-creation in consumer society is also undoubtedly right, but it does not require that that process occurs in a vacuum with respect to social inequality and status."[71] Schor also emphasizes the "inclusion of both the production and the consumption side in the analysis"[72] as a crucial and underappreciated component of Adorno and Horkheimer's critique. Indeed, it seems that many of the most compelling approaches to the study of consumption (and production, for that matter) are those that conceptualize their objects of study not as paradigms of social organization but rather as distinct but related moments in a larger social dynamic that includes, per force, a dialectical counterpoint.

Few critics have undertaken as lucid and as sustained a defense of the social figure of the user (a stand-in for the figure of the consumer) as Michel de Certeau did in *The Practice of Everyday Life* (1984). Certeau stakes his claims in the very first line of his book, where he defines his inquiry as "a continuing investigation of the ways in which users—commonly assumed to be passive and guided by established rules—operate."[73] Eager to highlight the agency exercised in the "operational logics" of everyday consumption, Certeau insists that the status of users and consumers as "the dominated element in society . . . does not mean that they are either passive or docile."[74] In so doing, he shows the kind of anxiety that often keeps us from regarding consumption with the deference we reserve for production. "Everyday life," Certeau argues, "invents itself by poaching in countless ways on the property of others."[75] But how can we account for poaching without coming to terms with its constitutive duplicity, the poking out and taking in, the shoving in and emptying out that poaching implies? What is it about the passive and docile that makes it inconsistent with the "models of action" Certeau reads in the uses of everyday life?

Evident in Certeau's effort to square out the passive and the agential is the more generalized lack of dialectical constructs of passivity, which remains—in Certeau's text as well as in the functionalist, productivist accounts against which he positions his argument—among the least understood and most egregiously gendered loci of human operations. The absence of the figure of the homemaker in the functionalist analyses of consumption by Adorno and Horkheimer is telling in this regard, given the fact that it was the homemaker who was at the center of the efforts to transform the domestic space into a space of consumption. For Certeau use and, by extension, consumption hold the possibility of creative appropriation. While it is certainly true that creative appropriation can be performed with the forcefulness and bravado championed by, for instance, Oswald de Andrade and like-minded proponents of consumption-as-*antropofagia*,[76] there are other ways to conceive of the links between people and objects beyond use and appropriation. In the chapter dedicated to Lygia Clark, I will have occasion to discuss at length Clark's proposals (particularly her *Estruturação do self*) for counterintuitive, potentially transformative relationships between subjects and objects. These relationships are premised on the idea that certain things—the relational objects Clark builds especially for her propositions—are alive with vitality and privileged in their capacity to disturb, by means of touch and texture, the boundaries within which we confine ourselves as embodied subjects.

At the heart of this latter phase of Clark's work is a notion of animated thinghood that calls to mind Marx's seminal theorization of commodity fetishism (as the projection of value and life from the producing subject to the object of production), but only to revert to an earlier Marx, to the Marx of the *Manuscripts*. Densely contradictory subjects, subjects that are active in their sensorial participation but passive to the transformations brought about by relational objects, are at the center of Clark's radical reconceptualization of the object and thinghood in the age of commodity capitalism. The people who take part in Clark's proposals make themselves available to a sensorial, affective engagement with the world and open themselves up to transformations that come from this engagement. Both consumption and production sustain this vision of a subject standing in passive relationship to the objects with which it interacts, either by virtue of being transformed by those very objects in the process of making them, or by virtue of using objects, consuming them, taking them into its own being. Passivity can qualify production as well as it can qualify the moment of consumption.

Early on in his book, Certeau makes a crucial qualification to the scope of his argument, which, he tells us, centers not on consumers proper but on "an operational logic whose models may go as far back as the age-old ruses of fishes and insects that disguise or transform themselves in order to survive, and which has in any case been concealed by the form of rationality current under Western culture."[77] There is a link here between, on the one hand, the "operational logic" of use and consumption and, on the other hand, the mimetic forms of disguise and adaptation that Taussig theorizes in an incisive reading of Benjamin, discussed at some length in the chapter on Brazilian concrete poetry. David Alfaro Siqueiros appeals to this regression as a fundamental aspect of our engagement with buildings, with architecture, and, by extension, with painting on a mural scale. Octavio Paz and the concrete poets stage this regression into the sensorial by means of a mimetic appropriation of the language of advertising. Lygia Clark, on her part, structures regression on the basis of what she calls relational objects. Regression for Clark, the kind of regression she stages using her relational objects, is constructivist, belonging to a well-defined art-historical genealogy, and constructive. It allows for a turn away from the discursive logic of language and toward constructions of the sensorial, all the while revealing new insights into the commodity form.

This mimetic operational logic is an important reference as we try to make sense of the tactical, tactile regressions staged by Siqueiros, by the Brazilian concrete poets, by Paz, and by Lygia Clark, all of whom appeal to a return to nondiscursive, nonlinear, preverbal registers of language and meaning. In the context of consumer culture, regression as I read it in the work of these poets and artists serves as a way of bracketing the enlightened, hierarchical idea of the subject as an essentially thinking being, invested with sensorial, embodied capacities but not fundamentally defined by them. Regression as I understand it in the works analyzed in this book marks a strong commitment to materialism and to ideas of cognition and subjectification corollary to materialism.

Something like a dialectics of production and consumption emerges from the writings of one of the Brazilian concrete poets, Décio Pignatari, who coined a revealing portmanteau (one of many that pepper the language of concrete poetry): *produssumo*. *Produssumo* names what Haroldo de Campos later characterizes as "the poetics of invention within mass consumption, beyond Adornian skepticism."[78] *Produssumo* mashes together the Portuguese words for "production" and "consumption" to designate both the productive and agential possibilities inherent in acts of consumption, possibilities very much in line with the new wave of critiques of consumption summarized above. *Produssumo* also highlights, in keeping with the critical tradition of *antropofagia*, the processes (implicit and explicit, mindless as well as voluntary) of absorption, ingestion, and citation that buttress even the most original of productions.

The term has a more historically specific meaning intended to address an aspect of culture that both Pignatari and Augusto de Campos argued was in ascendance in the 1960s, something that slips through the cracks of a cultural system defined dualistically as a rigid opposition between high and low culture, between authentic and replicate cultures, between serious and banal cultures, between cultures with complex production values demanding an active engagement from their publics and cultures that assume pliant, passive audiences ready to receive artworks mindlessly, without critical or intellectual involvement. The significance of *produssumo* would rest on its capacity to stake out a place beyond "the apparently inevitable option between production (erudite) artists and consumption (popular) artists," a place occupied emblematically by the Beatles and John Cage, and most of all by the Tropicália movement in Brazil.[79] Even if we subscribed to the view of mass culture as false consciousness (an increasingly unpopular position among contemporary critics of culture[80]), we still have to grapple with the fact that many of the procedures by which mass culture is said to function are the same procedures that are envisioned as ways out of false consciousness and into social, political, and historical awakeness.

A basis for a dialectical account of consumption can be drawn from Marx's *Economic and Philosophic Manuscripts of 1844*. Money, labor, private property, and wealth are the principal objects of study of the essays compiled in these manuscripts. The movement, the conflict, the contradiction between inner human lives and the objects, institutions, discourses, and physical entities that give structure to these lives are the principal subject matter of these essays. An insistent and much-commented humanist horizon makes itself present often in Marx's *Manuscripts*, in the "premise of positively annulled private property," wherein "man produces man—himself and the other man," wherein "the object, being the direct manifestation of his individuality, is simultaneously his own existence for the other man, the existence of the other man, and that existence for him."[81] This complex notion of a humanized object, an object that, without reifying human existence, stands for something human on account of they who made it, resonates in later formulations of the gift (by Marcel Mauss, Taussig, and others) as an object of exchange constituted within a social dynamic that exceeds the reifying logic of exchange-value. "To recapitulate," writes Marx, driving the point home while noting its limitations, "man is not lost in his object only when the object becomes for him a *human* object or objective man. This is possible only when the object becomes for him a *social* object, he himself for himself a social being, just as society becomes a being for him in this object."[82]

Jonathan Dettman reminds us of the care with which Marx constructs the antinomic relationship between consumption and production. "In the *Grundrisse*," Dettman writes, "Marx takes pains to establish that the relationship between production and consumption is not simply a unity of opposites, a direct identity of production and consumption which he says economists call 'productive consumption,' but one in which they mediate one another reciprocally."[83] Along with the oppositional logic underpinning these two terms, another, less manifest and ultimately more fundamental link exists between them: "a mediating movement takes place between the two," notes Dettman, citing the *Grundrisse*.[84] And beyond the more obvious sense of "consumption" denoting a complementary movement or antinomic character ("consumption" as something that feeds into production, each one of these terms providing the conditions that make the other necessary in an endless sequence of movements), Marx draws out, as a more negative sense of consumption, a consumption proper described by the German philosopher as "the destructive antithesis to production."[85] This destructive moment of consumption, mysterious and conceptually compelling, opens up a series of questions regarding the place of consumption and the way meaning and signification are formulated in societies organized by commodity capitalism. What kinds of powers are unleashed by a dialectical rendering of consumption? How does this change our understanding of power? If, according to Marx, the "enlightened political economy" shows that those "who look upon private property *only as an objective* substance confronting men, seem therefore to be *idolaters*, *fetishists*, *Catholics*,"[86] what would this political economy make of those who see consumption *only* as subjective desire, as something entirely within the sphere of human will and thus subject to complete coercion and control?

Recent scholarship furnishes us with concepts supple enough to approach these questions. Kojin Karatani's understanding of capitalism as a function of exchange is exemplary in this regard, as is his corollary relativization of the paradigm of production.[87] Closer to the specificities of the Latin American region, Verónica Gago argues for a richer understanding of neoliberalism as both the "series of macropolitics designed by imperialist centers"[88] and the micropolitics of subjectification established at the level of everyday knowledges and practices, beyond the total control of institutionalized powers. As its title indicates, Gago's book grapples with what she sharply defines as neoliberal reason or "neoliberalism as rationality, in the sense Foucault used the term: as the very constitution of governmentality, but also as a counterpoint to the ways in which that same rationality is appropriated, ruined, relaunched, and altered by those presumed to be victims and victims only."[89] Part of the appeal of Gago's framing is the idea that if neoliberalism is more than a macropolitical regime, if, indeed, as Gago argues, neoliberalism must also be understood as a force of social and affective organization driven by people and forces working at the personal level, then it follows that resistance to or the overcoming of neoliberalism cannot be conceived in exclusively macropolitical terms. Understanding neoliberalism, then, understanding the period after World War II when the structural bases for neoliberalism were established, entails an expansion of what we understand to be the logics of both consumption and neoliberalism, a repositioning that takes seriously the modes of operation of subjects traditionally conceived to be completely under the coercion of institutionalized structures of power.

The present inquiry, which looks at a moment in the history of Mexico and Brazil posterior to the consolidation of the nation-state in the Latin American region but prior to the dominance of neoliberal regimes, subscribes to this vision of an expanded rationality, a consumer reason explored in depth by scholars like García Canclini and further complicated by the categories I here propose as categories for an aesthetics of consumption. My intention is twofold. On the one hand, I want to reveal and make manifest the aesthetic operation at the heart of commodity capitalism. On the other hand, I seek to understand this operation as a logic of contrarity, not just as the result of a series of structural interventions coming from above (either from the state or from an increasingly private initiative) but also and crucially as a complex of subjective dispositions that feed into the logic of consumption without losing their capacity to disarm it or dissolve it.

Antecedents: Consumer Culture and the Avant-gardes

The book focuses on the two largest cultural economies in the region: Mexico and Brazil. It grapples with the work of artists and writers working out of these countries and active during the decades after World War II:

David Alfaro Siqueiros, the Brazilian concrete poets, Octavio Paz, and Lygia Clark. These are some of the most celebrated artists and writers of twentieth-century Latin America, and this book casts a new light on their legacy. In chapters dedicated to their respective trajectories, this book analyzes how each of them arrived at forms of aesthetic production drawn taut between high modernism and consumer culture. That some of these poets and artists showed a serious and sustained interest in consumption and consumer culture holds the promise of a vision into the commodity form beyond the reach of critical writings that broach the subject of commodity capitalism without taking into consideration its forms of making sense, its ways of meaning. In *One-Way Street*, Benjamin writes of a true vision, a real gaze, "the most real, mercantile gaze into the heart of things": the advertisement.[90] What gives the advertisement, this "mercantile gaze," its measure of reality is a brash proximity to the objects of its representations. This is the key to the sense of reality Benjamin reads in advertisements.

Perhaps the most obvious link between consumption, consumer culture, and art is to be found in the long history of intersections between advertising and the avant-gardes. Their first significant rapport took place in the dawn of the twentieth century, in the work of writers and artists intimately tied to the rise of radical art movements in Europe and elsewhere. Not long after the publication of *The Foundation and Manifesto of Futurism* in February 1909, a number of contemporaries of Filippo Marinetti, the movement's founder, began to remark on the distinctly commercial—the distinctly *Americanized*—approach Marinetti took to the promotion of Italian futurism.[91] Blaise Cendrars referred to advertising as "the flower of contemporary life,"[92] and he looked to advertisements when composing his *La prose du Transsibérien et de la petite Jehanne de France* (1913). The simultaneist vein in Cendrars's poem, the composition of which draws the eye to the watercolors and brush strokes by Sonia Delaunay-Terk as much as it does to its words and phrases, led Guillaume Apollinaire to suggest that the poem was an effort "to train the eye to read with one glance . . . as one reads with a single glance the plastic elements printed on a poster."[93] Apollinaire's characterization of Cendrars's poem is interesting insofar as it hints at both a shift in reading habits brought about by posters and at the capacity of Cendrars's poem to accustom readers to this shift. James Joyce's Bloom, the protagonist of his *Ulysses* (1922), was an ad man, a newspaper publicity agent. Both *Ulysses* and advertisements can be described as affronts to logic, to the communicative and discursive functions of language. And both participate in what Benjamin calls the "brutal heteronomies of economic chaos."[94] From Marinetti to Joyce runs a recurring theme of language and liberation, a freeing of words from the tyranny of syntax.[95] And throughout, advertisements play a fundamental role as models of what this liberation can look like and what this liberation says regarding the order from which language is freed: the order of syntax, of narrowly rational thought.

Many of the most compelling insights on the commodity form and on the ways in which commodity capitalism structures our way of conceiving ourselves and the world around us come from artists, writers, and thinkers who deliberately choose to work with consumption and consumer culture. This is the case with many of the Soviet artists active in Russia during the period described by Christina Kiaer as "the relatively peaceful and semicapitalist period in Soviet history known as the New Economic Policy, or NEP (1921–c. 1928)."[96] Aleksandr Rodchenko, Vladimir Mayakovsky, El Lissitzky, Gustav Klutsis, and others either incorporated forms characteristic of advertising into their artworks—for instance, the logotypes Lissitzky designed for a 1923 book with poems by Mayakovsky, *Dlia golosa*[97]—or else worked directly in merchandising and advertising. The work of the Russian constructivists was well known to the Latin American poets and artists grouped together in this book, and I'll have occasion to discuss concrete points of contact between these seemingly disparate figures of the avant-garde in the chapters that follow.

A continuum is drawn in the work of artists active during the NEP period between the art object and the house item, between works of art and the objects of everyday life. So much is evident in the manifesto of the journal *Veshch'/Gegenstand/Objet*, organized by Lissitzky and Ilya Ehrenburg in Berlin in 1922, where art is described as "the creation of new objects" and objects, in turn, are defined as more than "objects of everyday use." "Naturally," the manifesto goes on to note, "in factory-made utilitarian objects, in the aeroplane or car, we see genuine art. But we do not wish to limit the production of artists to utilitarian objects. Every organised work—a house, a poem or a painting—is an expedient object, not leading people away from life, but helping to organise it."[98] For artists associated with constructivism during this markedly experimental period, commitment to socialism was expressed in the everyday, utilitarian objects they conceived *as artists*, as well as in the advertising produced for the sale and distribution of these kinds of objects. Lissitzky wrote at some length on home furnishings and furniture in his 1928 treatise "The Artistic Pre-

Requisites for the Standardisation of Furniture." A chair of his design was produced for the Russian pavilion at the International Fur Trade Exhibition in Leipzig in 1930 and incorporated into houses he designed around that time.[99]

A vision of objects and of a way of relating to objects alternative to the one cultivated by commodity capitalism came to Rodchenko during a visit to Paris in 1925. The circumstances of the trip made for a revelatory experience. Far from the Soviet Union, in the heart of a society increasingly defined by consumption and consumer goods, Rodchenko imagines the promise of emancipation at the heart of socialism in terms not just of work, not just of the conditions of production, but also in terms of possible relationships to "our things," the objects of our everyday life. In a letter to his wife written during his stay in Paris, he writes: "the light from the East is not only the liberation of workers, the light from the East is in the new relation to the person, to woman, to things. Our things in our hands must be equals, comrades, and not these black and mournful slaves, as they are here."[100] "Here" for Rodchenko, his point of enunciation, is Paris, a privileged place to recognize and study the extraordinary capacity of the commodity to organize desire. For Rodchenko the revolutionary possibility he envisions in Paris—radical association, true collectiveness—begins with a renewed sense of the relationship between men and women but also between humans and objects. "Things take on meaning, become friends and comrades of the person, and the person learns how to laugh and be happy and converse with things."[101]

Kiaer's analysis of Rodchenko's letters from Paris insistently points to the complex force field of affect that is organized by the commodity form, a site of displaced desires (at times errant, at times captured) that Rodchenko confronts head-on with a new vision of the socialist object. The object theorized by Rodchenko during his visit to Paris and his "encounter with Parisian consumer culture in 1925" constitutes, in Kiaer's reading, "an especially vivid articulation of the Constructivist theory of a socialist object that encompasses, rather than represses, the desires organized by the Western commodity fetish, even as its goal is to construct new, transparent relations between subject and object that will lead to the collective ideal of social utopia illuminated by 'the light from the East.'"[102] What Kiaer wants to shed light on with the example of Rodchenko's visit to Paris is a productive compromise between the ideal constructivist object and the conditions of exchange and desire operating in 1920s Parisian commodity culture. This compromise, Kiaer argues, yields an object that moves away from ideology and dogma to become "an actor in the actual material, historical, and bodily circumstances of NEP Russia"; "the utilitarian Constructivist object," Kiaer writes, "loses its perfection, and a good bit of its transparency, but it gains in its potential ability to organize the object-desires of modernity as an alternative to the commodity form."[103] "The socialist object of Russian Constructivism," Kiaer argues, "offers an alternative model of how commodity desire can become comprehensible to us, and available for social transformation, as we try to imagine a response to our own overloaded object world at the beginning of the twenty-first century."[104]

Rodchenko was far from the only figure of the Soviet avant-garde to embrace this duplicitous vision of what Susan Buck-Morss describes as "'socialist' commodities that, as intersubjective partners, were to provide alternatives to objects of consumption in their reified, capitalist form."[105] Kiaer cites Hubertus Gassner, who imagines a "constructivist universe" where "objects exist solely as organs of human activity."[106] Kiaer also examines the figure of Boris Arvatov, fascinating for the complexity with which he approached that moment in Soviet history suspended between the pressing necessity for trade and market capitalism, on the one hand, and socialist ideology on the other. Arvatov, Kiaer argues, "mordantly opposed to capitalism and vehemently Marxist in his training and sympathies . . . recognized the affective power of the mass-produced objects of modernity."[107]

Earlier in the twentieth century, during the first years of Dada in Zurich, the space and stage of the cabaret was revised and reinterpreted by Emmy Hennings, Hugo Ball, Marcel Janco, Tristan Tzara, and other members of the movement. Soon after its opening in 1916, the Cabaret Voltaire became a space of irreverence in the face of bourgeois propriety, a space where contestation against the horrors of World War I took inventive and unexpected forms directly informed by the theater of variety.[108] It is striking that the cabaret, a precursor of modern forms of entertainment, beloved by publics and derided by a significant swath of the intelligentsia,[109] could be used so powerfully as a platform of dissent. The artists who collaborated in the Cabaret Voltaire embraced amusement and entertainment values, caustically revising them to perform what Leah Dickerman has described as "an exuberant infantilism that undercut any pose of high seriousness."[110] Furthermore, these artists envisioned a curative dimension to their cabaret work, a shock-like remedy for spirits both shattered and inured by the atrocities of mechanized war. Their conjugation of the aesthetic and the therapeutic and their appeal to primordial states of consciousness through exercises in regression anticipated (with different means and under very different conditions) the kind of work Lygia Clark set out to do in the 1970s in the space of her home with *Estruturação do self*. Sophie Taeuber's language of abstraction, informed by her training in the arts and crafts as well as by her expertise in the applied arts (her works were on view at the third São Paulo Biennal in 1955), provides further points of contrast and comparison for the kind of homework Clark set out to do in the last phase of her trajectory. Furthermore, in the early 1920s, Man Ray and Marcel Duchamp picked up on the tactics of Dada artists in Europe through their *New York Dada* magazine, a platform for parodic, subversive appropriations of advertisements of the kind later performed by the concrete poets in Brazil.

In Mexico, Estridentismo, the first avant-garde movement constituted as such, embraced the language and braggadocio of Italian futurism and commercial propaganda. The movement's inaugural manifesto was published in Mexico City in 1921 and shared with most other manifestos a rhetoric of advertising. Titled "*Actual* no. 1" and written by Manuel Maples Arce, the movement's leader, the manifesto was printed as a broadsheet and plastered on walls facing the street, with care taken to target city blocks housing university buildings. Like Marinetti, Maples Arce strove to magnify the polemics he hoped to spark with his manifesto. But whereas Marinetti called for the burning of libraries and museums, Maples Arce tagged names onto his attacks on cultural institutions, leading a charge first against Miguel Hidalgo y Costilla, "El Cura Hidalgo," founding figure of the Mexican nation, and later against Frédéric Chopin, condemned by Maples Arce to death by electric chair.

Maples Arce was keenly aware of the impact that this type of sensationalist quip could have on his desired audience. His attention to publicity value comes to the fore several times throughout the manifesto, and under several guises. The manifesto's subtitle presents it as a *comprimido estridentista*, a pill for the ailments of a society at pains to be modern, at least in the eye of the manifesto's author. Marinetti himself was known for coloring his pronouncements with a medical or surgical tone. He signed many of his early essays and programmatic writings as "Dr F. T. Marinetti."[111] Maples Arce, too, plays out the desire to bridge the gap between art and life in pharmaceutical terms. Facing a world transformed by modern technologies, he lays out a program for a literary movement modeled as a fast-and-furious treatment: a pill for the maladies of backwardness. This twist, another clever marketing ploy by a poet hungry for public notice, is telling of a larger sociocultural context in Mexico in the 1920s, where the urban landscape was being transformed by new technologies as much as it was being redrawn by a burgeoning advertising industry banked by the pharmaceutical and tobacco industries, the latter a key source of corporate support for the Estridentista movement.[112]

The use of large, bold typeface for the title and headline and the strategic placing of Maples Arce's photograph on the front of the broadsheet ensured that "*Actual* no. 1" would get its fair share of attention amid the plaster of posters where it made its public debut. In the course of laying out his literary platform, Maples Arce makes a point to emphasize his "passion for the literature of commercial advertisements."[113] Further down the manifesto, in its sixth point (among the most intriguing, for its imagery and for the craft of its language), Maples Arce gives voice to the exhilarating experience of riding a car across some of Mexico City's thoroughfares, weaving together architectural landmarks, advertisements, and visions of automobile parts in a stream-of-consciousness account of his experience. For Maples Arce, the modernity that he so feverishly extols breaks down to three key elements: buildings, communications, and advertisements. The language of poets and the craft of artists, he argues throughout the manifesto, should feed from and be in line with the aesthetic (the artistic, perceptual, and emotional) experiences afforded by these elements of urban life.

Examples of Brazilian poetry in dialogue with advertising can be found throughout the twentieth century. Flora Süssekind looks into this dialogue in "Poesia & media," an essay included in her *Papéis colados* (1993) and later republished in the compilation of her works entitled *Vidrieras astilladas* (2003). This title suggests a breaking of the putative incompatibility between, on the one hand, contestatory postures against dictatorship and violent developmentalism and, on the other hand, the platforms and discourses (the window displays and slogans) of market capitalism. Early-twentieth-century works by Brazilian poets employed in advertising, Süssekind notes, resulted in forms of rhymed propaganda.[114] "Advertising as a profession," Süssekind writes in *Cinematograph of Words* (1997), "attracted . . . many of the best-known men of letters in the twentieth century, who did not think twice before accepting the role of the sandwich man,"[115] a derogatory term designating men of letters working with or in advertising and evocative of the laborers who earn wages by wearing signs quite literally over their shoulders. She names several Brazilian poets working in advertising at the time—including Olavo Bilac, the most revered of the Parnassian poets in Brazil, who worked with Confeitaria Colombo, and Emílio de Menezes, who collaborated with a Bromil cough syrup publicity campaign in 1917.[116]

By the 1960s and in the face of vicious repression, everything, argues Süssekind, even those experiments with language that seem most distanced from (or even incompatible with) the pressing realities of life under authoritarianism, "can be explained in terms of the engine of oppression of the authoritarian state."[117] Süssekind's approach, remarkable for its plasticity and for its sophisticated take on the intersection of culture, capitalism, and politics, is among the first in Latin America to substitute the rigid dichotomy of subversion-or-integration for a spectrum of responses that differ not in their engagement with or their failure to engage authoritarianism and its violently complicit expansion of market capitalism, but in the play of irony, parody, and referentiality that distinct genres and styles can afford. "Whether it's a preference for parables," writes Süssekind, "or for a literature focused on autobiographical reveries, the key lies either in the stylistic detour or in individual delirium as indirect responses to the impossibility of artistic expression beyond the grip of censorship."[118] As Süssekind argues, censorship was hardly the only measure of control deployed by the repressive governments, dictatorial and pseudo-democratic, that exercised power in Latin America in the decades after World War II. Repression, cooptation, and the regime of spectacle functioned then, as they function now, as the more effective tools of domination of capitalism at its most expansive.[119]

In Brazil in the 1950s and early 1960s, constructivism was by and large the most important reference for avant-garde poets and artists. The embrace of constructivist principles in Brazil coincided with periods of accelerated economic growth and industrialization (the 1920s and 1950s),[120] an unsurprising fact given constructivism's complex articulation of aesthetic experiments with utilitarian production. Constructivism was a particularly formative influence for the Brazilian artists and poets whose work is analyzed in depth over the course of this book. Constructivism was also, along with the Bauhaus and the Ulm School of Design, one of the principal referents for the professional organizations and academic programs of study dedicated to design that opened in Brazil in the decades after World War II. A 2008 exhibition curated by Daniela Name and titled *Diálogo concreto: design e construtivismo no Brasil* focused on the many convergences between constructivist aesthetics, industrial design, and graphic design in Brazil, shedding light on facets of artistic production—advertising and merchandising work, graphic design, industrial design, furniture production—fundamental for the development of a canon of constructivist art in Brazil.

An early, interesting, and perhaps surprising instance of serious scholarly interest in Brazilian advertising comes from Gilberto Freyre, in his pioneering analysis of classified ads in the newspapers of imperial Brazil. In 1961, as Brazil left behind the developmentalist frenzy that gave rise to the construction of Brasília to enter into one of the grimmest moments of its modern history, Freyre inaugurates what he refers to as the Brazilian branch of *anunciologia*, a science dedicated to the study of advertisements. Notices of runaway slaves published throughout the nineteenth century are the principal source of analysis in Freyre's groundbreaking book-length study titled *O escravo nos anúncios de jornais brasileiros do século XIX* (1963), where Freyre insists on the significance of advertisements as documents for the study of society. Freyre goes as far as asserting that the value of advertisements as sources for historical, anthropological, and sociological accounts of slavery in Brazil is higher than that of the other sections of the newspapers.

Corpus

Why study consumption and consumer society in relation to societies that seem at the fringe of commodity capitalism, outside the consecrated centers of this form of capitalism (Paris, New York, Los Angeles, etc.)? The matter of developmental mismatch—the *desencuentro* between, on the one hand, the political economy of consumption forcefully implemented in much of the Latin American region from the 1950s onward and, on the other hand, the precapitalist, preconsumerist conditions of development that held (and still hold) in much of the region—is a compelling reason to study consumer culture from the margins. In his analysis of the proletarianization of peasant communities in Colombia and Bolivia, Taussig argues that "societies on the threshold of capitalist development necessarily interpret that development in terms of precapitalist beliefs and practices."[121] Something like a "precapitalist" or, more precisely, a preconsumerist attitude to the products of the culture industry characterizes the approach of the artists and writers here convened. "Preconsumerist" should be here understood not chronologically, as that which comes before consumerism, much less teleologically. Rather, what this term reveals is a disposition that seems regressive relative to the ideology of consumerism—and revelatory for that very reason.

A sideways view, the look into commodity capitalism from a place both abstruse and external to its center, is well positioned to confront contrarieties and ambiguities that are easy to conceal or neglect. Despite, or perhaps precisely because of, a relative lag in the development of industry, consumer capitalism took deep roots in Latin American countries primed for "development" by a North American neighbor eager to align the region to its own strategic and economic interests and eager to ward off the influence of the Axis powers during World War II (and of the Soviet Union after that, during the Cold War). The ground was prepared, so to speak, by extensive US spending both private and public on advertising in Latin America during and after the war, even during moments when the flow of US manufactured consumer goods diminished.

This book presents a contradiction. It is premised on the study of consumption but structured around studies of particular artists and poets, particular authors—producers, in short. Even though the book is announced as a book on consumption, more often than not it ends up commenting on conditions of *production*, on the ways in which artists and poets go about their work in the age of consumer culture. The apparent contrarity between the book's subject matter and the readings that make up its chapters reflects the dialectical understanding of consumption that emerges both from the work of the artists and poets analyzed in this book and from the ways in which these artists and poets consciously and deliberately integrate into their work the perspective of publics conceived as participants, clients, or consumers. The basic idea here is that the producers (poets and artists) chosen for this book operate with categories responsive to the position of consumers. In doing so they help us understand something about how art is produced in the age of consumer culture—and also something about how consumption itself works, how it produces.

What is distinctive about these poets and artists is not so much that they concern themselves with their publics, or that they research and engage with the perspective and the experience of their publics, but that they conceive of these publics as consumer publics. The difference is important. It is partly what allows the poets and artists brought together in this book to concern themselves with subjective dispositions and cognitive faculties that are more commonly linked to consumption and less commonly associated with the production of art and poetry. In sum, the focus of this book will lie not on consumers, nor on consumption as a distinct and separate moment in the social dynamic, but rather on conditions of production of art and poetry in societies structured as societies of consumption, and on consumption as *productive force*, as "a power in the realm of consciousness."

Siqueiros's decades-long investigation into mural painting and conditions of spectatorship is a case in point. The "subversive dialectic" he flags in the title of his first essay on the use of mechanical tools and industrial materials refers to the real and effective material and ideological transformation that his methods of production underwent after incorporating into his productive process considerations emerging from the perspective of the consumer. The Brazilian concrete poets' interest in the reading posture of the consumer (the *leitor de manchetes*) and the changes in the creation of poetry they envision vis-à-vis this posture is also telling, as is Lygia Clark's insistent investigation into the notion of participation as a constitutive element of the aesthetic experience.

All of the artists and poets here convened occupy prominent places in the history of Latin American art and literature. Siqueiros is one of the three "great ones" of Mexican muralism. Octavio Paz is a Nobel laureate and a cultural institution in his own right. The Brazilian concrete poets are synonymous with a watershed moment in the history of Brazilian poetry, and their legacy continues to divide Brazilian poets, critics, and scholars to this day. Lygia Clark is among the most critically acclaimed artists in Latin America. Jointly, this group stakes out a wide spectrum of creative choices and literary and artistic insertions in the wider social spectrum. Siqueiros is among the most visible representatives of muralism and the larger, regional wave of figurative art with strong, though not entirely determinant, links to social realism. Clark, by contrast, is a leading practitioner of abstraction, with direct filiations to a tradition of constructivism. Each of them represent different sides of a Latin American cultural sphere cleft in the mid-twentieth century by the Communist Party's embrace of social realism and the concurrent resistance of artists who practiced abstraction without abdicating art's possibility for social insertion.[122]

In critical accounts of the work of these artists published during the time in which they were active, the localized contrast between the respective positions they occupy in a wider constellation of modern art is too blinding, too critical, too strategic to allow for a comparative analysis of their respective tactics. In Brazil, the rise of abstraction and concretism as the dominant tendencies of advanced art was premised on the suppression of the kind of figurative, muralist, social-realist art that the figure of Cândido Portinari stood for.[123] In Mexico, a corresponding conflict took shape as muralism's overbearing legacy and its near monopoly over state commissions and a budding private market galvanized an oppositional wave of expressionism and abstraction. By bringing together two figures who occupy such distant, even contrary positions in the art field, as Siqueiros and Clark do, my intention is not to elide the differences that hold between them, but rather to provide a richer spectrum of artistic responses to the social conditions of consumer culture.

None of the artists and poets gathered here, except for the Brazilian concrete poets, are readily associated with consumer culture or with the culture industry, but most of the works here gathered came about through some kind of contact with the material culture of consumer capitalism. In all four cases studied over the course of the book's chapters, this contact took place in explicit awareness of the extent to which the market shapes societies in general and conditions of art production and reception in particular. Siqueiros noted that in the first decades of the twentieth century "manifestations of a new social type emerge, that is, manifestations of a new market."[124] "The world turns," Siqueiros continues, "to collective forms, to imposing masses of men, concentrations of tens and thousands of people appear in the everyday life of all peoples . . . and thus the need for new forms of advertising and art."[125] Haroldo de Campos writes of "a certain kind of contemporary mental form" imposed by "posters, slogans, headers, the diction of popular speech."[126] In "Los signos en rotación," his celebrated essay on poetics, Paz grapples with the power of mass and consumer culture to reconfigure the place of the sensorial in the production and reception of language at large and written language in particular. He writes: "Journalism, advertising, film, and other forms of visual reproducibility have transformed writing."[127] The experience of language, he concludes, "is once again physical, corporeal: today we apprehend the word through our ears, the word is embodied, it is incarnate."[128] Lygia Clark, for her part, begins and ends a decades-long artistic trajectory in the space of the home, crucial battlefield for the consolidation of consumer culture. She devotes the better part of her career to an earnest investigation of what she called relational objects, made from everyday materials of the kind one finds in households everywhere: plastic bags, rubber bands, tubes, Styrofoam, and so forth.

Including Brazilian concrete poetry and Lygia Clark in the same corpus and arguing for a certain continuity traceable across their respective bodies of work is contrary to what has been, for a long time, a commonly held belief regarding the opposition between the aesthetic projects represented by the concrete poets on the one hand and Clark on the other. Concrete poetics and aesthetics, the story goes, stand for the rigid, intellectualist, prescriptive, mechanized, antisubjective principles of art formulated by Theo van Doesburg in his "Concrete Art Manifesto" of 1930.[129] Neoconcretism, on the other hand, stands for an organic, vital, sensual, embodied approach to the production of art and to its insertion in the social milieu. This contrast is important for what Sérgio B. Martins has identified as the trace of teleological historicism in Ferreira Gullar's theory of the nonobject[130] as well as in other foundational accounts of contemporary art in Brazil. Recent scholarship on the Brazilian avant-gardes after World War II skews this "comparative cliché," as Martins calls it,[131] in favor of more complex, more nuanced accounts that trace the multiple points of difference and convergence between concretism and neoconcretism.[132]

The sharp contrast between concretism and neoconcretism was, in any case, built more on the differences between neoconcrete and concrete visual artists (figures like Lygia Clark and Hélio Oiticica, on the one hand, and Waldemar Cordeiro and Geraldo de Barros, on the other) than on the differences between neoconcrete artists and concrete poets. The heart of the dispute between the two movements was, of course, triggered by the publication of a manifesto written by one of the poets: Haroldo de Campos's "da fenomenologia da composição à matemática da composição" (1957). There Haroldo, and by extension the other concrete poets, embraced explicitly the dogmatic imposition of "mathematical" over "organic structure,"[133] a choice defended as a matter of principle by Cordeiro and Barros. But as subsequent collaborations between Haroldo de Campos, Augusto de Campos, and Hélio Oiticica[134] demonstrate, the rupture of neoconcrete art and concrete poetry was, in the long term, more strategic, less categorical, and much less definitive than the rupture between concrete and neoconcrete art proved to be.

Part of what I attempt to accomplish in my reading of concrete poetry might seem incongruous or outright foolish from the perspective of older narratives of concretism and neoconcretism, narratives that insist on celebrating the emancipating sensualness of the latter at the expense of a stifling cerebralness in the former. The case for concrete poetry's excessive rationality, the case for its narrow and dogmatic intellectualism, can and has been made strongly in reference to the rhetoric of its manifestos and in relation to the so-called orthodox phase of the movement, when the rhetorical devices and the visual components of concrete poetry were reduced to a minimum, and when concrete poetry fit rigidly within language structures derived from the modernist grid. But as I hope to demonstrate, the larger body of poems and programmatic texts of concrete poetry provide ample evidence of a transversal commitment to the material and sensorial dimensions of language, a commitment that proved fundamental to the concrete poets' understanding of language under market capitalism.

There are some direct biographical links between some of the figures convened here, though biographical connection was neither a guiding thread nor a preoccupation as I put together the corpus of this book. Rodolfo Mata writes that Paz first heard of Brazilian concrete poetry by way of e. e. cummings during a visit to New York in 1959.[135] Paz and Haroldo de Campos began writing to each other in 1968, discussing their views on poetry and sharing news of their respective publications. The exchange led to Campos's translation of Paz's *Blanco* and to the publication of a dossier of Brazilian concrete poetry in *Vuelta*, the literary magazine founded by Paz in 1976. Paz's encounter with Brazilian concrete poetry through his correspondence with Campos had a significant impact on his immediate and long-term projects. It sparked, in particular, a moment of marked attention to visuality in his poetry extending from the late 1960s to the early 1970s. His *Topopoemas* (1967), *Discos visuales* (1968), and *Blanco* all date from this period. In a letter to the Spanish-Mexican artist Vicente Rojo (with whom Paz collaborated on the publication of *Discos visuales*), Paz makes it clear just how much Brazilian concrete poetry influenced his turn toward the visual in poetry. Paz writes: "In a way, *Discos visuales* is a variation on the surrealist object-poem. Also, and above all, it has to do with the experiments of concrete poetry."[136]

Concrete poetry first appeared in Mexico in the work of Mathias Goeritz, the visionary artist whose tremendous legacy in Mexico City spans painting, urbanism (Ciudad Satélite), architecture (Museo Experimental El Eco), and visual poetry. It was Goeritz, keenly attuned to art and literary developments in Europe and elsewhere, who first came into contact with the ideas elaborated simultaneously and independently by poets in Brazil, in Switzerland, and elsewhere, the same ideas that would eventually coalesce into something like a global movement of concrete poetry. It was Goeritz, too, who first undertook the production of concrete poems in Mexico,[137] and he did so with distinction—integrating it into walls and other architectural features of buildings in a way that brought concrete poetry to the arts integration movement then in vogue in Mexico (Siqueiros was a vocal defender) and elsewhere in Latin America. Concrete poetry and Brazilian concrete poetry in particular were influential in Paz's turn toward visual poetry and his experimentation with forms of advertising, explored at length in chapter 3 of this book. Concrete poetry was first introduced to Mexican audiences during an initial, much-publicized and highly consequential exhibition entitled *Poesía concreta internacional*, organized by Goeritz at the Galería Universitaria Aristos in 1966.[138] The exhibition, with a catalog and posters designed by Vicente Rojo, was a major success both in terms of attendance and in terms of the impact it had in the local artistic and literary milieu.

The stature of both Paz and Siqueiros in the Mexican arts scene made it all but impossible for them not to be aware of each other's work. Paz in particular took an interest in Mexican muralism, and he wrote of Siqueiros's contribution to the preeminent Mexican visual arts movement. He expressed reservations about Siqueiros's dogmatic political outlook and recognized the pioneering role Siqueiros played in incorporating technologies of communication and industrial materials into the practice of painting. In reference to Siqueiros, Paz writes: "He was an innovator and explored many territories: aerial perspective and perspective in movement, photography and new materials and instruments."[139]

The midcentury outdoor murals of David Alfaro Siqueiros are studied in detail in chapter 1 of this book. This chapter revisits Siqueiros's legacy as a politically engaged artist in light of his experimentation with billboards and advertising as viable forms for the production of politicized art. Starting with a remarkable moment of experimentation in the 1930s that saw Siqueiros incorporate film and photography as key components of his mural painting, this chapter sets the ground for a revision of Siqueiros's billboard murals from the 1950s and for a closer examination of the tense, contradictory aesthetic and political program that these murals represent. The chapter works through the extensive writings published by Siqueiros throughout his life and includes photographs and several unpublished essays and lectures housed at the Sala de Arte Público Siqueiros in Mexico City and the Getty Research Institute in Los Angeles. Analysis of the mural works Siqueiros produced in Los Angeles and in Mexico City in the 1930s provides the background necessary for the discussion of the billboard murals he produced in Mexico in the 1950s. The tension I identify in my study of Siqueiros's billboard murals—the tension between a commitment to progressive political forces and an overt embrace of tourism and of commercial platforms—compels us, I submit, to revisit persistent assumptions about what politicized oppositional art is and how it should relate to the powers it opposes. The chapter includes a comparative reading of Siqueiros's writings on his use of mechanical tools and industrial materials and Benjamin's essay on reproducibility, written at just about the same time, with Siqueiros preceding Benjamin by a couple of years.

A possibility manifest in the work of Siqueiros (a "spectacular coup against the spectacularization of society")[140] comes to the fore in Brazilian concrete poetry, the subject of chapter 2. The allure that advertisements held for the Brazilian concrete poets is studied in detail over the course of this chapter, beginning with a reading of *Poetamenos* (1953), the visually captivating collection of poems by Augusto de Campos. Modeled after neon lights and originally intended as neon signs, these poems draw the senses as much as they draw the mind, and this, I submit, is crucial to our understanding of the regressions and the actual potentials of urban commodity capitalism. For if, as Fredric Jameson argues, "the most implacable theory of manipulation in mass culture . . . must somehow acknowledge the experiential moment in the mesmerization of the masses . . . if only then to dismiss it as the fix, addiction, false pleasure, or whatever,"[141] so, then, the reader of Brazilian concrete poetry must come to terms with the visual and perceptual fascination exerted by advertising, entangled as it is with the more "profound" semantic and political dimensions of concrete poems. This chapter works through poems by Augusto de Campos where his embrace of advertising is most evident. It also focuses on poems by Décio Pignatari that show traces of his time spent working in the advertising industry. The libidinal attraction thematized in Campos's *Poetamenos* and the alluring scatological nature of Pignatari's advertisement-poems set the terms for my reading of fascination as a principal category for an aesthetics of consumption. Readings of the extensive theoretical writings produced by the concrete poets constitute a significant part of this chapter. Special attention is paid to what critics—Ronaldo Brito and Roberto Schwarz foremost among them—have denounced as Brazilian concrete poetry's affinities with developmentalism and the ideology of progress. In this chapter, I consider these affinities as a crucial and problematic element of a larger critical engagement, an element that does not exhaust itself in the poets' enthusiastic embrace of the culture industry, contrary to what some of the movement's critics have implied.

Chapter 3 focuses on the intersection of consumer culture and poetry in the writings of Octavio Paz. Much has been said about Paz's views on modernity, but his thoughts on the techniques and technologies subtending consumer culture are lesser known and seldom discussed. In essays crossed by the teachings and writings of José Gaos, Martin Heidegger, and Alfonso Reyes, Paz grapples with a dialectic of enrichment and extraction at work in the language of culture under capitalism. He points to both to the potential unleashed in language by the language of advertising and consumer culture (its increased corporeality, its attraction and sensualness) and to the depletion of meaning and signification unfolding under market capitalism. In this as in other chapters of this book, I am most interested in highlighting an underlying ambiguity in poetry and in art toward the world of commodity capitalism, the ambiguity of a constitutional negation, a riposte that takes the form of replication. "Poetry," writes Paz, "has resisted modernity, and in resisting it, it has revitalized it. Poetry has been its antidote and its *réplica*."[142]

What I propose is a reading of opposition as *réplica*: as response, as copy, and as aftershock. The first and last senses of opposition I here offer—opposition as response and as aftershock—Paz himself illuminates in essays analyzed throughout the course of chapter 3. The middle term—opposition as copy, as reproduction—is one Paz was less eager to embrace, but it reveals much about the links between his poetry and the context of consumer culture to which his poetry responds. For at the heart of Paz's most experimental phase as poet (the phase of *Blanco*, of *Topopoemas*, and of *Discos visuales*), at the heart of the poetry he produced in the late 1960s, is an appropriation of forms from mass media and advertising. Readings of earlier poems frame the confrontation of lyric poetry and consumer culture as a longer, transversal concern in Paz's poetry, one that follows closely his interest in the city as lyric subject. As I hope to demonstrate, the earlier poems written before Paz's experimental phase present the city in frozen and metric stillness—in the vibrating stillness of the sonnet—by a lyrical voice traveling on foot, and, occasionally (quaintly) on tram. In "Entrada en materia" (1958–1961) as well as in subsequent poems, the city comes to life in all its fluorescent glory, in zigzagging verses, sharp, loud, and aggressive, the old Mixcoac of Paz's childhood flooding not with water but with an endless stream of cars making their way through streets plastered with store signs and neon lights.

The fourth and final chapter of this book focuses on the works and writings of Lygia Clark. My reading of Clark's work grapples with her return home, to the space of her apartment in Rio de Janeiro, the site and ground of her last major proposal, the *Estruturação do self*. Of all the figures convened in this book, Clark seems the one who is most distanced from the world of consumer culture. Yet, as I argue, her extensive body of work is guided by an investigation into the notions of home, homemaking, and being at home. Clark's interest in the notion of home is made explicit in the many works that feature this term in their titles as well as in her sustained interests in, and dialogue with, the discourse of architecture. A focus on the idea of home throws new light onto the series of artworks and proposals Clark grouped together under the title *objetos relacionais*, emphasizing the way they are made, their homely manufacture, as well as the everyday household materials with which they are made. In my reading, Clark's long and rigorous experimentation with what she called relational objects gives meaning and substance to a largely forgotten Marxist vision of our relationship to objects, a relationship essentially defined by consumption. The framing of Clark's relational objects against the background—real and conceptual—of the home provides new perspectives on Ferreira Gullar's notion of the nonobject, a term Gullar coined in reference to works by Clark from the late 1950s. The chapter builds on the idea of consciousness as consciousness with something, a twist on a well-known principle of phenomenology that posits all consciousness as consciousness of something. Objects as conceived by Clark, as relational objects, take on possibilities seldom envisioned by Marxist critiques of mass culture, burdened as these critiques usually are with a sense of puritanism vis-à-vis commodities and the commodity as form. Against a background of consumer culture, in the context of the larger historical moment—commodity capitalism—to which Clark's work belongs, the relational objects reveal another way of conceiving of objects and of the relationships that hold between subjects and objects.

ONE

Attention and Distraction

The Billboard as Mural Form

Siqueiros Goes Commercial

By far the most technically daring of the three "great ones" of Mexican muralism,[1] David Alfaro Siqueiros began to use mechanical tools and industrial materials in 1932 during a stay in Los Angeles. Two decades' worth of experiences with these tools and materials gave rise to Siqueiros's 1950s program for outdoor murals modeled after large-scale billboards. Most interesting about these projected murals is the political expediency to which they aspired. Conceived for major corridors of urban movement and projected in a visual language fit for apprehension in distraction, these murals sought to have a real, effective impact on immediate historical events. In what follows I revisit Siqueiros's legacy as a politically engaged artist with an emphasis on an aspect of his work—a form of vision made and meant for distracted publics—that goes mostly unremarked in the extant bibliography on the artist. Analysis of the mural works Siqueiros produced in the 1930s provides some necessary background for my reading of the billboard murals he began to envision in the 1950s. The tension I identify in Siqueiros's plan for billboard muralism—the tension between a commitment to progressive political causes and an overt embrace of commercial platforms—compels us to revisit persistent assumptions about what politicized oppositional art is and how it should relate to the powers it opposes.

Mural painting, then—politically committed, commercially modeled, and spectacularly proportioned: such is the tensely construed form of art Siqueiros pursues from the 1950s until the end of his artistic trajectory in the 1970s. The course of my analysis follows three steps in Siqueiros's pursuit of this form. First, the exteriorization of mural painting from indoor patios to walls facing the street and the concurrent employment of mechanical tools in painting. Second, the mapping of what Siqueiros called the topography of the spectator using technologies (the camera and film projector) and techniques (montage and photomontage) anchored in photography and film. And third, the adoption of visual strategies drawn from advertising, especially from billboards, for the production of this form of muralism. In all three steps, Siqueiros was guided by the conviction that his intended public was a distracted public, a public demanding a dynamic and participative rather than a static and contemplative engagement with art.

An outright embrace of advertisements as *the* reference for the production of artworks placed outdoors is likely to be met with surprise, even scorn, particularly when the embrace came from an artist like Siqueiros, outspoken as he was regarding his commitment to liberation and class struggle. He anticipates this kind of reaction, prefacing his praise of billboard advertisements (or "commercial muralism" as he called it) with a plea: "Don't be surprised!"[2] Most likely to arouse suspicion on the part of those who followed Siqueiros's politics since the early days of Mexican muralism was the fact that his embrace of "commercial muralism" in the 1950s did not seem to dampen his commitment to leftist ideology and the struggle against capitalism. In a moment of inflection during which the citizen and the consumer collapse into a single social category, outright appropriations of forms and techniques of advertising by a progressive, even radical, politically engaged artist would have raised more than a few eyebrows. Siqueiros was well aware of the resulting paradox (the paradox of progressive, political art made with commercial, capitalist forms), and he took it in stride.

Considered carefully, Siqueiros's sustained interest in both commercial forms and revolutionary struggle seems astute, even visionary, given what Jonathan Crary has theorized as "the paradoxical intersection, which has existed in many ways since the later nineteenth century, between an imperative of a concentrated attentiveness within the disciplinary organization of labor, education, and mass consumption and an ideal of sustained attentiveness as a constitutive element of a creative and free subjectivity."[3] The existence of this paradoxical intersection and its implications for the production of art under capitalism did not escape Siqueiros. In an unpublished document written in New York around 1934, Siqueiros argues that art "reflects the characteristics and the contradictions of the whole society that produces it," that art "suffers the same contingencies of the class or classes that propel it."[4] Most striking in this and other writings by Siqueiros is the exception he takes from the revolutionary purism[5] characteristic of so many prominent leftist intellectuals in the Americas and beyond: "the rise of a revolutionary class," writes Siqueiros, "carries with it the kernel of a revolutionary art that grows in the very body of a moribund society."[6] This, he goes on to argue, "produces an inevitable overlap of cultural elements (revolutionary and counter-revolutionary) in the artistic production as a whole."[7] This belief in the power of "heterogeneous, mixed, paradoxical aesthetic effects," this conviction in the face of revolutionary form manifest in "parasitic and decadent expressions"[8] is, I believe, one of the most fascinating, consequent, and suggestively formulated aspects of Siqueiros's aesthetic thought.

From the 1930s onward and in the 1950s in particular, Siqueiros's mural paintings aspired to a political expediency that seems to be at odds with the commercial forms, discourses, and techniques Siqueiros was building into those very murals. The tension he established and that I focus on in this chapter, the tension between an allegiance to revolutionary forces and an overt embedment with the world of commerce, gives us pause to weigh hardened assumptions about what politicized oppositional art is, what it looks like, and what its relationship to the powers it opposes (i.e., the market, consumerism) should be. This is not to suggest that the paradoxical combination of political art and forms of advertising was new in the theory and praxis of politicized art. A number of artists and writers from the Soviet avant-gardes (Mayakovsky, Lissitzky, and Klutsis foremost among them) moved prolifically between art production and the production of political and commercial propaganda. Benjamin himself was taken with what Christina Kiaer has characterized as "the commodity's dream-power,"[9] and it was his fascination with the mobilizing potential inherent in this dream-power that animated many of his most intriguing writings on the Parisian Arcades.[10]

We find glimpses of the link between commodity culture and politicized art early on in Siqueiros's trajectory, in a lecture he delivered in Paris in 1938. Siqueiros recalls that *El Machete* (an outlet first of the Syndicate of Technical Workers, Painters, and Sculptors [Sindicato de Obreros Técnicos, Pintores y Escultores] and later of the Communist Party in Mexico), the first of many journals Siqueiros had a hand in publishing, was of large dimensions, "larger than the widely-circulated bourgeois newspapers"; this, he argues, allowed its distributors to fix it on street walls, like a poster.[11] A few years before *El Machete* started circulating, "*Actual* no. 1" (1921) by Manuel Maples Arce, the first manifesto of the Estridentista movement (written and published under the marked influence of Siqueiros's own "Tres llamamientos de orientación actual a los pintores y escultores de la nueva generación americana," included in the first and only issue of *Vida Americana*[12]), was posted on Mexico City buildings, a modernist call to arms amid the plaster of advertisements covering walls and kiosks throughout the Mexican capital.

Such was the prevalence of posters and other forms of advertisements in the streets of Mexico City from the beginning of the twentieth century onward that what seems surprising is not that an artist would attempt to conjugate politicized aesthetics and commercial propaganda, but that more artists did not do so. In a recently published account of the development of consumer culture in Mexico in the last decades of the nineteenth century and the first decades of the twentieth, Steven Bunker makes a point of reminding us just how profuse the presence of advertisements was in the landscape of Mexico City. "A careful look at Porfirian- and Revolution-era photographs reveals a city whose brick and stone structures are blanketed with paper and painted advertising."[13] Bunker argues that by the time the Mexican Revolution started in 1910, advertising in the city was excessive enough to be regarded as a public interest issue.[14]

Three subsets of Siqueiros's murals, all of them painted after the foundational moment of Mexican muralism in Mexico City in the early 1920s, will be considered over the course of this chapter: first, two murals painted outdoors in Los Angeles, California; second, the two indoor murals he completed in the 1930s, in Argentina and in Mexico City; and third, the billboard and logotype murals he completed in the 1950s in the Mexican capital. Siqueiros's writings, which remain somewhat understudied relative to his artworks, will also be discussed here. Though this has been relatively unremarked in studies on the artist,[15] Siqueiros was a sharp and sophisticated art theorist; the sheer number of his articles on aesthetics and politics position him as one of the most prolific art writers among twentieth-century Latin American artists.[16] That said, a few words about Siqueiros's rhetoric and style are in order. His texts are often peppered with rhetorical flights of fancy and, on first reading, this makes them seem like so much fluff buttressed by too few statements of substance.

Multiple formulations of the same proposition are not uncommon across his writings. This is partially a consequence of the programmatic nature of his rhetoric—a necessary evil, so to speak, of the manifesto style Siqueiros cultivated most of his life. Defining traits of his style, like the constant repetition of clauses at the beginning of paragraphs, suit Siqueiros's pedagogic and propagandistic agenda. Numbering and listing are also common in his texts, as is a certain hyperbolic flare.

One other aspect of Siqueiros's writing style should be noted. It was often the case that he wrote effusively about breakthroughs before fully grasping their importance or lack thereof. In most but not all cases, his early enthusiasm was eventually confirmed as he delved deeper into the full significance of his technical findings. His writings on photography and film, the earliest of which date from 1921, are a case in point. Siqueiros began to experiment with photography and cinematography in earnest in Los Angeles in 1932. He wrote about this experience soon thereafter. Some of his most incisive writings on the significance of photography, however, come not from the early texts, but from writings penned in the late 1930s and the early 1940s. This is not to say that the earlier texts are rendered dispensable by the later ones; they are, in fact, strikingly similar in their details and substance. They differ in the calm sobriety with which the ideas that are jostled around in the early writings are laid out in the later texts. It is not uncommon for him to wax enthusiastic about a development only to admit its initial shortcomings years later, once he had moved beyond those shortcomings.[17]

Siqueiros Goes to Hollywood

In 1932, ten years after he painted his first murals in the Escuela Nacional Preparatoria in Mexico City and having spent the better part of the 1920s as a labor organizer and political agitator, Siqueiros traveled to the United States for a brief but pivotal stay in the city of Los Angeles, where he was commissioned to paint murals on walls facing the street.[18] He assembled a group of artists (the "Block of Mural Painters") and completed murals that gave him grounds to write a series of essays and lectures focused on what he argued was a new phase of muralism: an outdoor, public muralism, a collective form of muralism completed by teams of collaborators rather than individual artists, an art form and a mode of production better fit for political agitation in the age of mass publics. Two of the three murals Siqueiros painted in Los Angeles, *Mitin obrero* (1932) and *América tropi-*

cal (1932), were more or less visible from the street, and the move from indoor patios to walls facing the street completely overhauled the way Siqueiros thought about mural painting. In a lecture read in 1932 at the John Reed Club in Los Angeles, days before his forced departure from the United States under threat of political persecution, Siqueiros looks back at the first years of the muralist "renaissance" in Mexico and states:

> We were painters in the age of the easel painting, specifically, in the age of the framed painting, in the age of the frame. We were painters in a time during which the visual work of art corresponded to a static spectator. In Mexico, during our first muralist experience, we had done nothing but to move within the confines of the "paneux," that is, to work with the framed painting of larger proportions, or more clearly, to move toward the enlargement of the easel painting projected on the wall of an architectural site.[19]

During the first years of muralism, neither Siqueiros nor any of the other artists involved in the muralist movement recognized the limits of artworks meant for mass spectatorship but set in spaces of limited access. The muralists aspired to produce a truly public form of art, one that could reach not just informed and specialized audiences but the Mexican public at large. In truth, though, the spaces where the first murals were set (the interior patios of government buildings) significantly limited their potential for reaching mass audiences.

As he began to paint murals outdoors Siqueiros began to think about the site of mural painting as a determinant of its formal structure as well as of its potential political impact. Siqueiros realized that the mass urban public he sought to reach was distracted and in motion: walking, driving, and moving through the urban grid. He realized that images and language displayed outdoors elicit a viewing experience fundamentally different from the one rehearsed in museums and other traditional exhibition spaces. The fact that Siqueiros came to this realization in Los Angeles, a major city in the industrialized world and the world capital of the entertainment industry, is telling. A warm welcome given to both Diego Rivera and José Clemente Orozco in the United States a few years prior to Siqueiros's arrival in Los Angeles was a likely incentive for Siqueiros to make the move north, but his admiration for the United States' preeminent position as the leading industrialized nation of the inter-war period (an admiration that throws doubt on reductive assessments of the muralists and their relationship to the United States)[20] seems to have been another important factor behind his decision to live and work there.[21] His diatribes against American capitalism notwithstanding, Siqueiros considered the United States an ideal platform for artists to acquaint themselves with mechanical tools and industrial modes of production, which, he lamented, remained "unknown, inconceivably, to this day, to my fellow muralists in Mexico, unknown to the sub-snobs that follow contemporary trends in Paris, and generally unknown to artists of the world."[22]

The circumstances under which Siqueiros worked in Los Angeles brought about a fervent period of technical experimentation. With the move to Los Angeles he engaged more closely with the tools, the forms, and the world of cinema, building on interests and desires he began to develop a year earlier in Taxco, Mexico, in 1930–1931, in conversation with Sergei Eisenstein. Some of the key technical breakthroughs he arrived at during his time in Los Angeles are a direct consequence of working in close quarters with filmmakers and other professionals of the film industry based in Hollywood.[23] His interest in film dates back to 1921, to the publication of *Vida Americana* in Barcelona, which includes an article by Siqueiros called "Cinematografía mexicana." This brief text is a laudatory review of *El caporal* (1921), an early film produced in Mexico and directed by Miguel Contreras Torres. Siqueiros is particularly drawn to the affinities between Contreras and North American films; he takes this to be "the highest mark of solid modernity."[24] A decade after writing this, Siqueiros meets Eisenstein in Taxco, sparking a brief, intense, and mutually influencing relationship.[25] Siqueiros mentioned Eisenstein in praiseful terms in subsequent writings on film, and Eisenstein credited Siqueiros for the aesthetic of *¡Que Viva México!*, filmed in 1931 but only released posthumously in 1979. Eisenstein also contributed to Siqueiros's first solo exhibition at the Casino Español in Mexico City in 1932, writing a blurb for the catalog of the exhibition.[26]

Cinema turned into a key reference for Siqueiros as he tried to understand the kind of spectacle that his outdoor murals in Los Angeles could elicit among the publics for whom he intended them. *Mitin obrero* (1932), also known as *Mitin de fábrica* and *Mitin en la calle*, was the first one he completed as part of the seminar he taught at the Chouinard School of Arts. Misgivings on the part of the director of the Chouinard School resulted in the mural's placement outdoors. In the lecture delivered in Paris in the late 1930s, cited above, Siqueiros writes: "The director of the Chouinard School of Art considered it inappropriate to trust our group with one of the interior walls of her academy. . . . She was happy with us taking a wall on the exterior of the building to bring forth the completion of

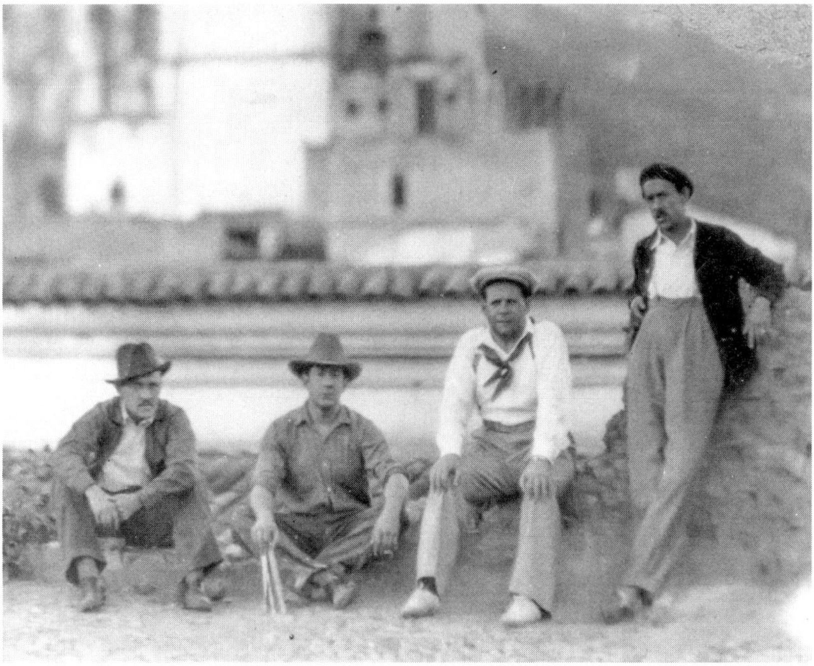

Figure 1.1. William Spratling, David Alfaro Siqueiros, Sergei Eisenstein, and Chano Urueta, on set for the filming of Eisenstein's *¡Que viva México!* in 1930 or 1931. Unknown photographer. Courtesy of the Instituto Nacional de Bellas Artes y Literatura.

our project."[27] In an unpublished document from 1932 (a draft of the lecture he delivered in Los Angeles that same year), Siqueiros wrote effusively (and not without exaggeration) on the significance that the ensuing events had for his future work:

> Due to its very situation our *exterior* work constituted a far-reaching public spectacle, unprecedented in modern art and, due to some of its physical traits, unprecedented in art in general. During the time when we began to sketch it out, we noticed thousands of people watched from the thousands and thousands of windows in the buildings around us. . . . Additionally, thousands and thousands of pedestrians stopped to look at it and they kept on looking as they walked by. . . . Without, in theory, meaning to do so, we had found . . . a superior vehicle for the modern art of modern life. An unquestionable form for the great masses![28]

The context of this passage seems to be intentionally vague about whether it refers to the execution of *Mitin obrero* or of *América tropical* (1932), the second outdoor mural Siqueiros completed in Los Angeles. But based on descriptions made by his collaborators and by critics and journalists who wrote about the murals soon after they were completed, it seems more likely that what Siqueiros has in mind here is *América tropical*.

América tropical, as its title suggests, is an allegory of the tropical latitudes of the American continent. It was painted on the exterior wall of a building in downtown Los Angeles, on Olvera Street. The mural was commissioned as a more or less celebratory depiction of motifs often associated with tropical America: lush vegetation, pyramids, and so forth. Siqueiros's take on the subject was brashly provocative. Instead of providing an idealized vision of the tropics and its dwellers, Siqueiros painted an Indian man crucified under the gaze of an eagle menacingly perched on top of a double cross, amid the rubble of a ruined stone pyramid.

Compared to the works of the first phase of muralism, this mural includes a relatively small number of graphic elements. Its figures are arranged around a crucifixion scene, the visual anchor point of the composition. To draft it, Siqueiros used a photograph from 1865 of the crucifixion of a colored servant accused of murdering his master's son,[29] a pointed choice for a Mexican artist working in the United States and cognizant of the systemic discrimination against, and the systemic oppression of, African Americans in the United States.[30] To the left of the crucifixion is a large tree-like figure; its disproportionately large dimensions serve to offset the asymmetry of the wall where the mural is set. The branches of the tree-like figure, like the curved torso and the limbs of the crucified man, are tubular, establishing a visual resonance between the crucified man and the vegetation around him and thus suggesting the extent to which this man is rooted in the tropical setting around him. The top of the trapezoidal pyramid behind the crucifixion scene is decorated with hieroglyphs that appear to be modeled after Maya and Aztec codices. To the right of the crucifixion, Siqueiros painted a porch around the actual door that pierces through the wall, cleverly integrating the preexisting architectural feature into the composition of his mural, in much the same way Rivera did in his murals at the Palacio Nacional and the Secretaría de Educación Pública in Mexico City. On top of the painted porch, two armed men in Mexican garb (an iconic look linked to the Mexican Revolution of 1910–1920) crouch down as they witness the crucifixion scene with an air of expectation, ready to intervene at a moment's notice.

We get a sense of the conditions of spectatorship afforded by the space where *América tropical* is set from recollections by Harold Lehman, an American artist who collaborated with Siqueiros first in Los Angeles and

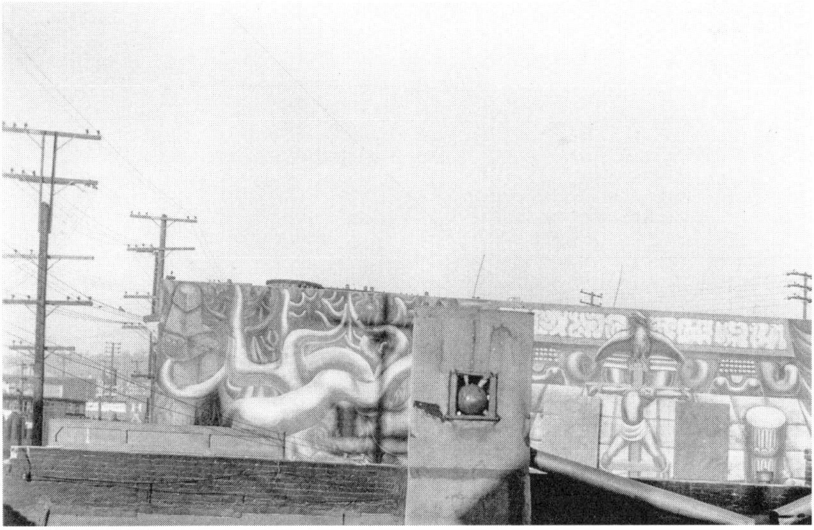

Figure 1.2. Rooftop view (in the middle ground, partially obstructed) of David Alfaro Siqueiros, *América tropical* (1932). Fresco on cement, 250 × 50 feet. Los Angeles, California. Photograph ca. 1932; photographer unknown. Courtesy of the Instituto Nacional de Bellas Artes y Literatura.

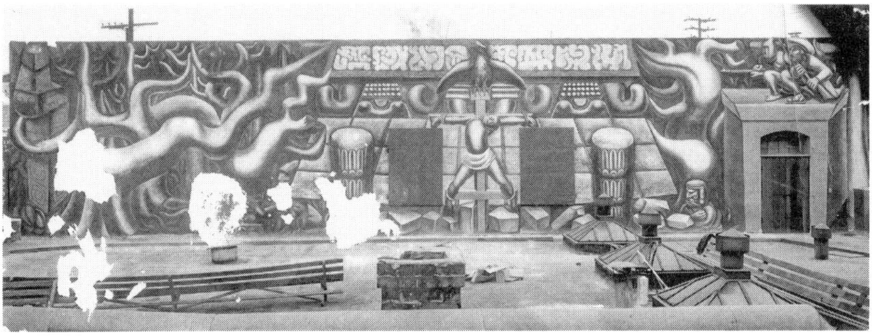

Figure 1.3. Rooftop view of David Alfaro Siqueiros, *América tropical* (1932). Cement fresco, 250 × 50 feet. Los Angeles, California. Actual architectural features (windows, door) visible on the center and right side of the mural. Photographer unknown. Courtesy of the Instituto Nacional de Bellas Artes y Literatura.

later in New York City (in the Experimental Workshop Siqueiros and his collaborators, among them Jackson Pollock, opened in Manhattan).[31] In an interview for the Archives of American Art of the Smithsonian Institution, Lehman speaks at length of his work with Siqueiros, providing a candid, firsthand account of the process of painting *América tropical*, the reactions elicited by the finished mural, and the whitewashing of the work following the public backlash caused by the mural's overt political tone.[32] He describes the space where the mural was set as being partially open and at least partially visible from the street: "they used to have an open staircase, right up the building onto the roof. They had a building that had a one level roof and then a raised wall with the fresco, and then the roof of the second part of the building. And they closed off the entry so that you could not get up to the roof to view it. However you could see it from a distance."[33]

Period photos of Olvera Street in Los Angeles, where *América tropical* is located, show a vivid scene at the site of Siqueiros's mural. Then as now, the part of downtown Los Angeles where the mural was set, around Olvera Street, was known for its large Mexican population and for its foot traffic, aided in large part by the proximity of a railroad terminal and of City Hall.[34] Some of the mural's compositional features indicate that it was in fact designed to be viewed from a distance. Most noticeably, the tree-like figure on the left side, which would seem disproportionately large to a viewer standing right in front of the mural, would look balanced when seen from afar and aside, from the street. For Siqueiros, acknowledging the dynamic nature of the spectator was a matter of recognizing that the public of *América tropical* was both massive and in transit, in motion, walking by and taking in the mural at the same time, thus presenting him with the challenge of arriving at an art form and a corresponding painting technique adapted to mass publics moving through large, public spaces.

The Mural as Spectacle: Photography and Society

The social condition of the spectator of outdoor murals was a subject of concern for Siqueiros. In his writings on aesthetics from the 1930s, he dedicates much space to a shift analogous to the one theorized by Walter Benjamin in his seminal essay on reproducibility, the shift experienced by the work of art as it moves from cult spaces to spaces of mass spectatorship. Benjamin focuses on the increasing scope for exhibition that technologies like film and photography bring to the work of art. This increase in exhibition value, Benjamin notes, takes place on several fronts. There is, of course, the sheer expansion of viewing sites made possible by photographic and cinematographic reproductions, an expansion that allows for the experience of a given work of art in places and settings far removed from it. There is also, perhaps more importantly, what Benjamin characterizes as the "qualitative transformation"[35] of the nature of the work of art: the transformation from cult object to mass object, the social shift from works of art made to be seen by a few to artworks conceived squarely in terms of their exhibition value.

The revolutionary force of mechanically produced artworks, writes Benjamin, rests firmly on this shift from an individual, ritualized, cult-like contemplation to a mass, collective reception. He singles out cinema as the form of art most fit to furnish experiences of simultaneous collective reception. But he also writes of buildings and works of architecture as objects that have provided and continue to provide these kinds of experiences. "Buildings," Benjamin writes, "are received in a twofold manner: by use and by perception. Or better: tactically and optically. . . . Tactile reception comes about not so much by way of attention as by way of habit. The latter largely determines even the optical reception of architecture, which spontaneously takes the form of casual noticing, rather than attentive observation."[36] This "form of casual noticing" that Benjamin goes on to call a reception in distraction is precisely what Siqueiros begins to ponder in Los Angeles in 1932 as he worked on murals set on walls facing the street. And he does so, tellingly, at the same time that he begins to incorporate the tools and techniques of photography and cinematography.

The impact Benjamin's writings on reproducibility have had on our understanding of art in the age of mass publics is a measure of the significance of Siqueiros's own 1930s research into public art, mural painting, revolutionary form, and mechanical tools. Anticipating some of the most incisive insights in Benjamin's essay on reproducibility, Siqueiros devotes a section of "Los vehículos de la pintura dialéctico-subversiva," the lecture he gave in 1932 at the John Reed Club prior to his departure from Los Angeles, to a list of mechanical devices he started using during his California stay. In it, he lists seven "new elements and instruments" that he began using in California: the drill gun, the cement gun, white waterproof cement, the spray-paint gun (which, Siqueiros notes, had been used "exclusively in commercial work"[37]), the blowtorch, the electric projector, and the cement mixer. "We repeat," Siqueiros emphasizes, dogmatically, "new instruments call for new aesthetics. Each instrument creates its own art expression."[38]

Whereas in "Los vehículos de la pintura dialéctico-subversiva" Siqueiros merely lists the mechanical instruments that he began to use in Los Angeles, in the unpublished version of this lecture he makes a persuasive case for the need to use those same instruments in the production of art intended for mass publics:

It is evident that an art destined to those new human realities, a physically superior art, infinitely superior to the one corresponding to previous demand, can only be a mechanical art, or rather, so as to not frighten anyone, a mechanically produced art. Clearly, it is one thing to produce for a circumscribed and reduced elite and another thing to produce for millions of people, in a dynamic gesture that is necessarily combative. It is unquestionable that it is one thing to produce for static contemplation and a very different thing to produce for the purpose of education and political agitation.[39]

Significantly, Siqueiros repeats the last sentence of this excerpt at the beginning of the paragraph that follows, stressing the shift away from static contemplation and toward active engagement. A couple of pages later, Siqueiros restates his point and makes a crucial connection between the need to mechanize art production and the political motivation underlying his artworks.[40] By making explicit that his conviction about the importance of incorporating mechanical means of production derives from his investment in the political expediency of artworks, Siqueiros clarifies that his defense of mechanization is based on the need to modernize the means of art production so as to adapt it to social conditions and political ends.

For Siqueiros, the use of mechanical tools in mural painting produced several different but related results. The immediate effect of the incorporation of mechanical tools into painting, he notes, was a drastic reduction in the amount of time required to complete a mural painting. Mechanical tools like the spray-paint gun allowed him to complete his work at a faster pace. "Our work," writes Siqueiros in reference to *Mitin obrero*, "was finished in two weeks (first and second week of July 1932), despite the physical dimensions of the space chosen for it (24 × 19 feet). We were able to do this thanks to the exclusive use of mechanical instruments."[41] The level of efficiency achieved was, in Siqueiros's estimation, one of the principal breakthroughs of his experience in Los Angeles.[42]

Siqueiros's writings on mechanical reproducibility and its impact in the production of revolutionary mural painting come a few years after the 1930 publication in *Mexican Folkways* (a principal source of criticism on Mexican art in the 1920s and 1930s) of a dossier edited by Diego Rivera on José Guadalupe Posada (1852–1913) and on the tradition of popular graphic arts in Mexico. Since at least the late nineteenth century and with renewed vigor during the years of the Mexican Revolution, cheaply produced, massively distributed prints and graphics played a key role in

Mexico in shaping the public perception of politics, public figures, and current events at large. Through the 1920s and into the 1930s, the influence of *gráfica popular* on the work of the muralists grew steadily, thanks in part to the early recognition of its enormous aesthetic and political value by the French-born, Mexican-based painter Jean Charlot. Siqueiros recognized the mass reach and the political and revolutionary expediency of the popular graphic arts, and in his writings as well as his collective work of the 1930s (the workshops and working groups he established in Los Angeles, in New York, in Argentina, and in Mexico City) engravings and prints feature as an important platform for the production of artworks meant for mass publics. But very early in his investigations into mechanically reproduced art forms, photography, more than engraving and print making, became Siqueiros's principal focus.

Photography's unmatched capacity for visual documentation did not escape Siqueiros, and neither did the potential political impact of its mechanical reproducibility. He envisioned at least two different roles that photography could play in muralism. First, photography was a source of visual documents of the figures and events used as subject matter in mural paintings, of the spaces designated for mural painting, and of the different vantage points afforded by those spaces. Second, photography could be used to expand the potential viewership of mural paintings. From 1932 onward, Siqueiros began to entertain the idea of making murals suited for photographic and cinematographic documentation and subsequent distribution in photo and film format, and he did so with complete awareness of the impact reproducibility could have on social intervention and political agitation. Photogenic painting, Siqueiros writes in 1932, "which can be precisely and infinitely reproduced by photographic systems, has enormous value as an engaging aspect of agitation propaganda."[43] Siqueiros stresses that paintings made to be photographically reproduced "must have the conditions that photography demands, which is to say, the conditions that enable the reproduction of visual art in the most precise and clear manner."[44] This visionary call for a form of painting suitable for photographic reproduction (a call made two years before Benjamin wrote his seminal essay on reproducibility)[45] would be noteworthy on its own, but the fact that Siqueiros actively and insistently links the need to make painting photogenic to his agenda of political agitation makes his engagement with photography the more noteworthy.

A third use of photography in muralism was the use of photography for the productions of photo-murals. Soviet artists like El Lissitzky and Gustav

Klutsis began working with the medium in the 1920s in large-scale installations and exhibition spaces, precursors of sorts to the large-scale photographic billboards and immersive advertising spaces like Times Square. In 1932, photo-mural production had some recognition in the United States, enough to consider it a viable precedent for Siqueiros's own experimentation with uses of photography in mural painting.[46] As Desmond Rochfort notes, "the context of the times suggests that the use of photography and by extension the use of the projector was current practice in some quarters and may well have influenced Siqueiros to take up this approach."[47]

Photography entered the dynamics of Siqueiros's work by way of a "half-crazy" member of his team at the Chouinard School "whose characteristic mania consisted of using the photo camera incessantly." "This young man," writes Siqueiros,

> followed us relentlessly with his machine, relentlessly keeping up with the process of our work. Every paint stroke provided a reason for him to use one of his photo frames. . . . He followed us methodically, tracing the movement of the spectator of our work, photographing our wall from every angle that we chose to organize its final execution. From very near, from very far, from the right side, from the left side.[48]

Siqueiros's initial skepticism toward the compulsive habits of this unnamed man was dispelled on the day he presented to Siqueiros "more than three hundred photographic documents, which constituted the graphic biography of our work throughout its process."[49] Siqueiros realized that the information contained in the "graphic biography" of his painting shed light on aspects of painting that are not registered by the naked eye. "The graphic documents," notes Siqueiros, "revealed to us with mathematical precision the different ways in which figures receded, depending on the angles from which they were seen."[50] Moreover, the series of photographs provided by Siqueiros's young collaborator constituted a register of the possible path followed by a spectator taking in the mural. Through the use of photographs, the possible paths taken by spectators as they go about the mural became predictable, measurable, and so did the multiplicity of viewpoints unfolding in the course of following those paths. The coincidence here of movement and vision is telling, for it points to what Jonathan Crary has called "a larger organization of perceptual consumption"[51] that comes hand in hand with the increasing power of spectacle. Historicizing how spectacle came to be taken "as an explanation of the contemporary operation of power," Crary points out that the term's "currency emerged from the activities in the late 1950s and early 1960s of the various configurations now designated as presituationist or situationist."[52] Siqueiros's writing from the 1930s is indicative of an earlier, preparatory inquiry into spectacle's theater of power, as well as an early appropriation of this form of power for the production of politicized art.

For the mural painting Siqueiros completed after his stay in Los Angeles—a work titled *Ejercicio plástico*, commissioned by Natalio Boltana and set in Don Torcuato, near Buenos Aires, Argentina—Siqueiros once again assembled a group of collaborators. The group included artists (Antonio Berni, Juan Carlos Castagnino, Lino Spilimbergo), a scenographer (Enrique Lázaro), and a filmmaker (León Klimovsky), collaborators who allowed Siqueiros more rigorous experimentation with mechanical equipment and with the possibility of making mural paintings for reproduction in film. The mural's location, in the dark basement of a private residence, called for the use of artificial lighting for the completion and viewing of the mural, drawing it closer to the experience of film and cinema—the experience of moving images—that Siqueiros had in mind as he went about completing the mural. In reference to the work that went into *Ejercicio plástico*, Siqueiros writes: "we made the camera into a visual machine corresponding to the active visual reality of the normal spectator."[53]

This identification between the camera's mechanical visual register of the world and "the active optic reality of the normal spectator" is telling. It hints at a kind of exchange, a transaction between the camera and a mode of experience that Siqueiros attributes to the active nature of the spectator. Siqueiros insists on the need to appropriate the camera to engage the visual reality of the spectator. He writes:

> Without the living document, without the irrefutable document of the photographic image, modern painters will not be able to draw a single drop of the new visual truth that lives intensely in mechanical thunder and in the torrent of the great masses agitated by the final class struggle. Without the photographic document they will not know anything, visually and materially speaking, of the daily, bloody repression of the exploiting class. They will know nothing of the tireless, heroic struggles of colonized people throughout the world, ransacked and tortured frenetically by imperialism. They will know nothing of the wars between empires that, from time to time, drown the world in a bloodbath. The faces of tens of millions of dead proletarians will be completely unknown to them. The brutal, miserable life of workers will be nothing but a vague reference

> for them. Without the photographic sketch, modern artists will keep on stumbling like blind romantics amid the rigid anatomies of machines, facing their abstract forms in movement. Blind to the intense social truth and blind as well to the intense visual value of modern mechanics, blind like the so-called modern painters of France and of the world over. Like them, artists will simply be *snobs* and their affect will contort into sterile cogitations. In a word, without the photographic sketch the painter will continue to live in a mystical state, which is to say, he will continue to live as a parasite of beauty.[54]

The way in which Siqueiros codes the disclosure that the camera performs on the optical experience of the artist and the spectator points to a resonance between the camera's visual register and the world in which the artist and the public live, the world that we perceive, both mechanized and in motion, modernized and violently repressive. This is what Siqueiros suggests when he identifies a correspondence between the camera as artifact and the optic reality of the spectator. It is not as if the camera transforms the spectator's visual engagement with the world. Rather, the camera corresponds to it, suggesting an exchange realized on the basis of a shared historical circumstance that sees the rise of photography and cinematography concurrently with the emergence of frames of cognition defined not by attention nor by contemplation but by distraction. There is a small section in Benjamin's article on reproducibility devoted to perception that resonates with Siqueiros's ideas on the correspondence between the camera and the optical reality of the modern, dynamic spectator. It begins by stating: "*Just as the entire mode of existence of human collectives changes over long historical periods, so too does their mode of perception*. The way in which human perception is organized—the medium in which it occurs—is conditioned not only by nature but by history."[55]

Beginning with the Los Angeles murals, Siqueiros thinks about the spectators' engagement with the spaces they inhabit, an engagement that, Siqueiros noted, takes place in motion. But awareness of the way the movement of the spectator affects the manner in which paintings are apprehended did not immediately translate into a corresponding composition for his murals. It was not until the completion of *Ejercicio plástico* (fig. 1.4) in the basement of a private residence near Buenos Aires that Siqueiros applied his observations of the transit of the spectator to the structure of his mural work. The mural, as its title suggests, is an exercise in visual experimentation. It lacks the politically charged subject matter of his other murals and has been described accurately by Laurance P. Hurl-

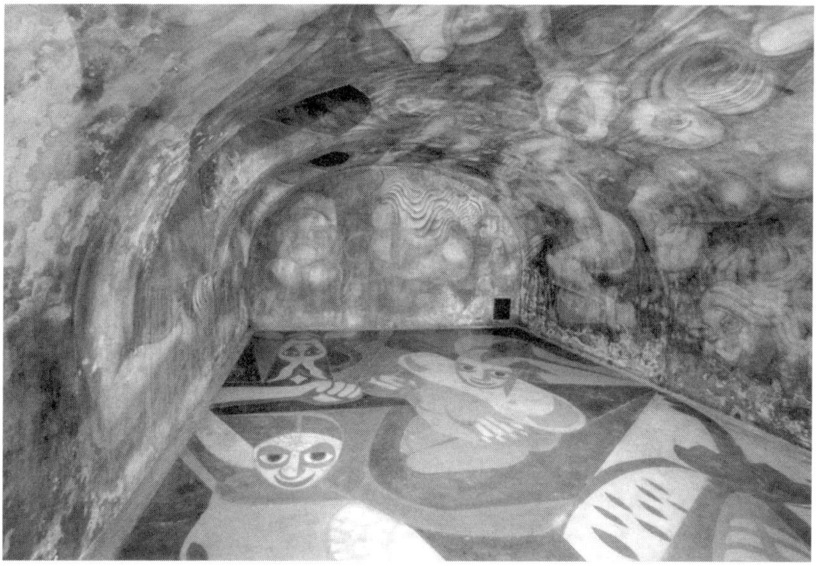

Figure 1.4. David Alfaro Siqueiros, *Ejercicio plástico* (1933). Fresco on cement, 2150 square feet. Antigua Finca Los Granados, Buenos Aires, Argentina. Photograph ca. 1980; photographer unknown. Courtesy of the Instituto Nacional de Bellas Artes y Literatura.

burt as a "spatial envelope,"[56] given that both the floor and ceiling are used as pictorial surfaces, along with the walls.

Preparatory work for *Ejercicio plástico* included photographing female models posing on glass platforms[57] as well as projections of hand-drawn sketches and photographs onto the walls where the mural was to be painted. The intent was to explore how a small, flat image could be grasped in its entirety in a glance, and how this image unfolded into dovetailing planes when blown up to cover the large physical proportions of a wall. The principal technical difficulty tackled by Siqueiros in completing *Ejercicio plástico* was how to account for the multiple points of view from which the mural could be regarded. He had to coordinate a manifold of perspectives within a single surface. This called for a structure that unfolds not from a unified point of view but from a multiplicity of perspectives that succeed each other as the spectator moves across the space of the mural. "The geometry of our wall," writes Siqueiros in reference to *Ejercicio plástico*, "was neither absolute nor static, but profoundly multiple and mobile. . . . In mural painting, the movement of the spectator activates the organic geometry of the wall, it 'distorts' it, transforms it."[58]

While *Ejercicio plástico* marks Siqueiros's first effective use of photographic equipment to document the multiple perspectives from which a mural painting can be seen, *Retrato de la burguesía* (1939–1940) stands as his first attempt to use montage and other filmic compositional devices in the making of his mural paintings. The appropriation of techniques and technologies from the film industry for the production of murals yielded fascinating results, results facilitated in large part by Siqueiros's collaboration with photomontage artists he met in Europe. In 1936 Siqueiros went to Spain to serve as head of propaganda efforts for the Republican side of the Spanish Civil War. On arrival, he gave up this task and went to the battlefield where he fought alongside prominent Spanish artists of the time, most notably Josep Renau, by then a renowned photomontage artist. Renau went to Mexico after the end of the war and collaborated with Siqueiros on *Retrato de la burguesía*, together with Antonio Pujol, Luis Arenal, Antonio Rodríguez Luna, and Miguel Prieto. All were members of the Grupo Internacional de Artistas Plásticos organized by Siqueiros for the completion of this mural (Renau, Rodríguez Luna, and Prieto were all Spanish exiles living in Mexico after the Spanish Civil War). This was Siqueiros's first commission upon returning to Mexico from Spain. It was also one of the first murals Siqueiros completed in Duco, or pyroxylin, a synthetic paint developed in the 1920s, widely used in the automobile industry throughout the twentieth century, and adopted by Siqueiros as his paint of choice from 1932 onward.[59]

Retrato de la burguesía (figs. 1.5–1.7) was commissioned for what was then the recently finished headquarters of the National Electricians' Union in Mexico City, with the stipulation that the mural would develop themes related to the electrical industries. The mural was meant to serve an educational and recreational purpose, a kind of edifying distraction for the members of the union. Siqueiros's plan and his final execution, though, put an emphasis on political agitation. Photography and its relatively objective capacity to document reality was a foremost concern for the group of artists collaborating on *Retrato de la burguesía*. The space where the mural was placed was also a matter of much interest for the artists, particularly for Siqueiros.[60] Siqueiros, Renau, and the team of artists assembled by Siqueiros for the completion of the mural produced an extensive study of the movements of people going up and down the staircase where the mural was to be set.[61] Renau came up with a series of numbered photomontages, some of which laid bare the spatial structure of the staircase where the mural was to be situated. Others mapped out the transit of a person moving up the staircase.

Renau identified six key perspectives where the gaze of spectators would likely rest as they climbed up the staircase. Following Renau's lead, Siqueiros devised a layout for the mural that presented a person going up the stairs with a stream of richly colored and tightly packed images of inflamed masses, of war, death, and destruction, of the electrical industry, of capitalism, empire, and class struggle. These images work like frames in a film. Like many of the prints then being produced by the Taller de Gráfica Popular in Mexico, the images in *Retrato de la burguesía* bear an overt, predominantly antifascist tone, a narrative that progresses within the physical confines of the mural from the rise of fascist regimes in Europe to a future, utopian defeat at the hands of the world proletariat. Both the research done prior to the mural's completion and the eventual disposition of its panels according to the movement of the spectator rendered the mural more than a figurative plane. *Retrato de la burguesía*, like *Ejercicio plástico*, works more like a topology; the experience of the mural and the revelation of its meanings rest as much on its visual elements as on the movements, the postures, the moving and still perspectives that the space of the mural affords.

To a spectator standing still from any point on the staircase, the mural remains a dizzying array of graphic elements, its parts arranged in a seemingly haphazard manner. But once the spectator begins to move from the bottom of the staircase up, the sequential, montage-like composition of the painting comes to life, revealing a carefully planned-out arrangement of motifs. The meaning of these motifs rests not in each motif alone but in its position relative to the visual elements that precede and follow it. Because the mural encompasses all the walls of the staircase cube in which it is situated, it is impossible to capture all components of the mural in a single photograph. Photographers negotiate the difficulty of documenting the mural by employing fish-eye or other wide-angle lenses or by providing a series of photographs that, when taken as a sequence, give a sense of the visual experience offered to the viewer moving up the stairs where the mural is set. A series of images, or one single moving image—a film of the mural—would most adequately reproduce the visual experience afforded by *Retrato de la burguesía*. It is a mural made for film, a cinegenic mural. It is arguably the first successful exercise in what Siqueiros conceived as a *plástica fílmica*, the making of visual artworks suitable for reproduction on film.

The first perspective or frame that spectators encounter to the left as they begin the ascent up the staircase features a depiction of machine works tended by a group of workers. Above this image and to the left

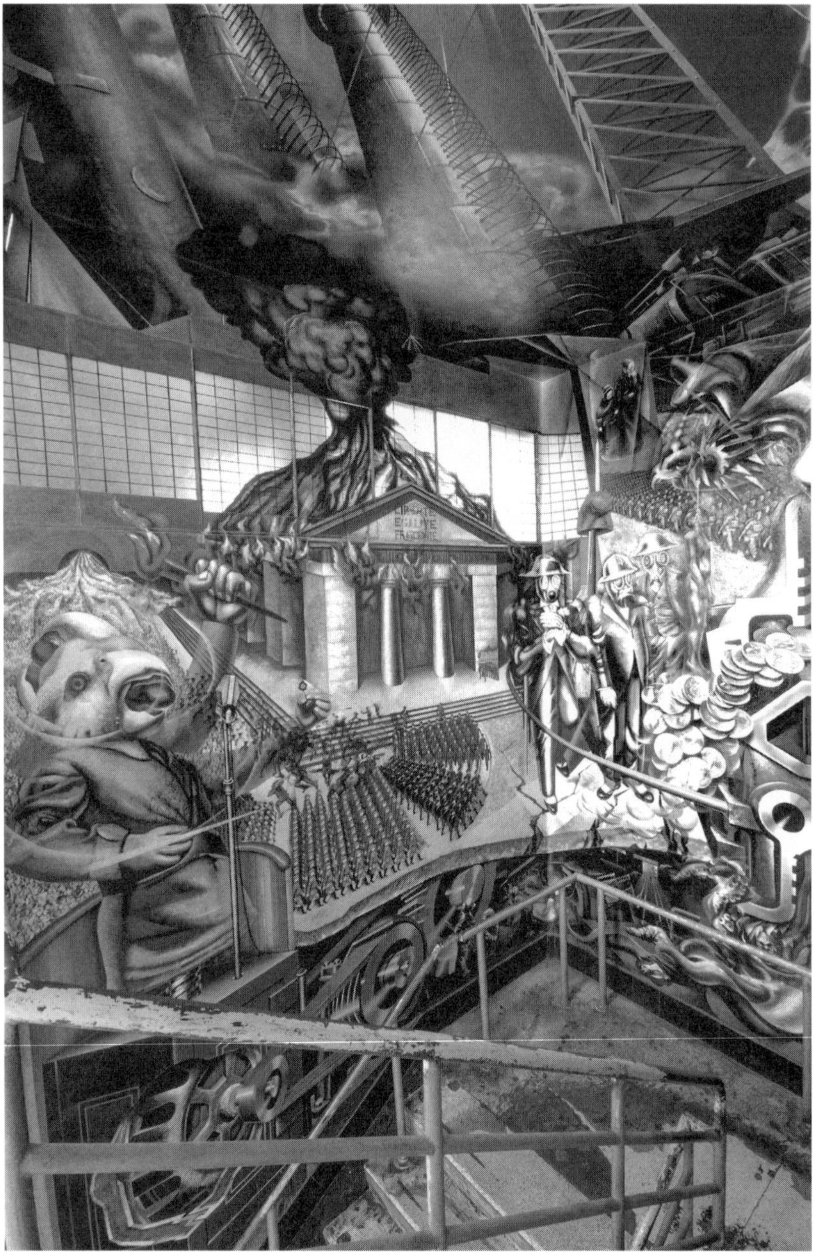

Figure 1.5. David Alfaro Siqueiros, in collaboration with José Renau, Antonio Pujol, Luis Arenal, Antonio Rodríguez Luna, and Miguel Prieto. *Retrato de la burguesía* (1939–1940). Sindicato Mexicano de Electricistas, Mexico City. Pyroxylin on cement, 1,000 square feet. Photograph ca. 2017, by Patricia Méndez Obregón. Courtesy of Sindicato Mexicano de Electricistas and the Instituto Nacional de Bellas Artes y Literatura.

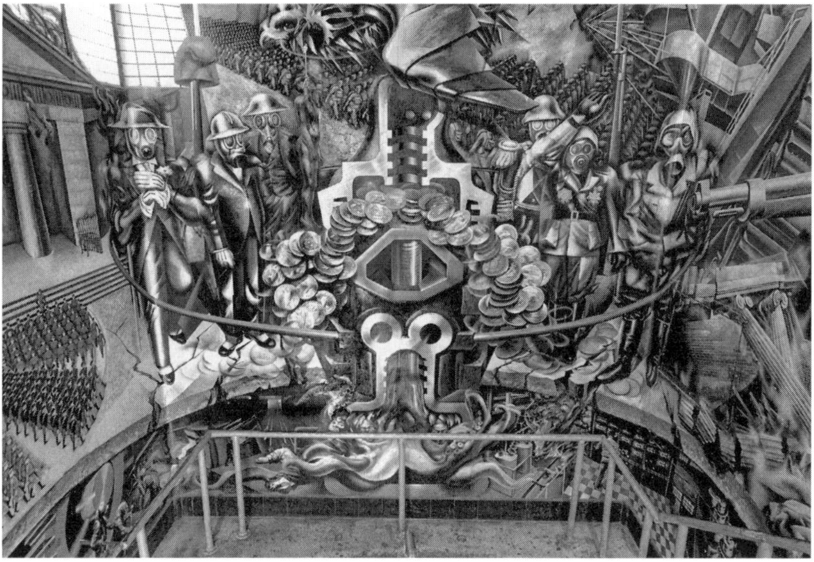

Figure 1.6. David Alfaro Siqueiros, in collaboration with José Renau, Antonio Pujol, Luis Arenal, Antonio Rodríguez Luna, and Miguel Prieto. *Retrato de la burguesía* (1939–1940). Sindicato Mexicano de Electricistas, Mexico City. Pyroxylin on cement, 1,000 square feet. Photograph ca. 2017, by Patricia Méndez Obregón. Courtesy of Sindicato Mexicano de Electricistas and the Instituto Nacional de Bellas Artes y Literatura.

("above ground" in the pictorial space of the painting) stands a demagogue in front of a microphone, both demagogue and microphone connected to the machine works below so as to suggest that both draw their power from it. To the right of the demagogue and also standing above the machine works is a large temple that bears on its façade the liberal values of the French Revolution. The temple is in flames. An esplanade spreads before troops dressed in the military garb of fascist regimes marching in close formation. At the center of the mural is a depiction of a moneymaking machine with gold coins coming out of it and blood flowing through its inner workings. Originally, the machine featured a grisly image of children's faces, eerily realistic (probably modeled after a photograph from the Spanish Civil War), crushed by the workings of the machine. There is a striking resemblance between this composition of child faces, machinery, and coins and a photograph by Lola Álvarez Bravo titled *El sueño de los pobres II* (1935), a photograph that may very well have served as the basis or inspiration for the composition in *Retrato de la burguesía*. Overall, the iconography of the mural is striking for its dynamism and for the general legibility of the figures and images that went into its composition.

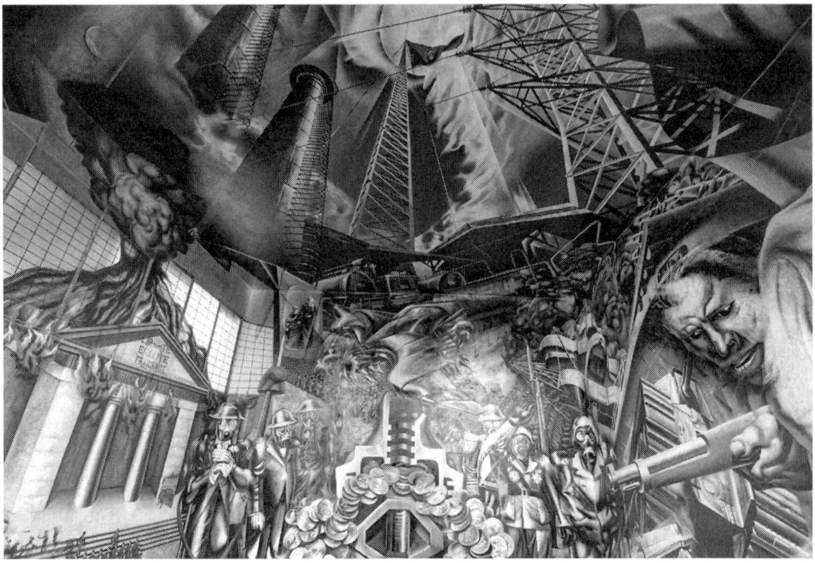

Figure 1.7. David Alfaro Siqueiros, in collaboration with José Renau, Antonio Pujol, Luis Arenal, Antonio Rodríguez Luna, and Miguel Prieto. *Retrato de la burguesía* (1939–1940). Sindicato Mexicano de Electricistas, Mexico City. Pyroxylin on cement, 1,000 square feet. Photograph ca. 1950, by Guillermo Zamora. Courtesy of Sindicato Mexicano de Electricistas and the Instituto Nacional de Bellas Artes y Literatura.

In preparation for this mural, Siqueiros and his team once again used photographs as models for many of the figures depicted in the mural. He and his team of collaborators drew widely from photographs, newspapers, magazines, other print sources, and known artworks, reinforcing, in the space of the mural, visual and narrative conventions familiar to most of the mural's intended spectators: working-class members of an electrician's union.[62] This preference for print culture and for the culture industry as references for the form and the drafting of figures in the mural—a preference made over and above the more allegorical and conventional art-historical citations of the first-wave murals in the early 1920s—can be read as a sign of recognition: recognition of the power that the culture industry and, increasingly, consumer culture wielded in shaping the way stories (even stories of class struggle) were told.

Of course, not all the references from mass culture that went into this and other murals by Siqueiros are drawn from sources ideologically aligned with the culture industry and consumer culture. In *Retrato de la burguesía*, and even more starkly in the agitational magazine *Frente a frente*, Siqueiros borrows from John Heartfield, the Dada artist, and Gustav Klutsis.[63] These artists (like Siqueiros, Renau, and the others who collaborated on *Retrato de la burguesía*) engaged in a complex series of appropriations from and interventions in mass culture, interventions that often include extensive work in political propaganda and sometimes in commercial advertising. The point here is that none of these artists felt their political commitments and ideological affiliations were compromised by their willingness to draw freely from mass culture and from platforms and materials (magazines, advertisements, and the like) eventually engulfed by consumer culture. In the Soviet Union of the early 1920s, Klutsis was hardly alone among artists working both on the forefront of leftist, politicized aesthetics and also on the various commercial enterprises that emerged during the NEP period. In late 1930s Mexico, and to this date, the confluence of politicized aesthetics and an interest in mass culture and commercial forms in the works of Siqueiros has hardly registered, except to point out, as is the case of Leonard Folgarait's reading of the last mural by Siqueiros (*La marcha de la humanidad en la tierra y hacia el cosmos*), not a tense conjugation, a productive ambiguity, but a complete abandonment of the commitment to class struggle and leftist politics Siqueiros embraced so vigorously in the early days of his trajectory.

Billboard Muralism: Siqueiros in the 1950s

Siqueiros's longest, most sophisticated reflection on the historical period that gives rise to what he theorized as "billboard muralism" is included in an unpublished document from 1932. This typewritten text, possibly titled "La pintura mural como vehículo de arte político revolucionario,"[64] expands on topics ranging from the polychromatic external finishes of pre-Columbian buildings to the repercussions of reproduction technologies on modern art. It is one of the most insightful pieces of prose written by Siqueiros. It is principally a description of the material circumstances under which the Los Angeles exterior murals were completed, and it weaves, along the way, a cogent account of the sociopolitical need for the kind of art form that Siqueiros was developing at the time he completed those murals.

The ambitious intent behind "La pintura mural como vehículo de arte político revolucionario" is made clear in its subtitle, "Dissertation on Ideas, Theories, and Uses of Materials and Instruments in Mural Painting"; the word "dissertation" is repeated once more in the first pages of the typed manuscript. The text opens with a categorical affirmation of the need to secure the latest technological means for the production of art, as well as the technical skills that new technologies nourish and demand. Siqueiros writes: "significant works of art cannot be produced under conditions of technological anachronism. The true work of art can only flourish in tandem with the technology of its time. Moreover: the true work of art is always an advance of the joint techno-industrial production of its time."[65] The document then moves on to a hasty account of mural painting that wants to demonstrate a historical link between, on the one hand, material conditions and social circumstances and, on the other hand, the technologies and materials predominantly used in painting during a given period in the history of art.

Siqueiros's narrative of the history of mural painting is divided into seven stages, the first few of which are described in highly speculative terms. The first stage is set in antiquity, and not much is said about it beyond its having been "the time of the integrative visual arts,"[66] a nod, no doubt, to his own increasing interest in the synthesis of the arts or "plástica integral," as Siqueiros called it in writings from the 1950s. The second and third stages correspond to the rise of propaganda art, of religious propaganda and Christian art. The description of the fourth stage is more substantial. It is a moment in the history of mural painting that coincides with changes in the economy of Christian society and with the rise of "aristocratic feudal lords."[67] During this stage, Siqueiros writes, "mural painting was no longer made for large, public sites of mass gathering; it moved into the private chapels of popes and into the 'pagan' palaces of the aristocracy."[68] This gives way to the fifth stage, during which "the size of mural painting was reduced, proportional to the reduction of its corresponding public."[69] The sixth stage sees mural painting in a time during which "the market of visual art undergoes a profound crisis . . . the bourgeois economy rises and with it another kind of market emerges, that is to say, a wider market, as wide as the new affluent class, and so the proportions of the moveable painting are reduced."[70]

It is at this point (the moment preceding Siqueiros's own place in the pipeline) that mural painting all but dies down, wiped out by the predominance of the small-scale canvas painting, much fitter as an object of exchange and much more suited to the economy in which it first thrived. Last on the list is the seventh stage, the stage corresponding to Siqueiros's own time. He describes it as follows:

> Currently, the market for visual art products goes through a profound crisis: a correlate in the cultural field to the larger crisis that affects society as the greater economic whole. At the same time, signs of a new social type begin to appear, which is to say, signs of a new market. The world turns according to the expressions of the basic, underlying economy of each society: it turns toward collective forms, toward imposing masses of men, as tens of thousands of people begin to appear everywhere in everyday life . . . and thus the need for new forms of advertising and art.[71]

The world turns toward collective, commercial forms, and art as envisioned by Siqueiros follows suit. In this regard, the relationship posed by Siqueiros between art and advertising in terms of their shared need to arrive at forms appropriate for addressing mass publics is suggestive. It is one of the earliest linkages between advertising and art on the part of Siqueiros, a linkage that will become increasingly significant in his artworks as well as his writings, reaching a kind of climax in the 1950s during the completion of both *Velocidad* (1953) and his three murals at Ciudad Universitaria: *Las fechas en la historia de México o el derecho a la cultura*, *Nuevo emblema universitario*, and *El pueblo a la universidad, la universidad al pueblo* (figs. 1.8 and 1.12), all completed between 1952 and 1956.

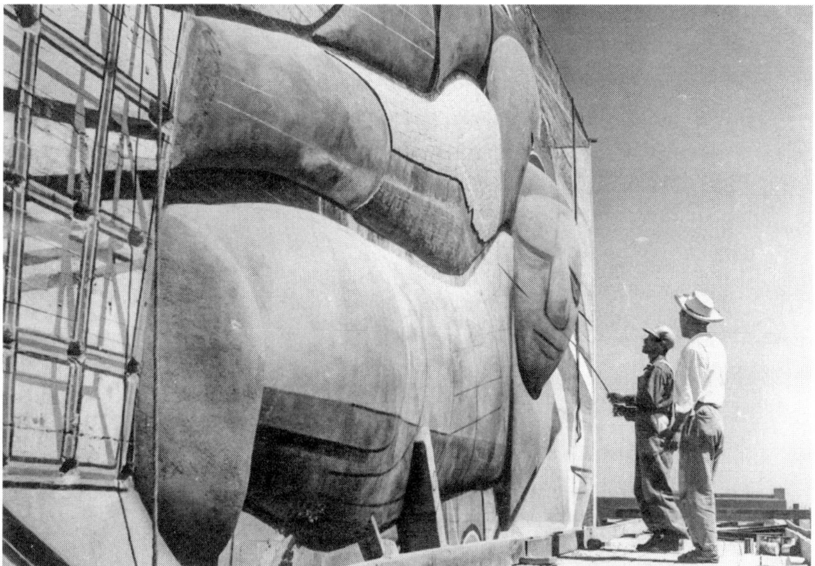

Figure 1.8. Collaborators of David Alfaro Siqueiros working on *El pueblo a la universidad, la universidad al pueblo*. Photograph ca. 1953; photographer unknown. Courtesy of the Instituto Nacional de Bellas Artes y Literatura.

The murals Siqueiros painted in Ciudad Universitaria are located, like his murals in Los Angeles (and like the large mural José Clemente Orozco completed in 1947 in the Escuela Nacional de Maestros[72]), outdoors, on walls visible from public space. Because of their location on a university campus and because of the way they thematize their location, these murals bring out crisply the "didactic concern for immediate political efficiency" that Luis Cardoza y Aragón identified as a central component of Siqueiros's aesthetic.[73] Education—its institutions, its formative and regulatory role in the constitution of a modern nation-state—features prominently in the history of Mexican muralism. The movement as such coalesced in the early 1920s during José Vasconcelos's term as minister of public education, in times of unprecedented interest and governmental support for public education in Mexico. Some of the most iconic works from the first phase of the muralist movement in Mexico in the 1920s were completed either in the school buildings of the Escuela Nacional Preparatoria or in the headquarters of the Ministry of Public Education, the Secretaría de Educación Pública. The construction of Ciudad Universitaria was itself a summons of sorts for three salient figures of Mexican muralism—Siqueiros, Rivera, and Juan O'Gorman—and for many more who completed art works both in the years immediately after the inauguration of the new campus and in the decades that followed.

What is distinctive about the murals Siqueiros completed in Ciudad Universitaria is the discursive baggage he brought to the commission, particularly his study of, and admiration for, commercial billboards as a form of muralism. By the time he completed his Ciudad Universitaria murals, commercial advertising was an important formal and compositional reference for Siqueiros's mural painting. It was also, crucially, a key reference for his thoughts on the link between aesthetics and politics. In the 1920s, 1930s, and 1940s, Siqueiros was among the fiercest critics of what he and others condemned as "Mexican curios," a repertoire of figures and styles used prolifically in popular and fine artworks made for the tourist market.[74] By the 1950s the nationalist spirit of 1920s postrevolution Mexico had given way to an outright embrace of foreign investment, to the rise of tourism, and to a booming market for consumer goods (automobiles and televisions foremost among them) as the driving forces of the political economy of Mexico. Siqueiros's enthusiasm for commercial advertising is shrewdly aligned with the spirit of the "Mexican miracle," the period after World War II characterized by a frantic pace of urbanization and industrialization.[75] His enthusiasm came at the far end of what Robin Greeley recently periodized as the moment in the history of postrevolution Mexico characterized by "the reversal of Cárdenas' socialist programs and the institutionalization of capitalism under Presidents Manuel Ávila Camacho (1940–1946), Miguel Alemán (1946–1952), and beyond."[76]

Rather than being troubled by the contradiction between this enthusiasm for advertising and the political expediency he desired for his mural works, Siqueiros instead saw in the forms of commercial propaganda a fresh source of formal innovation that could be adapted for the purposes of political agitation. In an article published in 1953 in *Arte público* (fig. 1.9),[77] a bulletin focused on promoting Siqueiros's vision for an arts synthesis movement integrated into the construction of Ciudad Universitaria, Siqueiros writes, dogmatically: "there is only one valid experience prior to our current muralist project, realist and placed outdoors: the experience of commercial propaganda, of the billboard that covers large outdoor city walls, financially, industrially, and commercially important for our times. And this is only because these billboards are precise in their figuration, ultra-realist, meant for outdoor spaces."[78] To stress his point, he refers to billboards as "commercial advertising muralism."[79]

By the 1950s, large-format advertisements, large-scale ads posted directly onto walls, and free-standing billboards placed up and down Mexico City's landscape captivated Siqueiros. In his formidable collection of photographs (an important part of which was lost during a flood in the archives of the Sala de Arte Público Siqueiros in Mexico City, the principal depository of his documents and unpublished texts), at least four photos of billboards survive, illustrative of the kind of advertisements Siqueiros may have seen throughout the Mexican capital. By the 1950s, at the height of his interest in large-scale outdoor advertising, Siqueiros's fervor for the billboard form was running so high that he went as far as calling it "the true muralism of the bourgeoisie":

> Don't be surprised! The living tradition . . . of *commercial muralism*, of the great commercial billboard that takes up large outdoor surfaces in modern cities, in the great metropolises of the capitalist world: a commercial muralism that I call . . . "the true muralism of the bourgeoisie," its only form of outdoor visual art. A tradition that clearly, and beyond its banality and ephemeralness, beyond the mercenary nature of its content, offers indisputably useful lessons for our purposes.[80]

There is more than just rhetoric to these words. By the time he penned this manifesto, a manifesto of billboard muralism, he was already incorpo-

PRIMER FOLLETO DE

ARTE PUBLICO

TRIBUNA DE PINTORES MURALISTAS, ESCULTORES, GRABADORES Y ARTISTAS DE LA ESTAMPA EN GENERAL

Revista editada por la "Sociedad de Amigos de la Pintura Mexicana Moderna".

MEXICO, D. F., FEBRERO DE 1953. $ 0.50 EJEMPLAR

18 Artículos Correspondientes a los Números Uno y Extra de Nuestra Publicación

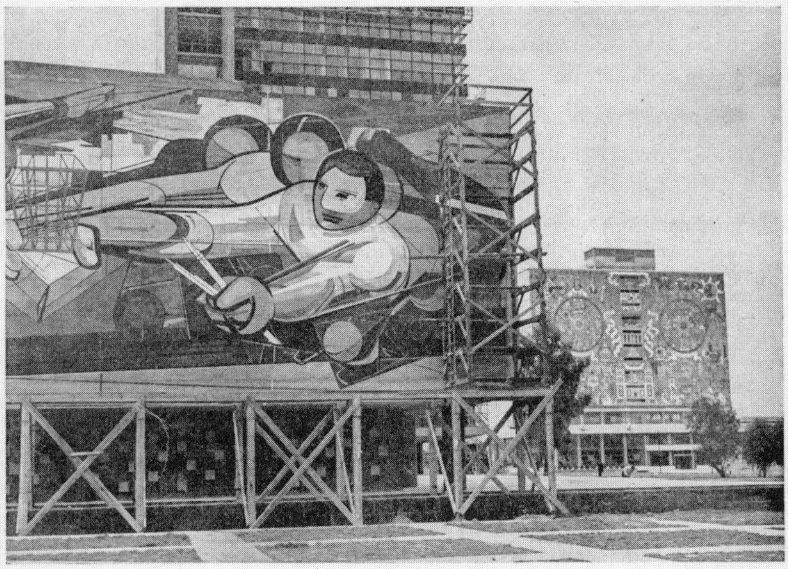

LOS MURALES EXTERIORES DE SIQUEIROS (EN PRIMER TERMINO) Y DE O'GORMAN (AL FONDO) EN LA CIUDAD UNIVERSITARIA.

EL DEL PRIMERO, EN PERIODO DE TRAZO; EL SEGUNDO, YA TERMINADO.

¿INTEGRACION PLASTICA CON COPIAS O REPLICAS DE ESTILOS TRADICIONALES MEXICANOS PRE-HISPANICOS, EJECUTADOS CON MEDIOS ARCAICOS, EN CONSTRUCCIONES DE ESTRUCTURA MODERNA INTERNACIONAL?

¿INTEGRACION PLASTICA MEDIANTE EL ENCUENTRO DE NUEVOS ESTILOS, COMO CONSECUENCIA LOGICA DEL ACATAMIENTO A UNA FUNCION NACIONAL HISTORICA CONCRETA DEL PRESENTE, MEDIANTE EL USO DE LOS MEDIOS MATERIALES MEJORES QUE PUEDA PROPORCIONAR LA CIENCIA, LA TECNICA Y LA INDUSTRIA DE HOY?

VEA PAGINAS DE LA 8 A LA 13, DE LA 14 A LA 17 Y DE LA 17 A LA 19.

Figure 1.9. Front page of the first bulletin of *Arte Público: tribuna de pintores muralistas, escultores, grabadores y artistas de la estampa en general*, edited by the Sociedad de Amigos de la Pintura Mexicana Moderna. Mexico City, 1953. Siqueiros's *El pueblo a la universidad, la universidad al pueblo* (1952–1956) is visible in the foreground, under construction. In the background, a partial view of Juan O'Gorman's *Representación histórica de la cultura* (1952). Courtesy of the Instituto Nacional de Bellas Artes y Literatura.

rating traits of commercial billboards into his praxis as mural painter. This expansion of the form of mural painting carried his mural practice to a threshold. An image of the city (the city under the increasingly firm grasp of commercial advertisers, the city under visual siege, so to speak) and a profile of citizens as consumers and distracted passers-by emerge side by side in Siqueiros's writings on art synthesis and public art, together with the more programmatic view of the function murals should serve in contemporary Mexican society and in Ciudad Universitaria in particular. The university itself, like other major universities in Latin America under expansion toward the middle of the twentieth century, thrived on increasing enrollments. The universities multiplied within the span of a few generations the ranks of an urban middle class, an educated class of professionals defined as much by their purchasing power—they made possible, as Diana Sorensen notes, the literary and cultural booms of the 1960s[81]—as by the more traditional markers of citizenship and civic engagement.

Increasingly from the 1950s forward, Siqueiros's mural work grew more integrationist, more cynical in its desire to be assimilated fully into the economies of consumption and tourism taking off forcefully in the decades after World War II. *Velocidad* (1953; figs. 1.10 and 1.11) was the first mural Siqueiros completed in the 1950s under this vision of mural painting. It is one of two murals (the other being *Ejercicio plástico*) with no explicit political content, and it is too graphically restrained to tell the kinds of stories mural paintings usually tell. It was commissioned for the façade of the Automex Factory in Mexico City, a subsidiary of the Chrysler Corporation and a sign of what was already shaping up to be a systemic return of foreign investment to Mexico after the nationalizing efforts of the Cárdenas administration.[82] The commission materialized thanks to the architects Guillermo Rossel de la Lama and Lorenzo Carrasco. The mural features a female figure placed inside an oval shape. A play on rising surfaces makes it more apt to be seen on approach, sideways as one moves toward the sloping curves of its raised concrete understructure. Graphically, the composition is simple, even more so than that of Siqueiros's Los Angeles murals. The central motif, the mythical figure of a woman, is set on a rectangle, within which an elongated elliptical shape has been placed at an angle, which itself contains a circle. The figure of the woman is anchored to the central circle, her extremities reaching for the two short sides of the rectangle in a centrifugal motion. She seems to be running, or spinning vertiginously, like the wheels of an automobile.

Just as the experience in Los Angeles catalyzed for Siqueiros a realiza-

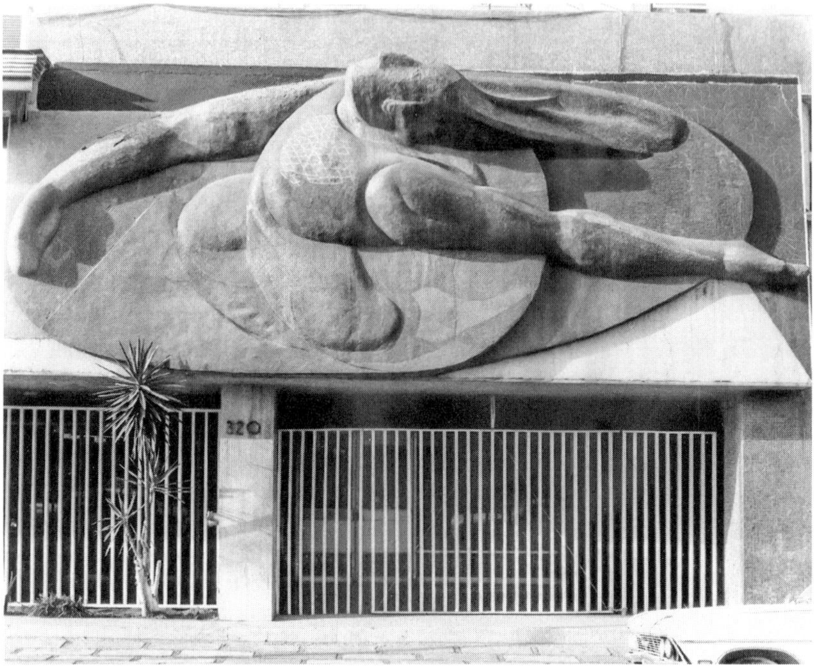

Figure 1.10. David Alfaro Siqueiros, *Velocidad* (1953). Fábrica Automex de Automóviles Chrysler, Mexico City. Mosaic, 240 square feet. Photograph by R. Arenas Betancourt. Courtesy of the Instituto Nacional de Bellas Artes y Literatura.

tion of the mobile nature of the outdoor spectator, so *Velocidad*, located on a wall facing the flow of car traffic, had Siqueiros thinking of a public in motion. This time around, the intended public was not just moving; it was motorized. "It was the public," writes Siqueiros in describing his decision to make mural paintings to be seen from automobiles and motorized vehicles:

> It was the public, it was pedestrians who guided us, with their actions alone, with their dynamic presence alone, in terms of how we should compose our works of the new style, works meant to be seen from hundreds of windows, from different levels, from all the floors in modern buildings; a work meant to be seen from automobiles and buses, from above and from below and from the most extreme angles.[83]

Anticipating a public taking in his murals from the seat of a moving car presented Siqueiros with a different set of challenges. There is, first and foremost, a set of social and economic considerations that emerged for him in assuming that the spectators of mural painting are either driving cars or riding buses. Siqueiros was quick to accommodate this kind of spectator. By the 1950s, the automobile was becoming a fixture of Mexico City's landscape, a consumer good within reach for an increasing percentage of the population. The automobile and its attendant ecology were transforming life and the landscape of Mexico City. Expanding car ownership gave the impression of a nation speeding up the goals of modernization dreamed up by successive postrevolution governments. So central was the place of the automobile in Mexico's plans for modernization and industrialization that in 1952 a television program on automobiles and highways, *Caminos de Anáhuac*, was produced for some of the earliest broadcasts of the medium.[84]

Looking at *Velocidad*, one is struck by its formal and thematic simplicity, which makes it much easier to see in passing. Its graphic restraint seems to be a nod to the limited attention range of a spectator in a moving vehicle. A profusion of motifs and details (a defining characteristic of, for instance, Diego Rivera's murals, to say nothing of the work of Juan O'Gorman—a frequent target of Siqueiros's critiques and contributor to the mural painting initiative at Ciudad Universitaria) would be lost to a

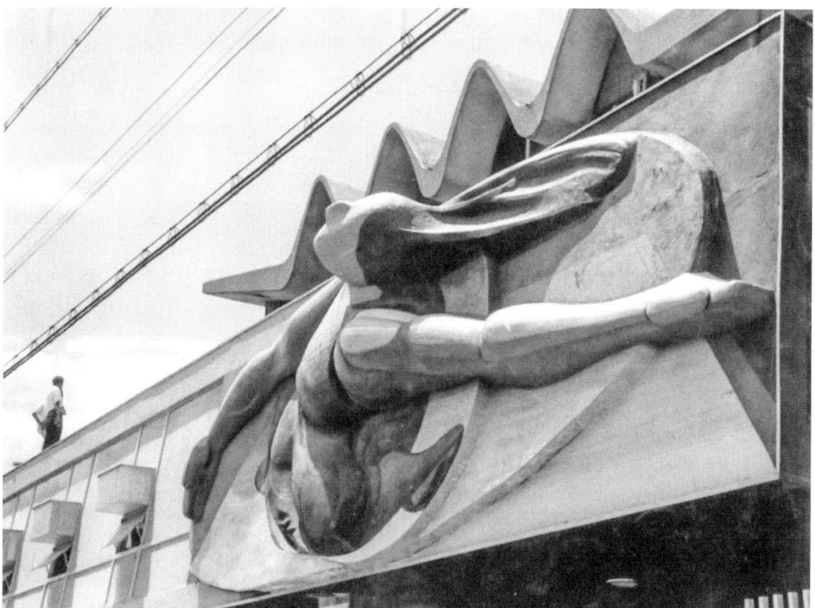

Figure 1.11. David Alfaro Siqueiros, *Velocidad* (1953). Mosaic, 240 square feet. Fábrica Automex de Automóviles Chrysler, Mexico City. Photograph by R. Arenas Betancourt. Courtesy of the Instituto Nacional de Bellas Artes y Literatura.

spectator taking in a mural from inside an automobile. By contrast, the lone motif of *Velocidad* is thrust forth unadorned and unobstructed, its attractiveness buttressed by a play on the textures and the surges in its concrete structure. The more one looks at it and the more one considers its graphic economy, the more one is inclined to think of it as a logotype for speed rather than an allegory of it. The analogy is not too far-fetched when we consider the extent to which Siqueiros praised publicity for devising graphic solutions to the problem of engaging the attention of urban dwellers and the earnest dedication with which he undertook the study of publicity and advertising as models for the production of exterior mural painting.

The mural, together with the works he completed for Ciudad Universitaria, is representative of Siqueiros's practice of what he called *escultopintura*, a technique that results in paintings bordering on the sculptural. "Outdoors," writes Siqueiros, "objectively flat pictorial forms lack pugnaciousness vis-à-vis the three-dimensional forms that surround them: houses, trees, vehicles, etc. . . . These considerations led me, as they led Rivera, to the use of a technique we call sculpto-painting."[85] Clearly and concisely, with an eye toward paintings as everyday objects placed outdoors, Siqueiros identifies the problem to be addressed, a problem of textures. "If," he writes, "to the greater size of a work of art, particularly to an outdoors mural painting, corresponds greater violence in the lines of the drawing as well greater intensity in its polychromy and its coloration as a whole, it seems clear to me that its texture or textures cannot be the same as the textures of an easel painting or the same as those of an indoor mural painting."[86] A wider, richer set of perceptual faculties is called into question by this problem of textures: the sense of touch and the different ways of feeling objects and regarding space are here summoned. That these other-than-optical faculties come into play in thinking about mural painting makes sense given the nature of the mural as medium, especially as it is theorized and put into practice by Siqueiros. Considered in its physical context, the outdoor mural conceived and produced by Siqueiros calls for categories of apprehension beyond the visual.

Benjamin's essay on reproducibility appeals to one such category: tactile reception. In a passage where he sketches out his idea of a reception in distraction, Benjamin cites architecture as another, older form of art where apprehension takes place in passing, in movement, in much the same way it happens with motion pictures. "Architecture," he writes, "has always offered the prototype of an artwork that is received in a state of distraction and through the collective. . . . Architecture has never had fallow periods. Its history is longer than that of any other art, and its effect ought to be recognized in any attempt to account for the relationship of the masses to the work of art."[87] A spectrum of attention emerges from Benjamin's careful analysis of tactile versus optical reception, a spectrum drawn taut between distraction and concentration, habit and attentive observation. In reference to this spectrum, the building wall, fully integrated into the architectural functions of the building to which it belongs, is seen tactilely, its volume and contours negotiated by users relying on faculties proper to bodies neither blind to nor entirely absorbed by the stimuli around them. The painting hanging on a wall, on the other hand, demands dedicated attention. It absorbs the gaze, its mode of use being such that the eye must focus on it attentively in order to gauge its measures of meaning.

Distraction neither forestalls the moment of analysis nor gives way to it completely. There is room in the idea of attention in distraction for a negative moment, a moment that takes away from a full engagement with the object of analysis. The subject of this mode of attention is pulled by the object of analysis, but drawn elsewhere. That this mode of attention would engage a range of perceptual faculties beyond the optical is made clear by Benjamin's recourse to architecture, for the compulsion to move about a building in order to receive it, in order to take it in, can hardly be described as a force exerted on and by the eyes alone. Both tactile reception—the mode of engagement Benjamin associates with architecture—and the play on textures Siqueiros builds into his sculpto-murals appeal to a regime of sense and knowledge that resides not in the still, contemplative eye, but in the "shifting, mobile, unruly fantasy relations"[88] that Kiaer ascribes to individual consumers and their relations to modern commodities.

Siqueiros poses the problem of textures as a problem of sculpture and painting, of architecture and muralism, of politicized art, and of commercial advertising. The reception he wants to cultivate in the 1950s with his sculptural billboard murals, the mode of engagement he envisioned with his first incursions into outdoor mural painting in 1932, is neither fully attentive nor wholly distracted. The range of attention Siqueiros envisions is tantamount to an analysis made in distraction, a moment of critical apprehension that happens in motion, an apprehension that need not arrest the eye. This mode of apprehension assumes crucial importance as consumer capitalism consolidates and begins to broker the language and the very rhythms of meaning formation operating in the vast majority of mass media platforms. Around the same time that Siqueiros was theorizing distraction, in the 1950s, Octavio Paz reads it as a form of distance from and resistance to "the dominant tendencies of our civilization": "A man that is distracted," Paz writes, "negates the whole modern world." Distraction for Paz is "attraction for the reverse side of this world."[89]

Benjamin draws the link between distraction as mode of apprehension and consumption since at least the early 1930s. In a fragment of writing titled "Theory of Distraction," he calls to our attention the need to examine the relationship between distraction and absorption or ingestion. Though too fragmentary to sustain any firm readings, this short text does seem to suggest a strong relation between distraction and consumption. "In its concern with educational value," Benjamin writes, "'The Author as Producer' disregards consumer value."[90] And further: "Educational value and consumer value converge, thus making possible a new kind of learning."[91] This new kind of learning, an education in distraction, is exactly what Siqueiros seems to be pursuing with his billboard murals of the 1950s, most of which he painted, appropriately enough, in the recently completed Ciudad Universitaria, the new and sprawling campus of the Universidad Autónoma de México (UNAM).

In an interview with Julio Scherer García published in *Excélsior*, a leading Mexico City newspaper, and later in *Arte público*, Siqueiros writes:

> The difference between outdoor mural painting set on the exterior walls of buildings and mural painting on interior walls is infinitely greater than that which exists between mural painting in general and easel painting. To start, I believe there are great optical differences between them: one is meant to be seen from twenty, thirty, forty, maybe fifty meters away, while the other is meant to be seen from hundreds of meters away, maybe even from kilometers away, and this calls for fundamental differences in composition. If it is true that the publics of indoor mural paintings establish the laws of pictorial composition according to their normal movement, we must agree that the basis of the "great spectacle" of outdoor painting calls for radically different solutions.[92]

Siqueiros took these ideas seriously enough to test them out in real life, with the help of his wife Angélica Arenal. As Valerie Fraser writes, in preparation for the outdoor murals Siqueiros completed in Ciudad Universitaria between 1952 and 1956, "Siqueiros had his wife Angélica [Arenal] drive him up and down Avenida Insurgentes at sixty miles an hour in

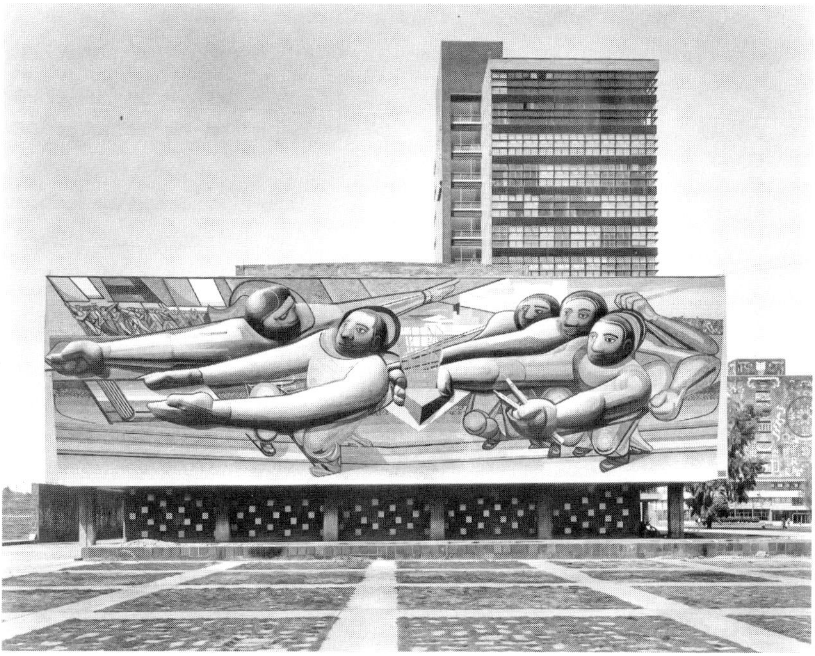

Figure 1.12. David Alfaro Siqueiros, *El pueblo a la universidad, la universidad al pueblo* (1952–1956). Low relief and mosaic, 3,000 square feet. Edificio de la Rectoría, Ciudad Universitaria, Mexico City. Photograph ca. 1956, by Guillermo Zamora. Courtesy of the Instituto Nacional de Bellas Artes y Literatura.

order to assess how the figures would indeed reach out in a forceful and dynamic way to those passing on the highway."[93]

Siqueiros planned three murals for one of the central buildings of the Ciudad Universitaria campus: *Las fechas en la historia de México o el derecho a la cultura*, *Nuevo emblema universitario*, and *El pueblo a la universidad, la universidad al pueblo*. He finished *El pueblo* and left the other two murals unfinished. All three murals bear a striking material and compositional resemblance to *Velocidad*. Like *Velocidad*, the murals at Ciudad Universitaria are characterized by a relative graphic simplicity that makes them legible quickly. Two of the murals, *Las fechas* and *El pueblo*, exhibit the sculptural painting technique used by Siqueiros to great effect in the completion of *Velocidad*. The raised surfaces and surges of concrete and mosaic that protrude out of these murals literally thrust the surfaces on which they are set forward, competing for the attention of the spectators walking and driving by them.

The texts Siqueiros wrote in tandem with the murals at the Ciudad Universitaria campus leave no doubt as to the link between these murals and advertising. "The style of David Alfaro Siqueiros," reads an unattributed text most likely penned by the muralist himself, "due to the expressed and manifest will of the painter, displays elements of the great billboard, of commercial muralism, without however losing the elements of traditional sculptural synthesis, which are common to his work in general."[94] Siqueiros appreciated the innovative use of technologies like neon light in advertising. In a short essay devoted expressly to billboards and commercial advertisements as precedents of his outdoor mural paintings, and citing a conversation with an unnamed American engineer, Siqueiros refers to electric billboards as "'a muralism where the conjunction of neon light and mechanical engines achieves the graphic expression of movement.'"[95]

By the 1960s, as the only surviving member of the three "great ones" of Mexican muralism, Siqueiros was strongly positioned as the foremost visual artist in Mexico. He was a towering figure in a cultural field too keen on—and remarkably good at—making institutions out of its most accomplished artists and writers. He was also well positioned to confront critically the cultural and economic juncture of Mexico in the 1960s, having worked as an artist with technology and mass media since the 1930s and having embraced in the 1950s a program of politicized muralism centered on the notion of the billboard mural. But as he began to work on his last, largest, and by all accounts most exorbitant mural project, *La marcha de la humanidad en la tierra y hacia el cosmos* (1964–1971), it became clear that the contest of conflicting desires that Siqueiros upheld so fruitfully for the better part of his career had been resolved in favor of commerce.

La marcha was completed in 1971 in the lobby of a large tourist hotel in Mexico City. The building was constructed expressly for the realization of Siqueiros's mural. As Leonard Folgarait writes, Manuel Suárez, the project's patron and principal financier of the hotel where the mural was set, "expected 85 per cent of the visitors to be American tourists."[96] Suárez was up front to the point of cynicism about the true function of Siqueiros's last mural. Referring to *La marcha*, he stated: "what you will see here has many aspects, but one single end: to capture the tourist market."[97] As Folgarait notes, "the Mexican tourist industry had enjoyed a boom since the 1950s, increasing its earnings an average of 12 percent each year until the early 1970s."[98] Predictably, US visitors accounted for much of that growth, and that growth in turn proved providential for the Mexican economy in the 1960s,[99] after the buoyant 1950s and before the devastating crises of the 1970s and 1980s.

Siqueiros did little to dislodge the impression that his last and most grandiose mural project (it is much too sculptural, much too architectural, much too monumental to refer to it as a painting) was anything other than that: at best an attraction, a verily awesome tourist attraction; at worst a tourist trap. Siqueiros claimed as his public "the rural populations of the third world,"[100] but nothing in the content of the mural (the subject matter is, as Folgarait notes, too universal to convincingly appeal to any one group of people) or in the conditions of spectatorship afforded by the mural (the mural itself is indoors, in a private space that required, and still requires, visitors to pay a fee) is in any way responsive to this half-hearted aspiration. Even supporters of the muralist despaired at the lack of cohesion of his last project, his final gesture. The resolution of Siqueiros's subversive dialectic in favor of private enterprise and commerce was so complete that it colored not just the production of his last mural but also his assessment of Mexican muralism as a whole. More than anything else, Siqueiros declared in the 1970s, muralism in Mexico had contributed "to the development of tourism."[101] In the end, tourism and commercial enterprise trumped subversion, dialectical or not. Billboard muralism turned out to be all billboard and no political agitation. There is no message in Siqueiros's last mural, not even a clear commercial message. The tug-of-war between consumer culture, art, and politics Siqueiros rehearsed so provocatively was over.

I don't think this makes the revision of his sustained dialogue with market capitalism any less interesting, any less urgent. As the most notorious cultural program to emerge from the revolutionary project in Mexico, the fate of Mexican muralism was sealed long before Siqueiros abandoned his aspirations to political struggle. The project failed, new social movements responded to more injustices at larger scales and under changing circumstances, and the art that emerged in tandem with these new movements materialized accordingly. Siqueiros the demagogue, arresting as he can be, would hardly seem any less reactionary now than he did then, during his own lifetime. But Siqueiros the appropriator, Siqueiros the replicant, the shrewd artist and activist too invested in political impact to resist what was most alluring about commercial culture, may still have something revealing to say to us. We live in a reality decisively more wrought by consumption and consumer culture than was the reality Siqueiros had to contend with. Even if the goal is to dismiss, once and for all, the promiscuous alternative Siqueiros represented, we might as well listen carefully to what he had to say.

TWO

Fascination; or, Enlightenment in the Age of Neon Light

A Case of Concrete Poetry

Brazilian concrete poetry enchants from the very beginning, starting with the first poetry volume published by a member of the movement: *Poetamenos* (1953) by Augusto de Campos.[1] Strictly speaking, *Poetamenos* is not a book. It's a set of placards thick enough to hang on a wall,[2] each one printed with a brightly colored poem. The most salient feature of these poems is their radiance. Their words and word fragments come printed in vivid colors, mimicking the vibrancy and movement of neon signs. In a letter to the US concrete poet Mary Ellen Solt, editor of an early anthology of concrete poetry, Campos recounts how for *Poetamenos* he wanted to use "luminous letters which could automatically switch on and off as in street advertisements . . . but there was no money."[3] He revisits this wish in an interview with Marjorie Perloff, where he states:

> I would say that in my case I kept a great interest in visual poetry, or rather, as we used to call it, using Joycean terminology, "verbivocovisual" poetry. But my own poetry evolved in the sense of appropriating new technologies that were explicit in our theories all along, but that we didn't have at our disposal at the time. When I wrote my first book of poems of the fifties, *Poetamenos* (*Poetminus*), I remember indulging in some wishful thinking: "Oh, if I could only have filled letters, luminous billboard letters, letters that light up!"[4]

Anton Webern's *klangfarbenmelodie* is often cited as the principal intertext of *Poetamenos*.[5] Music gets prime billing in the volume's own introductory text. But it seems to me that neon light—already falling out of use by the time *Poetamenos* was published—reveals as much as, if not more than, music about this work, about concrete poetry in general, and about concrete poetry's place in the larger social context from which it emerges and to which it responds.

The intention behind *Poetamenos*, the intention to write with neon light, emerges from the frenzied optimism of São Paulo in the 1950s. These poems don't just respond to or portray the wave of development and modernization that took hold of São Paulo in the years after World War II. They are also tuned to what Michael Taussig describes, in reference to advertisements, as a form of distraction, "a very different apperceptive mode, the type of flitting and barely conscious peripheral vision perception unleashed with great vigor by modern life at the crossroads of the city, the capitalist market, and modern technology."[6] A flickering mode of attention is revealed and exercised in *Poetamenos*, a mode of attention that flows easily from one source of meaning to another, distracted but not disengaged. A different posture, a different spirit is engaged by the childish allure of the bright colors in *Poetamenos*, the kind of spirit that could and would thrive in the world so aptly probed by Taussig when he states, reading Benjamin, that "the everyday is a question not of universal semiotics but of capitalist mimetics."[7]

Imitation in the age of consumer capitalism is what operates here, imitation as something more than simple mimicking, something more deliberate, more complex, and potentially much more disruptive. Poetry is what imitates, what behaves like something other than itself, and in so doing it models for us a form of vision crucial for our understanding of experience in the context of consumer capitalism. But Taussig sees higher stakes in the question of mimetics. Like Adorno before him, Taussig sees in mimesis, and in the mimetic and tactile aspects of Benjamin's writings in particular, an alternative to analytical interpretation, "a form which, in an age wherein analysis does little more than reconstitute the obvious, is capable of surprising us with the flash of a profane illumination."[8]

Something like a "flash of a profane illumination" shines as we work through the poems of *Poetamenos*. Illumination here comes in the form of contradiction. Adorno wrote that "the lyric spirit's idiosyncratic opposition to the superior power of material things is a form of reaction to the reification of the world, to the domination of human beings by commodities that has developed since the beginning of the modern era, since the industrial revolution became the dominant force in life."[9] But what happens when opposition looks more like imitation? How are we to understand the mimetic posture of Brazilian concrete poetry vis-à-vis the world of commodities that the aesthetic at large and the lyric in particular are supposed to resist? What I am after here is an alternative to the two options literary history and art criticism usually present us with when coming to terms with engagements with and appropriations of consumer culture: either banal celebration or immediate indictment, the kind that assumes that any affirmative contact with consumer culture evinces a will to assimilate to it. At stake in my reading of Brazilian concrete poetry and in the other chapters of this book is the possibility of reclaiming, by mimetic appropriation, certain categories singled out, colonized, and perfected by the culture industry, by consumer culture—categories like distraction, enchantment, fascination, and homemaking. These categories trade in ambiguity, and it is this ambiguity (the ambiguity of the deadly serious that appears to be banal; the ambiguity of the seemingly utilitarian that never quite delivers on its promise) that Brazilian concrete poetry claims in its dealings with consumer culture.

Capital Desire (Mimesis and Regression)

Taussig coins the term "capitalist mimetics" in a memorable reading of Walter Benjamin's writings on distraction. Mimesis is a key concern for both Adorno and Benjamin, but according to Taussig it was Benjamin who made this concern an integral part of his thought, disclosing in nineteenth-century technologies of visual reproduction "a process of demystification *and* reenchantment" that would end up becoming the basis for Benjamin's "own mimetic form of revolutionary poetics."[10] A passage from Benjamin's *One-Way Street*, a marvelous book of short writings attuned to the visual landscape of urban commodity capitalism, gives Taussig occasion for a concise assessment of how vision and everyday language work in the age of advertising. "What in the end makes advertisements so superior to criticism?" asks Benjamin, "Not what the moving red neon sign says—but the fiery pool reflecting it in the asphalt."[11] Like Benjamin, Taussig approaches commodity culture without the benefit of distance: he presses close to it and finds in this intimacy a measure of meaningful engagement, a gauge modeled on something other than the discursive, analytic aspects of narrowly defined, capitalist reason: "Not what the neon says, but the fiery pool reflecting it in the asphalt; not language, but image; and not just the image but its tactility."[12] Capitalist reading, a form of literacy aggressively limited to the barest, most denotative levels of meaning, is here opposed to—though not displaced by—seeing. Seeing, in turn, is not distanced, dispassionate, but tactile, regressive: "a vision-mode at home in the pre-Oedipal economy of the crawling infant, the eye grasping, as Gertrude Koch once put it, at what the hand cannot reach."[13]

This notion of a regressive, pre-Oedipal, presymbolic faculty finds echo in a passage at the beginning of *The Practice of Everyday Life* where Certeau points to the mimetic faculty as a primitive alternative to the reigning mode of cognition in Western culture, a form of consciousness that is rational but too narrow in its reasoning. In reference to practices of use and consumption, which are more or less coextensive in Certeau's account with the practice of everyday life, Certeau writes: "the question at hand concerns . . . an operational logic whose models may go as far back as the age-old ruses of fishes and insects that disguise or transform themselves in order to survive, and which has in any case been concealed by the form of rationality currently dominant in Western culture."[14] Certeau's "operational logic" of everyday life rests on a horizontal mode of vision, an engagement with the world leveled with experience and no longer abstracted to the higher, critically distanced vantage points of analytic vision. Taussig's reading of the mimetic faculty in Benjamin's writings goes a step further; his model of vision presses closer to the object of apprehension, resulting in a form of seeing that is not just horizontal, but tactile.[15]

In the more strident, more vibrant streak of Brazilian concrete poetry, the embrace of the tactile and the material in language comes hand in hand with a dismissal of communication as an exclusive or even primary function of language. Language in these poems communicates more than contents, more than verbal meanings, and the form of imitation they cultivate entails a careful and playful breakdown of the structures underlying communication in mass culture. Some poems in the concrete repertoire rely on parody, but not those in *Poetamenos*. Imitation in *Poetamenos* is faithful without being submissive. *Poetamenos* affirms the original (neon light), replicating it, but in a way the original alone could not have anticipated: it takes neon light seriously, kneading out of it a lyricism that is well beyond the spectrum of commercial culture. Like parody, *Poetamenos* goes too far, but it errs on the side of the solemn.

In Chile, there is an understudied precedent for this kind of playfully incisive mimicking of mass media: *El Quebrantahuesos* (1952), a collaboration between Nicanor Parra, Alejandro Jodorowsky, Enrique Lihn, and others. *El Quebrantahuesos* is an art proposal or action rather than a standalone work. It is comprised of a series of broadsheets and of the act of exhibiting them and displaying them in public spaces in the early 1950s in Santiago, Chile. These parodic mural newspapers were made with cutouts from newspapers and marked by a biting sense of humor, a ludic element absent in *Poetamenos* but present in other concrete poems. Soon after appearing in public in what amounted to proto-happenings in the city of Santiago, *El Quebrantahuesos* fell into oblivion. It was reproduced in 1975 in *Manuscritos*, the extraordinary arts magazine produced and published by Cristián Huneeus, Ronald Kay, and Catalina Parra in the midst of one the most repressive periods of the Pinochet dictatorship.

An antagonism neither named nor resolved takes shape in both *El Quebrantahuesos* and in the concrete poems most closely linked to newspapers, logotypes, and advertising. The form of these poems seems at odds with their subject matter. In the case of *Poetamenos*, verbal and visual images of desire and love are printed in bright colors and arranged like music, to be recited by as many voices as color fonts on the printed page. These images seem locked in a struggle with language. Of the six poems included in *Poetamenos*, four feature intricate word arrangements loaded with erotic imagery. Desire and love are at the center of what is perhaps the most memorable poem in the collection, "eis os amantes" (fig. 2.1). In it, words thick in sex and innuendo splay across the page, mixing and mingling in visual clusters that enact scenes of intercourse at once static and in movement. Portmanteaus dominate the verbal landscape of the poem. Below and on either side of the centered, orange column that anchors the top part of the poem, ten such word compounds are carefully arranged to suggest a movement of union and separation, fusion and fragmentation. A drama of kinship, sex, and love unfolds at every level of the poem: visually and verbally, in the makeup of each word compound and in the relationship between word units. Parts of words (he/she, one/other, this/that) come together in single composites. Complementary colors, orange and blue, mark the different parts of each arrangement. The color variations within a single word unit are used to great effect. We see the word composites and we also see the distinct parts that constitute them. A playful tension arises, a dilemma: at the same time that we come to recognize the complex meaning of each word compound, we see each one of its parts distinctly, in bright color. A visual scan of the poem from the top down coupled with a close reading of the color variations across and between

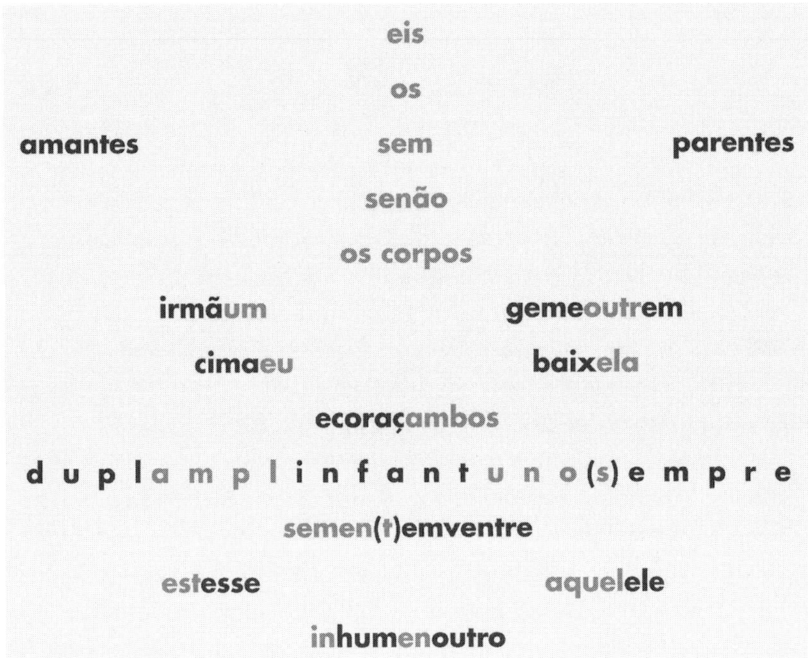

Figure 2.1. Augusto de Campos, "eis os amantes," in *Poetamenos* (1953). Originally printed in orange and blue fonts. © Augusto de Campos; courtesy, Augusto de Campos.

word units gives the reader a sense of a sequence, like a series of copulations leading to a morphological climax in two colors.

The images conjured by some of the portmanteaus (*cimaeu*, *baixela*, *semen(t)emventre*) leave no doubt as to their gendered, sexual nature. Words copulate, in much the same way we can imagine the lovers in the poem copulating. A dense image of contact is constructed in the poem, not by pronouns and adjectives alone, much less by syntax and description, but by collision and accumulation, by parataxis. Clusters of letters become the organs that split and splice word units, the same units from which those clusters derive. Words diffract in the color-movement of their own syllables, echoing the *subdivisions prismatiques de l'Idée* Stéphane Mallarmé recognized in his own spatial diffractions of the word. In diffraction, words offer a new reading. Different colors multiply the number of images and stories that coexist in the poem, adding an entire order of magnitude to the structures of meaning sustained by the words alone. If we take "eis os amantes" or any other poem in *Poetamenos* and compare it with an image of itself stripped of its chromatic structure, we can see how the use of colored fonts—and by extension the neon as referent—adds layers of organizational webbing, buttressing topographies of reading that are lost to the flatness of print matter, the flatness of the black and white. This is particularly evident in poems like "eis os amantes" where the two different colors mark divisions within the same words, within lines, and across lines, thus creating spatial configurations that visually flesh out the sexual encounter so powerfully suggested by the poem through nouns and pronouns (*irmã/gêmeo*, *um/outro*, *cima/baixo*, *eu/ela*) spliced and recombined. There is union in this coming together, but hardly any fulfillment. Traces of a critique of commodity fetishism can be seen in passing.

In "eis os amantes" desire is enacted as impossibility: synthetic as it may be, union in the poem is marked by difference, verbally and chromatically. The poem enacts closure in neon light, in its images of union, but it also performs movement and alternation within that union. It is as if the object of desire was plainly within view in the poem, but only as the spliced fragment of a disjointed whole. The poem thus functions, as Rachel Price writes in her reading of Brazilian concrete poetry, "a bit like a psychoanalytic fetish, reconciling presence and absence, avowed and disavowed beliefs."[16] A utopian drive characteristic of the early phase of concrete poetry is evident in this poem, a drive to use neon light to forge a new language, a language capable of expressing longing and love not beyond but within the manufactured world of commodities. Time and again in the concrete repertoire, we find evidence of how taken the concrete poets were with the commodity world's uncanny ability to organize desire. What is extraordinary about their approach is that it plays out as a struggle not with the commodity, not even with advertising, but with the language of consumer capitalism. In "eis os amantes," neon light is manipulated in a way that makes it object-oriented and rehumanized: it spells out not an object of desire but a language for longing. Desire, in turn, inasmuch as it is embodied in the material language of commodity culture, is brought closer to this culture, imploding it.

Mass Media, Manifestos, Classified Ads

Manifestos written by Augusto de Campos, Haroldo de Campos, and Décio Pignatari in the first five years of the movement leave the distinct impression that the world they belong to is as distinguished (Mallarmé, Ezra Pound, Joyce) as it is rarefied (the Mallarmé of *Un coup de dés*, the Pound of *The Cantos*, the Joyce of *Finnegans Wake*). The world they reach out to in these first manifestos is the world of high modernist poetry. Poetry in these writings is willfully removed from its immediate surroundings. It is autonomous, distinctly formalist. A shift in tone takes place toward the end of 1956, two years after Juscelino Kubitschek assumed power and the same year his Plano de Metas for the modernization and industrialization of Brazil was instituted. As Daniela Name argues, efforts to industrialize the Brazilian economy began earlier in the 1950s, just as the largest cities in the nation began growing in importance and at the same time that the concrete poetry movement and other Brazilian avant-garde movements of the period began to emerge.[17] Kubitschek galvanized the feelings of optimism and images of modernization that characterize this period in the history of Brazilian culture. His administration accomplished this most memorably through the construction of Brasília, the new Brazilian capital and capstone of the national development and construction ambitions of Kubitschek's presidency.

Writing on the many points of contact between the work of constructivist and concrete artists in Brazil and the fields of advertising, merchandising, and design, Name makes the case for the need to situate their artworks against the background of developmentalism and import-substitution industrialization.[18] Connections among art, poetry, and the emerging industries of design, marketing, and advertising took place not only at the level of production, with many avant-garde artists and poets of the period working for these industries, but also at the level of theoretical reflection. The concrete poets in particular wrote prolifically about art, poetry, and industry, mulling over and feeding into the feverish optimism of the period.

In "nova poesia: concreta," a manifesto written for the architecture and design magazine *ad—arquitetura e decoração*, Décio Pignatari, one of the three most prominent figures of Brazilian concrete poetry (together with the brothers Haroldo and Augusto de Campos: the *Noigandres* poets, as they are known collectively), places the discussion on language and concrete poetry squarely within the age of mass media. In terse language dispensing with capitalization, he writes: "verse: crisis. forces the reader of headlines (simultaneity) into a prosthetic posture."[19] The world Pignatari pictures here is a world he shares with the average reader, a world of newspapers and headlines, neon lights, comic books, radio, and television. It is this willingness to come to terms with a reality increasingly dominated by mass media and consumption that makes concrete poetry, in the eyes of Flora Süssekind, "one of the most productive dialogues between poetry,

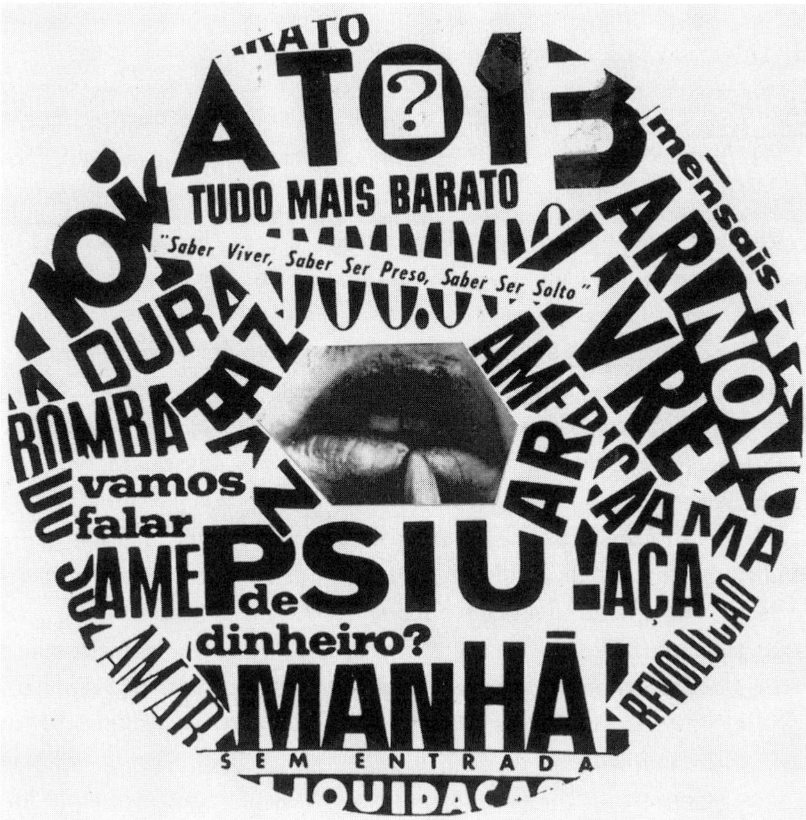

Figure 2.2. Augusto de Campos, "Psiu!" (1966). © Augusto de Campos; courtesy, Augusto de Campos.

technology, and spectacle in Brazil," a dialogue begun "at the peak of developmentalist optimism."[20] It was the concrete poets, Süssekind argues, "who, at the turn of the decade [1950s–1960s], redefined the book as object, seeking to modify the gaze of the poetry reader, now transformed into a spectator of the poem, as well."[21] This is the public that the concrete poets imagined facing hereafter, the consumer-public they turned their attention to: a reader who reads but mostly watches, a subject at home in print culture and in the world of television. The way Pignatari sees it, concrete poetry begins to move toward "a general language art. advertising, the press, radio, television, film. a popular art."[22]

As Charles Perrone has argued, even when it seems most removed from the events happening around it, years before it felt the need to make a "participatory leap" into the political arena, concrete poetry bears material traces of the social. Cutouts of magazines and newspapers pasted on the surface of a visual poem (as in Augusto de Campos's "Psiu!" from 1966; fig. 2.2) are the more obvious examples of direct use of the material culture subtending concrete poetry. Puns and a certain unmistakable rhythm—the rhythm of headlines and advertising copy: broken, staccato, too keen on alliteration and all the better for it—are less evident but no less vivid trace. The bright neon colors of *Poetamenos* can also be read as signs of social circumstance. What is social in these poems is electric light (or in the illusion of it), as channeled by advertising.

Toward the end years of the concrete movement as such, in 1974, Augusto de Campos was writing of a "universal intercommunicability" that made it "literally impossible for a common citizen to live his life without coming across Vietnam, the Beatles, strikes, 007, the Moon, Mao, or the Pope."[23] Earlier in 1969, Haroldo de Campos had already evoked a longer history of links between mass culture and language, citing Georg Wilhelm Friedrich Hegel's characterization of newspaper reading as a kind of "morning philosophical prayer"; Alphonse de Lamartine's prophetic vision of a world where "thought will spread around at the speed of light, instantaneously conceived, instantaneously written, and instantaneously understood in the most remote parts of the world"; and Mallarmé's fascination with the newspaper form.[24] Earlier, in 1957, Haroldo de Campos wrote of "the transformations that have occurred in the traditional practice of thinking; the cosmic vision," he goes on to argue, "that is now offered to us by the current state of science demands an analogous revolution in the structure of language."[25] The innovative use of typography and layout in *Un coup de dés* is related, Campos reminds us, to Mallarmé's interest in the visual and material aspects of newspapers.[26]

The fact that these statements first appeared in the *suplemento dominical* (Sunday supplement) of *Jornal do Brasil*, and the fact that this newspaper in particular had just undergone a striking overhaul of its graphic design, invests Haroldo de Campos's ideas with all the more immediacy, all the more meaning. The newspaper as document of shifts in language, the newspaper as record of the changes language brings about in the frames of cognition it subtends, the newspaper in this capacity was, for the reader of Haroldo's essay, more than a hypothetical scenario. It was a tangible object, a concrete thing, the printed platform of the essay where these shifts and changes were being considered.

In the late 1950s and early 1960s, the *suplemento dominical* of the *Jornal do Brasil* became the preferred platform for publication and debate for the most prominent figures of modern Brazilian poetry and art, particularly for those artists, poets, and critics either associated with or invested in the concrete and neoconcrete movements.[27] It was a marked shift in tone for a newspaper that was known just a decade earlier, in the 1940s, as the "jornal das cozinheiras," a nod to the newspaper's preeminent share of the market for classified ads, as well as to its reputation as a place to find and advertise employment in housekeeping and domestic work. Founded in Rio de Janeiro in 1891, the paper started out with a strong tradition of art and literary writing with contributions by the likes of Joaquim Nabuco and José Veríssimo. By the 1930s, financial troubles turned the newspaper mostly into a vehicle for classified ads. Twenty years later in the mid-1950s, the newspaper's directors undertook a general reform aimed at turning *Jornal do Brasil* into a beacon of modern journalism. Wilson Figuereido, journalist for the newspaper for over five decades and director of its editorial staff, situates the newspaper's transformation within a generalized process of professionalization of Brazilian journalism taking place in the 1950s,[28] in tandem with the country's push for industrialization and modernization and coinciding with Juscelino Kubitschek's rise to power. An overhaul of *Jornal do Brasil*'s layout, its typography, and its overall graphic design constituted the most visible aspect of the newspaper's reform, an overhaul undertaken, significantly, by an artist with concretist and neoconcretist filiations: Amilcar de Castro.

Castro, a sculptor who participated in the event that marked the division between concretism and neoconcretism (the 1ª Exposição Nacional de Arte Concreta in 1956), took on graphic design and layout responsibilities for *Jornal do Brasil* in 1957 at the behest of Reynaldo Jardim, an artist and the well-regarded director of Rádio Jornal do Brasil, the radio station owned by the newspaper's parent company. Changes in the newspaper look and layout were swift and decisively modernizing, starting with the pages of the *suplemento dominical* (formerly the women's section) and spreading in the late 1950s and early 1960s to the rest of the newspaper. Under Castro's direction, form and function took absolute precedence over the ornamental frames and vines that characterized the *Jornal do Brasil* for the better part of its history. Uniform, sans serif typography was adopted for the newspaper, along with more dynamic use of photographs informed in large part by Castro's previous work in the magazines *A Cigarra* and *Manchete*, the former a cultural publication with a largely female readership and the latter a modern photojournalism magazine in the style of *Paris Match*.

The most striking graphic reforms took place in the *suplemento dominical*, which quickly took on the role of principal platform for public debate and discussion for the foremost artists and poets of the period. It was in this section that the "Manifesto neoconcreto" first appeared in March 1959, signed by Castro himself, Cláudio Mello e Souza, Ferreira Gullar, Franz Weissmann, Lygia Clark, Lygia Pape, and Theon Spanudis. Vast, blank spaces on the two-page spread of the manifesto along with columns both rigid and playful in their disposition (one rises tall like a skyscraper, another reaches down to a graphic underground) dominate the layout of the manifesto, mimicking, as Daniela Name notes,[29] the free sense of rigor neoconcretism would assume as its trademark style.

Two facts about the transformation of the *suplemento dominical* strike me as significant for what they tell us about the material and economic conditions behind the publication of a newspaper supplement that achieved both mass circulation and a remarkably elevated level of critical inquiry in its content as well as in its graphic layout. There is, first, the origin of the *suplemento* as the women's section of the newspaper, the preferred vehicle of advertisements for the kind of consumer goods that flooded Brazilian markets in the 1950s. Second, perhaps more revealingly, there is the *Jornal*'s previous reputation as the "jornal das cozinheiras" along with the business model responsible for this kind of reputation. The paper's large share of classified ads and the significant revenue these ads produced are likely what allowed the newspaper's owner, the Countess Pereira Carneiro, to assume the risk of overhauling *Jornal do Brasil* after decades of journalistic ill repute.

By the 1960s, and in the words of Figuereido, the *Jornal do Brasil* took on the task of representing and responding to the needs of a rising middle class, "founders of a society of consumption, the symbol of which was the nationally produced automobile."[30] In Figuereido's account, it was the transformation from "jornal das cozinheiras" to newspaper for the consuming class that allowed *Jornal do Brasil*, which stayed in print until 2010, to survive the crisis of print journalism brought about by the rise of television and televised newscasts. And it was classified ads, in the first instance, that provided the material and economic conditions for the publication of a cultural supplement as advanced, rigorous, and influential as the *suplemento dominical* was in the late 1950s and early 1960s. What we find here is an early example of the kind of "telling disjunction between the material and the symbolic worlds" that Diana Sorensen reads as a generalized trait of the turbulent 1960s. "It was the economic bonanza of the postwar bourgeois world," Sorensen argues, "that produced the social context in which a new culture could flourish. Money and exchange came under suspicion, but they constituted the conditions of possibility for the prevailing sense of experimentation, artistic autonomy, and a generalized teleology of revolution."[31]

A striking document of the relationship between the *Jornal do Brasil*'s revolutionizing modernity and the business practices that provided the material conditions for the realization of such modernity can be found in the newspaper's front pages from 1959 and 1960, after Amilcar de Castro's graphic reform of the *suplemento* had spread to the rest of the paper but before it stopped depending so heavily on classified ads. There, large photographs, smart layouts, and modern typography appear literally framed by cleanly arranged rows of classified ads. Seen from the vantage point of the respected newspaper that the *Jornal do Brasil* would go on to become, this image of juxtaposed interests and desires looks almost obscene. It stands as a compelling document of the intimate and often overlooked links among avant-garde aesthetics, commercial interests, and consumer culture in Brazil and elsewhere.

For Haroldo de Campos, the link between Mallarmé's innovative use of layout and typography and his interest in newspapers functions like an endorsement of the convergences between mass culture and Brazilian concrete poetry. If at the heart of *Un coup de dés*, cornerstone of modernist poetics, lies a sustained and documented interest in journalism (and advertising: Benjamin sees *Un coup* as "the first to incorporate the graphic tensions of the advertisement in the printed page"),[32] then "a reverse in interests, from journalism toward the techniques of concrete poetry, wouldn't be so disconcerting."[33]

Décio Pignatari shared Haroldo de Campos's assessment of the importance of newspaper and journalism for poetry and for the understanding of modern culture in general. In a newspaper article titled "Graphic Arts and the Other Arts" and prefaced with lines from Oswald de Andrade, Pignatari tells the story of the advice he gave to a group of young artists in charge of a graphic arts stand in Tokyo. Pignatari instructed them to show "Brazilian newspapers, from the most respected to the most sensationalist, in order to offer a concrete sample of an important parcel of our visual culture, 'consumed' daily by millions of Brazilians."[34] By the time Pignatari wrote this, Brazilian writers and poets had been responding to transformations in the realm of mass media since at least the 1920s. Oswald de Andrade is a manifest precursor in this regard, with his *Memó-*

rias sentimentais de João Miramar (1924) standing as a foundational exercise of a Brazilian poetics of mass media.[35] Andrade's later, more widely celebrated formulation of *antropofagia* is also a crucial precedent.[36]

There is another overlap between the concrete poets and the poetics of Oswald de Andrade, more consequential but seldom discussed. It has to do with their shared embrace of the more promiscuous relationships that hold between, on the one hand, the literary and artistic event and, on the other hand, the more material and commercial, the more mundane dimensions of society. In "O caminho percorrido," a lecture delivered in 1944 in the city of Belo Horizonte, Andrade writes, intriguingly: "To inquire as to why there took place in our capital [the capital of the state of São Paulo] a literary renovation is the same as inquiring as to the reasons for the Inconfidência Mineira in Minas Gerais. Just as there were revolutions fueled by gold, so there were revolutions fueled by coffee."[37] And later: "We must understand *modernismo* together with its material and prolific causes, rooted entirely in São Paulo's industry . . . *modernismo* is a diagram of the bull market for coffee, of its bankruptcy, and of the Brazilian revolution."[38]

Awareness of the commercial and economic realities subtending their own historical circumstance also characterize the concrete poets' understanding of their work and its social context. Like pop artists in Britain in the decades after World War II, the concrete poets in Brazil called upon works by earlier avant-garde artists like El Lissitzky, John Heartfield, and Kurt Schwitters as precedents for an engagement with mass culture and commercial form.[39] Lissitzky's constructivist designs for a book of visual poetry signed by him and Mayakovsky were particularly salient for them. In an article published in 1962 in the literary supplement of *O Estado de São Paulo*, one of the largest newspapers in São Paulo and a main organ of diffusion for the concrete poetry movement (along with the *suplemento dominical* in *Jornal do Brasil*), Haroldo de Campos notes how Lissitzky "solved the problem of giving titles to poems by creating logotypes . . . the function of which was, first and foremost, to lay bare in an expressive synthesis the semantic weight of the poem."[40] The reference here is to a collection of poems by Vladimir Mayakovsky entitled *Dlia Golosa* (*For the Voice*, 1923). For *Dlia Golosa*, Lissitzky was responsible for the text's layout and its aggressively innovative typography, and he designed a kind of thumbnail image for each poem. These images are the logotypes Haroldo de Campos refers to. A quick glance at the first page of one of the poems in the collection, "Scum," gives one a hint of the parallels between the work of Lissitzky and the work with newspapers, advertisements, and logotypes produced by the concrete poets in Brazil almost fifty years later. Mayakovsky's poem, "hardly trying to be a poem," speaks to those that "stand there dumb," "nailed by verse," as if the very diagonal disposition of Lissitzky's layout and the tilted rectangle of his logo (which rests on a small circle, presumably the "scum" to which the poem refers to) could already perform a rattling of shackles, a crushing, a revolt against verse and the linguistic order verse stands for.

The more pressing question remains: whether the mimicking and adaptation of advertising evident in many a concrete poem amounts to an avowal of consumer culture and an underlying ideology of developmentalism. Mike Gonzalez and David Treece offer the most comprehensive affirmative answer to this question. "For the Concretists," they write, "modernization was not problematic or ambiguous. On the contrary, the perspective which overshadowed this period was one of uncritical identification with national capitalist development."[41] Gonzalez and Treece describe the concretists' view of poetry as "a 'pure,' autonomous and self-referring practice, the construction of objective, utilitarian forms or aesthetic 'commodities,' reproducing the mechanisms of mass production and consumption characteristic of industrial capitalism."[42] "What they all assumed," Gonzalez and Treece write, grouping together *poema/processo*, concretism, neoconcretism, and the Violão de Rua poets, "regardless of their position within the debate, was, first, an unproblematic view of the relationship between language and reality."[43]

The most devastating criticism raised by Gonzalez and Treece centers on what they refer to as "the central ideological question" of Brazilian concrete poetry, "the Concretists' uncritical identification of their project with that of post-war capitalist development."[44] It rests on the assumption that appropriating, replicating, or willfully inhabiting the field of forces that go into the expansion of consumer society is inherently complicit with the development and the expansion of capitalism. This is the assumption at work in Antonio Candido's admonition in "Literatura e subdesenvolvimento," where he praises concrete poetry's spirit of experimentalism and its capacity for social insertion before remarking upon the danger these "modern experiences" present as potential instruments of political manipulation.[45] Candido, however, like Gonzalez and Treece, fails to recognize that contestatory power can be forged and contested using the same techniques and forces that capitalism unleashes for its sustainment and growth. He fails to recognize the nature of commodity capitalism as a network of relational forces within which power is built up and exercised, but also contested and dispersed.

To denounce the use and appropriation of techniques of advertising as evidence of a will to developmentalism skirts a more pressing issue, the context of which becomes more fully defined precisely through the kind of complicit, culturally and politically embedded language theorized by the concrete poets. In a few broad strokes, Benjamin paints a compelling picture of this issue when he writes that against the "blizzard of changing, colorful, conflicting letters," a child can hardly be expected to understand "the archaic stillness of the book."[46] "Script," Benjamin writes, "—having found, in the book, a refuge in which to lead an autonomous existence—is pitilessly dragged out onto the street by advertisements and subjected to the brutal heteronomies of economic chaos."[47] Under this new order, language must now coexist with words and also with things. Concrete poetry, Augusto de Campos writes, is "tension of word-things in space-time."[48] The increasingly object-like nature of concrete poetry led poets like Ferreira Gullar and Osmar Dillon away from language-centered works and toward proposals like Dillon's *Lua* (1959–1960), more firmly anchored in sculpture and the visual arts.[49] The insistence, on the other hand, of the main group of concrete poets on replicating the order of things in the realm of poetry has often led to charges of reification. By mirroring the objectifying tendencies of commodity capitalism, the concrete poets are said to reify language, the word, and the consciousness that constitutes itself in that word. Language in concrete poetry, in this reading, has little to say about the social circumstance from which it emerges, and what is worse, potential readers feel neither interpellated by this poetry nor able to voice a response to it. After all, what kind of dialogue is to be established with a poem that looks like a logotype? The plurality of perspectives (the "gathering of the voices" of Gonzalez and Treece's book) is presumed to be effaced from the fierce materiality of the concrete poem, and readers, in turn, "whether viewed as consumers or as alienated workers [are] reduced to the status of a silent, faceless object."[50]

The force of concrete poetry and its potential contribution to our understanding of how language functions under conditions of market capitalism lie in the rigor, and the persistence, of its appeal to a mode of consciousness (distracted, captivated, fascinated) and its concurrent appeal to the social subject of this mode of consciousness (the "passive consumer"; the "silent, faceless object," often female or effeminate; the "uncritical" subject of consumption). This subject, assumed by the concrete poets (though not explicitly theorized by them), is attuned to the complexities of visual culture—the culture so fiercely exploited by market capitalism—but is either marginalized or triumphantly tuned out from the conventional (read narrowly linguistic) registers of the dialectic. Therein lies the crudeness of what Benjamin theorized as "the brutal heteronomies of economic chaos," the coarse silence of the subject at home in this chaos, its regressiveness. It rests squarely on the crisis of a logocentric order that must now go beyond, or beneath, the verbal. And therein lies the revelatory power of mimesis as theorized by Benjamin. To quote Mark Hansen, it comes from the way it "*historicizes* the linguistic (textualist) model of the cosmos as specific to a particular (if particularly long and important) phase in human existence," all the while distinguishing—without hierarchizing—the linguistic model from a "primitive, prelinguistic and embodied" mode of experience.[51] A "curious posthistorical form of preliteracy"—this is how Hansen describes the faculty that takes hold of experience at this historical juncture.[52] What is curious about this return is its conflicted temporality: a throwback to a "primitive, prelinguistic" and "prelogical affirmation of the world, in the sense that it takes place before the fact of *logos*," a throwback that also moves forward, beyond progression, beyond the idea of history as development.

Haroldo de Campos insists on this historicity of language in a 1957 manifesto where he singles out "the clarification of mental habits" as the task of the concrete poet.[53] What concrete poetry does, what it can do, is to "bring [immediate stimulation] to the clarification of mental habits, to the creation of new semantic reactions that stir the reader's perception of the real structure of everyday communication and prepare him for non-Aristotelian systems of communication."[54] In Campos's view, concrete poetry functions as a kind of decoder, an inoculator, a platform where dominant forms of communication are laid bare for the reader to recognize and better understand. It is worth teasing out the implications of Haroldo de Campos's characterization of language in the booming postwar period as "non-Aristotelian" language. What he seems to be after with this reference to Aristotelian thought is a set of principles, an ethics for poetics. Haroldo writes about the "value" of the task of concrete poetry and formulates it as follows: to take not feeling but sentimentality out of poetry, "to place the poem in correspondence with a series of speculations taking place in the science and philosophy of our times."[55] Three years later in 1960, Mário Pedrosa would insist on the importance of promoting communication between science and the arts in an article that picks up on the emerging concern for "concepts of force, of energetics, dynamics, intensification, etc." among artists of constructivist filiations.[56] Both Campos and Pedrosa assume in their calls for closer links between science and the arts a shared field of operations between these two forms of inquiry. For Campos, this resulted in an episodic but defining embrace of logic and mathematics as models for composition in poetry. For Pedrosa, it translated to a concern for the environment and the environmental as transversal principles of science, technology, and the arts.[57]

Until recently, readings of concrete poetry frequently focused on its embrace of logic and mathematical thought. The principal contention behind many of these readings is that concrete poetry is too embedded in consumer capitalism, too blinded by the allure of its logic, to produce a substantial response to it. No objection to concrete poetry in Brazil is as frequent and as damaging. Ronaldo Brito's rigorous critique of constructivism in general and concrete aesthetics in particular (first published as an article in 1976[58] and later expanded into a pioneering, book-length study of neoconcretism),[59] though concerned mostly with concrete and neoconcrete art, sets down the basis for this line of objection. Brito begins his study with a methodical analysis of the constructivist roots of concretism and neoconcretism. Both share, in Brito's estimation (and in accordance with the historicist principles for the interpretation of neoconcretism first established by Ferreira Gullar), a point of origin in their opposition to the denotative realism of Cândido Portinari's paintings. Both offer abstraction as an alternative to the politics of representation inherent to Portinari's brand of realism. In the process of doing so, both disclose the expediency of realist, figurative painting in the constitution of nationalist ideologies, national identities, and other forms of representational politics.[60] The key difference between concretism and neoconcretism according to Brito rests on the way in which each positions itself in the face of the conditions of production and consumption imposed by market capitalism. Concretism's embrace of design, like that of most other constructivist movements, is indicative of its integration to, and affirmation of, the market organization of capitalist economies. "For Western constructivist artists," writes Brito, "—from Mondrian and Van Doesburg to Max Bill and the concretists—the work of art can only be conceived as social insertion under two guises: as speculation and sublimation (as in the vaguely platonic deliriums of Mondrian), and/or as an integration, an almost necessarily acritical integration into the standing process of production (as in the Bauhaus, in part, and the Ulm School)."[61]

There is something more ambiguous, less "necessarily acritical" about concrete poetry's integrative approach to market capitalism. This ambiguity is what seems to move Lorenzo Mammì when he calls for more "verification and depth" in contemporary revisions of Brito's thesis on concretism and neoconcretism.[62] This ambiguity is also what Rachel Price points to when she suggests that concrete poetry's insertion into postwar consumer culture is concurrent with its investment in abstraction and nondetermination.[63] In the manifestos, however, the Brazilian concrete poets often affirm the consumer subject without qualification, and often their programmatic writings do seem to indicate a willingness to deliver the reading public to a regime of the senses dominated by consumption and market capitalism.

The concrete poets justify the affirmative, integrative vocation of their program by invoking a mission at times informative, at other times pedagogical: a call to tune readers in to what is most critical about everyday language in the age of mass culture. And insofar as they insist in this mission, without questioning how this aspect of language came to be operative or why the powers orchestrating market economies and mass culture capitalize on this aspect of language, they seem to deliver publics to the commodity world, to the world of exchange and consumption. But there is a caveat. The aspect of language they insist on emphasizing—the material aspect of language, prelinguistic and posthistorical—seems useless. It is useless because it doesn't stand for anything; it represents no one and communicates nothing, at least nothing clearly, nothing denotatively.

The material dimension of language that concrete poetry emphasizes, the sensorial in language (Roman Jakobson's poetic function, discussed below, but also the fiery pool of red in Benjamin's reading of neon light), inasmuch as it communicates no clear message, operates outside purpose. And yet in advertising this sensorial aspect of language (the concrete, visual, vocal, and tactile dimensions) *is* put to purpose. A reversal takes place here. "The aesthetic," Robert Kaufman writes, "while looking like conceptual-objective, 'useful,' content-determined thought or activity, quite precisely only *looks like* them, only mimes them at the level of form."[64] Advertising, on the other hand, and neon light in particular (its shine, its glow) appears (but only appears) to be functionally inconsequential. And yet the noncommunicative aspect of language in advertising, its gloss and glow, the intensity of its impact and shock, is precisely what drives desire and fuels the irresistible fascination consumer culture exerts on society. Fascination is put to purpose, rationally deployed in advertising and consumer culture at large. To reject the enchanting, the fascinating aspect of language for the way it mediates desire in commodity capitalism is to miss the dialectical character of fascination and enchantment, their nature as mediation with no stable value in their own right. This is the point Adorno makes when he writes that "art is motivated by a conflict: its enchantment, a vestige of its magical phase, is constantly repudiated as unmediated sensual immediacy by the progressive disenchantment of the world, yet without its ever being possible finally to obliterate this magical element. Only in it," Adorno continues, "is art's mimetic character preserved, and its truth is the critique that, by its sheer existence, it levels at a rationality that has become absolute."[65]

Similia Similibus Curantur

In "Publicidade o texto vivo" Pignatari draws an explicit link between the "nonverbal" aspects of language, mass media, and advertising:

> Given the need for faster and more precise communication, the importance that the nonverbal sphere has attained in all fields is now noticeable. Seeing is easier than reading. Words themselves do not escape that trend and their visual aspect is valued more and more. This concern for the visual aspect of words is evident, for instance, in brands and logos: "Esso,"[66] all curves inside its characteristic oval is decisively "seen" rather than "read."[67]

Esso had a remarkably strong presence in Brazilian and Mexican media and culture toward the middle of the twentieth century. Aside from the numerous television commercials advertising its energy products (where the roundness Pignatari mentions, the roundness of the letters in the name brand, the roundness of wheels proved time and again to be a central motif), Esso sponsored a radio news program in Brazil from 1941 onward. The program broadcasted reports on the US involvement in the war and was also a vehicle for vignettes of the American way of life, the kind that would prove so crucial for preparing Brazil as a major market for American-made consumer goods, the kind often sponsored and supported by the Office of the Coordinator of Inter-American Affairs. The 1965 inauguration of the Museo de Arte Moderno in Mexico City was celebrated with a painting prize sponsored by the oil company. That same year, Esso was the principal sponsor, in collaboration with the Organization of American States (OAS), of the 1965 Salón Esso at the Museo de Arte Moderno in Mexico City. The Esso-OAS partnership was the source of a larger effort to promote contemporary art in the Latin American region and included, among other interventions, the first Salón Intercol de Artistas Jóvenes in 1964 at the Museo de Arte Moderno de Bogotá in Colombia, and a collection of Puerto Rican prints in the 1970s.

For Pignatari, the use of language in logotypes and advertising campaigns like those of Esso were exemplary of a reigning economy of language. Compared to slogans and newspaper headlines, verse, Pignatari writes, is "anti-economical, it is not concentrated, it does not communicate quickly."[68] "Verse" here refers not to a unit in isolation but rather to the longer, distended measure of writing structured in stanzas and ordered by rhythms established within and between each line of verse. Thus interpreted, Pignatari's reasoning becomes more clear: verse forces readers of headlines and headings, readers of newspapers and magazines, into an unnatural attitude, a misleading position that makes them seek out longer sequences of language (sequences tending toward the linear, the discursive) when in fact, in everyday life, they are bombarded with clusters of signs and symbols that rely not on distension but on parataxis. Implicit here is a leveling of the visual and the verbal dimensions of language. The logotype, Pignatari notes, must be seen as well as read.

Pignatari's "hombre hambre hembra"[69] (1957; fig. 2.3) was published in 1958 in the fourth issue of *Noigandres*, the first publication dedicated expressly to the writings of the concrete poetry movement.[70] It is among the most minimal of the concrete repertoire, standing out even among other concrete poems similarly stripped of all but a few discursive elements. It features three Spanish-language words, "hombre" (man), "hambre" (hunger), and "hembra" (woman), repeated thrice. The image crafted in the poem (a verbivocovisual image, to use the Joycean term so dear to the concrete poets) suggests desire, need, hunger. Its structure is as simple as the instincts evoked by this image are basic. The nine words that make up the poem are laid out in three columns and four lines, the columns far more separated from each other than the lines. Every association suggested by the poem is a function of the visual relationships between the words. The syntax of the poem, its grammar, is therefore visual. Pignatari's merit consists in, as Augusto de Campos puts it in his reading of the poem, "substituting, for syntax, visual vectors that establish the connections between the words. The paronomastic cohesion is so intense that the poem cannot be written in Portuguese (*homem-fome-mulher*), nor translated into English (man-hunger-woman) without losing the poetic function."[71]

hombre hombre hombre
hambre hembra
hambre
hembra hembra hambre

Figure 2.3. Décio Pignatari, "hombre hambre hembra" (1958). In *Poesias pois é poesia* (Cotia, SP: Ateliê Editorial, 2004). © Décio Pignatari; courtesy of Dante Pignatari.

The poem brings to mind basic instincts: hunger and sex drive. It renders explicit the associations that hold between "hombre," "hembra," and "hambre" by visual and paratactic means alone. Clustered together, "hombre" and "hembra" form a unit away from "hambre," as if to suggest that the union of the former gives rise to the latter. The remaining possibilities of association and clustering by visual proximity ("hombre" and "hambre"; "hambre" and "hembra") yield comparable situations of lack or need. The moment the relationships between the three words are drawn syntactically, the sense of baseness that results from their arrangement and resulting series of associations is altogether lost. The meaning of the poem thus rests largely, but not entirely, on its capacity to make sense visually.

For critics like Mary Ellen Solt, the kind of emphasis on the visual dimension of language underlined by Pignatari takes poetry dangerously close to something that it is not—an object for vision, a visual object. "In addition to his preoccupation with the reduction of language," writes Solt, "the concrete poet is concerned with . . . making an object to be perceived rather than read."[72] Implicit in the logic of Solt's assertion is that seeing and reading are not just different things, but that they are also, somehow, mutually exclusive. But where Solt sees mutual exclusion, Pignatari argues for simultaneity. The extent to which this is achieved in this and other concrete poems is a measure of the success of Brazilian concrete poetry's attempt to articulate and give visibility to a cognitive frame of mind in synch with mediated forms of communication, forms of communication that rely on visual and spatial configurations of the word for the production of meaning. The concrete poetic function here rests largely, though not entirely, on the capacity of the poem to produce meaning based on relationships between its elements that take place at the level of its concrete, visual, and phonetic aspects.

Concrete poetry puts forth a challenge to seldom-acknowledged hierarchies of language operating in late capitalism, hierarchies whereby the nonverbal, nonlinear, "irrational" aspects of language, its vocal and visual dimensions, are deemed experientially enriching but ultimately inconsequential. The logic here is one of use, of purpose: language is judged in terms of its usefulness and reduced to being a vehicle of communication. This is the landscape, the historical reality against which modern poetry, and concrete poetry in particular, defines itself: poetry works against narrowly defined language, cultivating a play among different aspects of linguistic signification that resists the logic of purpose and wagers, instead, on recursiveness. This is the notion of poetry put forth by Mexican poet and writer Alfonso Reyes to describe his own experiments with visual and sound poetry, the *jitanjáforas*. In a book published in 1952, around the time of the rise of Brazilian concrete poetry, Reyes writes, referring to the experimental poetics of Mariano Brull's "Verdehalago": "Certainly, this poem is not directed at reason, but rather at sensation and fantasy. Words here do not seek a useful objective. They almost play alone."[73]

In "Linguistics and Poetics" (1958), a lecture delivered the same year Pignatari published "hombre hambre hembra," Roman Jakobson is careful to emphasize that the "intellectual" and verbal functions of language are not displaced or undermined in utterances where the poetic function plays a central role. To this effect, Jakobson states, citing Paul Valéry: "No doubt, verse is primarily a recurrent 'figure of sound.' Primarily, always, but never uniquely. Any attempts to confine such poetic conventions as meter, alliteration, or rhyme to the sound level are speculative reasonings without any empirical justifications. . . . Valéry's view of poetry as 'hesitation between the sound and the sense' is much more realistic and scientific than any bias of phonetic isolationism."[74] This sense of hesitation turns into a gesture of interruption in concrete poetry's critique of the communicative function of language. Poetry at large functions as a form of resistance against advancement as ideology.[75] Advancement is particularly troubled by the visual and paratactic structures of concrete poems. In the most accomplished of these poems, the eye constantly stumbles out of any kind of forward rhythm.

Pignatari's most well-known poem, "beba coca cola" (1957; fig. 2.4), is a good example of the way hesitation and interruption work in the language of concrete poems. It was published in the same issue where "hombre hambre hembra" first appeared and borrows the slogan from the iconic Coca Cola advertising campaign: "Drink Coca Cola" (in a later version it

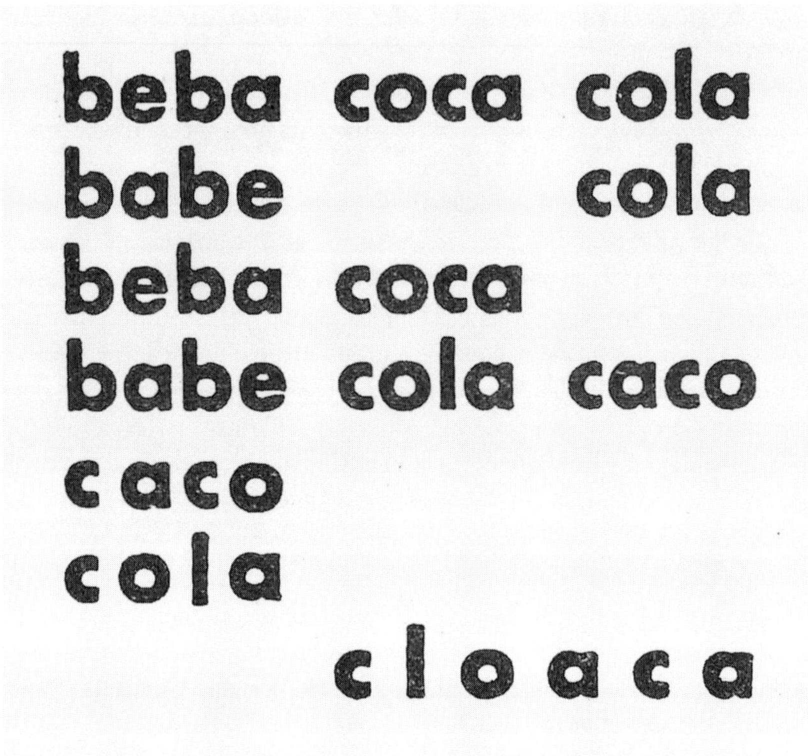

Figure 2.4. Décio Pignatari, "beba coca cola" (1957). In *Poesias pois é poesia* (Cotia, SP: Ateliê Editorial, 2004). © Décio Pignatari; courtesy of Dante Pignatari.

also borrows the trademark white and red color scheme of the Coca Cola brand). The majority of literary critics who have written on Brazilian concrete poetry pause over "beba coca cola," and for good reason. It offers one of the most suggestive convergences of concrete poetics and advertising in the concrete poetry repertoire. It exposes in its layout as well as in its semantics the unsightly side of the featured product: the drool, shards, and shit that come with the consumption, disposal, and excretion of soft drinks like Coca Cola.[76]

A resemblance exists between Pignatari's "beba coca cola" and the advertisement printed on the back cover of the first number of *Klaxon*, the official print outlet of the figures that participated in Brazil's Semana de Arte Moderna in 1922. The advertisement in *Klaxon* presents a simple but powerful slogan, "coma Lacta," bearing the same formulaic structure (imperative plus name of product advertised) at work in Coca Cola's well-known slogan. Augusto de Campos admires the ad's strategic use of space and typography and considers the Lacta ad one of the best poems published in *Klaxon* (the other ones he singles out are all advertisements, as well).[77]

Like other poems by Pignatari from the late 1950s, "beba coca cola" is characterized by the relative scarcity of its rhetorical devices, by the economy of its verbal content. It is printed in lowercase Futura font and structured around repetitions, variations, and rearrangements of a limited number of words, the three words in the Coca Cola slogan. Seen and read from top to bottom, the poem presents a series of puns on the words in "beba" and "coca," transforming "beba" to "babe" (Portuguese for "drool") and "coca" to "caco" (shard, bit, old relic) through simple but effective transpositions of the syllables in each word. The poem reads swiftly, easily; there is a sense of pleasure in the immediate recognition of the slogan appropriated in the poem, a pleasure that makes way for another, more obscene form of enjoyment that comes from seeing this same slogan twisted and turned, its words surrendering to phonic associations of drool, shit, and shards that suddenly seem to have been there all along.

The lines in "beba coca cola" are split into three columns, with the exception of the last line, where the letters that make up "Coca Cola" are recombined to form the word "cloaca," a Portuguese word for "sewer" that also brings to mind the cavity in birds and some mammals where the digestive tract, the urinary conducts, and the sexual organs converge. The sharp but playful diffraction of the original message "beba coca cola" brings forth a semantics of waste latent in the Portuguese-language version of the slogan. The two distinct and seemingly distant fields of soft drinks and sewers are thus brought together. And given that the poem ends with an image of excretion, the placing of the word "cloaca" in the lower part of the visual plane, its position in the bottom of the poem, reinforces the image of a sewer, a cesspool. Unhinged from the block constituted by the first six lines of the poem but still visibly underlying it, the image of waste ciphered by the word "cloaca" lingers at the bottom of the composition as the visible sediment of the foul bodily functions that go hand in hand with drinking Coca Cola.

The merit of a poem like "beba coca cola" rests largely on its effective appropriation of the range of associative techniques employed in advertising, techniques that are generally thought to be effective at the subliminal level but are considered less meaningful or significant as critical processes. This dissociation of the effective and the significant—an epistemological breach—is a dangerous one: we acknowledge something is of consequence, yet we refuse to categorize it as *really* meaningful, thus preempting any real attempts to understand it. Recognizing the way Pignatari uses advertising as matter and model to formulate a critique of consumption and consumer culture might lead us, metonymically, into recognizing consequential uses of the materiality of language in the products of the culture industry. This amounts to a kind of homeopathic reading of concrete poetry: concrete poetry as an exacerbation, an exaggeration of the signifying mechanisms of the culture industry. Pignatari himself suggests this reading in a passage in *Semiótica da arte e da arquitetura* (2004) where he writes: "Art does not simply 'monkey around' with science; it translates scientific and technological methods in a procedure that is, shall we say, homeopathic, based on the principle *similia similibus curantur*, with the intention of challenging and neutralizing these same methods critically as well as creatively."[78] In this reading, if advertising works by effectively, economically, and seductively conveying information about how the world works and how we should inhabit it, anti- or counter-advertisements like "beba coca cola" work not by resisting but by pushing further the mechanism of advertising, by being more witty, more seductive, and more materialistic than the original advertisement ever was, by showing more than what the advertisement was ready to show, revealing a less ideal, more physical level of reality behind the advertised product.

A different but kindred labor of revelation can be found in "carne leite pão" (1963) by José Lino Grünewald.[79] Grünewald started publishing poems in 1956 and joined the concrete poetry movement soon thereafter, adopting the rigid austerity of the orthodox phase of the movement, when verbal means were reduced to a minimum and the graphic presentation of poems was reduced to grids of words in sans serif, black-and-white font. Like Pignatari's "beba coca cola," Grünewald's "carne leite pão" focuses on three words that ring familiar to the eyes and ears of everyday consumers. The words in Grünewald's poem, however, correspond not to a slogan but to basic food staples: meat, milk, and bread. The triad of words is repeated fifteen times throughout the poem, alternating with voices in the imperative (invitations, summonses, commands) representative of messages typically found in commercial propaganda: "travel by jet," "dress well," "eat ice cream," and so forth. The effect is rhythmic, almost hypnotic, not unlike the effect achieved by litanies in religious rituals. The last two lines of the poem break with its overall rhythm by striking a tone closer to conventional rhyming poetry. Closer, too, both to the captivating ring of slogans, jingles, and other such advertising devices and to the pounding echo of political mottoes: "carne leite pão / não não e não." Negation in the last lines of this poem—negation both of the imperatives to consume listed throughout the poem and of the ideology of need implied by the notion of basic food staples—is unequivocal. That its effect is achieved with a minimum of rhetorical devices, in a voice that suggests both commercial and political propaganda, and in the language of everyday nourishment and consumption is, I think, noteworthy.

Among the Brazilian concrete poets, Pignatari was the one who worked most consistently in advertising and graphic design, the one most invested in the movement's links to design as discipline as well as its historical links to the Bauhaus and the Ulm School.[80] Pignatari worked in brand development for products like Lubrax motor oil and lectured at the Escola Superior de Desenho Industrial in Rio de Janeiro. He wrote extensively on graphic and industrial design, successfully translating his skills from industry to poetry and back to industry, in much the same way other artists of the period did (Hermelindo Fiaminghi, Alexandre Wollner, Geraldo de Barros, Willys de Castro, Hércules Barsotti, Waldemar Cordeiro, and Lygia Pape all come to mind, as do Andy Warhol, James Rosenquist, and Edward Ruscha). His work in advertising spanned copywriting, graphic design, and brand development, and he envisioned these fields as possible spheres of action for the visual and the verbal arts. Pignatari insisted, however, on the nonreducibility of art to industry.[81] Rather than place the visual and verbal arts at the service of industry, Pignatari envisioned uses of mass and consumer culture that had more to do with the critiques of consumer culture articulated around the same time by pop artists elsewhere in Latin America[82] as well as in England and the United States, critiques constructed using the very tools and materials, the techniques and the defining discourses of consumer culture.

In at least one case, though, Pignatari muddled the division between poetry and advertising. Both an ad and a poem, "disenfórmio" (1963; fig. 2.5)[83] is included in the fifth number of *Invenção*, the main publishing arm of Brazilian concrete poetry after *Noigandres*. The work is a collaboration between Pignatari and Rubem Martins, the owner of an advertising agency.[84] It is divided into two broad areas: a top part with seven lines where "DISEN" and "FÓRMIO" (the two halves of the name of the product being advertised) gradually come into the page from the sides as they crush the phrase "*perturbações intestinais*" into a bolus of letters; and a bottom part consisting primarily of technical information about the product. Seen and read from top to bottom, the composition of the ad gives the im-

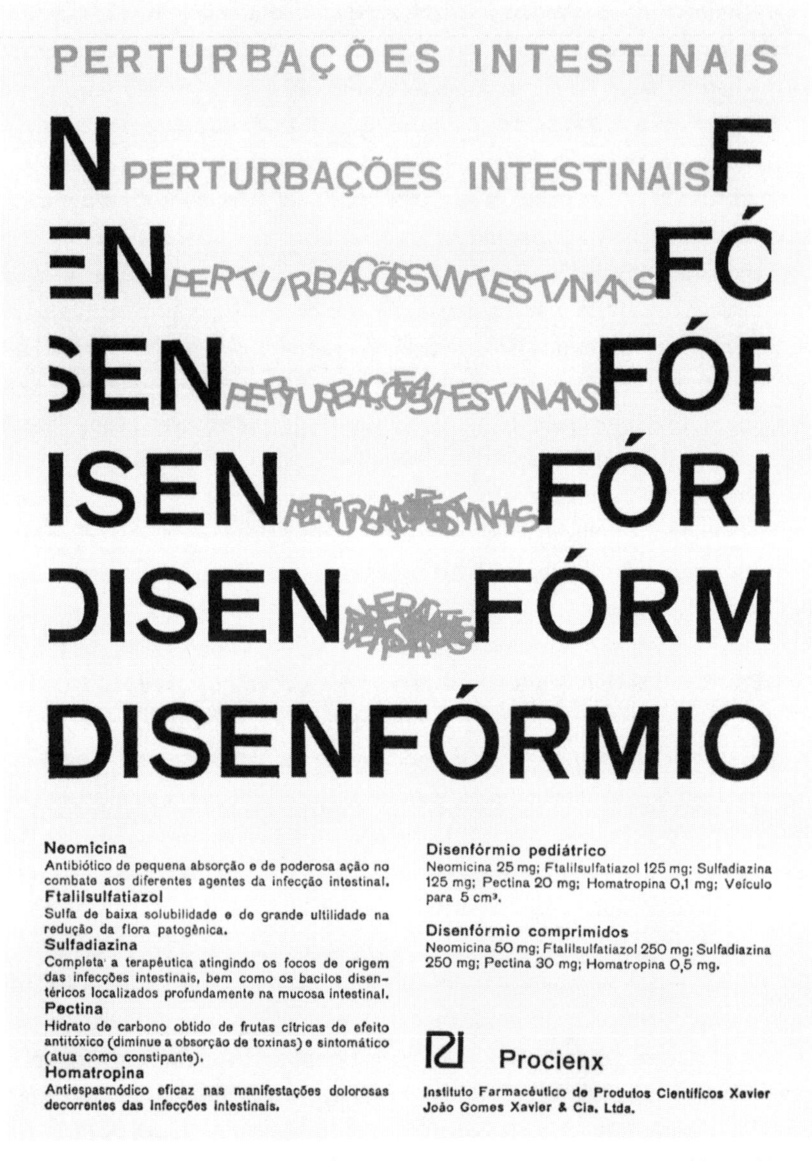

Figure 2.5. Décio Pignatari, "disenfórmio" (1963). In *Poesias pois é poesia* (Cotia, SP: Ateliê Editorial, 2004). © Décio Pignatari; courtesy of Dante Pignatari.

pression of a sense of movement at the same time that it reenacts, at the level of words and letters, the very result that the medication is supposed to effect: digestion.

The first line of the top part of the ad is entirely occupied by the capitalized words "*perturbações intestinais*," in red sans serif font. In the second line, the letters in these words begin to be pushed together by the two black letters in the middle of the word *DISENFÓRMIO* ("N" and "F") coming in from the sides of the page. As the eye moves down the ad, the larger black letters continue to make their way into the space of the page, simultaneously piling together the letters in "*perturbações intestinais*." By the sixth line the phrase has been completely mashed together by the two halves of the name of the medicine, forming a solid ball or stool out of the letters of what was once an "intestinal disturbance."[85] The effect of the ad is a cheeky, graphic rendition of the antidiarrheal effect the medication is supposed to have. Read from bottom to top, this effect is reversed: the words "*disen*" and "*fórmio*" are pushed out by unraveling "*perturbações intestinais*," the force of which can almost be felt as it finally stretches to full legibility at the top of the composition.

With its reference to feces and stool formation, "disenfórmio" puts front and center the scatological aspect of commodity culture that Aleksandr Rodchenko alludes to in his letters from Paris from 1925, where the Russian artist frequently mentions toilets, bidets, plumbing systems, buttocks, and shit.[86] H. G. Wells's famous accusation of a "cloacal obsession"[87] in James Joyce's *A Portrait of the Artist as a Young Man* (1916) also comes to mind, not least because the grounds for this accusation—that Joyce gathered all manner of linguistic debris from the streets, from the "sewers" of language and also, *most* repugnantly, from advertisements—hold just as well for Pignatari. Like Joyce, Pignatari prowled the language of his time searching for sediment, for discard and dispose. Pignatari's "disenfórmio" and his "beba coca cola" both take part in a cloacal compulsion, at more than a thematic level. What is more, Pignatari places this compulsion at the center of the design operation: a stool is quite literally formed by the advancing letters that make up words suggesting both design (*disen*) and form (*fórmio*). Smuggled into the signifying dynamic of the advertisement, the concepts of design and form profit from their association with the product being advertised, gaining a powerful if somewhat crude metaphor for their function: design and form, like the medication "disenfórmio," work by giving form to loose matter.

In an interview conducted twenty-five years after "beba coca cola" was published, Pignatari quips: "The first one in the world to write a poem about Coca Cola, in '57, was I! A quarter century ago. I don't need to make speeches to stand against multinationals."[88] The pride he takes in having dispensed with speeches, with discursive language, to mount a critique of transnationals must be understood in the context of the leap into political participation, the *salto participante*, that Brazilian concrete poetry took in the tumultuous political situation leading up to the military coup of 1964. "The sixties," writes Pignatari, "left a great lesson. I was very mature by that time but I was rejuvenated, because the countercultural revolution came to contradict a strictly industrialized vision."[89] The vision, that is, that permeated Brazilian concrete poetry in the first decade after its inception.

For Pignatari, breaking with the "strictly industrialized" vision of the early years of concrete poetry did not imply ceasing the experimentation with language that he and the other concrete poets had taken up in the early 1950s.[90] It did, however, imply the appropriation of the vehicles of expression (advertisements, newspapers, mass media, and mass culture in general) most often used by capitalist interests in Brazil.

The result is a tense rehearsal of experimental poetics that incorporates mass media, mass culture, and advertising without renouncing the contestatory streak that concrete poetry assumed in the 1960s in the face of violent oppression and the rise of a dictatorial regime. Describing his strategy of resistance, Pignatari states: "I go to the mass media and whenever I have to fight, you don't see me practicing short poems *à la* Neruda."[91] Whether Pignatari had any success intervening in the social and political debates of his time is a matter of debate. Gonzalo Aguilar argues that the "the high culture and avant-garde poetics of the concrete poets hardly fit the spectacular logic of media."[92] Given what Pignatari says about not needing to "make speeches" against multinational companies such as Coca Cola, it seems that any indictment of his aspirations for political consequence must first answer the question of whether the appropriation of forms of advertisements and the exacerbation of the signifying mechanisms of the culture industry do not in themselves constitute consequent interventions.

As to the literary virtues of advertisement-poems, a case can be made for their merit based on Pignatari's own suggestion of a homeopathic response to industrialization, development, and consumer capitalism. Benjamin, too, suggests a heightened capacity for action in forms of print that thrive outdoors, in "the inconspicuous forms" of popular printed matter—"leaflets, brochures, articles, and placards."[93] "Significant literary effectiveness," writes Benjamin, "can only come into being in a strict alternation between action and writing; it must nurture the inconspicuous forms that fit its influence in active communities better than does the pretentious, universal gesture of the book."[94] The emphasis on the pretentiousness of the book form is key. It makes one question the extent to which the critique of assimilative approaches to mass and consumer culture is founded on implicit assumptions of lettered superiority, as if remaining within the form of the book (that is to say, the form of prose, the form of the discursive argument, the form of literature and critique as institutions) was enough to guarantee resistance against the banality of consumer culture; as if any degree of intimacy with forms of consumer culture implied, on its own, a blind submission to it.

For some critics, this sense of openness or familiarity toward market capitalism is a source of suspicion, even alarm. In "Writing as Re-Writing" Marjorie Perloff argues that the collusion with advertising and graphic design manifest in a streak of concrete poetry puts in check its status as poetry, bringing it dangerously close to advertising. Concrete poetry, Perloff suggests, does not probe so much as it advances commercial interests and the logic that subtends these interests. Perloff reads identity (between the lyrical and the commercial or the industrial) where concrete poetry enacts replication and asks: "what happens when the identity of poem and industrial sign is complete? How, then, is art different from commerce, poetry from good design?"[95] Elsewhere, Perloff also questions "whether the conflation of Concrete poetry and advertising isn't a kind of dead end for the former; such texts as [Augusto de Campos's] 'CÓDIGO,' after all, function primarily as recognition symbols."[96] Aguilar shares in this reading when he writes that works like "disenfórmio," while interesting as experiments with the poetic in language, lack value as poetry: they "dissolve poetry" and fail to integrate it into everyday life.[97] Aguilar's argument hinges on presumed intentions of utility or lyricism behind works like "disenfórmio," intentions difficult to ascertain in the face of the poem's ludic twists, its dirty jokes. In principle, according to the logic formulated in programmatic writings, these poems were supposed to aspire, as Aguilar argues, to transparent, efficient utility. More often than not, though, they fail to meet this objective, and perhaps it is in this failure where the promise of their beauty as poems is revealed.

"Código" (1973; fig. 2.6), the poem-logotype designed by Augusto de Campos for the literary magazine of the same name, cleverly transforms the letters in the title of the publication into a series of concentric circles suggesting a labyrinth. The word "código" is readily legible in Augusto de Campos's design, as is the word "God." And just as these words are legible, so is the emblem, the image of a "code" formed by the concentric circles of the letters. The end result functions handsomely as a logotype, effectively conveying the meaning of the title for which it was designed at the verbal and visual levels. The effect is a suspension of the drive to either read the letters as forming a word or to see them as the elements of a figure: one reads *and* sees the word "código" and, likewise, one sees and also reads the maze-like figure. The concrete poets were keen on stressing that this double operation of language as both reading and seeing or hearing was

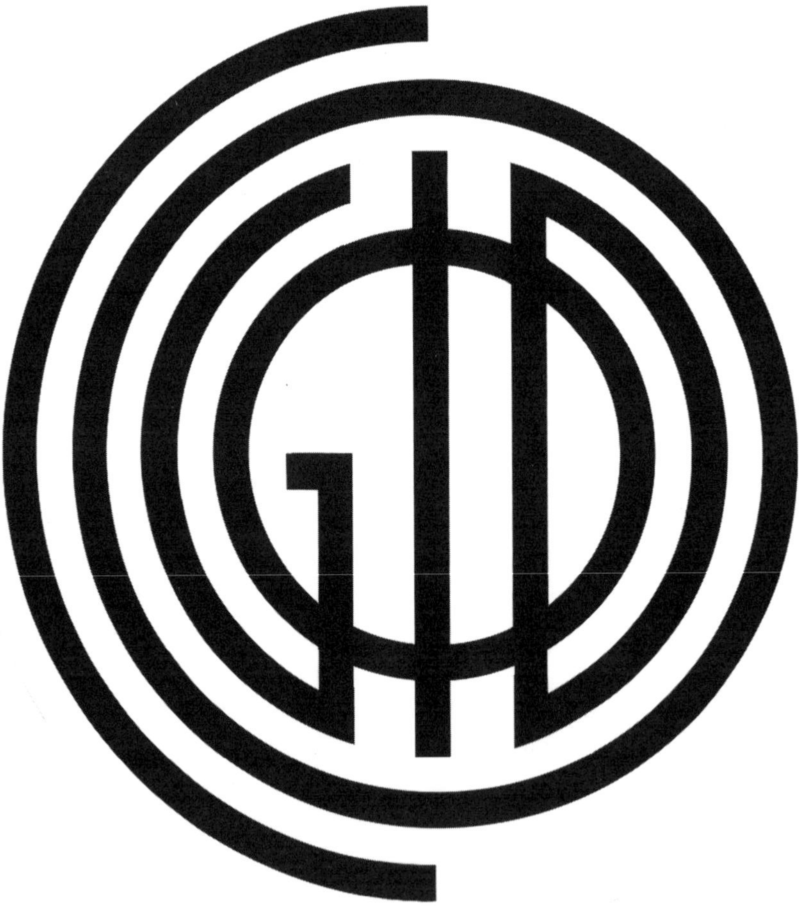

Figure 2.6. Augusto de Campos, "Código" (1966). © Augusto de Campos; courtesy, Augusto de Campos.

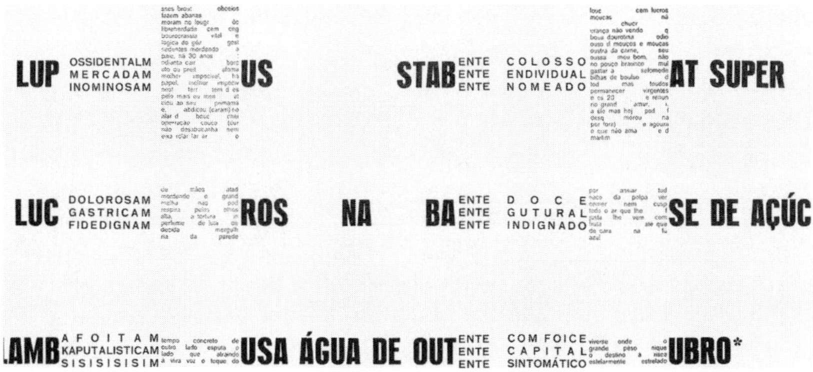

Figure 2.7. Décio Pignatari, "stèle pour vivre 3" (1962). Courtesy of Dante Pignatari.

not exclusive to advertising or concrete poetry, but rather a general aspect of all language. This is what Haroldo de Campos insists on when he argues for an "operational ambiguity" ("*uma ambigüidade operacional*") at the heart of everyday language, inasmuch as it is buttressed, unwittingly or not, by material and sensorial dimensions and also by its more explicit communicative functions.[98]

A different form of operational ambiguity, closely related to Mallarmé's play on the newspaper platform in *Un coup de dés*, is evident in Pignatari's "stèle pour vivre 3" (1964; fig. 2.7). It was published in the journal *Invenção* a few months after the Cuban missile crisis (the work is also known as "estela cubana"), a pivotal episode in hemispheric relations and one of the most tense episodes of the Cold War (the prospect of nuclear war loomed large during the crisis). The poem is a mixture of challenging accumulations of broken words and broken word orders. Three different blocks of text coexist in it, broken and staggered between each other. A mixture of broken Portuguese, Latin, Italian, and English keeps the reader grasping for meaning, the text relentlessly jumping from a "native" register (the language of the poet, Portuguese), a mother tongue (Italian), a classical language, and English, a language—the language—of empire. Some words appear complete, others in fragments; still others run into each other, creating suggestive word compounds. The political overtones are explicit.[99] Scattered in the mixture of languages and interrupted word orders are unequivocal references to the political circumstances of the poem's writing: "*tortura*"; "de mãos atad"; "mordendo o grand"; "*luta*"; "CAPITAL"; "USA."

A logic of breakage and interruption reigns over the poem, alternating with a language of the bodily: of the gastric (GASTRICAM), the guttural (GUTURAL), and the salivary (SPUTA). Pignatari calls the fragments in the poem in smaller font and lowercase (the fragments corresponding to the body of the text according to the typographic conventions of the newspaper) "(dead) body fragments." "Stèle pour vivre 5" mimics the conventions of the newspaper and its correlate constructs of truth, only to overturn these constructs. It does so by suspending the orders of information established in a newspaper page by means of font size, capitalization, and bold lettering. In the newspaper, each block of information—headline, subhead, body of text—occupies a distinct space in a vertical order of reading, a vertical montage of sorts: headline first; subhead second; body of text last. These blocks are arranged in a veritable, visible hierarchy of reading. The three clusters of text that make up the poem weave into each other along a long horizontal axis extended over a sheet of paper wider than it is longer. In "stèle pour vivre 3" the hierarchy is broken: the vertical order of the newspaper is rotated so that all three blocks of information—headline, subhead, body of text—are level with each other.

Consumption as Tmetic Drive

Concrete poetry's embrace of the "other materials at its disposal," its embrace of the nonverbal or nondiscursive registers of language, can be read as a compensatory gesture. This is what Charles Perrone points to when he writes that, for the concrete poets, "it was imperative to underscore not just the nonlinearity of the poetic approach but the intentional relativization of the semantic charge as well, especially in relation to the normally ignored, or underplayed, dimension of primary sensorial (visual) apprehension."[100] The mechanism of perception that directs our attention to both figure and background—or, in the case of the work of the concrete poets, to both verbal content and the physical, material vehicle of that content—is counter to the dynamics of perception and reading of a logocentric regime of language, wherein the material vehicle of language is more often than not overlooked in the construction and interpretation of meaning.

I would like to conclude this chapter with some thoughts on tmesis as a figure of speech that can well characterize Brazilian concrete poetry's fascination with consumption. Augusto de Campos's follow-up to *Poetamenos* is a collection of poems titled *Bestiário* (1955), which reads like a sonic anticipation of the "dialectic of eye and breath" that Augusto envisions a year later, in 1956.[101] Visually, *Bestiário* marks a shift away from *Poetamenos*. Whereas *Poetamenos* hinges on the tension between eye and voice, *Bestiá-*

rio moves from voice to breath and to a concurrent shift from the barely corporeal (the embodied void) register of the voice, to the resounding, fleshy quality of the breath, with all its connotations of warmth, stink, and moisture. Published two years after *Poetamenos*, *Bestiário* is visually more restrained, printed in black and white and with a single visual motif—a long, slender column centered vertically and horizontally. For the most part, the letters that make up each poem barely stray from their anchoring center. Grouped together, the letters in *Bestiário* look like black spinal columns holding together the white bodies of the pages around them, except for the third poem, where the winding movement of the letters suggests an ebb, a spiral, a staggered flow. The more one reads, the more explicitly visual some beastly figures (parasites, condors, zebras) become, gaining weight and substance in the reader's eye and peopling the compendium of beastly creatures the volume purports to be.

The title page gives us two reading cues for this assemblage of poems: music and growl. The poems in *Bestiário*, we learn, are poems for the bassoon, poems for the digestive tract. Augusto de Campos's sustained interest in music comes across loudly in this title page, as does the register of animals and beasts to which he has attuned his poems. But what kind of animal, what kind of beast emerges from these poems? Not the beast of lungs, not the animal that speaks, but the one with the gullet, the animal that growls and swallows, the beast that eats and gurgles. The first such beast is the poet himself, *o poeta*.

A first read of the opening poem gives us a good impression of how the whole series is organized and how we can make sense of it. As in *Poetamenos*, not all words are kept whole within a line of text; some are broken off into two or more lines, yet there is a more or less straightforward reading to be culled from the poem. It reads like a phrase cut to pieces by four parentheses, but easily recomposed: "*sim o poeta infinitesimal existe e se manifesta nesta animal espécie que lhe é funesta*." The suggestion is striking: yes, poetry persists, even in this fatal form, even in this baleful age. And it persists in that most distinctive of Brazilian avant-garde guises: the form of the cannibal, the form of *antropofagia*.

Tmese or tmesis is the first whole word to appear in the poems of *Bestiário*, and it strikes a discordant note among the string of fragmented words that make up the poem—it is too technical, too obtuse. Tmesis is a figure for cutting, but the most arresting examples of tmesis in literature do something more than cut. In Ovid's celebrated use ("they the man surrounded" / "*circum virum dant*"), it is not the man (*virum*) who cuts into those who surrounded (*circumdant*) him. It is they (the alluded, but also the words) who surround him, they who stand around him. The effect is a visual rendering of the action told. It is also a different way of giving an account of what takes place in this surrounding. A sense of the way words are held within fragments of other words begins to emerge from the visual and semantic operation at the heart of tmesis. Likewise, in Campos's poem, the words keyed into parentheses do something other than break the words and phrases around them.

A dialectics of consumption, a new take on *antropofagia*, begins to take shape here: words are encapsulated, taken in, digested, made other, synthesized by other words and by the things that populate the world. What do the nonverbal and the verbal have to do with the beastly and the human? What is the place of fascination, of neon light, in lyric poetry? What can be gleaned from comparing these two tensions, these two antagonisms that resist and complement each other? And what's the appropriate method to study them comparatively? Tmese here reads like an unfolding of the mimetic principle—language pressed against its subject matter until it bears its semblance. The semblance here belongs to tmese and its everyday exchanger: not development but envelopment, not advancement but surrounding, not progress but an engulfing that cuts.

Words in Augusto de Campos's and Décio Pignatari's poetry often act out these actions, these states of being. Often, though not always (lest the rigor of concrete poetry's mathematical phase be excessively underplayed), they do so in playful accord with formal structures suggested by mass media—logotypes, neon signs, newspapers. This image of words engulfed by other words, of advertisements surrounded by poetry and poetry immersed in advertising, could well function as a cipher for concrete poetry in its connections with consumer culture. In Augusto's *Poetamenos* the image gains dynamism, movement—flickering neon movement. But most importantly it gains a plot, a plot of poetry, if such a thing could ever exist.

THREE

Poetry, Replication, Late Capitalism

Octavio Paz as Concrete Poet

That Octavio Paz (1914–1998) wrote on mass media, technology, and advertising is hardly surprising. His collected works amount to a commanding fifteen volumes, spanning all but one major literary genre (the novel). The most celebrated writer from Mexico and among the most prolific, Paz wrote at length about a staggering array of subject matter. What seems striking, then, is not so much that he wrote about technology, the culture industry, and consumer culture, but that his thoughts on those subjects are central to his writings on poetry, a fact easily overlooked but all too present on second reading.[1] Two of the essays where he takes up the problem of language in the age of consumer culture are among his most compelling writings on poetry: "Los signos en rotación" (1965)[2] and "La nueva analogía: poesía y tecnología" (written in 1967, published in 1973).[3] Together, these essays mark the beginning of a transition in Paz's thought: from unease to earnest curiosity, from suspicion to vested interest in the power of mass media and the growing influence of consumer culture. The two-year span during which Paz published *Blanco* (1967), *Topopoemas* (1967), and *Discos visuales* (1968) sees the poet at the most experimental phase of his production. Paz's interest in mass media and consumer culture peaked during the years leading up to this period.[4] By the late 1970s, Paz leveled his growing influence shrewdly and effectively, first in relative independence from the Mexican state and later as its most prominent cultural representative. Throughout, Paz remained an engaged observer of language in the age of market capitalism, a fact that has remained relatively understudied in the extensive bibliography devoted to the study of Paz's work. The present chapter sets out to study this facet of Paz's thought and the way it is revealed in his essays and poetry from the 1960s and 1970s.

Much has been said about Paz's views on modernity[5] and the history of Mexico,[6] but his thoughts on technology and consumer capitalism in Mexico are lesser known and seldom discussed.[7] Over the course of the two essays cited above and in writings published in the 1950s, 1960s, and 1970s, Paz develops a two-pronged, "complementary" view of the relationship among poetry, language, and capitalist society. On the one hand, Paz writes, key developments in radio, film, advertising, and television facilitate a collective experience of language that foregrounds the vocal, visual, and material aspects of language. On the other hand, the growing demand for consumer goods and for the resources necessary to produce these goods reduces the world to use-value. Poetic practices responsive to this historical moment can appropriate the richer, sensually charged language of consumer culture, but they must do so, Paz argues, while facing the imperative to oppose the destruction of the world as image, its reduction to mere resource. This raises a question: how exactly does lyric poetry oppose a world ruled by the logic of markets while replicating the language of consumer capitalism? And how exactly does this opposition constitute a central problem for lyric poetry?

In this as in other chapters of this book, I want to focus on a term of ambiguity useful in understanding aesthetics in the age of consumer capitalism. "Poetry," writes Paz, "has resisted modernity, and in resisting it, it has revitalized it. Poetry has been its antidote and its *réplica*."[8] What I propose is a reading of opposition as *réplica*: as response, copy, and aftershock, as riposte that takes the form of replication. Opposition between poetry and the overriding principles of capitalist modernity (neither progress nor growth but linear efficiency and forward movement) serves as the basis upon which Paz conceives of the relationship between poetry and market capitalism. But as I hope to demonstrate over the course of this chapter, opposition for Paz stands for something more complicated than resistance or confrontation.[9] "The conflict," Paz writes, "between poetry and modernity is not accidental, it is consubstantial."[10] This sense of consubstantiality is manifest in the visual poems Paz wrote in the late 1960s, under the influence of Brazilian concrete poetry and in correspondence with one of its leading figures, Haroldo de Campos. These poems make use of the forms and the language of advertising and mass media, and they craft an experience of language that replicates and resists the logic of consumer culture.

Paz's thoughts on language, modernity, and consumer capitalism are informed by his readings of Alfonso Reyes and Martin Heidegger. Technology and Heidegger's notion of the world image play a central role in the two essays where Paz grapples most forcefully with the question of language and modernity. Architecture and the massive infrastructural developments in Mexico City in the 1950s and 1960s provide another set of references for Paz as he broaches this question. The poems where Paz most explicitly converses with consumer culture all establish, in different ways and to different extents, a dialogue with mass media and advertising. A reading of these poems is offered in the final section of this chapter; a review of Paz's earlier poems on Mexico City will ground my analysis of the more experimental phase of his production. My hope is to frame Paz's engagement with consumption and with the discourses that subtend consumer culture within the larger themes of his oeuvre and to suggest, in turn, new readings of his work informed by his brief but revealing period of experimentation with visual poetry and the language of commodity capitalism. Seen this way, Paz's Mexico City poems emerge under new light, as meditations on a metropolis just as it was undergoing a major transformation—a transformation dictated in no small measure by the demands of an emergent consumer economy and an attendant shift in culture.

"Entrada en materia"

The frantic pace of Mexico City's growth in the decades after World War II, during the period that came to be known as the "Mexican miracle,"[11] hit Paz right at home, in the Mixcoac of his childhood and youth.[12] He was, however, absent for the start of it. In 1944 and with the support of a Guggenheim fellowship, Paz left Mexico to begin a period of study in the United States, after which he settled in Paris, where he spent the better part of six years. In a series of public lectures delivered in Mexico City in 1975, Paz looks back at his return and states: "In 1953, after nine years, I came back to Mexico. It was a different city, still charming but already turning into the monster it is today."[13] The letters Paz sent to the poet and translator Jean-Clarence Lambert in the months after his return to Mexico capture a sense of unease in the face of rapid change. In 1954, Paz writes, with dread and resignation: "The atmosphere here is atrocious: the world of *The Waste Land* linked to that one region that Huxley describes in *Brave New World*. And there is no trace of the countryside, the true though petrified Mexico, because I'm moored to the city."[14]

The "wasteland" evoked by Paz was Mexico in the grip of furious development and industrialization, the result of major policy changes by Miguel Alemán and Adolfo Ruiz Cortines. Paz's dim outlook during these years stands in contrast with the heady optimism of this moment in the history of Mexico. Paz was far from alone in his pessimism. *Los olvidados*, Luis Buñuel's masterful depiction of urban abjection, was released in 1950. The general mood, however, was one of optimism, especially in Mexico City and especially among its ruling classes. Recalling this period twenty years later, Paz states: "In Mexico in 1955, satisfaction was widespread among politicians, bankers, union leaders, and farmworkers. Even a large group of intellectuals found that sense of optimism contagious."[15] In his writings of the period, Paz denounces cities, urban life, development, and the growing preponderance of market capitalism, but he rarely turns his attention away from all this. As Pere Gimferrer notes, the night and its festival of lights and advertisements captured Paz's imagination forcefully. Electric light in nocturnal Mexico City, argues Gimferrer, stood for Paz as a substitute for language, a theater of signs and symbols as dynamic as language itself.[16]

It was a stark contrast to the old Mixcoac, the place where Paz spent his childhood. Now integrated into Mexico City's ever-expanding limits, Mixcoac was once a stand-alone town connected by tram to the Mexican capital. In the poems Paz wrote upon his return to Mexico in 1953, Mixcoac serves as a kind of placeholder for a countryside lost to the spreading metropolis.[17] There is a feeling of defeat in these poems, a sense of powerlessness in the face of breakneck, uneven development. Neither raging nor nostalgic, the lyric voice in these poems finds its tone in resignation: no attempt to escape or somehow push back the expanding lines, real and symbolic, of the urban spread is entertained in them. Rather, contemplation takes the place of resistance: the lyric subject of these poems sees, from a distance, the growth of the city, the way the city absorbs, phagocyte-like, the countryside. The poet reflects on this dynamic of expansion and absorption, and in a sense he sees himself reflected in it.[18]

In Paz's poems, the lyric subject identifies with the city of its childhood, but only in dreams. The yearning for greenery and countryside that Paz often expresses in his early poems is beautifully laid out in "Visitas," first published in *Libertad bajo palabra*. In "Visitas," a dream-like sequence sees the lyrical I bearing witness to fields, leaves, and seas seeping "through the urban night":

A través de la noche urbana de piedra y sequía
entra el campo a mi cuarto.
Alarga brazos verdes con pulseras de pájaros,
con pulseras de hojas.
Lleva un río de la mano.
El cielo del campo también entra,
con su cesta de joyas acabadas de cortar.
Y el mar se sienta junto a mí,
extendiendo su cola blanquísima en el suelo.
Del silencio brota un árbol.
Del árbol cuelgan palabras hermosas
que brillan, maduran, caen.
En mi frente, cueva que habita un relámpago...
Pero todo se ha poblado de alas.[19]

The feeling of loss ("todo se ha poblado de alas") in the last verse turns into resignation in "Crepúsculos de la ciudad," where the lyrical is no longer at a distance, but wandering through the city:

Todo lo que me nombra o que me evoca
yace, ciudad, en ti, signo vacío
en tu pecho de piedra sepultado[20]

The poem takes the reader through nocturnal sites of decadence and decay. Its atmosphere is punctuated by an image of prostitutes standing like "pillars of the vain night" ("putas: pilares de la noche vana").[21] The image rings of Baudelaire's odes to the city,[22] and it adds to the atmosphere of grimness and desolation a firm sense of verticality that holds all the way down to the cold, metallic sky described in the fifth of this long string of sonnets. Toward the end of "Crepúsculos," the lyrical subject folds inward, sinking into itself, heavy with the pace, the dead weight of frantic city time. Witness the final sonnet:

Las horas, su intangible pesadumbre,
su peso que no pesa, su vacío,
abigarrado horror, la sed que expío
frente al espejo y su glacial vislumbre,

mi ser, que multiplica en muchedumbre
y luego niega en un reflejo impío,
todo, se arrastra, inexorable río,
hacia la nada, sola certidumbre.

Hacia mí mismo voy; hacia las mudas,
solitarias fronteras sin salida:
duras aguas, opacas y desnudas,

horadan lentamente mi conciencia
y van abriendo en mí secreta herida,
que mana sólo, estéril, impaciencia.[23]

City time, the "intangible sorrow" of empty hours: this is the time of impatience, the closing term of the poem, and it is also the rhythm the poem tries to capture, the temporality it tries to wrangle out of language. Impatience and the modern themes of mindless velocity and a blind drive to progress are suggested here. They come up again in "En la calzada," where Paz abandons the sonnet in favor of a looser form of verse, one where the piled-up movements of the city gain concrete meaning in the very layout of the poem, stacked as it is with different destinations, different objectives.[24] Here as in other city poems by Paz, a lyrical subject looks out to streets where everyone is doing something, going somewhere. The subject who sees sets himself apart as the only one distanced from the mindless movements of the city, the only one standing still, reflective amid the endless drifting. He takes the commotion from the sheltered peace of a green, shady road.

"En la calzada" anticipates what would become an obsessive confrontation of urban grim and country greenery in *Salamandra* (1958–1961). The first poem of *Salamandra*, "Noche en claro," dedicated to André Breton and Benjamin Péret, begins with an image of "forest steps arriving in the city"[25]:

A las diez de la noche en el Café de Inglaterra
salvo nosotros tres
                    no había nadie
Se oía afuera el paso húmedo del otoño
pasos de ciego gigante
pasos de bosque llegando a la ciudad[26]

A palpable transition is evident from the poems in *Libertad bajo palabra* to those in *Salamandra*. Whereas in the first collection of poems the city is presented almost entirely devoid of modern artifacts, in *Salamandra* there is marked attention to them and to the telltale signs of an emerging consumer culture.[27] The shift can be seen in the namesake poem, "Salamandra,"[28] the longest in the collection. The poem focuses on the mystifying reptile, the salamander, and it places it in increasingly evocative settings: "entre los fauces de la chimenea"; "en la pared de sal"; "en el pecho azul y negro del hierro"; "en la testa del himno"; "entre las baldosas desunidas / de un patio petrificado por la luna." The second series of settings is the city, described not in opposition to nature but in affirmation, almost in celebration of construction materials. Glass, cement, stone, and iron are the building blocks of a landscape heretofore unseen in Paz's poetry:

Salamandra
            en la ciudad abstracta
entre las geometrías vertiginosas
—vidrio cemento piedra hierro—[29]

This world of stone and of modern construction materials takes center stage in another poem of the same period, "Entrada en materia," the first in *Días hábiles* (1958–1961), a compendium of voices, figures, and places set against a city in the grip of market time, of business days, as the title of the book suggests. "Entrada en materia" is announced by its title as an introduction and an immersion into this matter. It confronts from the outset the gloss and grit of a city transformed by development and advertising. It opens with the following image of cars roaring under neon light:

Bramar de motores
                        río en crecida
silbidos latigazos
                        chirriar de frenos
algarabías
            El neón se desgrana
la luz eléctrica y sus navajazos
Noche multicolor
                        ataviada de signos
letras parpadeantes
obsceno guiño de los números[30]

Two verbs stand out in this opening stanza: *bramar*, to howl or roar, and *chirriar*, to screech. They embody in their respective semantic fields and in their phonetic structure (both are near onomatopoeias) a register of harsh sounds linked to the automobile, an increasingly common feature of life in Mexico City. The cars in the poem rattle the image of the city thanks to the vibrating sounds of the verbs used to evoke them. The neon signs, electric light, and winking ads, on the other hand, fragment that image; they cut it with their enveloping, unrelenting flicker, a flicker not unlike the one produced chromatically in Augusto de Campos's *Poetamenos*.

In some editions of this poem, the link between technology and fragmentation is matched in this stanza by a shift in visual form evident in the spiral-like disposition of verses. Spirals permeate Paz's poetry. They define the look and rhythm of poems like "Movimiento,"[31] "El día en Udaipur,"[32] "Vrindaban,"[33] "La exclamación,"[34] "Viento entero,"[35] "Poema circulatorio (para la desorientación general),"[36] and many others. Spirals frame Paz's understanding of how modernity works: they capture a play of mythic time and simultaneity, the pillars of his literary imagination. *Blanco*, too, discussed at length below, is a beautiful long spiral made of two side columns wrapped around a central column.

Paz revisits Mexico City almost a decade after *Días hábiles* in the triptych of poems entitled "Ciudad de México," included in *Vuelta*, his ninth collection of poems. *Vuelta* was written upon his second return to Mexico in 1968. In the lead-up to the state-sponsored massacre in Tlatelolco in 1968, Paz had been serving as ambassador to India. He renounced his post as a gesture of protest. The three "Ciudad de México" poems feature one recurring theme: broken words, broken sentences, broken language. "A la mitad de esta frase,"[37] the second in the series, exemplifies this trend. In it, words and sentences come fragmented and mashed together, a broken tongue spoken midsentence as the title of the poem suggests. It is as if city life was always taking place halfway through an utterance, halfway through an act but far from a purpose, far from an end, far from a realization as such.

Technology, World Image, Architecture

Paz's growing attention to cars, film, advertisements, and neon signs would not be much more than an interesting moment in his long literary trajectory were it not for the fact that it coincides with two of his most complex and widely discussed meditations on poetics: "Los signos en rotación" and "La nueva analogía: poesía y tecnología." In "Los signos en rotación" he runs through the litany of evils that one expects from a liberal intellectual writing about postwar society, paying particular attention to the dangers of advertising. Paz laments, for instance, "the docile adoption of forms of thought and forms of behavior rendered universally valid by advertising and political propaganda," as well as the irony of witnessing "a perfected communications system" alongside the "the annulment of interlocutors"; "personal life," Paz bemoans, "exalted by advertising, dissolves into anonymous existence."[38] A more substantial though still general take on the subject begins to take shape when Paz lists "the circumstances facing the new poets": "One of them is the loss of the world image; another is the emergence of a universal vocabulary made up of active signs: technique and technology; yet another, the crisis of signification."[39]

What does Paz mean by "image," by "world image"? And what does the loss of the "world image" mean to him? Paz dedicates an entire section of *El arco y la lira*, titled "La imagen," to the first question. He begins by noting that while the term has many meanings, only one, both vague and precise, interests him. In poetry, an image is "any verbal form, phrase, or group of phrases that the poet says and that together make up a poem."[40] He quickly moves on to a slightly more revealing definition: "Epic, dramatic, or lyric, condensed in a phrase or developed over the course of a thousand pages, every image brings together or joins together opposite realities, distant or indifferent. That is to say, the image brings into unity the plurality of the real."[41] Stones, a recurring feature in Paz's poetry, and feathers form an example of how the image in poetry works. "The poet names things: these are feathers, those are stones. And suddenly he says: feathers are stones, this is that."[42]

Provocatively and echoing Alfonso Reyes,[43] Paz affirms that what poetry does in its construction of images is not entirely distinct from what scientific and capitalist reason (coextensive, in Paz and Reyes's minds) do. Both bring "the plurality of the real into unity," both transform a manifold into a unit. But whereas capitalist reason brings together different objects and different realities by extracting them from their contexts and transforming them into abstract units ("a kilogram of stones," "a kilogram of feathers"), the image in poetry unites without extraction, without dismemberment: feathers are stones, this is that, and yet, in unison, both the lightness of the feathers and the weight of stones remain, in a way that foregrounds conflict. The image in poetry is an image of difference that unites.[44] It keeps paradox alive.

By the time Paz wrote "Los signos en rotación" he was well acquainted with Heidegger's writings on poetry and technology, and it seems clear that Paz's notion of the world image is indebted to his readings of Heidegger. Most present in Paz's writings is Heidegger's idea of a "world picture" (*Weltbild*), developed in a lecture by Heidegger from 1938 titled "The Age of the World Picture." In it and later in "The Question Concerning Technology" Heidegger argues that the modern era is defined not by a particular picture of the world but rather by the fact that we relate to the world in certain ways in so depicting it. "The world picture does not change from an earlier medieval one into a modern one," writes Heidegger, "but rather the fact that the world becomes picture at all is what distinguishes the essence of the modern age."[45] Forming a picture of the world signals the first step toward assuming mastery over it, an attitude at the heart of what Heidegger defines as technological being. "Now," writes Heidegger, referring to the constitution of the picture of the world, "for the first time is there any such thing as a 'position' of man. . . . There begins the way of being human which mans the realm of human capability as a domain given over to measuring and executing, for the purpose of gaining mastery over that which is a whole."[46]

Paz draws on architectural examples to illuminate the problem of technology. Architecture is so strong a reference for Paz that he names the first volume of his collected writings (the one that brings together his essays on poetry and history) "The House of Presence." "Among all the arts," he writes in 1975, "architecture is, in my opinion, the most dependent on history, the one that expresses most faithfully the circumstance of a given society."[47] True to this conviction, Paz theorizes language in reference to architecture. For Paz, pyramids, gothic churches, and ancient monuments are, first and foremost, symbols of the world and of a certain world order. In their physical proportions, in their placement in relation to other buildings, to geographical features, and to the stars in the firmament, ancient buildings tell us something about how place in the world was imagined, how those who constructed these buildings imagined themselves in the world. This is what Paz suggests when he writes: "A Mayan temple, a medieval cathedral, and a baroque palace were more than monuments: they were sensible points of space and time, privileged observatories for man to contemplate the world or the afterworld as a whole. Their orientation corresponded to a symbolic vision of the universe."[48]

Almost everything about Paz's example of the temple (save for the choice of civilization) corresponds to a notable series of passages in Heidegger's essay on "The Origin of the Work of Art," first published in 1950 and later included in *Poetry, Language, Thought*, a volume known to Paz and cited throughout his writings. Heidegger distinguishes the Greek temple from "representational art" and locates its nature as artwork not on what it says but on how it stands in the world and what it stands for. Both ancient and modern constructions are, of course, technological in a sense, but what Paz and Heidegger want to underline in stressing the difference between them is that, in very general terms, ancient buildings such as gothic churches and Mayan pyramids are placements in, and placeholders of, the universe (in the cosmic proportions of their architectural elements and in the very longevity they were invested with), whereas modern buildings generally forgo any nonfunctional correspondence to their surroundings and to the world where they are built.[49] This is what Paz points to when he writes: "the buildings of the past were replicas of the cosmic archetype, in the double sense of the word: copies of the model of the universe and human responses to the world."[50] Modern technological constructions, on the other hand, "do not represent: they are signs of action and not images of the world."[51]

What Paz is directing our attention to is a change in perspective, a shift in the way we conceive of the world through buildings and language. Whatever their function was at the time they were built, pyramids, gothic churches, and ancient monuments are, first and foremost, symbols of the world and of a certain world order. Their function is always a function derived from this trait rather than a condition to it. Airports, factories, and other similar constructions, on the other hand, are meant to intervene rather than stand for the world around them. Their function has nothing to do with how the world stands and everything to do with how it can be traversed and transformed. Paz writes:

> What do our hangars say, our train stations, our office buildings, our factories and our public monuments? They don't say: they are functions, not significations. They are centers of energy, monuments to the will, signs that radiate power, not meaning. Ancient buildings were a representation of reality, both real and imaginary; the constructions of modern technology are an intervention of reality.[52]

It is hard not to read these images of modern buildings and modern architecture as references to Mexico City in the 1960s, the Mexico City then being transformed by major development policies aimed at urbanization and the consolidation of a market economy. At the time, the Mexican capital was coming out of a major wave of infrastructural development initiated soon after the end of World War II. It started with the construction in the late 1940s of the first mass housing project, the Multifamiliar Miguel

Alemán, designed by Mario Pani in the spirit of Le Corbusier's functionalist architecture. Two decades later, the city's urban grid looked noticeably different. Jardines del Pedregal, an upscale urbanization project led by the architect Luis Barragán, broke ground in the 1940s. It was quickly followed by the planning and construction of Ciudad Satélite, a planned commuter city conceived in 1954 as a "city outside the city" but soon absorbed by the growth of the capital proper. The year 1954 was also the opening year of Ciudad Universitaria, a sprawling new campus for the Universidad Autónoma de México (UNAM) on the southern part of the capital and the site of mural and arts integration projects.[53] This was quickly followed by the construction of the Torre Latinoamericana (1956), then the tallest building in Latin America. The boom in construction and development came to a halt right around the time that the so-called Mexican miracle began to run out of steam. Its last major projects were the inauguration of the metro system in the late 1960s and the completion of the enormous, aggressively functional Unidad Habitacional Adolfo López Mateos, better known as Complejo Nonoalco-Tlatelolco, also by Pani. Soon after its inauguration, this massive and controversial housing project would become the site of a definitive moment in the history of twentieth-century Mexico: the massacre in Tlatelolco in 1968.

Photographers in Mexico were among the first to put forth a critical view of urban development. They did so using a most modern instrument: the photo camera. Initially a sight of curiosity, the construction sites of projects like the Torre Latinoamericana and the Unidad Habitacional Nonoalco-Tlatelolco soon became, in the lens of Nacho López and Rodrigo Moya, a revealing document of the contradictions at the heart of dreams of progress. At the time of their construction, all these buildings emerged from the midst of what remained an evidently impoverished metropolis. In the work of photographers and photojournalists of the period, most notably in the work of Enrique Metinides,[54] life in the city is imagined in terms of stark contrasts and violent contradictions, a sometimes deft and often crushing struggle between cars, buildings—symbols of a city daydreaming of progress—and people, people negotiating spaces that do not seem made for them, spaces not made in their image. So much is clear in one of the most unnerving visual documents of the period, an image of the clash between human flesh and modern construction: Héctor García's limpidly titled photograph *Niño en vientre de concreto* (1952).

A sense of modern constructions, of modern buildings as uncanny matrixes of human life (Heidegger's house of being, Paz's "casa de la presencia") comes forth in a passage in "Los signos en rotación" where Paz states: "Technology is a reality so powerfully real—visible, touchable, audible, ubiquitous—that true reality has ceased to be natural or supernatural: industry is our landscape, our heaven, and our hell."[55] The process of substitution that Paz describes here, wherein technology becomes the horizon, the landscape against which we define what is real, follows a dialectic of perception and visuality whereby "technology is interposed between us and the world, cancelling other possible perspectives: beyond its geometries of iron, glass, or aluminum, there is, strictly speaking, nothing, except the unknown, the region of the formless and the not yet transformed by man."[56] The logic behind Paz's assertion is clear: the more technology mediates experience, the harder it becomes to see the world beyond it as a world in and of itself and not as something to be transformed or intervened in, something that is not subject to our will, something that is other than us, that does not belong to us.

For Paz, the greatest danger development poses lies not in its unrelenting and unreciprocated demand for resources often associated with consumerism and consumer culture, what Susan Buck-Morss succinctly describes in *Dreamworld and Catastrophe* as capitalism's unwillingness to underwrite the costs of resource replenishment and reproduction, be they human or natural. It lies in the manner in which technology changes the way we imagine the world and the way we shape our relationship to it. "For technology," Paz writes, "the world is neither a sensible image of the idea nor a cosmic model: it is an obstacle that we must overcome and modify."[57] For Paz, as for Heidegger, the danger of technology lies in its very logic, in the way it renders the world something to be subdued, transformed, used, and mastered.

Language, Mass Media, Consumer Culture

As with buildings, Paz distinguishes between an older use of language and a modern one. The first use rests on a relationship of symbolic correspondence to the world (language matches the world/is in line with the way we conceive the world/represents the world), while the second rests on a relationship of intervention or interruption (language does not seek to match world/language intervenes world/language transforms it). Thus, when Paz states that "words no longer represent the true reality of things and things have turned opaque, mute,"[58] the implication is that language, too, has undergone the kind of transformation that buildings went through.

Language has ceased to be a depository of meaning capable of articulating a worldview and an image of the world in order to become a tool, an instrument, a function, something with which to change the world.[59]

Ambivalence marks Paz's writings on the language of his time, the language of cities overrun by advertising and mass media. At times his approach is predictably conservative, nostalgic for times when language seemed to be something better, something more meaningful, more wholesome: "the tattered language of cities," writes Paz, "is not language, it is the shreds of something that was once coherent and harmonious. Language in the city tends to petrify into formulas and slogans and so it suffers the same fate as popular art, industrialized as it is, and the fate of man himself, who goes from being a person to transforming into a mass."[60] Elsewhere, Paz voices a sense of purpose and urgency in the face of historical tendencies. Rather than lamenting change, what the poet must do, writes Paz, is to understand the language of the times and ultimately reveal the truth embodied in that language.

In Paz's reading, the turn toward everyday language, toward the language of the city, is what fueled the revolution in English-language poetry started by Ezra Pound, T. S. Eliot, and James Joyce. He makes one final distinction between the language of cities and popular language: the language of the city is not "the stylized 'popular' language of Juan Ramón Jiménez, Antonio Machado, García Lorca or Alberti," a language that is "no less artificial than the language of 'high' poetry."[61] Poetry needs to be responsive to the language of urban life, but in a different way. In *La otra voz* (1990) and in reference to what he perceived (wistfully, no doubt) as a shift toward hiring poets as faculty members in US universities, he warns poets against remaining too distanced from city life: "Poets seek refuge in universities the way they did in medieval times, but it would be devastating if they abandoned the city."[62] Later in that same book, writing in the prescriptive register he was cultivating with increasing frequency, he admonishes: "Poets must look for rhythms and forms more consonant with the language and the life of our cities."[63]

Like the Brazilian concrete poets, Paz recognized in mass media and in advertising a thickening of language, a pronounced emphasis on the materiality of language. Haroldo de Campos first contacted Paz in 1968, having read the latter's poetry and essays, and after encouragement from Celso Lafer. The exchange eventually led to Campos's translation of Paz's *Blanco* and the publication of the translated poem and the correspondence between the two poets in *Transblanco* (1986).[64] But even before they established contact, Paz was familiar with concrete poetry. Mathias Goeritz organized an exhibition of it titled *Poesía concreta internacional* at the Galería Universitaria Aristos in 1966.[65] The exhibition was a success, and it seems to have had a significant impact on the literary and artistic scene in Mexico City. Vicente Rojo, Paz's graphic designer for *Discos visuales*, designed posters and the catalog for this exhibition, and the exhibition itself would have been on their minds as they collaborated on the *Discos*. Goeritz, the visionary artist and architect behind construction projects like Ciudad Satélite and the Museo Experimental El Eco, was the first to produce concrete poems in Mexico, "concrete" in both a conceptual and a literal manner (the poems were built into walls and buildings).

Prior to the correspondence between Haroldo de Campos and Paz, and before the introduction of concrete poetry in Mexico by way of Goeritz, Paz's writings on language, history, and society mirrored in some ways the terms under which the concrete poets conceived of the relationship between poetry and society. When Paz writes in the 1950s that "journalism, advertising, film, and other forms of visual reproduction transformed writing, which had been almost completely stifled by typography,"[66] Paz points to an experience of language mediated by mass media and consumer culture. Paz credits concrete poetry for identifying these transformations of language and redeploying them in the space of the poem. He also credits the concrete poets for a renewed attention to typography and layout in poetry, a reprise of concerns first foregrounded by the historical avant-gardes. He points to the increasing *thingness*, the growing object-like qualities of the book: "Spoken word or visual text, the poem grows separate from the book and transforms itself into an autonomous sound or plastic object."[67] This thickening, this increased emphasis on the material, goes beyond language. Paz writes: "what distinguishes the modern attitude from what prevailed even fifteen or twenty years ago" is that "experience is once again physical, corporeal: today, language comes to us through the ears, it embodies, it incarnates . . . the embodiment of the word and its collective incarnation corresponds to the displacement of the book by other means of communication and to the displacement of the written sign by the voice."[68]

In a letter to Haroldo de Campos dated 1968, Paz reads the thickened materiality of the concrete poem as an interruption of the forward logic of language in the age of capitalism, of language as mere discourse. He writes: "due to its immediate and total character, the concrete poem is a critique of discursive thought. Negation of the course—of the course and the discourse."[69] The "immediate character" of the concrete poem that Paz writes about rests in its emphasis on the visual and vocal dimensions of language, an emphasis on meaning apprehended visually (by seeing how a poems looks) and vocally (by hearing how it sounds). Insofar as a reader must alternate the act of reading with attention to the poem's appearance and its sound when spoken, the material aspects of language—its vocal, visual, and physical features—interrupt the drive to make language as efficient and clear as possible. Interruption functions here by way of interdiction: where discourse means to say something, to expound, to explain and move forward, the material aspects of language work recursively. The materiality of language presents meaning semantically; it remains verbal, but it does so in direct correlation to the way language incarnates—the way it is written, printed, voiced, and materialized. Interruption also works by impeding the designative function of language. The more language draws attention to itself as embodied sign, the less it points to objects, events, and meanings other than itself. Put another way, the more language becomes materially thickened—the more it becomes materially opaque—the less it can function as a transparent and unobtrusive vehicle of meaning.

Paz is making a case against the instrumentalization of language. He begins this work from the very first pages of "Poesía y poema," the first essay in *El arco y la lira*, where he writes of the deformation inherent to instrumentalization. He contrasts this with the attention to materiality at the heart of poetry, defined by its ability to signify not through but with and in language. Beginning with a reference to stones, the recurring motif in his poetry, Paz writes: "The triumph of stone is in sculpture, its humiliation in the staircase. Color is resplendent in painting; so is the movement of the body in dance. Matter, defeated or deformed in the instrument, gains back its splendor in the work of art."[70] Poetry and prose stand respectively as language horizons of freedom and instrumentalization.[71] Instrumentalization for Paz, as for Georg Lukács and Alfonso Reyes, is a condition of the objective, scientific mind. It is also a sign of its alienation. And although prose serves Paz as the register wherein strictly useful, transparent, instrumentalized language is most visible, it bears noting the obvious: that just as instrumentalized language can make its way to verse, so, then, there is a kind of prose capable of nurturing the material freedom of language crucial for its possibilities beyond mere use-value. The presumption of a purely instrumentalized language, in prose or in verse, rests on the existence of an illusion, for language is never just one thing; it is never just this or that, neither pure communication nor pure materiality. That is, the ideal of instrumentalized language rests on a false premise: a condition of transparency, of furious efficiency. Narrowly rational prose, narrowly *useful* prose, is the ideal language of capitalist modernity. The same cannot be said of the actual language of consumer culture and consumer capitalism, often banal, but also, usually, wasteful, sometimes brilliantly so, and perhaps the better for it.

In *El arco y la lira* Paz doubles down on his argument about prose as a historically specific form of language, thus exposing a generalized, effective, and dangerous presumption: that prose language is somehow more realistic, that it is somehow more natural than verse and other forms of rhythmic, nonlinear language. Prose, Paz affirms, is a late development in language: "Prose is a late genre, begotten by the mind's wariness of the natural tendencies of language."[72] He then continues:

> Prose, primordially an instrument of criticism and analysis, demands a slow process of maturation and is only produced after a long series of efforts leaning toward dominion over speech. Its advancement is measured by the degree of control thought can exert over words. Prose grows in a permanent struggle against the natural inclinations of language, and its most accomplished genres are speeches and demonstrations, in which rhythm and its incessant back-and-forth give way to the forward movement of thought.[73]

Paz takes this reading of the historical tendency toward linear, discursive, narrowly rational language as a cue to situate Mallarmé's *Un coup de dés* in the larger context of the history of language. He reads it as a turning point not just in modernist poetics but also as part of a larger social context: as a step in the history of the link between power and narrowly defined reason. In reference to Mallarmé's celebrated work, Paz writes: "The most profound poetic uprising of the century took place exactly in that place where the discursive spirit had taken almost complete control over language, to the extent that it appeared to be stripped of its rhythmic powers. In the heart of a people gripped by reason there emerged a forest of images, a new cavalry order, armed to the teeth with poisonous weapons."[74] The image of Mallarmé as quixotic antagonist to the discursive spirit is a powerful one. It gives *Un coup de dés* its proper measure. It also points to the fraught futility of resisting the language of narrow reason, which is the language of capitalism. The whole enterprise is useless. Perhaps this is its weapon, its poison, as Paz suggests.

Replication, or Paz's Experimental Poetry

There comes a moment in the poetry of Paz where he, like the Brazilian concrete poets, gravitates toward replication: replication of the world taking shape in the decades after World War II. In *El arco y la lira* Paz gives us a glimpse of how he understands replication and the place of mimesis in poetry. He begins by quoting Aristotle: "'Poetry in general seems to have sprung from two causes, each of them lying deep in our nature. First, the instinct for imitation is implanted in man from childhood . . . second, everyone takes pleasure in mimetic reproductions.'"[75] Paz then goes on to distinguish between the way imitation worked for the Greeks and the way it works in modern times. The key difference is in the model and object of imitation: whereas the Greeks took nature as their model, we no longer look to nature or, indeed, are able to look to nature as unmediated object of imitation.

What, then, is the object of imitation of modern poetry? According to Paz, it is mass media and advertising, technology or *técnica*, as he calls it, in the face of which poetry stands not in simple antagonism but in complementary opposition:

> The links between technology and poetry are unusual: on the one hand poetry, like all the other arts, tends to use technology, especially in the realm of mass media: radio, television, sound recordings, cinematography, etc.; on the other hand, poetry must oppose the negation of the image of the world. In the first case, poetry leans on technology; in the second case, it opposes it. This opposition is complementary.[76]

In the late 1960s, Paz started looking at advertisements and mass culture as models for the writing of his own poetry. Echoing a proposition developed at length by the concrete poets and by Walter J. Ong, Marshall McLuhan, and others, Paz argues that the homogenization of language in conventionally printed texts facilitates reading and thinking at the expense of sensorial stimulation. Accordingly, with the advent of print and printed prose language "poetry was purged of music, calligraphy, and of illustration; it was paired down until it became almost exclusively an art of the understanding."[77] By contrast, newspapers, advertisements, and posters capitalize on the texture of printed language, its visual and material features. With the development of modern, more visually invested print media, and with the advent of film, television, and other new media where written language could appear (as it does in televised advertisements) with visual and vocal traits that enrich its meaning, written language is jolted out of the homogeneity of conventionally printed text.

Discos visuales (1968; figs. 3.2–3.4) is the most strikingly visual, and among the most unusual, of Paz's poetry publications. A glance at the four colorful cardboard plates where the *Discos visuales* are printed is enough to draw the eye not just to the words—in fact, not primarily to the words—but to a vibrant suite of colors evocative of the mod aesthetic of the 1960s. The eye is so drawn to the graphic element of the discs that the words quickly recede into the background. They pop right back up with every rotation of the discs, only to withdraw once again when the discs are back at rest. In order for any meaning to be extracted from them, the poems must be seen and handled as much as, perhaps more than, they are read. Put another way, the poems demand an engagement at the sensory level as much as they demand a more narrowly rational engagement, assuming (falsely, for the sake of the distinction being made here) that the two faculties are separate and distinct.

Discos visuales is among the unconventional, object-like poetry publications Paz produced in the 1960s (the first was *Vrindaban*, published in Geneva in 1966; the second was *Blanco*, discussed below), in a moment of marked experimentation for the poet. Each disc is richly colored in a bold palette of orange, magenta, purple, and blue against a dark-gray background. The format and size of the discs, together with the casing of the volume and the title of the publication, bring to mind vinyl records, the primary medium for music reproduction at the time the *Discos visuales* were published. An advertisement served as the direct model for what would become the *Discos visuales*. Mass culture, in sum, in all its rich variety, is the proper context for the *Discos visuales*. Paz got the idea for them from an ingenious traveler's guide—an advertisement, really—for the now-defunct Trans World Airlines (TWA; fig. 3.1), which presented information about the airline's destinations and their respective time zones using stacked, rotating paper discs. Paz was so taken with the signifying potential of the clever little TWA guide that he mailed a copy to Vicente Rojo, along with his first pitch for a volume of poems printed on a similar platform.

Aside from shedding light on how *Discos visuales* and *Blanco* were con-

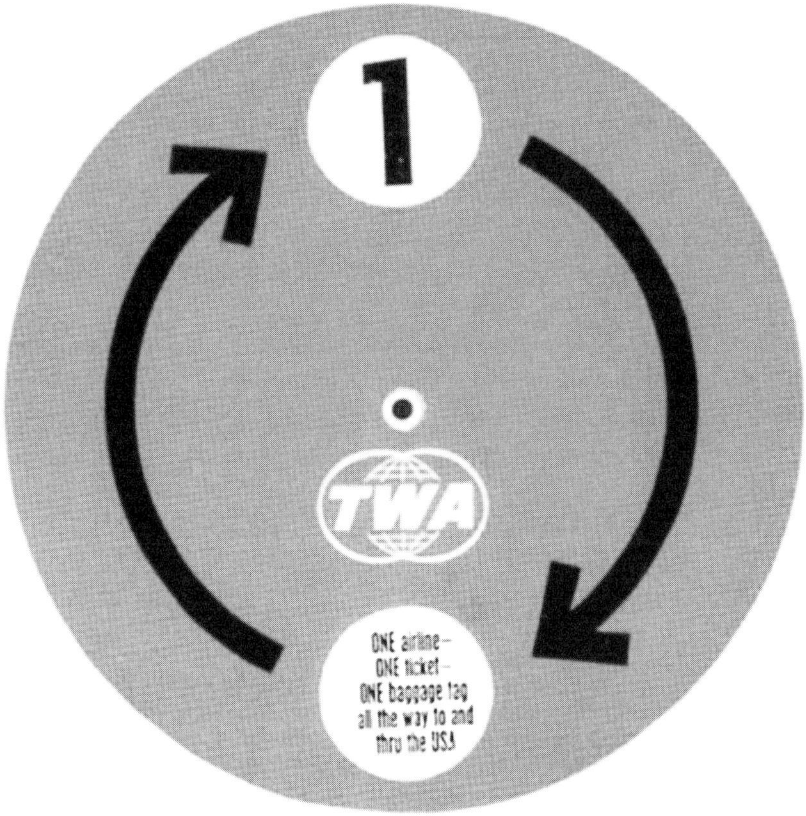

Figure 3.1. A Trans World Airlines (TWA) advertisement.

ceived, the letters exchanged between Paz and Rojo provide insights into Paz's view of the state of mass media in Mexico in the 1950s and 1960s. Paz writes: "It is inadmissible that radio and television are in private hands but it would also be deplorable if they were to be state monopolies. Thus, we ought to look for a mixed solution, where producers (technicians, workers, artists, teachers, and intellectuals) and consumers can participate decisively and where they can be employed in mass media."[78] A will to participate more directly as artist in the direction and production of mass media is visible in this brief statement, as is a hint of recognition of the consumer as new social category. Most revealing, perhaps, is the perspective of Paz the liberal intellectual, particularly given the way he himself would negotiate his relationship with the state (his own "mixed solution") in the last few decades of his life, having left the diplomatic corps and having formalized his commitment to the media conglomerate Televisa.

The result of Paz's collaboration with Rojo is essentially an attempt to replicate the TWA advertisement in a volume of poetry. Each *disco* features multiple cutouts, anywhere from two to ten. An introductory text printed on the inside of the volume's jacket indicates that Rojo was the one to design and project the four round objects. It also points out that these objects "are strictly speaking neither drawings nor designs nor toys nor tools to make poetry: they are part of the very substance of the poem."[79] Each poem is composed of a few word blocks printed on the bottom disc. The circular cutouts on the top disc structure the order of reading, allowing some word blocks to be read simultaneously while excluding other blocks of text. Rotating the disc hides the previously visible number and text, revealing new textual arrangements. Smaller cutouts on the outer edge of the disk indicate the starting point as well as the reading (the spinning) direction of each disk. The result is more controlled, much more linear,

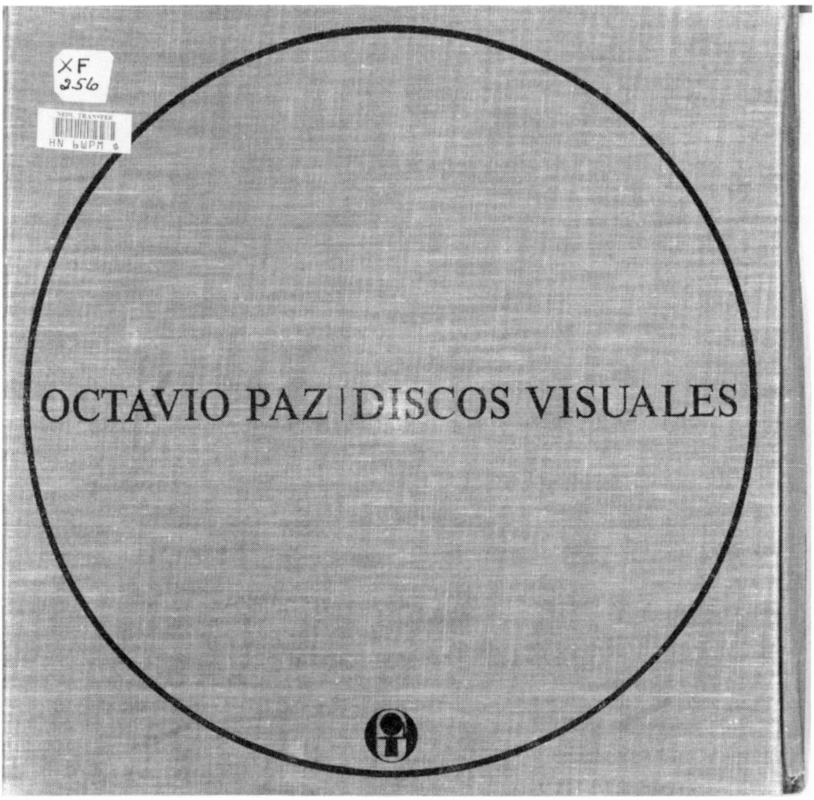

Figure 3.2. Octavio Paz, *Discos visuales* (1968), front cover. © Octavio Paz; courtesy, Marie José Paz.

and much less equivocal than what the roundness of the printed disks might suggest.

It is hard to overstate the importance of Rojo's participation in this project. For all his insight into the visual arts (he wrote prolifically and often brilliantly about the visual arts both in Mexico and abroad), Paz had modest talents for graphic design and graphic art.[80] We need look no further than his *Topopoemas* to assess the limitations the poet confronted when assuming graphic design responsibilities for his own projects. In the late 1960s when Paz conceived the *Discos*, there were few artists as prepared to undertake this project as Vicente Rojo. A trained painter and one of a wave of Spanish exiles living in Mexico in the aftermath of the Spanish Civil War, Rojo excelled more than anything as a graphic artist, and from the 1950s onward he made a name for himself as the leading figure

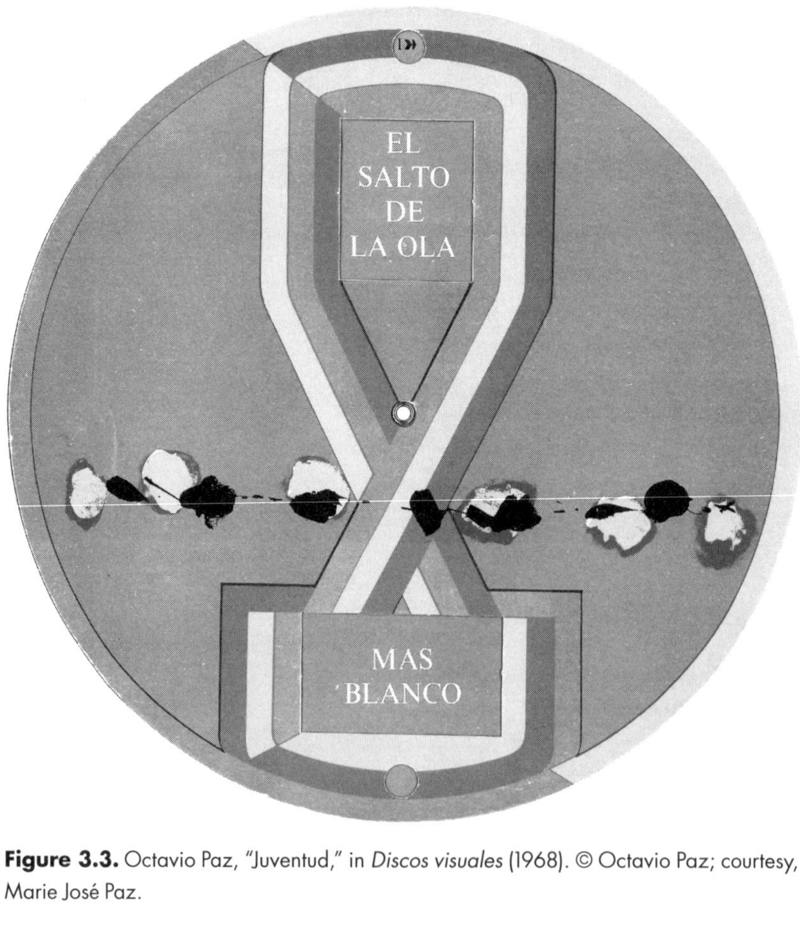

Figure 3.3. Octavio Paz, "Juventud," in *Discos visuales* (1968). © Octavio Paz; courtesy, Marie José Paz.

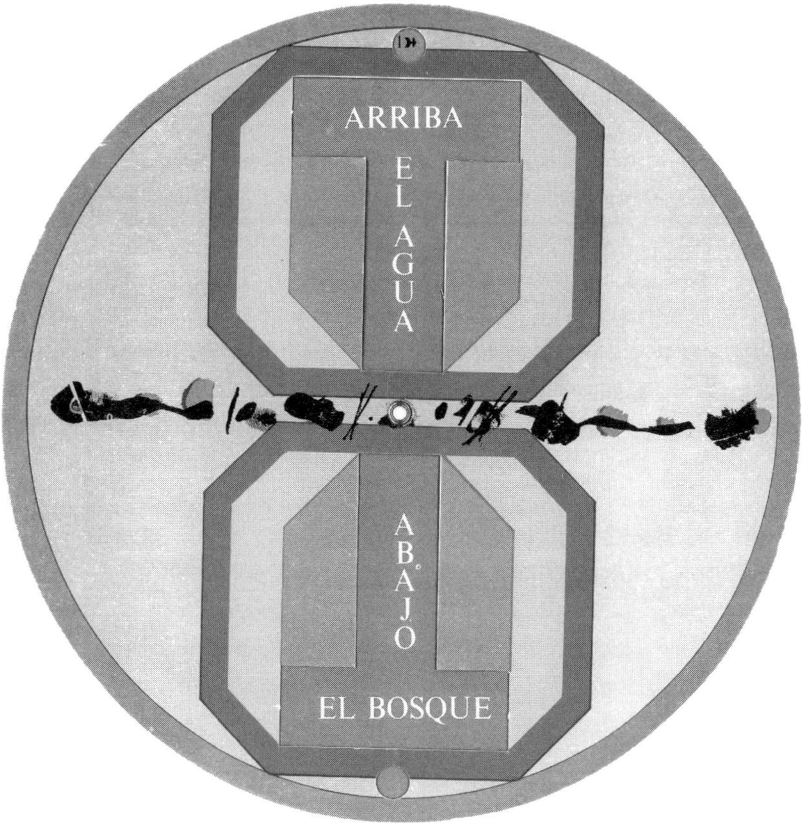

Figure 3.4. Octavio Paz, "Concorde," in *Discos visuales* (1968). © Octavio Paz; courtesy, Marie José Paz.

in the emerging field of graphic design. Rojo also built a tremendous reputation as book publisher and designer. He was a founder of Ediciones Era, the publishing house behind a splendid volume on Marcel Duchamp that includes Paz's essay on the artist (later republished, as *Apariencia desnuda*, in 1973), and he masterminded the graphic concept of a number of journals and newspapers, including *Plural* and *La Jornada*.

Themes of time and travel are vaguely interweaved throughout the four *Discos*, titled "Juventud," "Pasaje," "Concorde" (an homage to the ultrasonic aircraft), and "Aspa." "Juventud," haiku-like, packs a powerful meditation on mortality. "Pasaje" features only two arrangements and is perhaps the most accomplished in terms of its circularity and the cyclical movement within and between different word arrangements. "Concorde," as its name indicates, is the one thematically closest to modernity and consumer culture. It reads like a take on landscape poetry that grapples with the marvelous collapse of sky and earth experienced by those who travel by plane. "Aspa" is the most erotic of the set, and the most complex.

In an interview with Rita Guibert, Paz lists the two objectives he pursued in making his *Discos visuales*: "first, to invest the text with mobility through visual rhythm; second, to slow down the reading. Nowadays it is fashionable to read quickly, and there's even schools devoted to that. An abomination . . . I believe it is necessary to learn to read slowly, especially when it comes to poetry."[81] A fissure opens up here, wedged apart by the contradictory objectives Paz and the Brazilian concrete poets pursue in producing poetry with techniques derived from advertising and mass culture. The concrete poets, as we saw, set out to understand and cultivate faster reading habits. In this sense, the reading posture they encouraged, their approach to language and to temporality in language, is mimetic. Paz, on the other hand, wants to slow down reading, opposing what we usually take to be the overarching, primary rhythm of language in mass media and consumer culture: fast, furious, unrelenting. Slow reading emerges as another strategy of resistance to the forward logic of efficient communication.

Blanco

Paz wrote and published *Blanco* (1967) before the publication of his *Discos visuales*, and in many ways this long poem—one of his longest and perhaps his most ambitious—anticipates the defining characteristics of his other works of visual poetry. As Enrico Mario Santí notes, citing the poet himself, Paz conceived of *Blanco* in continuity with "Los signos en rotación," one of two essays where he broaches the problem of language, modernity, and capitalism most explicitly.[82] *Blanco* is printed on a long sheet of paper set in square binding. It uses two different fonts and two different font colors, red and black, a nod, perhaps, to a type of coloration Miguel León Portilla identifies as symbolic of extraordinary knowledge in Nahuatl thought.[83] Spread out over twenty-three distinct panels printed on one long sheet of paper, the poem is folded between the covers of a book to form an accordion or scroll that draws the eye up and down, like a column. The very act of handling the text brings estrangement to the reader's relationship with books. The volume must be turned on its side for the reading to begin.

More so than conventionally printed books, *Blanco* demands that readers physically engage with it in order to glean its meanings, in order to bring it to life. Of course, all books require some sort of ergonomics, some sort of manipulation. Pages must be turned in order for reading to take place. In *Blanco*, however, the lack of pagination together with the unusual format of the sheet of paper on which it is printed complicate the handling of the text, opening up the possibility of a noncontinuous reading of the pages or panels.[84] Multiple reading orders or reading itineraries are suggested, much like in Julio Cortázar's *Rayuela* (1963), in the instructions Paz included with the first edition of the text. Parallels between Paz's *Blanco* and Cortázar's work can also be traced in reference to two other works by the Argentinian writer: *La vuelta al día en ochenta mundos* (1967) and *Último round* (1969). Haroldo de Campos mentions the first of these inventively printed volumes--curiously cut along the horizontal axes of the printed page, giving way to two different but interacting series of texts—in his correspondence with Paz.[85] Both books, experimental in their structure and their physical form, reference the newspaper, and both can be read productively as responses to Mallarmé's *Un coup de dés*, itself indebted to the newspaper form.[86] The notes printed at the end of the volume indicate that *Blanco* can be read as three distinct poems, each set out in one of the three columns that run down the length of the scroll where the poem is printed. The center column is a meditation on language ("un poema cuyo tema es el tránsito de la palabra, del silencio al silencio"[87]). The second poem, on the right column, is a suite of variations on a theme: the different aspects of cognition ("cuatro variaciones sobre la sensación, la percepción, la imaginación y el entendimiento").[88] The third poem, on the left column, is an erotic poem.

The extant bibliography on *Blanco* mulls over the reading possibilities that the poem affords. Paz himself included in the volume where *Blanco* is published precise indications regarding the possible reading orders in the poem.[89] The accordion-like format of the volume allows for the random juxtaposition of panels, building an element of dynamism and randomness into the very physical structure of the poem. Unlike a conventional book, the scroll or accordion onto which the poem is printed allows for one panel to be seen and read together with a panel that might not be immediately adjacent to it. Thus, for instance, in the hands of a playful reader, panel 2 might end up next to panel 17, panel 5 next to panel 12, and so forth. This brings to mind other open works of literature from the period, works that experiment with the platform of the printed text to multiply the number of arrangements and perform a kind of *ars combinatoria*.

In the space unfolded by the poem, silence is pictured in the voids of the page that come before the first and after the last panel of the poem. This is a graphic feature that was important to Paz, as evinced in the letters he sent to Joaquín Díez-Canedo, the editor of *Blanco*, in the months preceding the volume's publication. When read as a unified whole rather than as three separate poems, the central column of *Blanco* works as a pillar of sorts. As Paz puts it, it follows the transit of the word from silence to silence, from the silence that precedes enunciation to the silence that comes after it, enacting along the way—and at several different levels that I hope to make explicit—the embodiment of language Paz links to advertisements and to the language of consumer culture.

Existing studies of the poem have shed light on its major defining features: its length and its place in the history of the long poem in Latin America,[90] its link to Eastern thought[91] and to the figure of the mandala,[92] and its spatial form.[93] Critics have also remarked on the poem's links to mass and consumer culture, with most commentaries limited to Paz's plans for a film adaptation of the poem. There is a tenuous but discernible link to the newspaper format in the poem's binding. Handling the long scroll where the panels are printed can very easily lead to a shuffling and rearranging of pages not unlike the experience of folding and unfolding a newspaper page. In a sense, the physical handling that *Blanco* calls for, and the rewarding effect that playing with the order of its panels might yield, is a sort of preparatory step, in the sense that it alerts the reader to the importance of physically engaging with the text in order to make it bear its meaning.

Like Haroldo de Campos's *Galáxias* (1984),[94] *Blanco* begins reflexively, with a meditation on beginnings:

el comienzo
        el cimiento
la simiente
          latente[95]

This play on words sets up, as Julio Ortega and David Draper point out,[96] a three-pronged origin: a temporal beginning ("el comienzo"), a spatial foundation ("el cimiento"), and a vital generation ("la simiente"). The rest of the first panel (the words of which are printed, like those in the six panels of the central column, in a noticeably thinner font, suggesting a language coming into and fading out of visual being) reinforces the theme of a beginning and grounds it in terms of language, or rather, of prelanguage, of that which comes before language: "la palabra en la punta de la lengua":

inaudita   inaudible
impar
grávida   nula[97]

Together, these five adjectives speak of the state of incipiency of this "word on the tip of the tongue," a word unheard of and without precedent.

From the very beginning of the poem we find ourselves confronted with the sheer physicality of language, of spoken language. Alliteration between the three words that follow ("inaudita/inaudible/impar") gives concrete meaning to the image of words at the tip of the tongue. As we speak it, the word before us, a word "unheard," "inaudible," "unmatched," stops us in our (lingual) tracks. From the outset the emphasis on sound sets up a critique of signification in language without departing from sense completely, in a strategy Paz formulates (in a letter to Haroldo de Campos) as a recourse against discourse, a strategy culled, homeopathically, from discursivity itself.[98]

If the first panel of *Blanco* stages the moment before language is realized, the lapse between silence and utterance, the second and third panel are jointly the space where it bursts into existence. As in the first panel, in the second and third panels the text appears in the center column, the one dedicated to a meditation about language. The first three lines set up an image of a well-like depth, an uninhabited mine from which, the reader might well suppose, language will be culled:

Sube y baja,
Escalera de escapulario
El lenguaje deshabitado[99]

In the notes accompanying the republication of *Blanco*, Paz writes that "escalera de escapulario" refers to the hanging ladder used by miners to climb in and out of vertical shafts. The mineral/metallic theme is developed further in the remainder of the panel, where the theme of language rising is relayed alternatively as a lamp and as a flower. This paves the way for a vision of language as electric light.

An image begins to take shape here, the image of an electric lamp, flickering at first, shining bright and blinding toward the end of the third panel. It brings to mind the sight of cinema, of the film screen lighting up, a vision of the first flashes of light making way for the moving images to come. This reading, which might seem tendentious, is grounded on the imagery built into these two panels, on the situation presented by the panel that follows it and, more importantly, on the stage directions Paz left for the film adaptation of *Blanco*, which call for a simple setup of three people reading the poem with no props other than reading desks and reading lights.[100] Squarely seen, the "tallo de cobre" mentioned in the poem is a faintly disguised reference to the arm of a lamp and the copper wire therein contained, the same lamp mentioned at the beginning of the panel. A few lines later in the next panel, the verses "Un girasol / Ya luz carbonizada"[101] suggest the sight of a lightbulb, beautifully capturing an image of shining, charred filaments. The scene built around the lamp bleeds into the next panel, where the side columns first make an appearance.

The first feature that comes across in scanning the side columns of *Blanco* is the use of colored fonts. A reading and a careful look at them reveals that these fonts graphically illustrate the sexual encounter described in them. In panel 4, the first one where the two side columns appear, the columns are placed separate from each other. As Santí observes in his close reading of the poem, the imagery of shadows on a wall present in this panel suggest a couple in a sex act.[102] The scene continues in panel 8, where two consecutive lines (*entrar en mí / al entrar en tu cuerpo*) allude explicitly to the sexual act described later in the poem.

The columns in panel 8 are closer to each other than those on panel 4, suggesting the movement of two lovers toward each other. By the time we get to panel 12, the columns are fused together, zigzagging, almost swaying back and forth, the color of the fonts being the only thing that marks the limit between them. In panel 16, where the sexual act finally takes place ("*lluvia de tus talones en mi espalda*"),[103] the columns are again placed very close to each other, but not exactly next to each other (fig. 3.5). The lines in each column are ever so slightly off level relative to the lines in the other column, echoing in their very disposition on the page the graphic (sordid, some might say) piling up of bodies described there. Two more elements top the list of graphic traits that reinforce the theme of sex in panel 16: first, the relative density of text on the page (twenty lines, compared to fifteen elsewhere) suggesting—or, better yet, performing—a pressing together of verse, rife with physicality; and second, the sudden penetration of the column on the left by the column on the right in line 7, repeated less drastically from that point onward. Here again, the

caes de tu cuerpo a tu sombra *no allá sino en mis ojos*
en un caer inmóvil de cascada *cielo y suelo se juntan*
caes de tu sombra a tu nombre *intocable horizonte*
te precipitas en tus semejanzas *yo soy tu lejanía*
caes de tu nombre a tu cuerpo *el más allá de la mirada*
en un presente que no acaba *las imaginaciones de la arena*
caes en tu comienzo *las disipadas fábulas del viento*
derramada en mi cuerpo *yo soy la estela de tus erosiones*
tú te repartes como el lenguaje *espacio dios descuartizado*
tú me repartes en tus partes *altar el pensamiento y el cuchillo*
vientre teatro de la sangre *eje de los solsticios*
yedra arbórea lengua tizón de frescura *el firmamento es macho y hembra*
temblor de tierra de tu grupa *testigos los testículos solares*
lluvia de tus talones en mi espalda *falo el pensar y vulva la palabra*
ojo jaguar en espesura de pestañas *espacio es cuerpo signo pensamiento*
la hendidura encarnada en la maleza *siempre dos sílabas enamoradas*
los labios negros de la profetisa *A d i v i n a n z a*
entera en cada parte te repartes *las espirales transfiguraciones*
tu cuerpo son los cuerpos del instante *es·cuerpo el tiempo el mundo*
visto tocado desvanecido *pensamiento sin cuerpo el cuerpo imaginario*

contemplada por mis oídos *Horizonte de música tendida*
olida por mis ojos *Puente colgante del color al aroma*
acariciada por mi olfato *Olor desnudez en las manos del aire*
oída por mi lengua *Cántico de los sabores*
comida por mi tacto *Festín de niebla*

habitar tu nombre *Despoblar tu cuerpo*
caer en tu grito contigo *Casa del viento*

La irrealidad de lo mirado
Da realidad a la mirada

Figure 3.5. Octavio Paz, excerpt from *Blanco* (1967). © Octavio Paz; courtesy, Marie José Paz.

only thing distinguishing the two columns (at least until one notices the slightly off-level layout of the columns relative to each other) is the color of the fonts. A strong resonance exists between this part of *Blanco* and Augusto de Campos's "eis os amantes." Together, these works draw a spectrum of the possibilities that a more playful layout in the style of posters and advertising offers for even the most solemn of poems.

Unlike *Discos visuales*—directly derived from advertising—film and cinema are the two principal models Paz had in mind as he produced *Blanco*. Paz's most explicit remarks on the convergence between cinema and poetry are clustered in "El ocaso de la vanguardia" (1972), an essay included in his book *Los hijos del limo* (1974). His thoughts center on an expansive reading of simultaneism, the avant-garde movement of the 1910s closely linked, as Paz notes, to cubism and futurism. Like cubism, simultaneism sought to present objects and situations by providing a manifold of perspectives simultaneously, in contrast to the fixed-perspective model of representation that dominated the visual arts until the emergence of cubism in the early twentieth century. In poetry, this approach to presentation and representation was taken up fruitfully by Blaise Cendrars, whose long poem *La prose du Transsibérien et de la petite Jehanne de France* (1913), with its colored typography, its innovative layout, and its expressive prints by Sonia Delaunay-Terk, stands as direct precursor to Paz's *Blanco*. In *Los hijos del limo* (1974), Paz makes note of the parallelism between the principles of simultaneism and those of montage, "especially as it was practiced and theorized by Sergei Eisenstein."[104] Expanding on this observation, Paz argues that in *La prose* Cendrars relies on a broken compositional method that "comes and goes, with anticipations, irruptions, digressions, and unforeseen links," a method that brings Cendrars's poem "closer to film than to painting, closer to montage than collage."[105]

In a lecture delivered in Mexico City in 1975, Paz states that in composing *Blanco* he sought out "a kind of correspondence between the temporal and the spatial."[106] His points of departure were, he writes, the exercises in simultaneism he completed as a young poet.[107] Paz reads in the stochastic logic of Cendrars's *La prose* the trace of "everyday language, the language of the everyday that flows and elapses"; it was through this kind of language, Paz argues, that "real time, simultaneous and discontinuous time entered into the poetry of our century."[108] Implicit in these assertions is an argument for the resonance between montage as organizational principle and the "real time" characteristic of modern, urban settings. Implicit, too, is the possibility of tracing the stochastic and multi-perspectival nature of montage onto literature and printed poems. The simplest way of doing this is to juxtapose and contrast two series in a poem and allow for combinations and collisions between them, much like montage allows for the combination and collision of different images and different strips of film. The result is a simultaneous presentation of two different verse lines, two different points of view. In *Blanco*, the overlapping of different perspectives so characteristic of montage takes place both within a single panel (in those parts where the side columns appear together but separated by different-color fonts) and across panels, to the extent that every panel can be juxtaposed with a different one depending on how the reader decides to unfold the long vertical sheet where the poem is printed.

In the letters he sent to Joaquín Díez-Canedo, editor of both *Blanco* and *Discos visuales*, and to Vicente Rojo, Paz invariably returns to the subject of the film version of *Blanco*. He pitches ideas about how the adaptation would take place and how it could be financed, and he goes so far as writing out stage directions. The film never materialized in Paz's lifetime, but the notes written by Paz toward its realization provide enough material to pose questions about the function of film and film form in *Blanco*. The idea of bringing *Blanco* to film was present in Paz's mind from the very conception of the poem. Initially, he sought to work with Mexican theater director José Luis Ibáñez, whose adaptation of a Carlos Fuentes story to film had brought him considerable prominence.[109] Ibáñez took no interest in the project, and Paz sought out Rojo. A letter written by Paz to Rojo dated March 6, 1968, summarizes the poet's intentions and ideas for the film adaptation of Blanco:

> For a long while, I've been concerned with the relationships among sound, the visual arts, and words. *Blanco*, among other works of mine, responds to this concern, which is not exclusively aesthetic. There lies the origin of my interest in the film version of the poem, which I envision as a projection of the book (and of the act of reading it) on a screen. This film would combine dynamically letters, spoken word, audio and visual sensations, and the different senses. That is to say: it would be the translation of interior subjective movement (reading) to exterior objective motion (the projection of the camera).[110]

Paz's ideas for a film adaptation of *Blanco* as well as his collaboration with Rojo in the making of *Discos visuales* form part of a larger, generational moment in Mexico that sees a renewed interest in interartistic collaboration, unseen since the 1920s. *Poesía en voz alta*, a turning point in the history of Mexican theater, is exemplary in this regard. Conceived by Juan José Arreola, it brought together a select group of artists and writers from the emerging "rupture" in Mexican visual arts and set out to revitalize theater and the scenic arts in Mexico, building on Arreola's conviction that theater is, at heart, spoken poetry. The initiative was defined from the outset as an interartistic and interdisciplinary effort, with theater and poetry as the two principal disciplines structuring the proposals and the programming that came out of the initiative. Soon after the opening of its first production in 1956, Paz joined the initiative's leadership, incorporating contemporary theater (including his own play, *La hija de Rapaccini*) to the initial classical repertoire.

A sustained effort to explore the performative dimensions of poetry and theater characterizes the activities organized under the rubric of *Poesía en voz alta*. And it is this emphasis on the performative dimension of the act of reading that is most intriguing about Paz's proposal for a film adaptation of *Blanco*. Time and again, Paz insisted that the adaptation to film had to work as a film projection not of the book itself but of the act of reading it, a detail important enough for him to reiterate it almost every time he wrote about the project of taking *Blanco* to the cinema screen. In another letter to Rojo, Paz insists: "What I'm really proposing to you is the cinematographic projection of the book, or, better said, the projection of its reading (silent at times, out loud at other times)."[111]

The more he insists on this, the more it seems, at least to this reader, that what Paz intends to achieve through the cinematic projection of the reading of *Blanco* is analogous to what Edmund Husserl attempted to do fifty years earlier in his *Lectures*: to bracket out both the object of perceptual experience (the poem) and the subject who experiences said object (the reader) in order to make the pure phenomenon of experience (the reading) available for scrutiny. Pere Gimferrer makes the case for this idea of *Blanco* as Husserlian bracketing or phenomenological reduction when he argues that "what *Blanco* narrates" is "pure phenomenological suspension."[112] Earlier, Haroldo de Campos described Mallarmé's poetic praxis (the most insistent precursor for both Paz and the Brazilian concrete poets) as a "phenomenological reduction of the poetic object."[113]

I find it useful to interpret the analogy between Paz's attempt to provide an experience of the act of reading by means of a projection of his poem *Blanco* and Husserl's phenomenological reduction of the act of perception (the bracketing out of the perceived object and the perceiving subject to arrive at an act of pure perception) in reference to Susan

Buck-Morss's argument in "The Cinema Screen as Prosthesis of Perception," where she makes the case for the cinema screen as a model for the complex philosophical operations behind Husserl's phenomenological reduction. Rather than reproducing or paraphrasing the rigorous philosophical exercise that underlies Husserl's argument, she directs the reader to the movie theater, because, she states, "if we wish to have a vision of the pure object, this 'self-given', 'absolute datum,' which is neither physical thing nor psychological fact but (—wondrous phrase!—) an 'intentionally inexistent entity', we would do best to put down the text, leave the lecture, and go to the movies."[114] Citing liberally from Husserl's lectures, she remarks that while the cinematic image transcends itself, its referents always belonging to a wider reality, "this transcendent reality is never 'given' in the cinema images themselves, [which] 'neither are nor genuinely contain the objects.'"[115] She goes on to explain how the subject, too, is bracketed out from the phenomenological experience of the cinema. "The cinema image," she writes, "although constructed by particular human beings (director, camera-person, editor), is not dependent on these or any other individual, psychological subjects for its meaning," for "that which it shows us is both given (in the pieces of the film) and constructed (in the juxtaposition that gives these pieces meaning)."[116] In the movie theater, Buck-Morss contends, the "reductions" that Husserl places at the center of his philosophical method (the bracketing out of the object and the subject from the experience of cognitive perception) take place by virtue of the mediation of cinema alone.

Considered in reference to Paz's theory of language and technology, the film adaptation of *Blanco* seems intent on isolating the act of pure reading, in an analogous way. Paz distinguished between two different kinds of language functions, one associated with a mythological or pretechnological era and the other linked to mass and consumer culture. In the first instance, language presents us with an image of the world as something inherently meaningful, something to be recorded and understood by means of language. In the second instance, the world no longer appears as something meaningful; it is conceived as something to be transformed. The first offers a sensible image of the world, while the second presents language as an opaque, perceptible entity capable of actively intervening the world. In the film adaptation of *Blanco*, both the world as sensible image and language as instrument are bracketed out to make way for the act of reading—the linguistic act, isolated, as it were, from both the world of which it speaks and the subject who speaks it.

In his letters to Rojo, Paz also entertained the possibility of television screenings with a candor rarely if ever displayed in his previous writings on poetry and mass media.[117] Television for Paz could potentially return poetry to the public forum via public, broadcasted readings of poetry.[118] His optimism unbounded, Paz goes so far as to bet on television as the new medium for poetry, after print.[119] Though his plans never materialized, Paz's interest in television did not subside. As Néstor García Canclini writes, toward the end of Paz's life the poet's criticism of the Mexican government is matched proportionally by his commitments to mass media and to the Televisa media conglomerate in particular, which secured exclusive rights to television appearances by the poet.[120]

The years during which Paz experimented with visual poetry and with the concrete dimensions of language cast a new light on his body of poetry and on the relationship between his poetry and the social juncture from which it emerges and to which it responds. Perhaps more importantly, at least in terms of the extant scholarship on the poet, the years during which Paz embraced both concrete poetry and the relationship between poetry and the language forms of consumer culture compel us to revisit Paz's long and complex meditation on poetry, language, and history. Language for Paz, as for the concrete poets and for Benjamin before them, is historical. It changed with capitalism; it changed for capitalism, growing brighter, more material, and more sensual at the same time that it lost those aspects of its capacity to make meaning that could not be subjected to utility and purpose. On their own, Paz's prolific writings on poetry and contemporary society make a compelling case for poetry's vocation as a spirit of opposition in the face of capitalist abstraction and extraction. What changes in light of Paz's more visual, more experimental poems are the terms under which we can describe this spirit of opposition. "In a world ruled by the logic of the market and, in communist countries, by the logic of efficiency, poetry is a zero-yield activity. . . . Poetry: expense, squander, waste."[121] In a world subtended by discourse, poetry is resistance and contestation as much as it is accursed share. It is riposte as much as it is mimesis. The replicas of mass culture and advertising Paz built into his most experimental poems emerge as powerful reflections on language in the age of consumer culture. Nothing more and nothing less than flights of fancy.

FOUR

Lygia Clark, at Home with Objects

An image comes to mind as I try to come to terms with the extraordinary trajectory of Brazilian artist Lygia Clark. It's an image of Clark working from home,[1] in her living room, with the relational objects she constructed and, later, with her "clients" who used these relational objects. This is how Yve-Alain Bois remembers her in his preface to a short selection of writings by Clark.[2] This, too, is the way Suely Rolnik evokes Clark: "We're in a room in Lygia Clark's apartment in Rio de Janeiro. An unusual space littered with endless objects of all kinds, objects that the artist calls 'Relational.'"[3] Home, the home as place of turmoil, is the point of departure for Clark the artist. She begins making art in 1947 as a way to cope with the crisis that overcame her after the birth of her third child.[4] Three decades later, having spent extended periods of time in Paris and after a brief stint in California, she returns home, home to Rio de Janeiro, home to the space of her living room and home to the rhythms of everyday life. In the present and final chapter of this book, I want to suggest that home and homemaking, in the greater sense of those terms, in their existential sense—the place we call home for the way we live in it; the things we do when we find ourselves at home—are apt measures of Clark's ambition, of her legacy.

How fitting, to bring this book to an end by bringing it to bear on the space of the home, a battleground of every major effort to expand commodity capitalism and so the quintessential space of consumption. How fitting, and how problematic. The risk, of course, is surrendering too easily to gendered commonplaces about the home and homemaking. The greater risk is looking past the different approaches to shelter and home made by Clark and by other artists in the decades after World War II.[5] Though it has not been stressed enough in extant studies on the artist, a sustained concern with the notions of home and the materials of homemaking is more or less evident in Clark's rigorous studies in framing, envelopment, environment, and embodiment, as well as in her long and well-documented research into what she called *objetos relacionais*, constructions made from household materials. Thus read, a new dimension of Clark's work comes to the fore, one that aligns her with artists from the first wave of the avant-gardes—from Dada, the Bauhaus,[6] and Russian constructivism in particular—as well as with women artists active in the decades after World War II. All these artists (Sophie Taeuber,[7] Lyubov Popova, Aleksandr Rodchenko, Varvara Stepanova, Vladimir Tatlin, Gego, Eva Hesse, Mira Schendel) broke with enduring expectations about the place of the artwork and the role art can play in the context of everyday life. They did so partly by making art using the kind of labor traditionally associated with women who work from home: crafts, decoration, homemaking.[8]

The crossroads between aesthetics, the everyday labor associated with homemaking, and the objects that populate a home serves as a framing device for my reading of Clark's work. For most of her long and prolific trajectory, Clark broached the larger question of what being at home means, a question that she posed in ways verging on the universal but always grounded on the concreteness of matter and texture. Clark's notion of architectural environment as something that is "'in itself expressive'" constitutes, in my reading, an early and decisive step toward the relational understanding of objects and bodies, of things and embodied subjects at the heart of her most forceful propositions.

In the following pages, I'll parse Clark's long-standing concern with frames, planes, shelters, houses, and other terms conversant with the discourse of architecture. I will also spend some time exploring a related concern with both objects and theories of objects, a concern shared by many of her contemporaries affiliated with the neoconcrete movement and formulated, most prominently by Ferreira Gullar when he coined, in reference to a work by Clark from the late 1950s, his theory of the non-object. Many of Clark's creative contemporaries devoted themselves to hybrid careers as artists and as professionals in the applied and industrial arts: furniture production, toy making, advertising, graphic design, and so forth, and the work of some, especially that of the neoconcrete artist Lygia Pape, will be discussed in some detail. My ambition here is to develop, through a study of Clark's relational objects, a more nuanced understanding of the home as a crucial context for our understanding of consumer culture and the commodity as form.

Frames, Doors, Penetrable Surfaces

Representations of real space, space to be entered and lived in, features prominently in Clark's early work, in a series of drawings and paintings she completed under the instruction of Fernand Léger. The figure of the staircase seen in many of these works, pregnant as it is with implications of spiraling movement, is representative in this regard. By her own account these early images of staircases and of other, less obviously architectural features aspired to be forms of lived environments, of real space. "I started with geometry," Clark writes, "but I was searching for an organic kind of space that made it possible for someone to enter into the painting."[9] Architecture as form and sensibility, as a way of structuring the artwork and as a way of thinking about the experience the artwork elicits, becomes a key reference for Clark early in her trajectory. Architecture helped Clark engage real space rigorously, directing her interest away from painting as figuration and toward a more topological understanding of pictorial surface. Architecture also serves as the first in a series of disciplines (architecture and industry in the 1950s and 1960s; a rarefied form of craft in the 1960s and 1970s; pedagogy and psychology in the 1970s and 1980s) to provide a point of triangulation for Clark the artist, all the while helping her maintain a degree of distance from the discursive constraints of the fine arts, both in her method of production and in the reception of her work.

In 1947, Clark begins an apprenticeship with Brazilian landscape architect and artist Roberto Burle Marx. It comes as no surprise, then, that architecture and architectural thinking have such a strong presence in her early works. As Luis Pérez-Oramas writes, one gets the sense that Clark "approached painting as architecture, as a science of topology, an operator of place"; her sense of painting, Pérez-Oramas argues, was always "fundamentally topological."[10] Some of her works and proposals bear this referent manifestly. Some others have an abstruse but distinct relationship to architectural thinking, especially those works that involve some sort of garment or structure to be worn on the body as a kind of portable shelter.

By the 1960s, a series of works explicit in their embrace of the language of shelter (*Construa você mesmo seu espaço de viver*, 1960; *Abrigo poético*, 1964; *A casa do poeta*, 1964; *A casa é o corpo*, 1968; *Arquiteturas biológicas*, 1968–1969) thread together the larger concerns that animate Clark's interest in architecture: home, a sense of doing or making crossed by *poïesis*, embodiment, a concern for objects, a link to what is vital.[11]

Clark's interest in geometric space that can be entered or inhabited is manifest in the series of architectural models she presented at the second Grupo Frente exhibition in 1955 (*Maquetes para interior*; fig. 4.1), models for rooms that echo, in their stark but rhythmic geometry, El Lissitzky's *Proun Room* of 1923. A breakthrough in Clark's study of penetrable space conceived within the flatness of the painted, two-dimensional surface takes place in an oil painting titled *Quebra da moldura* from 1954 (fig. 4.2). Here, Clark's probing of the line dividing what goes into and out of the pictorial plane is made explicit from the very title, an announcement of sorts of the breaking of the frame that these paintings sought to achieve visually and conceptually.

Boundary, frame, and outline are all carefully controlled and deliberately put to work in these paintings. The boundaries of and in the painting call for attention without demanding it, without the outburst and the

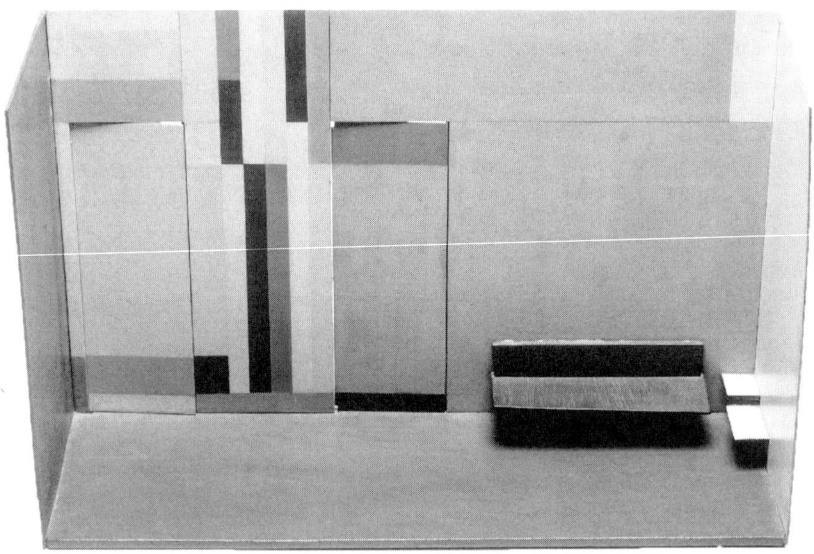

Figure 4.1. Lygia Clark, *Maquete para interior no. 1* (1955). Industrial paint on wood. 11 × 18 × 5 inches. Photograph by Marcelo Ribeiro Alvares Corrêa. Courtesy of Associação Cultural "O Mundo de Lygia Clark."

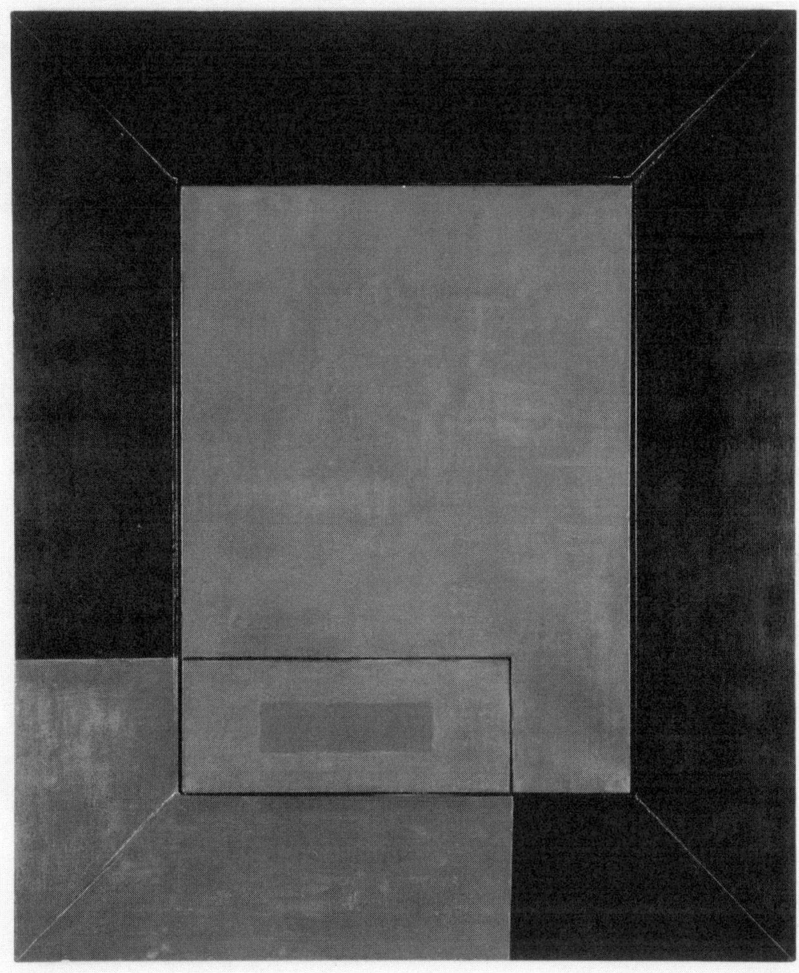

Figure 4.2. Lygia Clark, *Quebra da moldura. Composição no. 5* (1954). Oil and wood on canvas. 41 × 35 inches. Photograph by Mark Morosse. Courtesy of Associação Cultural "O Mundo de Lygia Clark."

graphic aggressiveness of, for instance, the painted, shaped frames produced by artists working with Arte Madí and Arte Concreto-Invención in Buenos Aires in the 1940s. Clark's is a softer, more controlled, more disciplined call for attention to framing devices: a line just thin enough to be visible, a dovetailing of different levels of depths just sharp enough to be noticeable. The resulting object is a two-dimensional pictorial surface that opens up to the space around it, gesturing to the wall where it hangs and activating the openings, crevices, and cornices that mark the architecture to which that wall belongs. The attendant experience sustained by this art object is an increase in the distinctly sensorial, markedly embodied consciousness of the space that surrounds us when we find ourselves aware of being indoors, sheltered.

A statement by Oscar Niemeyer in an article from 1957 picks up on the relationship between Clark's paintings and the architecture of the spaces where these paintings are shown. Notably, Niemeyer reads a social dimension in Clark's work. Clark, he writes,

> is not content with the specific problems of contemporary painting. Her restless spirit scans in the new social concepts for a new content for her work. She searches for a solution which is more closely connected to the problems of construction and enables a broader, fairer use. For Lygia Clark the usual architectural elements—doors, windows, etc.—are not obstacles or interruptions in the composition; they are modules or rhythms which are capable of enriching or disciplining themselves.[12]

The series of paintings on wood from 1955 titled *Superfície modulada* takes Clark's research further. In them, she does away with canvas and works entirely with interlocking wood panels, moving away from the traditional tools of fine art production and embracing a more industrial method that includes the use of the spray-paint gun (Clark is photographed holding one for an April 1959 feature in the women's magazine *Querida*)[13] and industrial-grade acrylic paints. The frame itself becomes the surface and plane that Clark seeks to intervene. The use of separate wood panels within the same painting creates real, visible divisions between different colors, investing these paintings with a restrained, refined, and uncanny sense of depth, as if the space separating each block of color was more than a line and closer to a crevice. That these narrow clefts in the surface of the painting alternate with flat lines dividing single panels into different blocks of color makes the real crevices in the surface of the painting the more unsettling. They force the viewer to come closer to the paintings to determine whether a dividing line is flatly pictorial or whether it constitutes a true break between panels.

A different posture is cultivated here, a different kind of viewing, still contemplative but anticipating the concerns for participation that would become a hallmark of Clark's later works. Bright greens, clay reds, and sky blues dominate the palette of these paintings, an echo, perhaps, of Clark's training with Burle Marx. In the space of a few years, these colors would subside into a more somber black, white, and gray-blue palette, the same one Clark used in the rigorous series of paintings she produced in the second half of the 1950s: *Planos em superfície modulada*, *Espaços modulados*, and *Unidades*.

Like the *Superfícies moduladas*, the *Planos em superfície modulada* are made from distinct, discrete wood panels. Up close, narrow openings like faults or fissures are visible throughout these paintings. The pictorial planes in these paintings are modulated on the basis of protrusion and recession. Looking at the *Superfícies*, one gets the distinct feeling of perceptual ambivalence we have learned to associate with Gestalt experiments where one image can sustain two distinct visual experiences: a rabbit or a duck in the example famously cited by Ludwig Wittgenstein; a Necker cube. In Clark's research into this elementary but compelling visual effect, an inquiry contemporary to Josef Alber's *Structural Constellations*, the gaze of the viewer is simultaneously drawn in and pushed out as it glides across the surface, in a play on perception that alternates between impressions of height and impressions of depth. Through this alternation, a larger, more fully embodied perceptual experience begins to develop. Depending on how we look at the modulated surfaces, we see them as either rising or enveloping—they either draw us in or push us out. An organic, ambiguous sense of both enveloping and expulsive space soon turns into one of Clark's signature elements of form, an element she highlights in works like the *Casulos* (1959–1960), the last series of paintings she completes in the lead-up to her breakthrough, the works she's most celebrated for: the *Bichos*. A strong sense of relationship to the world comes forth in the spatially inflected geometric works of the 1950s—to the extent that they stage, in a very concrete way, experiences that mediate the body's place in the home and in the environment.

There is much insight to be gained regarding Clark's views on the relationship between art and architecture from a lecture she delivered in 1956 at the Belo Horizonte National School of Architecture (Escola Nacional de Arquitetura in Belo Horizonte). Belo Horizonte is the city where Clark was born, so the lecture marks a homecoming of sorts for the artist after years living and working in Rio de Janeiro. Clark begins by making a case for collaboration between artists and architects, around the same time that David Alfaro Siqueiros was arguing for the same kind of collaboration in the construction of Ciudad Universitaria in Mexico City. Clark argues for the environment as the shared field of operations for both architects and artists. She writes: "I firmly believe in the search for a fusion between 'art and life.' It is not possible for man to have this supposed indifference in relation to the environment in which he lives. If man seeks for beauty and harmony in a work of art, there are no valid reasons for him not to wish for a harmonious atmosphere in which to work and live."[14] The fusion of art and architecture coincides, in Clark's estimation, with the rise of concrete poetry and art; a case can be made for Brazilian concrete poetry as the first major literary movement in Brazil to integrate meaningfully and consistently the language of architecture.

For Clark, the absence of expressive content or the recognition of this kind of content in aspects of the work of art previously understood to be mere background marks the difference between constructivism and concretism, on the one hand, and other forms of abstraction. This sets the ground for Clark's inquiry into environment as more than plane of expression, an idea of environment as something that is "'in itself expressive.'"[15] Environment not just as plane but as substance of expression: this is an insight germane to phenomenological reflections on background and embodiment of the kind most forcefully articulated by Maurice Merleau-Ponty. Philosophically, this insight frees reflection from idealism, allowing it to dwell productively on singular, material embodied matters ("foul existence," in Hegel's estimation). For Clark and her contemporaries this same insight is what frees the poet and the artist to work on matters related to the sensorial, to the material, to the everyday, with the certainty that this work is not in any way preliminary to some other, higher, more properly artistic or more rigorously aesthetic production.

For Clark as well as for the concrete poets, faith in the expressive content of background and environment translates into powerful deployments of the embodied and the sensorial (the concrete) aspects of the work of art. These deployments, in turn, work positively, as affirmations of certain features (color, sound, texture) and certain platforms (medium, home, environment) that recede as background whenever a strict division is enforced between form and content, between medium and substance. Consumer culture thrives on an apparent recognition of the values of the material, the embodied, and the home, and to the extent that it does, consumer culture seems to erase the divisions outlined above, redeeming the material and the sensorial. Put another way, consumer culture, and advertising in particular, appears to recognize value in the material, in the sensorial and the sensual, in the home and in the environments we live in. And yet it tramples this value, subsuming it wholly to the order of capital, the order of abstraction and extraction. The practice of embodiment and the emphasis on the sensory as practiced by Clark and the concrete poets work negatively, as indictments of the logic of abstraction and extraction that operates at the heart of capitalism and is sustained, in turn, by the hierarchies of meaning of a logocentric order. But they also work positively, as an affirmation of values that are successfully deployed by, but are not reducible to, consumption and consumer culture.

Industry, Enterprise, Mass Production

Optimism and an almost electric sense of possibility dominated Brazilian culture in the 1950s,[16] and neither Clark nor the other artists associated with the neoconcrete movement were exempt from this mood. Beginning in the 1950s, high yearly growth rates coupled with structural shifts in the political economy of Brazil invested the industrial sector with a lasting and unprecedented, though qualified, degree of import.[17] The administration of Juscelino Kubitschek (1956–1961) quickly capitalized on the symbolic weight of these levels of growth, brandishing them as signs of the social and economic possibilities opened up by its politics of modernization and development.

Possibility for the artists working during the heady years of the Kubitschek administration took many shapes and forms, often around the vision of a sphere of action for the arts both expanded (in industry, particularly in graphic and industrial design) and synthesized (as evident in Siqueiros' 1950s program for Ciudad Universitaria in Mexico City and in comparable discourses in Argentina, Venezuela, and Brazil). It was in 1950 when the Escola Superior de Propaganda e Marketing opened in São Paulo, under the auspices of the Museu de Arte Moderna (MASP). A year later in 1951, Pietro Maria and Lina Bo Bardi launched the Instituto de Arte Contemporânea do Museu de Arte de São Paulo (IAC/MASP). This was followed by the opening of a number of Brazilian design firms such as Form-Inform, a collaboration between Alexandre Wollner, Geraldo de Barros, Rubem de Freitas Martins, and Walter Macedo. In 1963, the Escola Superior de Desenho Industrial opened its doors in Rio de Janeiro, marking yet another step in the professionalization and institutionalization of design in Brazil.

Cases of concrete artists working in and for industry are known and well studied, but the collusion of neoconcrete art and business interests is seldom discussed. Some poets and artists who worked in industry (Décio Pignatari and Waldemar Cordeiro) were firmly linked to the concrete movement and remained close to it after the split with the neoconcrete group. Some others (Abraham Palatnik, Aluísio Carvalho, Amilcar de Castro) belong to the group of Rio de Janeiro–based artists who subscribed early on to the concrete movement and later to neoconcretism. Some others (Mary Vieira, Almir Mavignier) were early practitioners of abstract geometric and concrete art in Brazil who later relocated to Europe. All of them left a significant body of work more properly situated in the field of industrial and graphic design. Save for a few scholarly works and a recent exhibition focused on constructivist design in Brazil, discussed below, this body of work remains relatively understudied.

There's good reason for this. Until recently, most critics found it useful to distinguish sharply between concretism and neoconcretism, ascribing to concrete artists and poets a suspect intimacy with the world of commerce while drawing distance between neoconcrete artists and the trappings of industry. This neat contrast, however, has been called into question by recent scholarship that sheds light on the many overlaps between the work of artists and writers associated with the neoconcrete movements and the industries that were beginning to gain traction in post–World War II Brazil, industrial design and advertising foremost among them.

It makes sense that neoconcretism has been conceived as separate and distinct from any kind of industry. As Sérgio B. Martins convincingly argues,[18] a teleological reading of modernism in Ferreira Gullar's theory of the nonobject and in subsequent critical accounts of Brazilian art sets up neoconcretism both as a point of origin and a foundational moment for Brazilian contemporary art, with Hélio Oiticica and Clark as founding figures. According to this narrative, the collusion of high modernist aesthetics and industry would be a misstep attributable to concrete art and poetry alone,[19] a lapse avoided by neoconcrete artists removed from politics, industry, and everything else that might compromise the nondetermination of their works.

Clark's *Bichos* (1960–1966), her most widely discussed works, started out with a plan for mass production and distribution. The *Bichos* occupy a productively problematic place in the history of art, as a key development in the history of abstract sculpture and also as a privileged example of what Ferreira Gullar called the nonobject. Since the publication of Gullar's essay (and not always to Clark's agreement) the *Bichos* are cited as exemplary models of the nonobject. They embody, like few other artworks of the period, the three negative conditions that Mónica Amor lists as characteristics of the nonobject—"not painting, not relief, not sculpture"[20]—to which we could add, following Gullar's initial formulation: not commodity. And yet Clark's *Bichos*, her most widely celebrated works, were initially intended as trade objects, as objects of mass consumption, things to be bought and sold on street corners, indistinguishable in at least one important sense from what Gullar sought to negate when he conceived of the nonobject.

Early in the creative process, Clark contemplated the possibility of taking the *Bichos* to industrial production. This fact about her original intentions remains relatively obscure, despite the implications of the hypothetical scenario of *Bichos* available for mass consumption. In an unpublished journal entry dated 1963, Clark writes: "my initial plan for the *Bichos* did not include museums or *marchands*. What I wanted to do was to make a whole bunch of them and sell them everywhere, even on street corners with street vendors. Mário Pedrosa said it would be suicide but I very much regret not doing this because I believe this is really what I should have done."[21] Had Clark gone ahead with her original intentions, some of the most intriguing aspects of these works—participation, relationality, an insistent sense of free play—would have gained in substance, but only at the risk of trivialization. Mass production and consumption of the *Bichos* might well have changed their fate in the historical record, from consecrated masterpieces to curious toys—beautifully constructed, consummately abstract toys—a quirk in the long and distinguished career of a foremost artist of the twentieth century.

Like Luiz Sacilotto's aluminum sculpture *Concreção 5730* (1957),[22] Clark's *Bichos* rest directly on the surface where they are placed, dispensing with a base. Some are large enough to fill the space of a coffee table but not so large that they can't be handled by a single person using both hands. When handled, some behave queerly, like four-way folios, their planes folding like pages of a book constructed with two spines and two ways of unfolding: left and right, up and down. Some, like the *Bicho-monumento: Monumento a todas as situações* (shaped liked a square, monumental in spirit: an homage to constructivism) are less flexible, even stiff. Most present resistance to the person handling them—they are pliable but not wieldy. The intricacy of the folds and hinge structures of the *Bichos* makes it all but impossible to predict what kind of movements will be produced with any one particular way of handling it. Their edges are smooth and geometrical, perfectly rounded or straight lines. They are hinged in a way that the movement of one surface or plane causes a movement in another one of the *Bicho*'s planes or surfaces.

Clark writes that the hinges in the *Bichos* remind her of spinal columns, and she insists that the *Bichos* have no reverse side. In an entry in her unpublished journal, she takes great pride in recounting an anecdote about a tinsmith who bought from her the equipment she was using to make the *Bichos*.[23] Having no previous knowledge of the nature of Clark's artworks, he reckoned that the *Bichos* had no reverse side. "After asking me what I was doing with this machine, I showed him the little *bicho* without saying a word. He saw it and took it in his hands, turning it this way and that way and every other way and saying: 'How interesting, it doesn't have a reverse side.'"[24] What's important for Clark is not so much the absence of a reverse side but rather the lack of a distinct inner dimension, the intentional diffusion of the line dividing what is external from what is internal.

A short text by Clark dated 1983 lists the basic traits of the *Bichos*.[25] There, Clark insists on their organic, living nature, and she reinforces this vitality with the title she gives to the series: *bichos*, animals. The *Bichos* are famously interactive. They demand participation and sustain it integrally, establishing a kind of dialogue with those who handle them, "a dialogue in which the *Bicho* has very well-defined answers of its own to the spectator's stimuli."[26] In a letter to Hélio Oiticica, Clark defines the importance of the interactivity built into the *Bichos* as the ability to unveil and make evident immanent capacities for relation in the object and in ourselves. "It is precisely this 'relationship within itself,'" Clark writes to Oiticica, "which makes [participation] alive and important."[27]

Clark's desire to make objects for mass consumption comes at a moment when the production of art in Brazil was markedly influenced both by the legacy of European constructivist movements and their pivot to industry and by developmentalist policies of industrialization and modernization vigorously instituted in Brazil throughout the 1950s. She was far from the only Brazilian artist of her generation to be drawn to industry and mass production. In reference to his own embrace of graphic and industrial design, Wollner writes: "If I left painting it was because I wanted a dialogue not with ten but with ten thousand or a million people, among other reasons."[28] At its most generic, this desire for a wider audience, for a larger dialogue, can be interpreted as a wish for a contemporary kind of subject—a consumer or mass subject. And often this desire was explicitly political.

In "Esquema geral da nova objetividade," written by Hélio Oiticica in response to the *Nova objetividade brasileira* show held at the Museu de Arte Moderna in Rio de Janeiro in April 1967, Oiticica defines "new objectivity" on the basis of six core principles: (1) a "general will toward the constructive"; (2) the "tendency toward the negation of the object and the overcoming of the canvas painting"; (3) "participation of the spectator (corporeal, tactile, visual, semantic, etc.)"; (4) "taking a stand vis-à-vis social, political, and ethical problems"; (5) a "tendency toward collective proposals"; and (6) the "reemergence and the new formulation of the concept of anti-art."[29] The production of interactive, open works of art[30] (what the artist calls, citing Mário Pedrosa and Ferreira Gullar, "anti-art") lies at the center of Oiticica's call for "new objectivity," as does the need to increase exponentially the order of production and consumption of the art object. Oiticica writes,

> You can now see that the artist has a great need not just to create but also to communicate something that for him is fundamental, but that communication should take place on a large scale, not at the level of a small elite of "experts" but even against that elite, through the proposition of unfinished works, "open" works. That is the fundamental key of the new concept of anti-art: not just a hammering against the art of the past or against old concepts . . . but the creation of new experimental conditions wherein the artist assumes the role of "proposer," or "entrepreneur," or even "educator."[31]

The role of the artist as proposer was at the core of neoconcrete aesthetics. It was embraced and theorized with particular vigor by both Oiticica and Clark. Mário Pedrosa had already made the case for the artist as educator in 1955, in the catalog for the second exhibition of the Grupo Frente, which included works by both Oiticica and Clark.[32] There isn't anything noteworthy about Oiticica's embrace of these two possibilities (the artist as proposer and the artist as educator) for the social insertion of art. What seems striking is the candor with which Oiticica conjugates the role of artist and entrepreneur. For him as for Wollner and Clark, the need for a dialogue more massive than that afforded by conventional methods of exhibition and production superseded concerns about the dangers of colluding aesthetics and industry. To my knowledge, Oiticica never quite clarified how exactly artists could or would assume the role of entrepreneurs, but the fact that he entertained this possibility is indicative of the interest neoconcrete artists had in industry and mass culture,[33] an interest that is much more complicated and widespread than what older accounts of neoconcretism would have us believe.

The manifesto where Oiticica broaches the notion of new objectivity is peppered with vaguely Marxist language—the term "dialectical" occurs no fewer than ten times over the course of fifteen pages. Oiticica's talk of "pictorial-dialectic propositions" rings strongly of the deliberately exalting Marxist rhetoric used by David Alfaro Siqueiros in many of his manifestos and programmatic writings, beginning with his 1932 lecture titled "The Vehicles of Dialectical-Subversive Painting." Siqueiros's writings are unlikely to have had any influence on the Brazilian artist, but the resonance remains suggestive, especially given their shared interest in the intersection of painting and the urban environment and given Oiticica's eventual dismissal of mural painting as a viable form of socially inserted and politicized art. Converging ideas by Oiticica and Siqueiros on art, aesthetics, politics, and industry are indicative of a shared interest: an interest in industrially viable, commercially attractive, politically disruptive art, an interest that is more than episodic, shared by two very different artists working under very different circumstances.

Throughout Oiticica's article, Clark is singled out as the most influential among the neoconcretists, as she had been in Gullar's earlier account of the movement in 1960.[34] It was Clark, Oiticica writes, who gestured toward the abandonment of the frame in painting and the base in sculpture, and it was Clark who heralded the subsequent embrace of process and participation as the primary dimensions of aesthetic experience. Participation is at the heart of what Oiticica defines as a new notion of realism, one that has little to do with figuration (though the return to figuration in the work of the "nova objetividade" artists was certainly an important factor, especially among those associated with *Nova figuração*). In short, the realist art envisioned by Oiticica, the art form that would succeed in establishing a wider dialogue with mass and consumer publics, is an abstract art. Abstraction and politics do not collide in this vision of art, and neither do political commitment and a sense of entrepreneurship. A rich field of tensions emerges from the conjugation of these terms, a field of tensions in some ways comparable to the juxtaposition of art, politics, and commercial forms operating at the heart of Siqueiros's practice of billboard muralism and in Décio Pignatari's disdain for politicized poetics "à la Neruda" in favor of an embrace of mass and consumer forms.

Evidence of political commitment in core members of neonconcretism can be found early on, in the figure of Mário Pedrosa, the principal theorist of the movement. Pedrosa was, as Sérgio B. Martins notes, "a former Trotskyist militant . . . committed to political transformation" and "convinced that the role of art in this process was not simply illustrative."[35] For Martins, Pedrosa's commitment to a politically expedient notion of art resolves itself by recourse to the formalist notion of defamiliarization. In

Martins's reading of the political in Pedrosa's understanding of art, "art would simply communicate the promise of a renewed perception (based on the notion of 'good form'), one that contained, in its turn, the potential of breaking with the established, utilitarian relations that structured capitalist society."[36] The grounds for this sort of intervention are, Martins argues, the autonomy of the art form, the specificity of its purposelessness, "its privileged position for tackling form at its purest . . . and subsequently inform[ing] other spheres of activity from a 'spiritually' elevated viewpoint."[37]

Design, Environment, Object Relations

Functionality is the main concern Jean Baudrillard raises in "Design and Environment," where he theorizes design as a rationalizing, aestheticized bridge between beauty and industry. Baudrillard cites the Bauhaus as the movement responsible for a radically functional understanding of both object and environment. "It is the Bauhaus," Baudrillard argues, "that institutes this universal semantization of the environment in which everything becomes the object of a calculus of function and signification."[38] Baudrillard is keen to emphasize the universal reach of the Bauhaus principle of functionality, its grand design for a total and thorough organization of lived environments and the objects therein contained. The Bauhaus, Baudrillard writes, "projects the basis of a rational conception of environmental totality for the first time";[39] it derives "from the will of functionalism to impose itself in its order (like political economy in its order) as the *dominant rationality*, susceptible to giving account of everything and to directing all processes."[40]

In line with the primacy of function, the object theorized by the Bauhaus undergoes radical severance or alienation, consisting, in essence, of "the dissociation of every complex subject-object relation into simple, analytic, rational elements that can be recombined in functional ensembles and which then take on status as the environment."[41] Baudrillard situates this vision of objects as separate, autonomous, self-enclosed entities within a larger history of political economy. In the opening sentences of his essay, Baudrillard notes that "not all cultures produce objects: the concept is peculiar to ours, born of the industrial revolution."[42] Like Marx before him and like Taussig after him, Baudrillard reads alienation, the dissociation of human life from society and environment, as the more expansive correlate of the detachment operated by design, the detachment of people from the objects they produce and consume, from the objects of work and the objects of home: the objects we live with. Viewed as such, design and commodity capitalism—the political economy of the sign, as Baudrillard reads it—are part and parcel of the same logic of alienation.

The interpretive power of Baudrillard's poststructuralist approach to the understanding of capitalism is evident in its capacity to distinguish between thing, object, and commodity form. In Baudrillard's reading, capitalism would move the object away from the opacity of the thing and toward the abstract, rational transparency of the commodity. This operation is constituted, much like the operation of the sign, by virtue of a split or bifurcation.[43] It works, in other words, by abstraction. This, in turn, makes the object available for operations of equivalence: a value can be assigned to the object once it has been split from its context, a value entirely removed from its nature as thing. And just like the thing-turned-commodity loses all ambivalence and value beyond its use- and exchange-value, so, then, the object of design is radically reduced to two functions: beauty and utility.[44]

Baudrillard reads a perversion of the aesthetic in the way it is made to work rationally and functionally under the logic of design. The aesthetic here, what stands for the aesthetic under the principles of design, is never gratuitous, never without purpose. Baudrillard hammers this point home by drawing a link between the puritanism of the bourgeois revolution and the asceticism (the will to functionality above all ornament, above all excess, above all pleasure) of the Bauhaus and of design. "Like the capitalist revolution that instituted the 'spirit of enterprise' and the basis of political economy as early as the sixteenth century," Baudrillard writes, "the Bauhaus revolution is *puritan*. Functionalism is ascetic."[45]

Puritanism and ascetic functionalism do not encompass the range of design projects Daniela Name gathered together for *Diálogo concreto*, a 2008 exhibition of constructivism and Brazilian design. Some of the design work included in this exhibition (Wollner's logotype for Sardinhas Coqueiro, for example) certainly does fit the description of design as ascetic functionalism. Asceticism here is a function of rationality and calculation, of the way they often override any other dimensions of what we define as design. But some other forms of design, such as Lygia Pape's work for the Piraquê brand of crackers and biscuits, are animated by a warm kind of joy. For this reason, Name's choice of memory and seduction as the curatorial threads that bring together her exhibition is noteworthy. Recalling the conversations that led to the focus on affective memory, Name writes: "Each 'I remember' [uttered in conversation] worked, throughout the last few months, like one more brick in the conceptual foundation of *Diálogo concreto*: the understanding that the primordial goal of these design projects seems to be precisely to captivate and seduce spectators by means of their own memory. . . . Memory as bond and complicity. Memory as seduction."[46]

Like many of her peers, Pape (1927–2004) worked with a wide range of media and alternated her work as artist with projects linked to industry. With the Grupo Frente in Rio de Janeiro and alongside Lygia Clark, Pape produced and exhibited abstract geometric paintings in the 1950s, later moving on to sculpture. Pape showed early interest in the concrete movement and constructed poems rendered with light (*Poemas luz*, 1956–1957) as well as three-dimensional object-poems (*Poemas objeto*, 1956–1957). Later, she signed the "Neoconcrete Manifesto" (1957) and with the poet Reynaldo Jardim (1926–) she conceived and staged the *Ballet Neoconcreto* (1958) and *Ballet Neoconcreto II* (1959),[47] the first featuring dancers dressed as geometrical figures moving across a stage, and the second pushing the level of abstraction further to a precise play of surfaces oscillating between foreground and figure, figure and background.

A period television advertisement for matches by Fósforos de Brazil features animated matchboxes and matches marching in a castle-like setting, of their own accord, a "legion" of handy home goods in the service of the homemaker. The stark geometric shapes of the matchboxes and the matches, together with the animated nature of these shapes, bears a striking resemblance to the spectacle of the *Ballet Neoconcreto*, which may or may not have been the inspiration for the TV ad. What they share in common, both *Ballet* and television advertisement, is the uncanny vision of living, moving geometric shapes: a nightmarish realization of the neoconcrete dream of making geometric form organic, alive.

From the late 1950s to the early 1960s, Pape worked on a trilogy of book-objects—*Livro da criação*, *Livro da arquitetura*, *Livro do tempo*—extraordinary in their use of photography, landscape, and abstraction. Later she worked on film merchandising, designing posters for celebrated examples of Cinema Novo (Nelson Pereira dos Santos's *Vidas secas* and Glauber Rocha's *Deus e o Diabo na Terra do Sol*). She also produced short experimental films of her own. In 1968, the year of the Ato Institucional Número Cinco (AI-5), Pape produced and organized one of her most memorable works, *Divisor*. Part public performance and part living sculpture, *Divisor* is staged with a large white panel of fabric with holes just large enough for people to poke their heads through. In its first unveiling in 1968 as well as in a recent reenactment for the twenty-ninth São Paulo Biennial (2010), a small mass of people wore the panel of fabric collectively on their shoulders, moving in precarious and spontaneous unison. *Divisor* is a powerful display of simultaneous distance and unity, in the same spirit as Lygia Clark's "biological architectures" from the 1960s.

From the 1960s onward Pape conjugated art with her work as creative director of merchandising ("visual programmer," as she and several of her colleagues working in graphic design called themselves) for the Piraquê brand of crackers. She describes her work for Piraquê in an interview from 2003, where she states:

> It was a moment during which we experimented greatly in all areas. I particularly did not like being restricted to any one medium. I enjoyed framing dialogues between different media and I ended up taking sculpture to the work I completed as visual programmer. I always had a lot of fun working on the packaging for Piraquê. I loved going to the printing press, I would rush to Madureira to check on the proofs. . . . The red color in the packaging really popped in the supermarket aisles. You could see the products from a distance.[48]

In Pape's eyes, no conflict exists between her work as artist and her work in merchandising. On the contrary, for Pape these two facets of her creative output belong to one continuum. That a sense of continuity exists between her abstract, experimental artworks and the work she completed for industry is, I think, precisely what makes her work so compelling. Pape's work demands a reading that places this continuity as part of a larger tradition of experimental avant-garde artists making their way in and out of industry—a tradition leading back to the many fascinating points of contact between abstraction and the decorative arts in Zurich Dada[49]—and between abstraction and utilitarianism in Russian constructivism.[50]

Constructivist principles are clearly at work in Pape's designs for the Piraquê brand. Like the logotypes designed by Wollner and other Brazilian artists during this period, the logotype Pape designed for Piraquê is starkly minimalist and made entirely of geometric figures: two circles, one large and one smaller, one inside the other, and a line uniting the center of the smaller circle with the edge of the larger one. These are all the elements of her design. The effect is simple but effective, evocative of both the letter "P" (the first letter of the brand advertised) and the round shape of the crackers and cheese puffs sold under the brand. Grids are the main principle of organization that Pape uses in the design of the packaging, and as Name notes, Pape's take on the grid, like Oiticica's, has a playfulness to it that puts it at a distance from the rigidity of the modernist grid.[51] The use of real crackers and cheese puffs for the production of photographic images printed onto the packaging (another innovation by Pape) falls in line with the desire to showcase the texture, the *faktura*, the tectonics of the materials used in the products advertised.

As part of her merchandising work for the Piraquê brand, Pape designed a now-familiar type of packaging that was, however, very innovative at the time Pape created it. This packaging stays close to the actual shape of cookies and crackers (circles, squares) to yield long, elongated, cylindrically shaped parcels with a distinctly sculptural quality to them. As Name notes, the new parcels entailed a new approach to the way packaging materials were cut and glued together.[52] This is the kind of industrial innovation that constructivist artists aspired to achieve in their experimental "laboratory" work in Russia in the 1920s.[53] What Pape's design does is to make a commercial product distinctive, easily identifiable, memorable, and worthy of attention. Attention is what's at stake here, as is memory (remembering what the packaging looks like, creating lasting memories woven into and out of the visual impact of the packaging) and seduction (drawing the viewer's eye, awakening desire, making consumers want one product over similar ones). Inasmuch as packaging mediates the presentation of objects in market capitalism, Pape's commitment to it and the artistic rigor with which she approaches it constitute a forceful, formal investigation into the workings of desire in consumer culture. What's notable is that this work was completed both with artistic ambition and for commercial purposes. Yet this portion of Pape's work is barely mentioned in the extant bibliography on neoconcretism. Perhaps the success of Pape's design work (her packaging is still used, with modifications, by the Piraquê brand, and her sculptural way of parceling crackers is now standard worldwide) was also its undoing as artwork. More precisely, perhaps it was the site of Pape's success, the field of operations where this was achieved, that erases her design work from the canons of art history. New ways of seeing, new ways of feeling emerge from Pape's "visual programming," but these ways of seeing and ways of feeling belong at home, to everyday interaction with objects.

Relational Objects, "Routine Gestures," the Fetishism of Commodities

It is not uncommon for critics to remark on the soundness with which Lygia Clark moved from one stage of her work to the next. A progression in her concerns with interactivity, with participation, with embodiment, and with abstraction can be seen from her early, architecturally informed, abstract geometric paintings to the unfolding of the vertical plane in the hinged structures of the *Bichos*. The next step in this narrative is more diffuse, much less wieldy. It begins with *Caminhando* (1963; fig. 4.3), her first attempt at dislodging her propositions from any kind of permanent, fetishized object form, and her first foray into the ritualized, meditative, immersive experiences that would characterize the last quarter century of her production. With her knack for finding evocatively synthetic titles for her works and proposals, Clark referred to this stage of her trajectory as *nostalgia for the body*:

> I have called that phase of my work, the most varied of all: *Nostalgia do corpo*. I understood afterward that one of the properties of *Caminhando* had been radicalized here: The *proposition* (the word "work," which denotes the passivity of the result of a previous labor, is not the right one here) *makes us aware of our own bodies*. I assembled a large number of worthless materials which, when grasped, rediscovered by the touch, induced a stimulating trauma.[54]

After *Nostalgia do corpo*, the rediscovery of the overlooked, "worthless" materials of quotidian existence soon becomes a driving force behind Clark's work. The rationale for this rediscovery lies not in the materials themselves—Clark goes on to talk about the abandonment, the "suppression" of objects. It lies in the sense of embodiment that the texture of these materials brings to consciousness. Eliciting awareness of one's own body was the principal objective of the series of simple, relational objects that Clark began to construct from 1966 onward. The importance of these objects for our understanding of Clark's work is paramount. Every one of the proposals Clark formulated in the last two decades of her life was structured around these worthless objects. The insistence with which she returns to them begs closer analysis.

As Clark began working in earnest on her relational objects, the manual labor they required—the physical production of her relational objects—began to look more and more like the work of arts and crafts, the kind of labor one associates with domestic spaces and female subjects. Already

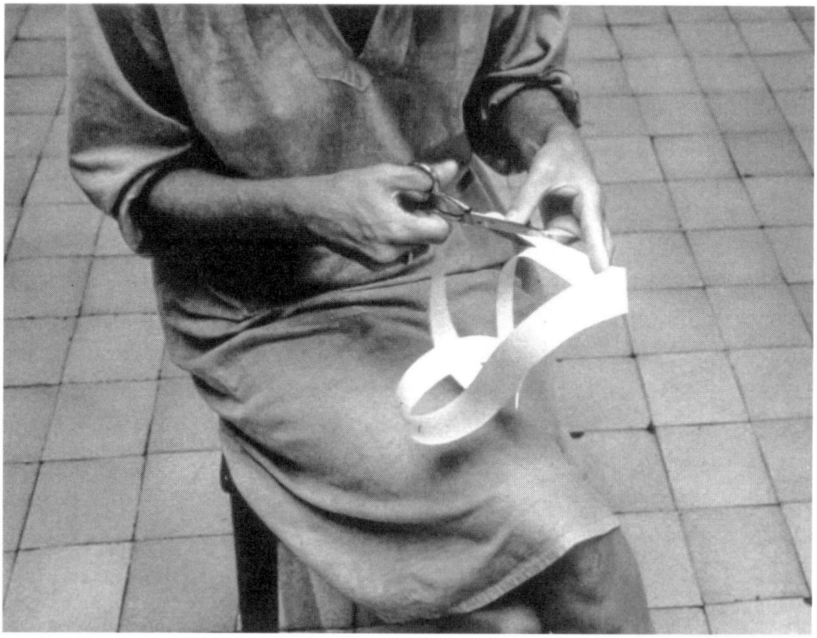

Figure 4.3. Lygia Clark making a *Caminhando* (1963), with paper and scissors. Photographer unknown. Courtesy of Associação Cultural "O Mundo de Lygia Clark."

with the *Bichos*, which she constructed with tools for metalworking, Clark had distanced her methods of production from the rarefied forms of artisanship characteristic of painting and sculpture. With the relational objects, Clark builds on this trend, moving further from traditional methods of art making and closer to the methods of arts and crafts.

Clark begins her work on a new vision of the object, the relational object, in Paris, under conditions of need and precariousness. She recalls the beginning of this enterprise in a letter to Oiticica from 1968 where she writes: "I've already begun work by collecting pebbles on the street, because there's no money for materials! I use everything that comes my way, such as empty potato sacks, onion sacks, the plastic film used to wrap clothing from the dry cleaners, and even the gloves I use to dye my hair!"[55] Clark laid out the basic conceptual scaffolding of her *objetos relacionais* in retrospect, in an article titled "Da supressão do objetos (anotações)" published in the legendary single-issue journal *Navilouca* (1974).[56] The title of her article gives a measure of the conflicted views on the notion of the object Clark was then contemplating. In her estimation, the object had "lost its meaning as a platform of communication,"[57] but even so, Clark invested the object with an increased capacity for relation, for relationality, though not the kind of relationship established by means of language or other such forms of symbolic communication. "By means of small objects without any value, like elastic bands, stones, plastic bags, I formulate sensorial objects, the touch of which provokes sensations which I immediately identify with the body."[58]

The first relational object Clark produced under these conditions was *Pedra e ar* (1966; fig. 4.4), striking for the manner in which it synthesizes all the major concerns in Clark's proposals of the period (participation, embodiment, ritual). The proposal is simple enough: take a plastic bag, fill it up with your own breath, and seal it, then place a pebble on one of its corners and let it rest there while you hold the bag with both hands. Simple as it is, the proposal demands full attention. Any movement of the hands, any change in the pressure the hands exert either lifts the pebble, risking its ejection, or lets it sink into the air-filled bag. A ritual sets in. The warmth of one's own breath trapped inside the bag adds sensuality to the experience. The title of the relational object anchors this experience in natural materials—rocks, air—and in the basic physical qualities of these materials: firmness and solidity, lightness and etherealness.

Relational objects are timely meditations on the notion of objectivity, in a moment when our understanding of objects and things was being redrawn against a logic of commodity capitalism. Consumer culture is the proper context for Clark's relational objects, the background against which they gain their measure and their meaning. In Clark's work with relational objects, the simplicity of the thing (simplicity as opaqueness and not as transparency) gains significance as part of an expanded field of relational ontologies.

Clark's inquiry into object relations overlaps with a wave of studies on objects and objectification, part of a renewed interest in consumption and consumer culture in the 1970s (Herbert Marcuse, Jean-Paul Sartre) and 1980s (Jean Baudrillard, Daniel Miller, Sut Jhally). Baudrillard stresses the semiotic constitution of objects by a "political economy of signs." Jhally, on his part, argues for an understanding of objects as symbols. In line with Baudrillard's critique of the "ideological genesis of needs," Jhally writes: "the recognition of the fundamentally symbolic aspect of people's use of things must be the minimum starting point for a discourse that concerns objects. Specifically, the old distinction between basic (physical) and secondary (psychological) needs must be superseded."[59] Jhally extends this argument to encompass what he calls "the symbolic constitu-

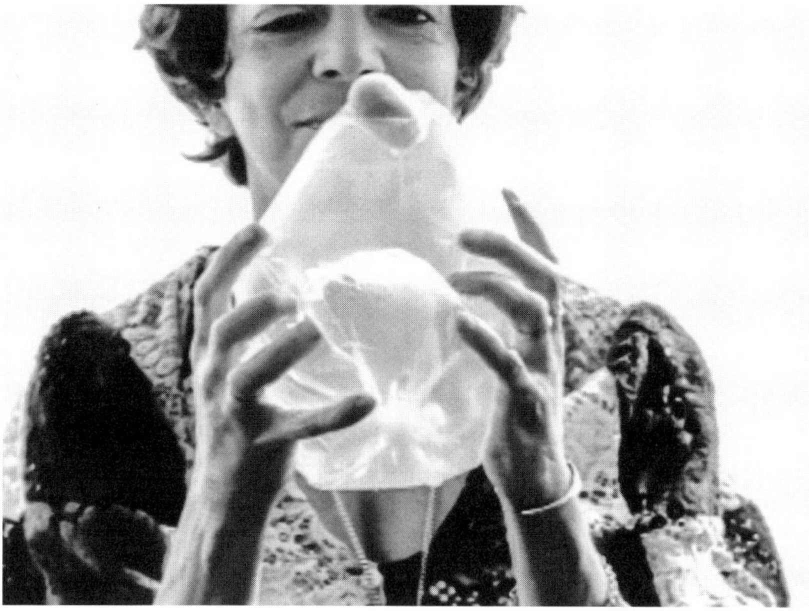

Figure 4.4. Lygia Clark, *Pedra e ar* (1966). Courtesy of Associação Cultural "O Mundo de Lygia Clark."

tion of utility."[60] For Jhally, the fundamental question confronting scholars interested in objectification and commodity capitalism is a matter of making distinctions fine enough to differentiate between terms that are intimately related—objects and objectification, the material and the materialistic—but that merit a closer look: "the problem of capitalist commodities," Jhally argues, "has not been sufficiently distinguished from the problem of objects in general."[61]

In the short text titled "To Rediscover the Meaning of Our Routine Gestures," Clark recounts how a fractured wrist after a car accident provided the materials for her first relational object:

> I had fractured my wrist in a car accident. It was coated in a kind of paste that had to be kept hot: My hand was imprisoned in a plastic bag kept in place by an elastic band, forming a sort of watertight sheath. One day I tore off the plastic bag, blew it up and sealed it with the elastic band; taking a small stone, I tried to hold it in place by pressing the bag with both hands on one of the points of the air pocket; then I let it be engulfed, thus mimicking an extremely disturbing birth. I was bowled over by the experience, which also marked the end of my crisis. I started to make a huge number of quite different new propositions.[62]

There is much symbolism in Clark's description of how she constructs this first relational object (the vision of the moving pebble as "an extremely disturbing birth" is a case in point), but not in the way she actually constructs the object. The materials she chooses are stripped of meaning beyond texture. This allows them to blend into the background of everyday experience. This is what makes them worthless things. It is as if Clark was deliberately resisting the displacement at work in symbolism. Indeed, for Clark the challenge is to create rituals and objects that allow a person to cultivate radical forms of presence and intensive experiences of perception. "If something exists," Clark states in an interview dated 1968, "to try to place a symbolic sense upon it is only to weaken it."[63]

Precariousness and creativity seem closely linked together in this story of how the relational objects came to be, but Clark is quick to shut down any comparisons between the work she undertakes, *arte povera*, and other art movements that, in Clark's reading, fetishize the status of refuse. The enveloping, sensorial qualities of the materials Clark uses in the construction of her relational objects plays a role as significant as their status as objects of refuse. In any case, what seems true is that situations of emotional, affective, or psychic precariousness—the crises Clark so often identified as preludes to periods of intense creativity—are triggers as strong, if not stronger, for Clark's work as was the poverty and lack of access to "art materials" that gave rise to her use of refuse in the construction of the relational objects.

Kurt Schwitters's use of refuse in the making of art objects is a revealing precedent for Clark's use of disposable materials. A key figure in the Hanover Dada movement, Schwitters embodies like few other artists from the historical avant-gardes the shift theorized by Haroldo de Campos when he writes that while "the tendency in classical aesthetics is to consider the art object *sub specie aeternitatis*, contemporary art . . . seems to have incorporated the relative and the transitory as an aspect of [the art object's] very being."[64] Campos identifies Schwitters as the one artist who marks "the defeat of the *primado incontrastável* of noble materials—marble, perennial bronze—in sculpture," a defeat exemplified by Schwitters's *merz*-column, "constructed out of the most diverse fragments taken from everyday refuse."[65] In line with his narrative of a modernist path leading to neoconcretism, Ferreira Gullar presents Schwitters's use of found objects and refuse as a moment in a process later expanded by the nonobject.[66]

At the same time that she formulated the notion of relational objects, Clark became aware of the potential for political incisiveness latent in her work and her proposals. For Clark, the immediate impact of these objects on social and political events is grounded in their power to draw our consciousness to "routine gestures," as the title of the article cited above suggests. "It was at that time," Clark writes, "that the political and social nature of my work became evident to me: Since it was a liberation for man, the release of a repressed desire, since the participant rediscovered a sensory energy deliberately numbed by our social habits, those experiments had a revolutionary impact and were also received as such."[67]

To date, most (though certainly not all) critical assessments of Clark's oeuvre remain somewhat timid about the political dimension of her work. This is a function of the nature of Clark's works and proposals, their abstruseness and the tenacity with which they resist reductive readings. This is also, to a large extent, a remnant of earlier, influential readings of Clark's works and neoconcretism in general. Brito's study of neoconcretism is a case in point. His stance regarding the link between neoconcrete art and industry also holds for his assessment of the political inflection of neoconcretism. It seems clear to me, however, as it does to others, that a palpable and at times explicit sense of politicization is manifest in the work of Lygia Clark. That the political dimension of Clark's work remains more or less invisible, or more or less articulated, is a function of the categories we use to distinguish between politicized and "apolitical" artworks. In Clark's case, a language of micropolitics as theorized by Suely Rolnik, or a theory of sensorial politics—the intervention in current social events at the level of the sensorial—as elaborated by Davide Panagia, and my own revisioning of homemaking, domestic space, and the materials that populate domestic space (the materials that sustain "the meaning of our routine gestures," to use Clark's formulation) all generate political readings of her work.

Guy Brett points to one such reading in his interpretation of Clark's relational objects as effective agents of integration (of subjects and objects, of material worlds and inner lives), in an essay where he argues for Clark's work as a gesture of resistance to what Jonathan Crary historicizes as a separation of perceiving subjects and objects of perception. In Brett's reading, "it becomes fascinating to interpret Lygia Clark's experiments in the 1960s as a pioneering attempt to re-integrate visual perception with the body as a whole, to reconnect the interior and the exterior world, and the knower and the known."[68] Theorizing her attempts at this reintegration of perceiving subject and perceived object, Clark makes reference to the psychoanalytic notion of introjection, a key concept in her understanding of the experiences she intended to trigger with her proposals. "Organicity, the full void," Clark writes, "all the concepts I proposed before in the object are now introverted in the interior of the person. Man, object of himself, as Mário Pedrosa says."[69]

Paulo Herkenhoff takes the point further, emphasizing Clark's will to create situations of interpretation beyond the self and the body, situations where the body, and by implication the self, is made porous to (and ultimately consubstantial with) other bodies, other objects. "This correlation of self which is completed in the world," Herkenhoff writes, "defines the politics of alterity. It is difficult to hold that Neo-Concrete art was made by apolitical artists. . . . The aesthetics of the senses implies a politics of the senses."[70] The difficulty, as Herkenhoff notes, is finding a language and a conceptual framework that allow us to recognize the relevance of neoconcrete art to immediate social events without thereby reducing it to "the 'ideological servitude' of committed art."[71] The challenge, then, is learning to recognize political expediency in artworks and proposals like those of Clark without doing away with the nondetermination that keeps them vital.

Here is another way to conceive of the political weight of Clark's relational objects. It has to do with the way consciousness changes with the rediscovery of the "sensory energy" latent in our everyday gestures. More to the point, it has to do with the way our consciousness of objects, of subjects, and of the relationships that hold between subjects and objects changes by means of the kind of attention Clark cultivates: attention to our everyday routines and to the materials that sustain these routines. The term "relational objects" highlights what was most important about these propositions: neither the objects (themselves precarious, ephemeral, startling in their material and formal simplicity and stripped of anything that might make them valuable in and of themselves) nor the vitality participants bring to these objects but rather the kind of relations these objects can sustain. The *objetos relacionais* work with sensation. They work with feeling. And they don't work until they are manipulated, which doesn't mean that they are inert or entirely passive. The effects produced within the framework of participation and manipulation of the *objetos relacionais* do not suggest a transposition of qualities from subject to relational object and vice versa so much as they reveal the dialogic tension within each of these terms. Relational objects behave, then, agentially. They move and they seem to know how to move, as Clark suggests in reference to the *Bichos*. Subjects, in turn, are relieved from the chokehold of symbolism, free to dwell on meanings immanent to the material dimensions (the textures) of relational objects.

We get a better sense of the larger implications of Clark's work in reference to what Michael Taussig theorizes as the "dominance of 'thinghood,'"[72] an ontology and a structure of power resting on principles of identity and self-containment avowed over and above the social and human relations sustaining everything that we hold as existing. For Taussig, the "dominance of thinghood" takes place when conditions of labor and production are subsumed to the logic of commodity capitalism. Thinghood as ontology gains further grounding with the dissemination of the products of this system of labor, products invested with as high a degree of self-containment and abstraction as the labor-time used to produce them. The theory of objects and objectivity that emerges from the neoconcrete movement and from the notion of relational objects in particular can be read against just such dissemination.

Close analysis of Clark's relational objects reveals opportunities for a revision of the subject/object dichotomy, such that certain imbrications, confusions, and transpositions of the figures of the subject and the object can be recognized as something other than the result of an alienated consciousness, something perhaps quite the opposite of this: a figure for liberation, in the most polemical and compelling reading. Through objectification we can envision the incipience of a concrete ethics: the recognition of and regard for something other than the self—something that is, in the first instance, another object, another body. Regard for texture and other such intensive sensorial experiences provides the basis for this new ethic, this thoroughly ethical aesthetic. Regard for texture, for feeling, and for objects of texture and feeling would constitute a first and necessary step toward recognition of alterity. But alterity arrived at by means of texture is a different kind of alterity. It is more intimate, more involved, a recognition that implies something more than mere regarding, something closer to holding or physically introjecting.

To argue, then, for the vindication of sensation and the sensorial even when they operate as the primary modes of engagement of commodity culture is not to recast our relationships with commodities in a positive, affirmative light, but rather to extricate the object from the fetters that the commodity form has imposed on it and, by extension, on our relationship to it. This work, of course, must be conceived in terms of our relationships to objects as much as it must be conceived as a shift in our relationships with each other.

A culture of consumption thrives on the presence of objects, and Clark's work picks up on this burgeoning presence of objects and the function they play as mediators of relationships. The emphasis in neoconcrete theory on the relational nature of the nonobject, an emphasis made evident in works by Clark and in her relational objects in particular, can be read as a gesture of resistance, or better, as an indictment against the presumptive self-containment of objects, the apparent naturalness of their self-containment and their self-bounded nature. Clark's relational objects can also be read as a form of contestation to the notion of subjectivity that corresponds to the ontology of objects as self-contained, self-bounded units. Clark's work thus rises as a form of resistance to what Suely Rolnik describes, in her reading of Clark's artworks, as "the figure of the 'individual,' a self-enclosed entity who extracts his or her feeling from an image lived as essence and maintains itself identical to itself, immune to otherness and its turbulent effects."[73]

Relational objects thus function as ways of imagining the relational nature not just of experience but of the very constitution of both subjects and objects of experience. They operate as that which Irene V. Small theorizes, in reference to the work of Oiticica, as "an epistemological device, that is, *as a material, embodied model of emergent knowledge*."[74] As epistemological device, the relational object is aesthetic (in the larger, richer sense of term elaborated by Terry Eagleton, Susan Buck-Morss, and others), inasmuch as the forms of knowledge it reveals operate at the level of sense perception. And as aesthetic device, the *objeto relacional* models emergent knowledges as much as it models rising processes of subjectification, structuring new sensibilities and new possibilities of experience, sensibilities defiant in how they embrace materiality during a moment of history defined by vicious appropriations—real and symbolic—of material cultures. Not just what becomes available for cognition (texture, in all its turbulence) but the way the subject stands (material, embodied) in the face of what is cognizable is what the relational object forces us to reckon with. That it does so precisely during a moment when the tangible and the material dimensions of experience are being colonized by the ascendant ambitions of consumer capitalism is the more compelling, for what this tells us about possible objects, viable subjectivities, and plausible courses of action that remain immanent to a capitalist social order and available for deviant appropriations.

What I'm proposing here is a reading of the *objetos relacionais* that sees them existing and operating not only outside the frameworks on the art institution but within the space and the temporality of the home, and so of the social and material conditions of consumer culture. Previous readings of the *objetos relacionais* see their fierce resistance to conventional frameworks of art reception and exhibition as evidence of their ability to defy the logic of exhibition, reification, spectacle, and commodification. For Clark, though, the move beyond art seems to be animated, in my view, less by a sense of abandonment (of museums, galleries, art) or escape than by a desire to affirm and release the suppressed pleasures, cognitive and bodily, of everyday experience. Thus read, the move from one institutional context to the next (from exhibition to classroom to therapy room to her own living room) registers less as a critique of or reaction against the objectification and commodification of the artwork and more as an inquiry into the possibilities an object (a special kind of object: a relational object) has to offer outside the frame of the museum, in quotidian space. Each stop in the series of institutional spaces traveled by the *objetos relacionais* reveals one such possibility: as props in participatory art, as objects of knowledge and theoretical devices, as therapeutic tools, as instruments for structuring a self. Put another way, what animates the itinerancy of Clark's *objetos relacionais* seems to be less an overcoming of the artwork as object (Gullar's vision for the nonobject) and more an openness to object relations as integral components of knowledge formation and of subjectification, processes that extend well beyond the institutional confines of art.

At Home, with Objects, Structuring a Self

Psychology and psychoanalysis loom large in Clark's work. In Brazil in the 1950s, Clark and other members of the neoconcrete movement were influenced by Mário Pedrosa's interest in Gestalt theory, which became a theoretical basis for the movement,[75] together with Maurice Merleau-Ponty's writings on phenomenology. Clark spent time under analysis in Paris, including a two-year period with Pierre Fèdida from 1972 to 1974. Extant studies of Clark's work stress her admiration for Donald Winnicott, whose work on object relations theory has clear points of contact with Clark's *objetos relacionais* and with her *Estruturação do self*. Both concepts, Christine Macel argues, are derived directly from Winnicott's work and from his writings on transitional objects in particular.[76] Winnicott and Didier Anzieu, Macel argues, are the two figures who most influenced Clark. Clark herself singles out Eugen Herrigel's *Zen and the Art of Archery*

(1948) as the book that most influenced her; it mirrors some of her concerns and reflections in a way that deserves more attention. It seems to me, though, that the psychoanalyst who comes closer to Clark's thought is Marion Milner. It is unclear to me whether Clark read Milner's writings, but in any case (direct influence is not crucial for the comparative approach I'm pursuing here), it seems sensible to include Milner in the constellation of object relations theorists important for our understanding of Clark's *objetos relacionais*. Comparing Clark's works to Milner's writings on art and psychology allows for mutual illumination of two approaches to the notion of the object. It is not, as it may seem on first reading, an accounting of the direction or the provenance of influence.

The most generative aspect of comparatively reading the work of Clark and Milner lies in their shared approach to the study of the relationships that hold between conscious subjects and the objects that people their existence. Like Clark, Milner began writing not as an analyst but as an artist with a gift for self-observation and a marked interest in the creative process. Milner wrote at length about "hallucinatory" moments, "moments when the original 'poet' in each of us created the outside world for us, by finding the familiar in the unfamiliar"; these moments, Milner argues, "are perhaps forgotten by most people; or else they are guarded in some secret place of memory because they were too much like visitations of the gods to be mixed with everyday thinking."[77] Milner's vision is astounding for the power with which she bridges two registers—the poetic and the divine—that are crucially intertwined, though rarely rendered together with such vision and such clarity.

A concern for the divine comes through in Clark's writings from the 1960s onward. In "The Full-Emptiness" (1960) she writes: "art is only valid in the ethico-religious sense, internally connected to the inner elaboration of the artist in its deepest sense, which is existential."[78] Later, in 1983, Clark returns to this language of the spiritual: "That which was previously an element of spiritual wealth has today lost all meaning. In this apparent emptiness, man finds it difficult to understand the new field which has been opened to him as a benefit, as this new field as not yet been incorporated within his sense of being. . . . It is from the spiritual emptiness that the new meaning will arise."[79] Milner, on her part, grounds her discussion of spirituality on a fundamental belief in creativity as the original, determinant aspect of human nature, the innate capacity to make and shape a world guided neither by precepts nor by universal principles, but by the interaction between the material world and the inner life of the subject.

The "original" poet, then: not just (not only) she who writes poetry, but she who makes a world "by finding the familiar in the unfamiliar."

The more one reads through the body of writings that Milner left behind, the more this finding of the familiar in the unfamiliar shapes up to be a very broad but very precise kind of interaction with the world—the kind that allows one to leave an imprint of one's own self in people and places one inhabits, the kind that also leaves us open to the world, expanding our capacity to regard it, to hold it, to incorporate parts of it and give ourselves to it. Two aspects of the divine are here encompassed: the world-creating faculty and the ability to hold, womb-like, the world and those who live in it. A third aspect, while crucial, is not self-evident. "Visitation" brings to mind the appearance of the divine as something transformative: as epiphany (as apparition and revelation) but also as possible disaster. To the extent that the "visitation of the gods," the creative act turned event of creation, is powerful enough to reveal new ways of relating self to world, it is also powerful enough to destabilize us, pushing dangerously close to destruction or dissolution, far away from the structures we rely on to make sense of ourselves and the world.

The danger of subjective dissolution was well known by Clark, who witnessed destabilization in the people who interacted with her works after she exhibited the *objetos relacionais* at the Venice Biennale in 1968. Later on, the potential to unsettle latent in her works would become more and more patent. Students who took part in the seminar she taught at the Sorbonne in the 1970s, discussed below, often left the exercises staged by Clark feeling disturbed, and Clark recognized this. In reference to *Corpo coletivo*, the name she gave to the experiences formulated at the Sorbonne, Clark writes: "this exchange is not a pleasant thing. The idea is that a person 'vomits' life-experience when taking part of a proposition. This 'vomit' is going to be swallowed by the others, who will immediately vomit their inner 'contents' too. It is therefore an exchange of psychic qualities and the word communication is too weak to express what happens in the group."[80] Guy Brett remarked on the discomfort that sometimes overcame the people who put on Clark's *Máscaras sensoriais*. "Experiences of participants might not be blissful: They might be disturbing or terrifying, just as the abyss, or the void, may be experienced in a positive or a negative way."[81]

The disturbances caused by Clark's *Máscaras sensoriais*, by her *Arquiteturas biológicas*, and by other related propositions can be read therapeutically, as ways to address larger, more baleful ills. Milner cites William

Blake to draw a link between the expedient imagination, the imagination of "narrow purpose"—an echo of capitalist reason defined as purpose-driven, narrowly defined reason—and suffering. She locates the therapeutic moment precisely in the overcoming of this narrow mode of attention: "when anyone discovers how to stop seeing the world with the narrow focused attention of expediency, stops interfering and trying to use it for his own purposes . . . something like a miracle can happen, the whole world can become transfigured."[82] What's crucial for Milner is the ability to engage the world creatively, which is to say, to engage it in a manner that is different from any form that has come to function prescriptively.[83] Milner argues that this is a kind of engagement with the world to which we had access as children. "And it is surely," she writes, "a state that is known at moments, to all of us, in childhood, but so often entirely lost in the purpose-driven life of adulthood; although we can find it again either actively or vicariously, through the arts."[84]

In an essay titled "The Role of Illusion in Symbol Formation" and in reference to the work of Herbert Read, Milner reflects on the function of creative and symbolic thought, arguing that "the original function (demonstrable in the history of civilization) of the identification underlying symbolism was a means of adaptation to reality"; "what later generations know and regard only as a symbol," Milner writes, "had in earlier stages of mental life full and real meaning and value."[85] What Milner is trying to demonstrate in this essay is "the possibility that some form of artistic ecstasy may be an essential phase in adaptation to reality, since it marks the moment in which new and vital identifications are established."[86] The invitation Milner makes here is to see symbolism and symbol-making in a fuller light, in such a way that we see a place for symbolic thought beyond the physical, mental, and developmental spaces to which it is mostly confined: childhood, the world of the imaginary, the world of make-believe.

Regression[87] and a childlike disposition toward language and the world emerges in the writings of Mário Pedrosa from the late 1940s and early 1950s as a possible affirmative, desirable outcome of the aesthetic experience. In "Arte, necessidade vital," a lecture he delivered for the closing of an art exhibition at the Centro Psiquiátrico Nacional in Rio de Janeiro, Pedrosa cites Charles Baudelaire to make the case for artistic genius as "*childhood recovered* at will."[88] In the context of an art exhibition where works by mentally ill patients were on view, and in the larger context of the experiments in art and psychiatry then being led by Dr. Nise da Silveira in the same psychiatric center where these works were on view,[89]

Pedrosa's point must be read as an affirmation of the creative capacities of children and the mentally ill as much as it should be read as a critical relativization of the rational and intellectual faculties predominant in functional adults. In his closing lecture, Pedrosa combines the cursory vindication of the unconscious and subconscious as domains of creativity and liberation with more suggestive remarks on the importance of trivial, everyday deeds (what Clark theorizes as "the meaning of our routine gestures") for psychological and psychiatric inquiry. "Even seemingly meaningless or unimportant acts," writes Pedrosa, "that are practiced automatically—inconsequential movements, mistakes, scribbles, awkward drawings thoughtlessly made on paper—have become objects of interest and study. . . . It was discovered that, beyond the express, apparently formal meaning of man's actions and words there might be another, truer hidden meaning."[90] The displacement of "truer meaning" from what was then—as it is now—a predominant register of the unconscious to the more trivial, everyday world of meaningless gestures and unimportant acts is key. It speaks of a regressive capacity and an attendant potential for creation and construction that cannot be confined within, much less reduced to, the institutional parameters of art and psychiatry. And it reveals, in turn, a new field of operation for both art and psychiatry, an emergent site for intervention and creation.

Clark herself embraced the creative, constructive potential of regression.[91] But unlike Milner, she did not appeal to symbolic thought. Her focus was on something more concrete, a cognitive capacity resting in our ability to feel texture and an attendant experience of embodiment and subjectification. Her work on relational objects as well as the experiences she proposed on the basis of these objects constitutes an initial, programmatic regress away from verbal, analytic capacities and into the more embodied registers of sense and meaning. The work she encompasses under the name *Estruturação do self* stands as the fullest realization of this constructive regress, the most elusive proposal in her oeuvre, both from the perspective of the art world and in the eyes of psychologists and psychoanalysts.[92] A statement by Clark in her essay on the suppression of the object captures succinctly the objectives she pursued with the *Estruturação*: "To receive perceptions raw, to live them out, to elaborate oneself by means of the process, regressing and growing outwards, to the world."[93] The work of regression here and the intended process of "growing outwards" brings to mind what José Bleger theorized in his 1967 treatise on object relations as a state of "primitive undifferentiation," which, he clarifies, "is not actually a *state* of undifferentiation but a different *structure* or organization that always includes the subject and the subject's environment, though not as differentiated entities."[94] Bleger, an influential figure in Argentinian psychoanalysis and notorious exponent of object relations theory in Latin America, stressed the importance of the body and bodily registers in his own clinical practice and in the process of reintrojection in particular.[95]

Clark goes to work on her *Estruturação do self* in earnest in late 1975 or early 1976, following her return to Rio de Janeiro after a second long period living in Paris. She envisioned a therapeutic dimension to her work earlier while in Paris, around the same time during which she was invited to facilitate a class titled "The Gesture of Communication" at the Centre Saint Charles at the Sorbonne in Paris.[96] The structure of the class, with its regular meeting times (three hours, twice a week) spread over an extended period of time, provided Clark with a stable working group for her collective proposals and for a collective deployment of her relational objects. Prior to her experience at the Sorbonne, Clark's opportunity to work with a stable group of participants over the course of a few days was limited to her time in California. Beginning in 1981, Clark trained a few professionals in behavioral health (Gina Ferreira, Lula Wanderley) in the techniques of the *Estruturação*. The *Estruturação do self* evolved up until 1988, shortly before Clark's death.

A short, unpublished text by Lygia Clark provides insight into the origins of the *Estruturação*. For Clark, there is a clear sense of continuity between individual sessions and the collective exercises she organized in the pedagogical context of the Sorbonne. While in Paris, Clark's engagement with the notion of relaxation was influenced by the work of Michel Sapir, whom Clark sought out following the advice of Pierre Fèdida. Clark herself underwent relaxation exercises in Paris in the months leading up to her return to Rio de Janeiro,[97] and her experience as a patient informed the work that went into the formulation of the *Estruturação do self*. Early sessions of the *Estruturação* included an element directly derived from Sapir's relaxation exercises, a verbal induction Clark used toward the beginning of the exercise. But Clark quickly did away with this,[98] and it seems that she eliminated it not out of some kind of anxiety of influence but rather to focus the *Estruturação do self* on the sensory, placing it firmly on the level of the preverbal. Recalling her first trials of the *Estruturação*, Clark writes: "at the time I would treat the client with Sapir's relaxation and with some of my objects. Little by little, I did away with Sapir's verbal induction and I began working exclusively with my own objects."[99] Lacanian *imago* as a leaving-home (a departure from a state of undifferentiation, from a kind of oceanic existence) and a leaving-behind (of unstable, unstructured, amorphous existence) comes to mind here. What Clark suggests is a return to a state left behind—the topological metaphor here begins to show its limitations—a regression of sorts, a step back before leaping forward. This step back as a way to step forward is something that captures her imagination at certain moments in her journals—she reads about this in the work of other artists and intellectuals and sees her own methods validated.

The *Estruturação do self* gains meaning in contrast to talking therapies. Clark's work is fundamentally linked to language; even after abandoning the idea of verbal induction, Clark set aside a moment at the end of each session for the client to verbalize the experience they had undergone. The session itself took place in silence, save for the sounds made by the objects as they are handled and placed on the client's body. After the session, language serves a different purpose, or rather, it finds itself in a different place: displaced, at least temporarily. The outlines of a new landscape of meanings begin to form, one where language serves not as all-encompassing totality but as limit, as the border of other, fundamentally different, sensorial experiences.

Clark describes the logistics of a session of *Estruturação do self* in an unpublished text titled "O objeto, o método e a prática."[100] The clients, as Clark called them, underwent the *Estruturação* stripped to their underwear and lying down on a mattress-like relational object made with sheets and filled with small Styrofoam balls (fig. 4.5). In this and other writings, Clark underlines that the mattress was soft enough to allow the weight of the client's body to carve a space for itself. During the first session, Clark asked the clients to rub their bodies with relational objects shaped like pillows and to verbalize the sensations this produced in them. In later sessions, it was Clark herself who rubbed these and other objects on the bodies of her clients. Clark also used her hands to rub and massage the bodies of her clients, taking care not touch their genitals or their breasts. After placing a number of relational objects strategically over different parts of the body and letting them rest there, Clark would let the clients lie in silence, with the objects resting over their bodies. This was the longest part of the session and the most important one. After removing the objects, Clark asked her clients to stretch "like animals."[101] Sitting up, the clients would receive one last relational object, a plastic bag filled with air

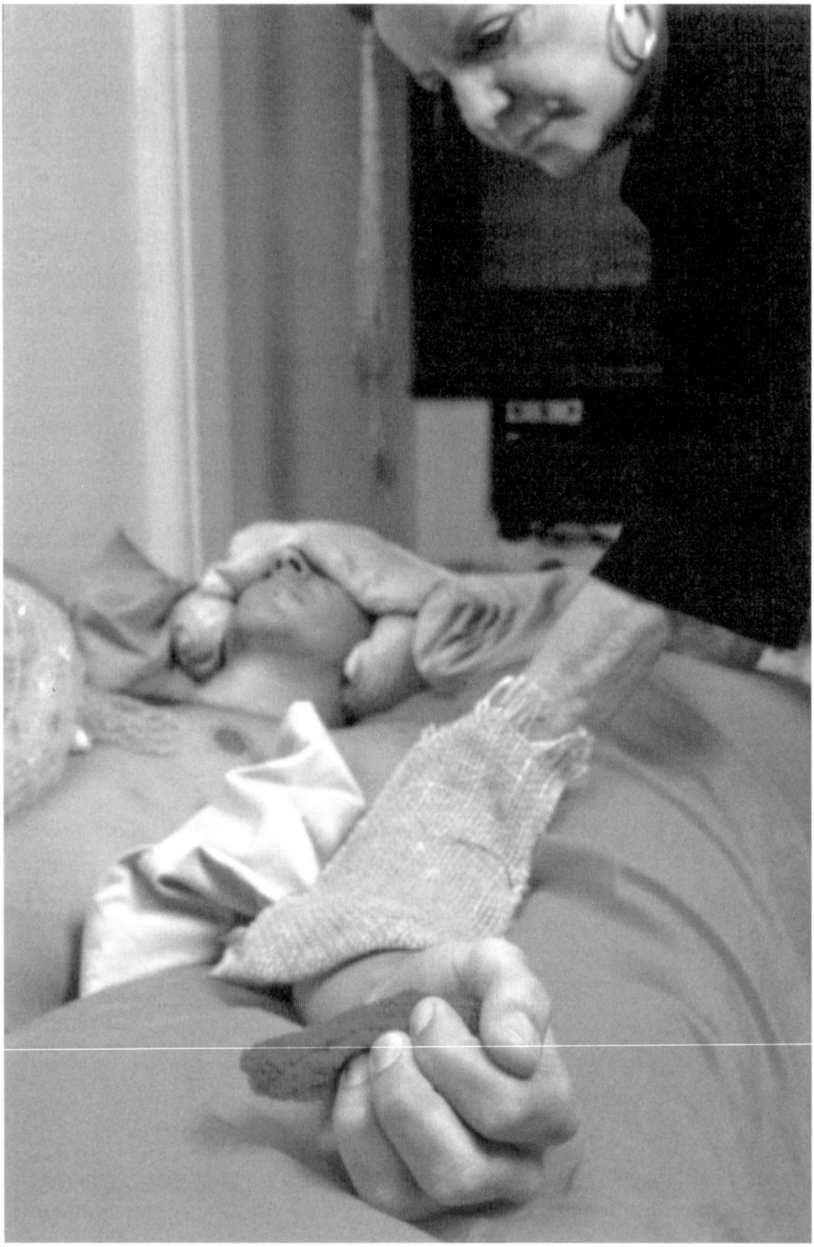

Figure 4.5. Lygia Clark, *Estruturação do self* (1976). Courtesy of Associação Cultural "O Mundo de Lygia Clark."

that Clark offered for destruction to those clients wanting to vent aggression at the end of the session. To those that chose to destroy the plastic bag, Clark would hand another empty bag and ask them to blow it up with their own breath to allow these clients to remake what they destroyed. The final part of the session was for clients to verbalize their experiences, a return to the world mediated by a turn back to language.

As she had been doing since 1966, in the *Estruturação do self* Clark works with materials taken from everyday life: plastic bags, plastic film (the kind used to wrap dry-cleaned clothing), plastic gloves, plastic balls, tubes, cardboard tubes, sheets, a mattress, Styrofoam, water, honey,[102] and pebbles. Some of the objects Clark used for the *Estruturação do self* (plastic bags filled with air, water, sand, seeds, and seashells; objects made with nets, pantyhose, plastic bags, stones, balls) are recognizable from earlier phases of her work. Some others (pillows, mattresses, blankets) Clark created expressly for the *Estruturação do self*. These last objects bear in their shape and in the name Clark gives to them a distinct relationship to the space of the home. As with her other relational objects, what is most important for Clark is not any symbolism behind the objects but rather the sensations that they are able to produce, although the symbolic weight of these objects as objects of the home still carries meaning in the experience of the *Estruturação*.

Photographs of the objects Clark used for this proposal, accounts of the process written by Clark and her collaborators, and their recollections of clients' statements made during the length of each treatment constitute the sources we have at our disposal as we try to make sense of Clark's last proposal. A film by Mário de Carneiro (*Memória do corpo*, 1984) documenting one of the sessions led by Lygia Clark is another important source of information on this work. Clark used the relational objects directly on the bodies of her clients, rubbing them, laying the objects on their bodies, using them to cover clients' ears, their eyes, their limbs, and their genitals in a sequence of movements choreographed by Clark herself and adapted to each client in each different session.

The *Estruturação* is a choreographed ritual that took place in Clark's presence, under her guidance. It took place much like therapy: in a controlled environment, for a set amount of time (about an hour), over a period of time, and at regular intervals. One effect Clark sought to elicit with the *Estruturação* would be to touch on sites of the body holding embodied memories of trauma, what Clark generally referred to as the phantasmagoria of the body. This is a first step in the process of releasing or "throwing up" these ghosts, these traumas, impediments to the normal functioning, the normal flux, of the body.[103] The image of the clients lying flat on the floor, floating on a bed of Styrofoam balls and covered with Clark's relational objects, is an image of strange fusion. It is, as Rolnik as noted, as if the client and the object formed a unity, "a single body, lined, as it were, with its visceral innards."[104]

For Rolnik, the principal merit of Clark's *Estruturação* lies in its ability to engage what he calls the "vibratory body," the *corpo vibrátil*, a form of embodiment attuned to perceptual experiences sustained at the sensorial level. The vibratory body as defined by Rolnik is the form of embodiment that is most attuned to microperception, to perception of intensities and not of clearly defined forms. The vibratory body is thus defined by a relationship of complementary difference with a more stable form of embodiment, the form of embodiment of everyday, intersubjective experience, the kind of embodiment that distinguishes between self and other and is not consumed by intensive, sensorial experiences. Stable embodiment, Rolnik argues, is useful for negotiating the demands of everyday life inasmuch as it helps maintain a clear vision of the world, a vision in which objects are clearly differentiated from each other and, most importantly, a vision in which objects and other subjects are distinctly separate from our selves. The price one pays for this useful, stable perception is a certain degree of fixedness and rigidity. Need, utility—the form of embodiment most tuned to utility and everyday use—is here, as in other chapters of this book, a fundamental concern, something in need of alternatives and resistance.

What Clark's *Estruturação do self* does is at once analogous and profoundly opposed to neoliberal politics of subjectification. In her *objetos relacionais* and especially in the *Estruturação do self*, Clark labors to release creative energies in the minds and the bodies of the people that come into contact with her work. The result—in direct opposition to the illusory freedoms and creativity promoted by market ideology—is a form of resistance to instrumentalization and the instrumentalization of creativity in particular. And so the therapeutic nature of the relational objects that Clark used in the *Estruturação do self* gains sharper contours. These objects heal inasmuch as they dispel a distressing fantasy—what Taussig calls "the fictional naturalness of identities on which the society depends and that guarantees its concepts of objects and objectivity"[105]—to reveal a vision of objects that feels more real and more grounded. This vision features ourselves and others as makers of those objects, but it also features these objects in an uncanny relationship of agency in relation to us—objects perceive us, as Paul Klee once suggested,[106] and they also make us who and what we are.

This vision of objects reveals for us the constitutive relationships that hold between us and the objects that surround our existence. The "new objectivity" (Oiticica *dixit*) in Clark's work is a harbinger of a new vision of social relations inasmuch as it stands for a dissolution of a capitalist ontology of thinghood and its attendant politics of subjectification: the dissolution, in short, of the presumptive self-containment of subjects and objects, the dissolution of static and rigid notions of both objectivity and subjectivity and of the criteria we use to distinguish between them. This translates in Clark's work to a productive confusion of objects, subjects, and the categories we attribute to each of them. Vitality, organicity, and objectivity are interchangeably attributed to objects like the *Bichos* and to the subjects of the experiences afforded by the *objetos relacionais*, the *Arquiteturas biológicas*, and the *Estruturação do self*. Anonymity and a sense of opaqueness, in turn, begin to qualify Clark's understanding of the body as she moves forward with her experimentation with objects.

The bridge between art and life—the common place of avant-garde aesthetics—gains an unexpected and productive interpretation in the work of Lygia Clark. And it does so with a simple but crucial change of terms, which itself implies a change of proportions. What Clark insists on is not ways to bring together art and life. Rather, what she pursues, with increasing clarity after 1960, is a crafting of objects carefully conceived to sustain experiences of the aesthetic within the space of the home, in everyday, intimate contexts, in the artist's own apartment, away from galleries and museums. What is remarkable—indeed, extraordinary—about Clark is the manner in which she goes about this pursuit: aesthetic in the most rigorous sense of the term. The objects Clark produced after the 1960s are not art objects; neither are they objects of design. Their rigor lies in the insistence with which they broach a single and complex problem of experience and perception, an aesthetic problem. These objects probe the relation of the inner life with the life of the world, and in so doing, they realize and make concrete the extent to which the most human of desires—the desire to create, the desire to make, the desire to inhabit—always and necessarily involves things beyond ourselves. Clark's *objetos relacionais* constitute a first and forceful step toward notions of perception, materialism, objectivity, and subjectivity that cannot be fully apprehended without revising our ideas about the commodity form and alienation. Consumer culture and the establishment of a form of capitalism subtended by the burgeoning presence of consumer goods is the larger background for Clark's revision of what objects are and how we relate to them.

Conclusion

The development of market economies and consumer culture in the decades after World War II, the rise of military regimes in Latin America in the 1960s and 1970s, and the transition to democratic governments in the 1980s and 1990s can all be read as steps in the rise of neoliberal regimes throughout the region. Put another way, it was within political and economic configurations staged during the Cold War that emerging neoliberal regimes throughout the Americas began to consolidate and rise to power. This is not to suggest a teleological reading of the events that defined the Americas in the second half of the twentieth century. The series of imbricated, intertwined historical transformations here alluded to is more complex than a linear progression from one period to the next might suggest. History, here as elsewhere, is less wieldy than the use of prefixes—suggesting clear preludes, codas, and postscripts—would have us believe. More than progression, repetition and *réplica* (as copy, as rhetorical device, and as telluric movement) are the two tropes that bind together the hemispheric history of the Americas, and of US influence and domination over the region. Taken out of line, read not as a step in a forward process but as a moment in a larger cycle of historical turns defined by capital, neoliberalism starts to look repetitive. The freedom neoliberalism defends (freedom of the markets) first dawned in the decades straddling the nineteenth and twentieth centuries and was later defended with increasing violence in the 1950s and 1960s. By the 1970s, Laura Randall writes, consumption levels in Latin American countries began to approach those of the United States.[1]

Consumption as colonial force has proved to be tremendously efficient. It subsumes under its interests whatever energies and tendencies toward creative liberation emerge from human ingenuity. Most specious about this appropriation is that once consumer capitalism appropriates something, it seems that what has been appropriated is immediately and decisively at odds with anything that aspires to resistance and emancipation.

Put another way, once a set of creative forces is deemed to have been appropriated by capitalism, once creativity is subsumed under their logic and placed under the service of its operations of power, other means must be found in order to imagine modes of contestation that can resist, or at least interrupt, the capitalist order. The revolution will not be televised, nor consumed, nor advertised, or so the wisdom goes. Left ideology betrays its puritan strain here, that vein of "institutionalized revolutionary puritanism" so shrewdly formulated by the Argentinian artist Roberto Jacoby in his own promiscuous dealings with both market forces and the contestation of these very forces.[2]

More than an affirmation of the terms I proposed in this book as terms for an aesthetics in the age of consumer culture, much more than a redemption of the aspects of consumption and consumer culture interpellated by the artworks and the poems studied throughout, my hope is to have sparked a spirit of ambiguity — of doubt and curiosity, however modest. Doubt in the face of conventions and intellectual divisions that insist, implicitly and explicitly, on a hierarchy between production and consumption. Curiosity in the face of the silly things that pepper our existence — the often foolish, sometimes foul debris of a world depleted by consumerist desire. Doubt and curiosity most of all, in the postures we assume, the positions we take, as we make sense of a world reduced to rubble.

Notes

Introduction

1. Marx introduces his idea of labor as "a power in the realm of consciousness" toward the beginning of the third of his *Economic and Philosophic Manuscripts of 1844* (Mineola, New York: Dover, 2007), which reads: "The *subjective essence* of private property—*private property* as activity for itself, as *subject*, as *person*—is *labour*. It is therefore self-evident that only the political economy which acknowledged *labour* as its principle (Adam Smith), and which therefore no longer looked upon private property as a mere *condition* external to man—that it is this political economy which has to be regarded on the one hand as a product of the real *energy* and the real *movement* of private property—as a product of modern *industry*—and on the other hand, as a force which has quickened and glorified the energy and development of modern *industry* and made it a power in the realm of *consciousness*" (93).

2. Ibid., 93–94.

3. Ibid.: "That the entire revolutionary movement necessarily finds both its empirical and its theoretical basis in the movement of *private property*—in that of the economy, to be precise—is easy to see. This *material*, immediately *sensuous* private property is the material sensuous expression of *estranged human* life. Its movement—production and consumption—is the *sensuous* revelation of the movement of all production hitherto—i.e., the realisation or the reality of man."

4. Hal Foster writes that "what unites the different strands of Pop art might be . . . a common recognition that consumerism had changed the appearance of the world, perhaps even the nature of appearance, and that art must draw on new contents and develop new forms accordingly." See Foster, "Survey," in *Pop*, ed. Mark Francis (New York: Phaidon, 2005), 18.

5. See Laura Randall, "Introduction," in *The Political Economy of Latin America in the Postwar Period* (Austin: University of Texas Press, 1997), 3: "Development style shifted from export-led growth and government provision of infrastructure before World War I to increasing attention to development of the domestic market. The closing of world markets during World War I, preferential trading agreements during the Great Depression, and disruptions to trade during World War II made export-led growth appear to be unduly risky."

6. Paulo Herkenhoff contextualizes the work of Lygia Clark against not one but

three postwar settings. See Herkenhoff, "Lygia Clark," in Lygia Clark, *Lygia Clark* (Barcelona: Fundació Antoni Tapies, 1998), 36: "It was the end of three wars: The World War, the Populist Dictatorship of Vargas and Modernist Literature . . . It is within this context that Lygia Clark began her studies."

7. José Bleger, *Symbiosis and Ambiguity: A Psychoanalytic Study* (1967) (New York: Routledge, 2013), 164: "Hence, I wish to underscore that *ambiguity is not confusion*, but the persistence of or regression to a state of primitive fusion or undifferentiation, which characterises the earliest adumbrations of psychological organisation (glischro-caric position). In other words, ambiguous subjects have not yet reached the stage of giving shape to contradictions. Equally, *they have not yet been able to discriminate different terms*, which for them are comparable, equivalent or co-existent. This is the basic characteristic of ambiguity and of the glischro-caric position or position of primitive undifferentiation (syncretism), and of ambiguity due to the persistence of the glischro-caric position or regression to it."

8. The idea here is that remaining flexible, adaptable vis-à-vis the terms of capitalist domination, is not necessarily a straightforward corroboration of these same terms. Adjustability here refers to the margin necessary to adjust our understanding of and responses to terms of domination that are subject to historical change. George Yúdice makes a related point when he writes: "civil society is also the society of consumption and spectacle. However, recognition of this does not mean that older Marxist notions such as the commodity fetish and alienation necessarily apply in the same ways in which the concepts were originally formulated." See George Yúdice, *The Expediency of Culture: Uses of Culture in the Global Era* (Durham, NC: Duke University Press, 2003), 169.

9. Michael Taussig, *The Nervous System* (New York: Routledge, 1992), 147.

10. In a text written for the *Mitos vadios* event in São Paulo and originally published in *Diário de São Paulo* on November 12, 1978, Hélio Oiticica states: "As ruas e as bobagens do nosso daydream diário se enriquecem / vê-se que elas não são bobagens nem trouvailles sem conseqüencia / são o pé calçado pronto para o delirium ambulatorium / renovado a cada dia." Cited in Moacir dos Anjos, "As ruas e as bobagens: anotações sobre o *delirium ambulatorium* de Hélio Oiticica," in *Ars* 10.20 (2012): 43. See also Irene V. Small, "Permanent Evolution: Hélio Oiticica and the Return to Rio, 1978–80," in Lynn Zelevansky et al., *Hélio Oiticica, To Organize Delirium* (Pittsburgh: Carnegie Museum of Art, 2016), 258: "Perambulating the city as part of what he called *delírio ambulatório*, he made *flash-vislumbre-anotações* (flash-revelation-notations) for works on index cards, often dating to the minute. He displaced and modified found objects—chunks of pavement, colored plastic bottles encircled with rubber bands, trays of sand—projected plans for environmental structures, invented new *Parangolés*, organized events, realized a host of maquettes for chromatic architectures he called *Magic Squares*."

11. Adorno, "Theodor Adorno: Letters to Walter Benjamin," in *Aesthetics and Politics* (New York: Verso, 2007), 123.

12. The editors of a recent anthology of Benjamin's writings on media distinguish between moments in his writing when he uses "distraction" in an affirmative sense (the sense he seems to have in mind when he argues for a "reception in distraction" in

the essay on reproducibility) and moments when he uses the term in a negative sense (the sense of entertainment, close to what Adorno seems to have in mind in his correspondence with Benjamin). See Benjamin, "The Work of Art in the Age of Its Technological Reproducibility," in *The Work of Art in the Age of its Technological Reproducibility, and Other Writings on Media* (Cambridge, MA: Harvard University Press, 2008), 54n33.

13. Benjamin, "Work of Art," in *Work of Art*, 40.

14. Theodor W. Adorno, *Aesthetic Theory* (1970), translated by Robert Hullot-Kentor (New York: Continuum, 2002), 13. My emphasis.

15. Ibid.: "It counts among the most profound insights of Hegel's aesthetics that long before constructivism it recognized this truly dialectical relation and located the subjective success of the artwork in the disappearance of the subject in the artwork. Only by way of this disappearance, not by cozying up to reality, does the artwork break through merely subjective reason."

16. Years after dismissing Benjamin's incipient theory of distraction despite its "shock-like seduction," Adorno goes on to theorize the dialectical moment of subjective disappearance into the object of art in terms of shock. See Adorno, *Aesthetic Theory*, 244: "The shock aroused by important works is not employed to trigger personal, otherwise repressed emotions. Rather, this shock is the moment in which recipients forget themselves and disappear into the work; it is the moment of being shaken. The recipients lose their footing; the possibility of truth, embodied in the aesthetic image, becomes tangible. This immediacy, in the fullest sense, of relation to artworks is a function of mediation, of penetrating and encompassing experience [Erfahrung]; it takes shape in the fraction of an instant, and for this the whole of consciousness is required, not isolated stimuli and responses."

17. Paul Virilio, *The Vision Machine*, trans. Julie Rose (Bloomington: Indiana University Press, 1994), 12.

18. Ibid.

19. Ibid., 14.

20. Jonathan Crary, *Suspensions of Perception: Attention, Spectacle, and Modern Culture* (Cambridge, MA: MIT Press, 1999), 3.

21. Ibid., 13. Crary is careful to maintain the dialogical tension of the historical moment he's describing. The relocation of perception, he writes, "also stands behind the astonishing burst of visual invention and experimentation in European art in the second half of the nineteenth century."

22. Ibid., 3.

23. For an extended analysis of Mesmer's place in Enlightenment thought, see Robert Darnton, *Mesmerism and the End of Enlightenment in France* (Cambridge, MA: Harvard University Press, 1968).

24. As Robert Hullot-Kentor argues in a timely and captivating analysis of contemporary usage of this term, "the culture industry," in all its current transparency, masks a fundamental antagonism that was all too present, all too *obvious* for those who coined the term: the antagonism between enterprise and culture, between a world of commercial purpose and a reserve of uselessness. See Hullot-Kentor, "The Exact Sense in Which the Culture Industry No Longer Exists," in *Culture Industry Today*, ed. Fabio Akcelrud Durão (Newcastle upon Tyne: Cambridge Scholars Publishing, 2010), 7–8.

25. Fredric Jameson, *Late Marxism: Adorno, or, The Persistence of the Dialectic* (New York: Verso, 1990), 146.

26. Theodor W. Adorno, *Prisms* (1967) (Cambridge, MA: MIT Press, 1997), 84.

27. Ibid., 86: "Luxury has a dual character. Veblen concentrates his spotlight on one side of it: that part of the social product which does not benefit human needs and contribute to human happiness but instead is squandered in order to preserve an obsolete system. The other side of luxury is the use of parts of the social product which serve not the reproduction of expended labour, directly or indirectly, but of man in so far as he is not entirely under the sway of the utility principle."

28. John Sinclair and Anna Cristina Pertierra, eds., *Consumer Culture in Latin America* (New York: Palgrave Macmillan, 2012), 11.

29. Daniel Miller, "Consumption as the Vanguard of History: A Polemic by Way of an Introduction," in *Acknowledging Consumption: A Review of New Studies*, edited by Daniel Miller (London: Routledge, 1995), 8–9: "It is by focusing upon the housewife as the global dictator that the ironies of power may be most directly confronted. It is ironic in the sense that the housewife is often stereotyped as herself both modest and denigrated. She commands little respect in the social world she inhabits. Her labour in shopping, her skills of thrift and comparative purchasing are largely disregarded and unvalorised. Yet it is she (or at least the consumption she stands for) who may have displaced the top-hat capitalist as the aggregate 'global dictator.'" And later (34): "the quintessence of power in the modern world lies objectified in the image of the First World housewife. Indeed, I termed the housewife a global dictator in recognition of the sheer authority that the collective decision-making, which she stands for, now exercises. . . . The housewife may stand as the key figure in both my negative and positive reading of the historical position of contemporary consumption. She commands the fate of developing countries as one of poverty or relative affluence. But she also commands the progressive activity by which consumption is used to extract culture as the self-construction of humanity from the intractable but essential institutions of the modern world, such as the market or bureaucracy."

30. Ulrike Müller, *Bauhaus Women: Art, Handicraft, Design* (Paris: Flammarion, 2009), 104.

31. Hubert Dreyfus defines cultural paradigms in reference to Heidegger's idea of an openness or clearing where all objects that can be regarded as objects show up. It is a kind of background without which nothing would be apprehensible. Like the clearing in Heidegger's thought, a cultural paradigm as defined by Dreyfus "collects the scattered practices of a group, unifies them into coherent possibilities for action, and holds them up to the people who can then act and relate to each other in terms of that exemplar." The cultural paradigm works like a background for things to become available for cognition, a kind of baseline conceptual category that is shared among a people as more than a simple cultural trait. As a set of social practices, the cultural paradigm functions, then, "as an understanding of what it is for anything to be at all." See Dreyfus, "Heidegger on the Connection between Nihilism, Art, Technology and Politics," in *The Cambridge Companion to Heidegger*, ed. Charles Guignon (New York: Cambridge University), 351–354. The cultural paradigm is not subject to discursive definition—it remains beyond conceptual formulation. Heidegger's terminology gets this

point across succinctly, with images of the clearing as the emptiness, the void wherein objects show up and take form, a clearing that cannot itself be anything defined and delineated. Recognizing consumption as cultural paradigm constitutes, in my reading, a first and necessary step toward envisioning modes of experience and forms of life other than those perfected by consumer society. In this respect, I take Robert Hullot-Kentor to heart when he writes, citing Adorno: "The only way out then, Adorno was sure, is through. Any real possibility would have to be pursued, developed and heightened out of the actual potentials of what we have become." See Hullot-Kentor, "A New Type of Human Being and Who We Really Are," in *The Brooklyn Rail: Critical Perspectives on Art, Politics, and Culture* (Nov. 10, 2008), http://brooklynrail.org/2008/11/art/a-new-type-of-human-being-and-who-we-really-are.

32. Steven B. Bunker, *Creating Mexican Consumer Culture in the Age of Porfirio Díaz* (Albuquerque: University of New Mexico Press, 2012): 3.

33. Ibid., 2.

34. Ibid., 4.

35. "Wars and depressions," Albert O. Hirschman writes, "have historically no doubt been most important in bringing industries to countries of the 'periphery' which up to then had firmly remained in the nonindustrial category. . . . Wars cause interruption of, or hazards for, *all* international commodity flows, essential or nonessential, and therefore provide a general unbiased stimulus to domestic production of previously imported goods. The same is true for the stimulus emanating from the gradual growth of markets." See Hirschman, "The Political Economy of Import-Substituting Industrialization in Latin America," in *The Essential Hirschman*, ed. Jeremy Adelman (Princeton, NJ: Princeton University Press, 2013), 105–107.

36. See Miguel Ramírez, "Mexico," in Randall, *Political Economy of Latin America*, 118–120.

37. News of an economic "miracle" going on in Brazil started circulating during the military administration of General Emílio Médici in the late 1960s and early 1970s, the years during which violent oppression in Brazil recrudesced to levels unseen since the beginning of the dictatorship in 1964. See Nelson do Valle Silva, "Brazilian Society: Continuity and Change, 1930–2000," in *The Cambridge History of Latin America*, ed. Leslie Bethell (New York: Cambridge University Press, 1984–2008), 484: "Brazil's GDP grew at an average annual rate of 6–7 percent in the late 1950s. Between 1967 and 1973 it reached an average rate of 11.2 percent a year, with an historic high of 14 percent in 1973. This was the well-known and officially trumpeted 'Brazilian miracle.'"

38. For a historiographical account of this term, see Julio Moreno, *Yankee Don't Go Home: Mexican Nationalism, American Business Culture, and the Shaping of Modern Mexico* (Chapel Hill: University of North Carolina Press, 2003), 236n11.

39. It appears that early customers at this department store were notoriously impatient, zealous shoppers. See Moreno, *Yankee Don't Go Home*, 2: "Employees panicked 'as a sea of hands thrust pesos toward them, into their pockets, into their blouses, anywhere—just to complete a purchase.'"

40. Ibid.

41. See George F. Flaherty, "Uncanny Tlatelolco, Uncomfortable Juxtapositions," in *Defying Stability: Artistic Processes in Mexico 1952–1967*, ed. Rita Eder (Mexico City:

Turner, 2014), 401. Flaherty describes the projects undertaken during the construction boom of the Mexican "miracle" as "gestures of the state's magnanimity at a moment when its speculative transformation of the capital city into a city of capital appeared uneven if not structurally unsound. Indeed," Flaherty writes, "the success of these projects . . . depended as much on managing public perception as on providing verifiable improvement of Mexico's infrastructure."

42. The expediency of these investments in the infrastructure of Mexican culture has not gone unnoticed. See, for instance, Gabriela Álvarez and María García Holley, "Museums for Modernization," in Eder, *Defying Stability*, 341: "In 1964, Mexico City's vast cultural and educational infrastructure boasted some forty museums, most of them newly created. This increase in the city's recreational supply was a result of modernization strategies and developmentalist policies, which, aiming to position the country in a competitive global marketplace without leaving behind its national identity, placed Mexican culture as the country's cover letter to the world. This made educational and cultural policies a crucial part of economic growth." And later: "The modernization of cultural facilities was one of the factors in López Mateos's national project. Museums became the new cultural cathedrals that would guard the cultural and historical myths of the country, following the model established around 1900 by the United States, which transformed museums into centers for public education and enlightenment" (343). And a few pages later: "Adolfo López Mateos's term in office was marked by a fostering of culture and education intended to place Mexico on an international level. In this way, tradition and national identity worked as bargaining chips for a technologically and educationally struggling—but developing—country" (351).

43. Álvaro Vázquez Mantecón points to 1958 as "a turning point in the social opposition to the project of developmentalism in Mexico." See Vázquez Mantecón, "The Dissident Image: Discrepancies to the Modernization Project in the Cinema and Photography During the Fifties and Sixties," in Eder, *Defying Stability*, 331–335: "That year saw strong demonstrations of a fundamentally different nature: university students protesting against transportation fare rises in Mexico City, and teacher, rail worker and telegraph union rallies demanding higher wages, but also freedom of association. This was the dark side of the 'Mexican miracle,' which required worker docility to keep labor cheap."

44. Octavio Paz, "Tamayo en la pintura mexicana" (1950), in *Obras completas de Octavio Paz*, vol. 7 (Mexico City: Fondo de Cultura Económica, 1994), 257–264.

45. See José Luis Cuevas, "El mural efímero," in *Letras Libres* (February 1999): 69–71.

46. Werner Baer and Claudio Paiva, "Brazil," in Randall, *Political Economy of Latin America*, 72.

47. Ibid., 73.

48. Industrialization in Brazil triggered massive waves of immigration that changed the face of cities throughout the Brazilian territory, but industrialization was, strictly speaking, a regional phenomenon overwhelmingly concentrated in the city of São Paulo and surrounding areas. Nelson do Valle Silva makes this point. See Silva, "Brazilian Society," in Bethell, *Cambridge History*, 491.

49. Ibid., 496.

50. Flora Süssekind makes note of the expansionist policies of the Castelo Branco

administration and singles out "the hyperdevelopment of mass media, and particularly of television" as one of its key components. See Süssekind, *Vidrieras astilladas: ensayos críticos sobre la cultura brasileña de los sesenta a los ochenta* (Buenos Aires: Ediciones Corregidor, 2003), 19.

51. As Elena Shtromberg notes, this initial moment in the history of television in Brazil hardly translated into an experience for mass audiences, though by 1970 the number of Brazilian households with access to television had increased exponentially. See Shtromberg, *Art Systems: Brazil and the 1970s* (Austin: University of Texas Press, 2016), 94: "in 1950 when TV Tupi debuted, there were only two hundred television sets in Brazil, the majority of which had been imported by Chateaubriand himself. This was quickly rectified by Invictus, a São Paulo factory that began to manufacture a seventeen-inch television model in Brazil in 1952 for the newly emerging market. For the better part of the 1950s, the television was a gadget predominantly owned by Brazil's wealthier class and continued to be a luxury item imported from the United States. . . . The number of homes that owned a television grew at an accelerated pace, from two hundred sets purchased in 1950 to three million in 1965 (by which time the majority were manufactured in Brazil), to well over six million by the early 1970s."

52. For a detailed account of Chateaubriand's life, see the biography by Fernando Morais, *Chatô, o rei do Brasil* (São Paulo: Companhia das Letras, 1994).

53. See Marialva Barbosa and Ana Paula Goulart Ribeiro, "Telejornalismo na Globo: vestigios, narrativa e temporalidade," in Valério Cruz Brittos and César Ricardo Siqueira Bolaño, *Rede Globo—40 anos de poder e hegemonia*. For links between developments in the communications sector and art movements in Brazil, see Felipe Scovino, "Brasileiros em Ulm: vanguarda e ruptura," in Daniela Name, *Diálogo concreto: design e construtivismo no Brasil* (Rio de Janeiro: Caixa Cultural, 2008), 43. For a brief discussion of the history of the film and radio industries in Brazil, see Rogério Duarte, "The Culture Industry in Brazil," in Durão, *Culture Industry Today* (Newcastle upon Tyne: Cambridge Scholars Publishing, 2010), 93–112.

54. Silva, "Brazilian Society," in Bethell, *Cambridge History*, 496.

55. See Aleca Le Blanc, "Under Construction: Calder at Rio de Janeiro's Museu de Arte Moderna in 1959," in *Modernidad y vanguardia: rutas de intercambio entre España y Latinoamérica (1920–1970)*, ed. Paula Barreiro López et al. (Museo Nacional Centro de Arte Reina Sofía, 2015): 209.

56. See Ferreira Gullar, "Arte concreta no Brasil: etapas da pintura contemporânea XXXIX—arte concreta V," *Jornal do Brasil: suplemento dominical*, August 6, 1960, 3: "A I Bienal do Museu de Arte Moderna de São Paulo, inaugurada em outubro de 1951, viria dar um impulso decisivo ao movimiento nascente, proporcionando aos artistas e críticos brasileiros o conhecimento das obras abstratas ou concretas de Sofia Taeuber-Arp, Max Bill, Richard P. Lohse, Walter Bodmer, Oskar Dalvit, Leo Leuppi, e outros, que integravam a representação da Suíca."

57. Glória Ferreira, "The Permanent Revolution of the Critic," in *Mário Pedrosa: Primary Documents*, edited by Glória Ferreira and Paulo Herkenhoff (New York: Museum of Modern Art, 2015), 14.

58. Le Blanc, "Under Construction," 210.

59. See Pyr Marcondes, *Uma história da propaganda brasileira: as melhores cam-*

panhas, gênios da criação, personagens (Rio de Janeiro: Ediouro, 2001), 38: "A publicidade viverá o que se pode chamar de seu maior momento de expansão, como setor que ainda luta por sua consolidação. Em 1957, acontece o *1° Congresso Brasileiro de Propaganda*, o início de um programa de institucionalização e regulamentação da atividade."

60. For a detailed account of the history of design in Brazil, see Lucy Niemeyer, *Design no Brasil: origens e instalação* (Rio de Janeiro: 2AB, 1998).

61. Néstor García Canclini, *Consumers and Citizens: Globalization and Multicultural Conflicts*, trans. George Yúdice (Minneapolis: University of Minnesota Press, 2001), 37.

62. Ibid., 38.

63. Ibid., 40. Emphasis in the original.

64. Ibid. Emphasis in the original.

65. Gareth Williams, "From Populism to Neoliberalism: Formalities of Identity, Citizenship, and Consumption in Contemporary Latin Americanism," in *Dispositio* 22.49 (Jan. 1, 1997), 21. For Francine Masiello's discussion of García Canclini's writings on citizenship and consumption, for her compelling defense of "a future that might recuperate the role of popular subjects," and for her critique of First World silencing of the "emancipatory powers of popular leanings," see Masiello, *The Art of Transition: Latin American Culture and Neoliberal Crisis* (Durham, NC: Duke University Press, 2001), 36–38.

66. Ibid., 34.

67. Ibid.

68. Yúdice, *Expediency of Culture*, 164.

69. Juliet B. Schor, "In Defense of Consumer Critique: Revisiting the Consumption Debates of the Twentieth Century," in *Annals of the American Academy of Political and Social Science* 611 (May 2007), 16.

70. Ibid., 22.

71. Ibid., 21.

72. Ibid., 23.

73. Michel de Certeau, *The Practice of Everyday Life* (Berkeley: University of California Press, 1984): xi.

74. Ibid., xi–xii.

75. Ibid., xi–xii.

76. Certeau envisions *antropofagia*'s decolonizing gesture, without citing the movement. For Certeau, the fate of the "products" of the colonial order (imperial languages, religions, artifacts, customs), in the hands of the people of Latin America, harbor the possibility of creative appropriation in modern consumer culture. See Certeau, *Practice of Everyday Life*, 32. Certeau had in mind here the colonial subjects of Latin America, particularly the Portuguese colonization of Brazil. For a critical assessment of the legacy of *antropofagia*, see Adam Joseph Shellhorse, "Subversions of the Sensible: The Poetics of Antropofagia in Brazilian Concrete Poetry, *Revista Hispánica Moderna* 68.2 (December 2015): 165–190.

77. Ibid., xi.

78. Haroldo de Campos, "Da razão antropofágica: diálogo e diferença na cultura brasileira" (1981), in *Metalinguagem & outras metas* (São Paulo: Perspectiva, 2006), 249:

"O *produssumo*, como o definiu D. Pignatari: a poética de invenção no consumo de massa, para além do ceticismo adorniano."

79. Augusto de Campos, *Balanço da bossa e outras bossas* (São Paulo: Editora Perspectiva, 1974), 185: "A opção, aparentemente inevitável, entre artistas de produção (eruditos) e artistas de consumo (populares), ganha com os Beatles uma nova alternativa—aquilo que Décio Pignatari chama de '*produssumo*' (produção e consumo reunidos)."

80. See Yúdice, *Expediency of Culture*, 166: "[Fredric] Jameson's notion of the explosion of culture (or, as Baudrillard would say, the 'implosion' of everything into it) so as to exhaust the space of the social has recently been echoed by critics who feel that culture can no longer be construed as false consciousness, as something 'foisted on the gullible populations by hype and the lust for profit.'"

81. Marx, *Economic and Philosophic Manuscripts*, 103. Emphasis in the original.

82. Ibid., 107.

83. Jonathan Dettman, "Consumption and the Culture Industry," in Durão, *Culture Industry Today*, 144.

84. Ibid., 145.

85. Marx, *Grundrisse*, cited in Dettman, "Consumption and the Culture Industry," in Durão, *Culture Industry Today*, 144–145.

86. Marx, *Economic and Philosophic Manuscripts*, 93. Emphasis in the original.

87. See Kojin Karatani, *The Structure of World History: From Modes of Production to Modes of Exchange*, trans. Michael K. Bourdaghs (Durham, NC: Duke University Press, 2014).

88. Verónica Gago, *La razón neoliberal: economías barrocas y pragmática popular* (Buenos Aires: Tinta Limón Ediciones, 2014), 14–15: "Tres lugares, entonces, a desarmar de los cuales depende la arquitectura discursiva que sólo explica el neoliberalismo desde arriba. Primero, que el neoliberalismo se trata sólo de un conjunto de macropolíticas diseñadas por centros imperialistas [. . .] Segundo punto a descomponer: que el neoliberalismo se trata de una racionalidad que compete sólo a grandes actores políticos y económicos, sean transnacionales, regionales o locales [. . .] Finalmente, si sólo se lo concibe en términos macropolíticos, se considera que su superación (si aún puede valer ese término) depende básicamente—en relación a los puntos anteriores—de políticas macroestatales llevadas adelante por actores de la misma talla."

89. Ibid., 303: "La razón neoliberal, en este sentido, es una fórmula para mostrar al neoliberalismo como racionalidad, en el sentido que Foucault le ha dado al término: como constitución misma de la gubernamentalidad, pero también para contrapuntearla con las maneras en que esa racionalidad es apropiada, arruinada, relanzada y alterada por quienes, se supone, sólo son sus víctimas."

90. Walter Benjamin, *One-Way Street*, trans. Edmund Jephcott (Cambridge, MA: Harvard University Press, 2016), 76. This volume, writes Michael Jennings in the introduction to the 2016 edition, "contains a number of Benjamin's earliest attempts to derive from a reading of a seemingly debased object a new perceptual or political potential" (16).

91. As a way of distancing futurism from "those who defend the aesthetics of Nature," F. T. Marinetti calls to mind, in a typically exhilarated tone, images of "multi-

colored billboards in the green meadows, iron bridges which chain the hills together, surgical trains that cut through the blue belly of the mountains," (45) in Marinetti, *Critical Writings*, ed. Günter Berghaus (New York: Farrar, Straus, and Giroux), 2006. He compares his *parole in libertà* to "luminous billboards": "only the great, luminous billboards of Words-in-Freedom will live on, for they are the only poetry which needs to be seen" (412). He grapples with luminous billboards again in his "Gli avvisi luminosi. Lettera aperta a S. E. Mussolini." My sincere gratitude to Günter Berghaus for pointing out these and other revealing moments in Marinetti's writings.

92. Cited in Rubén Gallo, *Mexican Modernity: The Avant-Garde and the Technological Revolution* (Cambridge, MA: MIT Press, 2005): 147.

93. Apollinaire, cited in Marjorie Perloff, *The Futurist Moment: Avant-garde, Avant Guerre, and the Language of Rupture* (Chicago: University of Chicago Press, 2003), 9.

94. Benjamin, *One-Way Street*, 42.

95. See Louis Gillet, "Joyce's Way" (1925), in *Claybook for James Joyce 1876–1943* (London: Abelard-Schuman, 1958), 42: "For a long time novels have emphasized the contrast between clear thought and this confused medley of feelings and instincts. Poetry and even the theatre strive to delve more and more, at the expense of rationality, into this domain of chiaroscuro and confusion, gloom and inarticulateness. It is a matter of breaking down the barriers, of pulling the sentence off the hinge-pins of logic (*[prends] l'eloquence et tords-lui son cou*), of liberating words from syntax and of connecting them spontaneously, or even of not connecting them at all: utmost purity of decadent art, since the times of Arthur Rimbaud and the famous Floupette." Gillet's text is an early reading of Joyce by a foremost literary critic in France, one whose initial mix of awe and skepticism vis-à-vis the force of Joycean prose gave way to unremitting praise.

96. Christina Kiaer, *Imagine No Possessions: The Socialist Objects of Russian Constructivism* (Cambridge, MA: MIT Press, 2005), 2.

97. For a translation of Mayakovsky's poems and reproductions of Lissitzky's logotypes and graphic design of the original book, see Vladimir Mayakovsky, *For the Voice* (Cambridge, MA: MIT Press, 2000).

98. *Veshch'*, cited in Christina Lodder, *Russian Constructivism* (New Haven: Yale University Press, 1983), 81.

99. Ibid., 158–159.

100. Rodchenko, cited in Kiaer, *Imagine No Possessions*, 199. Rodchenko's reference to race, blackness, and slavery highlights the balefulness of property relations, and how deplorable these relations are when exercised over human beings. These various forms of property relations, Rodchenko seems to suggest, are not entirely unrelated, even if they belong to entirely different moral orders.

101. Rodchenko, cited in Kiaer, *Imagine No Possessions*, 236.

102. Ibid., 200.

103. Ibid., 211.

104. Ibid., 7.

105. Susan Buck-Morss, *Dreamworld and Catastrophe: The Passing of Mass Utopia in East and West* (Cambridge, MA: MIT Press), 120.

106. Hubertus Gassner, cited in Kiaer, *Imagine No Possessions*, 210.

107. Kiaer, *Imagine No Possessions*, 27.

108. This assessment of a political bent in the inaugural actions of Zurich Dada and the Cabaret Voltaire in particular is made retrospectively by Richard Huelsenbeck, one of its principal collaborators. See Huelsenbeck, cited in Leah Dickerman, "Zurich," in *Dada: Zurich, Berlin, Hannover, Cologne, New York, Paris* (Washington, DC: National Gallery of Art, 2005): "This beginning of Dada was really a humanitarian reaction against mass murder in Europe, the political abuse of technology, and especially the Kaiser, on whom we, particularly the Germans, blamed the war."

109. Rodchenko was one such critic. He wrote indignantly about the cabaret and about the way women are objectified in it during his visit to Paris in 1925. See Rodchenko, cited in Kiaer, *Imagine No Possessions*, 216: "Here there are masses of theaters where the entire evening, naked women in expensive and enormous feathers walk on and off the scene in silence against expensive backdrops and that's all, they walk through and that's it. . . . And they are silent and don't dance and don't move. But simply walk through . . . one . . . another . . . a third . . . five at once, twenty at once . . . and that's it . . ."

110. Dickerman, "Zurich," in *Dada*, 25.

111. See Günter Berghaus, *Italian Futurist Theatre, 1909–1944* (Oxford: Clarendon, 1998), 398–399.

112. For more on the links between the Estridentista movement and the tobacco and pharmaceutical companies that financed it, see Rubén Gallo, "Wireless Modernity: Mexican Estridentistas, Italian and Russian Futurism," in *International Yearbook of Futurism Studies* 2.1 (2012): 24–26. See also Gallo, *Mexican Modernity*, 141–156.

113. Manuel Maples Arce, "*Actual* no. 1: hoja de vanguardia; comprimido estridentista," December 1921, Museo Nacional de Arte, Mexico City.

114. Flora Süssekind, *Vidrieras astilladas*, 175. See also Eduardo Ledesma, *Radical Poetry: Aesthetics, Politics, Technology, and the Ibero-American Avant-Gardes, 1900–2015* (Albany, NY: SUNY Press, 2016), 210–222.

115. Süssekind, *Cinematograph of Words* (Palo Alto, CA: Stanford University Press, 1997), 40–41.

116. Ibid., 37–47. In Mexico, the poet and writer Salvador Novo is often credited with the authorship of some of the nation's most memorable slogans, including the iconic "Mejor Mejora Mejoral," created for a brand of cold medicine and remembered widely and dearly.

117. Süssekind, *Vidrieras astilladas*, 15: "¿Realismo mágico, alegorías, parábolas, *ego-trips* poéticos? Todo se explica en función del aparato represivo del Estado autoritario."

118. Ibid.: "Ya sea la preferencia por las parábolas o por una literatura centrada en viajes autobiográficos, la clave estaría en el desvío estilístico o en el *desbunde* individual como respuestas indirectas a la imposibilidad de una expresión artística sin las barreras de la censura."

119. Ibid., 18–41. The Brazilian dictatorship is noteworthy for its early and widespread use of television as platform for dissemination of its nationalist values. See Shtromberg, *Art Systems*, 93: "On September 16, 1965, shortly after the inauguration of the military government, the Empresa Brasileira de Telecomunicações (Brazilian Telecommunications Enterprises), most often referred to as Embratel, was established to

oversee the expansion of telecommunications technology throughout Brazil's vast territories. Embratel's motto was 'Communication is integration,' signaling the drive to unite all of Brazil via new technologies. In 1967, just two months before *Tropicália* was exhibited, a new government entity, the Ministry of Communications, was created to administer telecommunications expansion and aggressively pursue satellite infrastructure. . . . The newly extended communications network enabled the government to access all corners of Brazil, and television became the apparatus through which the state was able to broadcast and promote its ideological agenda remotely. Television thus became an unparalleled vehicle for mobilizing mass audiences on demand, a characteristic that is as viable today as it was during the late 1960s and 1970s."

120. Felipe Scovino makes this point. See Scovino, "Brasileiros em Ulm," in Name, *Diálogo concreto*, 43: "O projeto construtivo em arte no Brasil ia de par com projetos semelhantes no campo econômico, político e social—a implantação da indústria siderúrgica, a exploração do petróleo, o Plano de Metas de Kubitschek, a importação de bens duráveis e o plano-piloto de Brasília."

121. Michael Taussig, *The Devil and Commodity Fetishism in South America* (Chapel Hill: University of North Carolina Press, 1980), 11.

122. Irene V. Small recounts an episode of this polemic involving concrete artists from Argentina and Brazil as well as the Brazilian concrete poet Décio Pignatari. See Small, *Hélio Oiticica: Folding the Frame* (Chicago: University of Chicago Press, 2016), 23: "That year [1953], Brazilians Décio Pignatari and Waldemar Cordeiro met several of these artists when they passed through Buenos Aires on their way to Santiago de Chile to attend a congress on Latin American culture. There Pignatari, Cordeiro, and Maldonado all vigorously rejected the Communist Party's advocacy of socialist realism."

123. See Gullar, "Arte concreta no Brasil": "Por volta de 1951, surgiram no Brasil as primeiras manifestações de arte concreta e essas manifestações não brotavam como resultado natural da evolução da moderna pintura brasileira e sim como reação a ela. Àquela altura, o ambiente artístico do país nesse setor era dominado ainda pela figura de Cândido Portinari, posto pela crítica acima de qualquer discussão [. . .] Foi então que Mário Pedrosa, depois de ter criticado duramente uma das últimas obras murais de Portinari (o Tiradentes), começõu a chamar a atenção da crítica e dos artistas para a arte abstrata e, posteriormente, para a arte concreta."

124. David Alfaro Siqueiros, "Folio 9.1.15," 254: "aparecen manifestaciones de un nuevo tipo social, es decir, de un nuevo mercado."

125. Ibid.: "El mundo se orienta según todas la manifestaciones de la economía base vital de los pueblos, hacia formas colectivas, masas imponentes de hombres, concentraciones de decenas y miles de personas aparecen en la vida diaria de todos los pueblos... y con ellas la necesidad de nuevas formas de publicidad y de arte."

126. Haroldo de Campos, "evolução de formas," in Augusto de Campos, Décio Pignatari, and Haroldo de Campos, *Teoria da poesia concreta: textos críticos e manifestos 1950–1960* (São Paulo: Ateliê Editorial, 2006), 81: "um certo tipo de 'forma mentis' contemporânea: aquele que impõe os cartazes, os slogans, as manchetes, as dicções contidas no anedotário popular."

127. Octavio Paz, "Los signos en rotación," in *Obras completas*, vol. 1, 269: "El perio-

dismo, la publicidad, el cine y otros medios de reproducción visual han transformado la escritura."

128. Octavio Paz, "La nueva analogía: poesía y tecnología," (1973), in *Obras completas*, vol. 1, 306: "la experiencia vuelve a ser física, corporal: hoy la palabra nos entra por los oídos, toma cuerpo, encarna."

129. See Theo Van Doesburg, "Concrete Art Manifesto," in *Abstraction in Artificial Intelligence and Complex Systems*, ed. Lorenza Saitta and Jean-Daniel Zucker (New York: Springer, 2013), 413–414.

130. See Sérgio B. Martins, *Constructing an Avant-Garde: Art in Brazil, 1949–1979* (Cambridge, MA: MIT Press, 2013), 40: "the very last sentence of [Gullar's 'Brancusi and the Problem of the Base in Sculpture'] leaves no doubt as to Gullar's ultimate aim: 'There is in Brancusi, as well, the path to the nonobject.' This assertion, to be clearer, bears the mark of teleological historicism."

131. Ibid., 19: "What I want to avoid is a facile opposition between an earlier concretism characterized as too 'rationalistic' and its more 'intuitive' adversary, neoconcretism; or at least, the internalization of these adjectives as essential attributes of well-defined movements. This comparative cliché can be traced back to an article by Pedrosa, in which he singles out the discrepancies between the São Paulo and Rio de Janeiro representations in the 1956–1957 'National Exhibition of Concrete Art' that took place in each city successively."

132. For a discussion of points of contact between concrete poets and artists, see Claus Clüver, "The Noigandres Poets and Concrete Art," *Ciberletras: Revista de Crítica Literaria y de Cultura* 17 (2007), n.p., http://www.lehman.cuny.edu/ciberletras/v17/cluver.htm. See also Rachel Price, *The Object of the Atlantic: Concrete Aesthetics in Cuba, Brazil, and Spain, 1868–1968* (Evanston, IL: Northwestern University Press, 2014), 165: "Rather than describe a mathematical, overly rational concretism giving way to a soft, organic neoconcretism, as some period documents assert, I want to argue that at the heart of both concrete and neoconcrete poetics lies a void." What Price argues against, what she resists in her account, is the kind of teleology that reads concretism as a step in the development of an aesthetics of neoconcretism that is more progressive, more "advanced" than the rigid, developmentalist principles of concretism. Price offers an alternative model, in *Object of the Atlantic*, 171: "I prefer to visualize the relation between the movements with recourse to a figure from the period, in which Cordeiro began to experiment with computer art: as a collection of punch cards each conveying different information but sharing the common logic of perforations or voids."

133. See Haroldo de Campos, "da fenomenologia da composicão à matemática da composição," in Campos, Pignatari, and Campos, *Teoria da poesia concreta*, 133: "A poesia concreta caminha para a rejeição da estrutura orgânica em prol de uma estrutura matemática (ou quase-matemática)." Even the rhetoric of this statement, the centerpiece of the polemics that marks the split between concrete and neoconcrete aesthetics, is uncharacteristically tentative: concrete poetry, in Haroldo de Campos's words, wasn't so much committed as motioning toward the embrace of the mathematical over and above the organic. Haroldo's own *Galáxias* (written between 1963 and 1976, published in 1984) would end up veering closer to a vital, affective, organic

proliferation of words and sounds and away from a rigid arrangement of language in accordance with rational principles. For a reading of the place of sound and music in *Galáxias*, see K. David Jackson, "Music of the Spheres in Galáxias," in *Haroldo de Campos: A Dialogue with the Brazilian Concrete Poet*, ed. K. David Jackson (Oxford: Centre of Brazilian Studies, Oxford University, 2005), 119–128.

134. See Gonzalo Aguilar, "Hélio Oiticica, Haroldo y Augusto de Campos: el diálogo velado—la aspiración a lo blanco," *O Eixo e a Roda: Revista de Literatura Brasileira* 13 (Dec 31 2006): 55–84.

135. See Rodolfo Mata, "Haroldo de Campos y Octavio Paz: del diálogo creativo a la mediación institucional," in *Anuario Latinoamérica* 32 (2001), n.p. Mata provides an extended account of the relationship between Paz and Haroldo de Campos, their dialogue, and the way they leveled this dialogue in their respective cultural contexts.

136. Octavio Paz and Vicente Rojo, "La fragua de dos libros," *Syntaxis* 25 (1991), 128: "En cierto modo, [*Discos visuales*] se trata de una variante del poema-objeto de los surrealistas. También, y sobre todo, tiene que ver con los experimentos de la poesía concreta."

137. For a brief account of Goeritz's work with concrete poetry, see Alicia Sánchez-Mejorada, "Poesía concreta," in *Los ecos de Mathias Goeritz*, ed. Mathias Goeritz (Mexico City: Instituto Nacional de Bellas Artes, 1997).

138. Jennifer Josten identifies this exhibition as the first of its kind in a Spanish-speaking country. See Josten, "Concrete Poetry," in Eder, *Defying Stability*, 107.

139. Octavio Paz, "El águila, el jaguar y la Virgen," in *Obras completas*, vol. 2, 66: "Fue un innovador y exploró muchos territorios: la perspectiva aérea y en movimiento, la fotografía y los nuevos materiales e instrumentos."

140. Flora Süssekind articulates this possibility in her reading of the Brazilian concrete poets and their engagement with the Tropicália movement. See Süssekind, *Vidrieras astilladas*, 178–179: "Cupo a los concretos también, en especial a Augusto de Campos, en ese cuerpo a cuerpo con los procedimientos característicos de la industria cultural, la percepción, entre otras cosas, del hábil golpe espectacular contra la espectacularización de la sociedad brasileña—incentivada sobre todo a través de la televisión por parte de los gobiernos militares—que era el Tropicalismo, que es el uso crítico de los propios recursos de los *media*."

141. Jameson, *Late Marxism*, 146.

142. Paz, *La otra voz: poesía y fin de siglo*, in *Obras completas*, vol. 1., 590: "La poesía ha resistido a la modernidad y al negarla, la ha vivificado. Ha sido su réplica y su antídoto."

Chapter 1: Attention and Distraction

1. Luis Cardoza y Aragón, fierce critic of Siqueiros's grandiloquent rhetoric and propagandistic style, singled out Siqueiros as one of the few artists in contemporary Mexico to envision and investigate new horizons of experimentation in the visual and plastic arts. See Cardoza y Aragón, *Pintura mexicana contemporánea* (Mexico City: Imprenta Universitaria, 1953), 186: "Penetración en nuevos campos de la plástica, investigación propiamente dicha en las posibilidades de la expresión, las tenemos muy

contadas, y hasta podríamos decir que apenas se han intentado, con excepción—casi única—de Alfaro Siqueiros."

2. David Alfaro Siqueiros, "Un problema técnico sin precedente en la historia del arte: el muralismo figurativo y realista en el exterior," in *Palabras de Siqueiros*, ed. Raquel Tibol (Mexico City: Fondo de Cultura Económica, 1996), 348: "¡No asombrarse!"

3. Crary, *Suspensions of Perception*, 1–2.

4. Siqueiros, "Por el materialismo marxista sabemos" (n.d., typescript, Getty Research Institute, Los Angeles, California), n.p.: "Que el arte refleja las características y contradicciones de la sociedad entera en que se produce. Que sufre las mimas contingencias de la clase o clases que lo impulsan."

5. In a rigorous and brilliant blow to the pretension of purism subtending what she theorizes as the revolutionary imagination of the Americas, María Josefina Saldaña-Portillo argues that both revolutionary discourse and the discourse of development "depend on a particular rendition of fully modern masculinity as the basis for full citizenship in either a developed or a revolutionary society." See Saldaña-Portillo, *The Revolutionary Imagination in the Americas in the Age of Development* (Durham, NC: Duke University Press, 2003), 43.

6. Siqueiros, "Por el materialismo marxista sabemos": "Que el surgimiento de una clase revolucionaria (burguesía o proletariado) trae consigo el embrión de un arte revolucionario que se desarrolla en el propio organismo de la sociedad moribunda."

7. Ibid.: "Que esa realidad produce una inevitable superposición de elementos culturales (revolucionarios y contra-revolucionarios) en la producción artística general."

8. Ibid.: "Que tal hecho crea efectos estéticos heterogéneos, mixtos, paradojales. Esto es, formas técnicas revolucionarias en expresiones parasitarias y decadentes y formas académicas, arqueológicas, contrarrevolucionarias, en impulsos políticamente revolucionarios."

9. Kiaer, *Imagine No Possessions*, 225.

10. Ibid.: "Benjamin's conception of the commodity's dream-power—of the individual consumer's shifting, mobile, unruly fantasy relations to modern commodities—departs from the model of the commodity fetish, both in Marx's sense (because Benjamin devotes much more attention to the political significance of the desires subsumed for Marx under the category exchange-value) and in the popular-Freudian sense (because the Benjaminian consumer doesn't fixate on the object)."

11. Siqueiros, "L'art dans la bataille sociale contemporaine" (1938, typescript, Sala de Arte Público Siqueiros, Mexico City). Original in French.

12. An arts journal published by Siqueiros in Barcelona in 1921.

13. Bunker, *Creating Mexican Consumer Culture*, 65.

14. Ibid., 76: "The chaos and exuberance of public bill posting decried by [Ildefonso] Estrada long predated and superseded his kiosks. As representatives of respectable society, the [Mexico City] council had long sought to bring bureaucratic rationalization to bill posting and other forms of public advertising. Throughout the Restored Republic and the Porfiriato, the Comisión de Policía lamented the popular production of store signs and advertisements that failed to comply with an 1833 law prohibiting the painting of 'ridiculous images' on storefronts and demanding proper orthography.

In 1875 the ayuntamiento even passed the commission's recommendation to rescind the business licenses as a penalty for noncompliance, but complaints by members of council for the next thirty years suggest enforcement was futile."

15. The bulk of Siqueiros's published writings are found in Tibol, *Palabras de Siqueiros*. It includes over eighty items, just over five hundred pages of print. A selection of Siqueiros's writings is available in English translation, in Siqueiros, *Art and Revolution*, trans. Sylvia Calles (London: Lawrence and Wishart, 1975). More recently, Héctor Jaimes edited three of Siqueiros's manuscripts held at the Getty Research Institute in Los Angeles. See *Fundación del muralismo mexicano: textos inéditos de David Alfaro Siqueiros*, ed. Héctor Jaimes (Mexico City: Siglo Veintiuno Editores, 2012). Mari Carmen Ramírez is among those to have engaged critically with Siqueiros's writings. She writes: "Siqueiros's theoretical clarity is an exceptional case in the confines of our continent's plastic arts." See Ramírez, "The Masses Are the Matrix: Theory and Practice of the Cinematographic Mural in Siqueiros," in David Alfaro Siqueiros, *Portrait of a Decade: David Alfaro Siqueiros, 1930–1940* (Mexico City: Instituto Nacional de Bellas Artes, 1997), 70. See also Héctor Jaimes, *Filosofía del muralismo mexicano: Orozco, Rivera y Siqueiros* (Mexico City: Plaza y Valdés, 2012).

16. Following is a list of books Siqueiros published during his lifetime: *No hay más ruta que la nuestra* (Mexico City: Talleres gráficos núm. 1 de la S. E. P, 1945); *Cómo se pinta un mural* (Mexico City: Ediciones Mexicanas, 1951); *Mi respuesta: la historia de una insidia. ¿Quiénes son los traidores a la patria?* (Mexico City: Ediciones de Arte Público, 1960); *La trácala: mi réplica a un gobierno fiscal-juez* (Mexico City: [n.p.], 1962); *Me llamaban el Coronelazo: memorias* (Mexico City: Grijalbo, 1977). The list of articles by Siqueiros is extensive, as is his correspondence with artists and intellectuals of the time. As stated before, the most comprehensive anthology of his articles, letters, lectures, and other short writings was put together by Tibol in *Palabras de Siqueiros* to commemorate the one hundredth anniversary of the author's birth.

17. In a letter written from New York to his then-partner María Asúnsolo dated April 6, 1936, and in reference to the experiments he carried out in New York with synthetic paint and the spray gun, Siqueiros writes: "debo decirte que ya por fin puedo conocer la utilidad verdadera de la brocha mecánica o brocha de aire, pues debo confesarte que antes de este experimento sufrí muchas secretas desilusiones por este veleidoso aparato inventado por el industrialismo capitalista." See Siqueiros, "Cartas a María Asúnsolo," in Tibol, *Palabras de Siqueiros*, 130. Siqueiros began to use the spray gun in 1932, and the writings that he produced around that time betray nothing of the trepidation he admits to four years later in his letter to Asúnsolo.

18. Siqueiros entertained the possibility of painting outdoors early in his career. In 1911, as a student in the Academy of San Carlos in Mexico City, Siqueiros took part in a strike against the school's traditional methods of teaching. This strike resulted in the establishment of the first open-air painting school in Mexico, the Barbizon school at Santa Anita. In many ways, his participation in the first phase of Mexican muralism a decade later can be read as a continuation of this original move away from institutional spaces of art production and exhibition and toward a less confined, more accessible environment for the production and reception of art. For an account of Siqueiros's participation in the San Carlos strike and his role in founding the Out-

door Schools, see Elsa Rogo, "David Alfaro Siqueiros," in *Parnassus* 6.4 (Apr 1, 1934), 5: "From the very first moments of his initiation into life as an art-student at the school of Santa Anita, the first of the Outdoor Painting Schools, his life has been a flame of discussion. The whole painting movement had its inception in the founding of these schools, brought about by a six-month long strike on the part of the students. Siqueiros, then only thirteen years of age, was a student in the School of Fine Arts, the Academy of Mexico City."

19. See Siqueiros, "Folio 9.1.15" (1932, typescript, Sala de Arte Público Siqueiros, Mexico City), 268: "éramos pintores de la edad del cuadro de caballete, más elocuentemente, de la edad del cuadro enmarcado, de la edad del marco. Éramos pintores de un tiempo en que la obra plástica correspondía a un espectador inmóvil. En México, en nuestra primera experiencia muralista, no habíamos hecho más que trasladarnos al 'paneux,' es decir, al cuadro encuadrado de mayores proporciones, o más claramente, a la amplificación del cuadro de caballete sobre el muro de una arquitectura." The text appears to belong to a text titled "La pintura mural como vehículo de arte político revolucionario." An English-language version of this text, also dated 1932 and written in Los Angeles, is housed at the Getty Research Institute in Los Angeles, California.

20. See, for instance, Mihai G. Grünfeld, *Antología de la poesía latinoamericana de vanguardia 1916–1935* (Madrid: Hiperión, 1995), 12: "en México los muralistas luchaban en contra del perpetuo imperialismo estadounidense y europeo buscando en el trasfondo indígena y popular una manera y voz colectiva." The muralist fight against imperialism, with clear anti-US overtones in the 1920s, had a decisive shift in tone in the 1930s and 1940s, when World War II and the rise of fascist regimes in Europe and Japan galvanized leftist intellectuals in Mexico against fascism, in turn deemphasizing a latent but strategic and qualified resistance to US imperialism. The importance that the move to the United States had for all three members of the Mexican mural movement points to the extent to which the United States functioned as a reference in the development of the arts and culture of postrevolutionary Mexico. See Desmond Rochfort, *Mexican Muralists: Orozco, Rivera, Siqueiros* (London: L. King, 1993), especially the chapter titled "The Technology of Utopia," where Rochfort distinguishes between the murals completed by Orozco, Rivera, and Siqueiros during their respective stays in the United States. Orozco's murals of the period, Rochfort writes, represent "the world of industrial and technological modernity . . . in a pictorial discourse with a moral and judgmental thrust, often harsh, deeply sombre and pessimistic" (121). "In Rivera's work," Rochfort argues, "the dualities of the modern world were treated to a conflicting combination of positions, either in an uncritical mythologized vision of American modernity or through the rhetoric of his revolutionary socialism" (122). For Siqueiros, on the other hand, the United States "proved to be a catalyst for an engagement with new methods of production, like capitalist industry itself, as well as providing thematic background for his continuous preoccupation with revolutionary struggle" (121).

21. For more on Rivera's, Orozco's, and Siqueiros's stays in the United States, see Anna Indych-López, *Muralism without Walls: Rivera, Orozco, and Siqueiros in the United States, 1927–1940* (Pittsburgh: University of Pittsburgh Press, 2009). See also Laurance P. Hurlburt, *The Mexican Muralists in the United States* (Albuquerque: University

of New Mexico Press, 1989). The opportunity to travel to Los Angeles was presented to the artist while under house arrest in Taxco, a mining town south of Mexico City known at the time as an enclave of artists and artistically inclined expatriates from the United States and elsewhere. For more on Siqueiros's stay in Taxco, see Rochfort, *Mexican Muralists*, 145. For an account of how the commissions of the murals Siqueiros painted in Los Angeles materialized in Taxco, see Shifra M. Goldman, "Siqueiros and Three Early Murals in Los Angeles," in *Art Journal* 33.4 (Summer 1974): 322.

22. Siqueiros, "Nuestra experiencia en Los Ángeles, California" (1940, typescript, Sala de Arte Público Siqueiros, Mexico City), 406: "desconocidas, inconcebiblemente, hasta hoy mismo, tanto por mis colegas muralistas de México, como por los sub-snobs de las corrientes contemporáneas de París y por los artistas en general del mundo entero."

23. See Rochfort, *Mexican Muralists*, 147: "The introduction and use of the photograph and projector in both of Siqueiros's Los Angeles murals owes much to the influence of Eisenstein. Hollywood film directors were the first to use the technique of photo-murals as it proved more economical than using scene-painters to paint backdrops." Shifra Goldman, on her part, writes that the team formed by Siqueiros in Los Angeles "included, among others, artists from the movie industry" (Goldman, "Siqueiros and Three Early Murals," 327n26).

24. Siqueiros, "Cinematografía mexicana," in Tibol, *Palabras de Siqueiros*, 21: "el *film* norteamericano, que el más alto significado de sólida modernidad: dinamismo, sana alegría infantil, vigor, destreza y *sencillez*." Emphasis in the original.

25. For more on Siqueiros's encounter with Eisenstein, see Ramírez, "Masses Are the Matrix," in Siqueiros, *Portrait of a Decade*, 68–99. See also William Richardson, "Siqueiros soviético: David Alfaro Siqueiros en el imaginario soviético," in *Otras rutas hacia Siqueiros*, ed. Olivier Debroise (Mexico City: Instituto Nacional de Bellas Artes, 1996), 285–298. See also Peter Wollen's "Perhaps . . ." *October* 88 (Spring 1999): 45–50.

26. Sergei Eisenstein, "Síntesis de las opiniones emitidas sobre la obra de Siqueiros" (1932, catalog, Sala de Arte Público Siqueiros, Mexico City), 2: "Siqueiros es la mejor prueba de que un pintor verdaderamente grande es, ante todo, una gran concepción social y una convicción ideológica [. . .] Siqueiros no es el registrador fielmente caligráfico del concepto que de una gran idea tienen las masas popularizadas. Ni es el alarido extático del individuo simplemente inflamado por la lava del entusiasmo de las masas. Siqueiros es la maravillosa síntesis entre la concepción de las masas y su representación percibida individualmente."

27. Siqueiros, "L'art dans la bataille," 91.

28. Siqueiros, "Folio 9.1.15," 266–267: "Por su propia situación nuestra obra *exterior* constituía un espectáculo público de gran envergadura, sin precedente en el arte moderno y por ciertas características físicas suyas, sin precendente en la historia del arte de todos los tiempos. En el momento mismo de iniciar su trazado observamos que millares de personas lo observaban desde los millares y millares de ventanas de los edificios que le eran circundantes. Desde las ventanas de enfrente, desde las ventanas de enfrente y de arriba a la vez, desde las ventanas de los flancos, también en este caso, de abajo y de arriba, etc., etc. Además, millares y millares de transeúntes se detenían en su marcha para observarlo y lo seguían observando en el proceso de su marcha. La

curiosidad de todos era enorme. ¡Claro, nuestro muro era exterior, estaba en la calle, bajo el cielo, podría ser visto de frente, oblicuamente por sus dos costados, desde abajo y desde arriba, de cerca, de lejos y desde gran distancia! ¡Pero es que habíamos inaugurado una forma interesantísima de arte público! ¡de arte para un espectador dinámico y múltiple! Sin pretenderlo teóricamente, habíamos encontrado en suma, un vehículo superior, estratégicamente hablando, para el arte moderno de la vida moderna. ¡Una forma indiscutible para grandes masas!"

29. Mexican art restorer Tomás Zurián first identified the photograph used by Siqueiros to model the central motif of *América tropical* as he browsed through an edition of William Ewing's *Body: Photographs of the Human Form* (San Francisco: Chronicle Books, 1994). See Zurián, "Arte y significación ideológica en Siqueiros: hallazgo iconográfico de América tropical," in *La Jornada* (13 Sep 1997): 2.

30. In a lecture delivered in Buenos Aires, Argentina, where he spoke at length of his experience in Los Angeles, Siqueiros states: "Vivíamos en el país más imperialista de la tierra: los Estados Unidos, en el país de las 'feroces contradicciones-férreas construcciones' y que presenta el espectáculo de la catástrofe imperialista más aguda que registra la historia del mundo y que ha vivido la época de prosperidad más grande del mundo y que, sin embargo, está sufriendo la crisis más tremenda, más grande que sufren los hombres! ¿Podíamos permanecer nosotros, pintores, hombres superiores, según se dice, dueños de una técnica formidable, al margen de esas realidades? [. . .] ¿Podíamos permanecer indiferentes ante la más cruel explotación de 18 millones de negros que son linchados impunemente por los más insignificantes delitos? ¿Podíamos permanecer indiferentes cuando se les están asesinando ante nosotros mismos y cuando se están haciendo leyes para impedir todo propósito de mejoramiento de la clase trabajadora norteamericana?" See Siqueiros, "Conferencia en Argentina," in Jaimes, *Fundación del muralismo mexicano*, 29–27. The other mural Siqueiros painted in Los Angeles, *Mitin obrero*, depicted black and white workers in a scene of apparent labor organization. This, it seems, together with the attention Siqueiros himself brought to the political overtones of his work, was the main reason for pressuring Siqueiros to leave the United States soon after he finished his murals.

31. The Experimental Workshop in New York was an important incubator for Siqueiros's research into industrial materials (particularly the synthetic paint pyroxylin), agitation and propaganda forms, and what Siqueiros formalized as the theory and practice of "controlled accidents," experiments with the forms and shapes synthetic paint would take when manipulated in unconventional ways (dripping, splashing, saturating) with or without the use of solvents. In Octavio Paz's estimation, Siqueiros's notion of controlled accidents stands among his most intriguing innovations. See Paz, "Re/visiones: la pintura mural" (1986), in *Obras completas*, vol. 7 (Mexico City: Fondo de Cultura Económica, 1994), 220.

32. After decades of neglect and disrepair, efforts to uncover and restore *América tropical* began in earnest in 1988. Brief notes on the history of the restoration of the mural can be found in a news article by Suzanne Muchnic for the *Los Angeles Times*, "Events Put David Alfaro Siqueiros Back in the Spotlight," http://articles.latimes.com/2010/sep/12/entertainment/la-ca-siqueiros-20100912.

33. Harold Lehman. Oral history interview with Harold Lehman.

34. Goldman, "Siqueiros and Three Early Murals," 324: "To Siqueiros, an outdoor wall in Olvera Street, located in a part of downtown Los Angeles then known as Sonora Town (because of its large Mexican population), close to the railroad terminal and City Hall, literally available to the 'flow of traffic and millions of people,' must have been especially attractive."

35. Benjamin, "Work of Art," in *Work of Art*, 25: "The scope for exhibiting the work of art has increased so enormously with the various methods of technologically reproducing it that, as happened in prehistoric times, a quantitative shift between the two poles [exhibition value/cult value] of the artwork has led to a qualitative transformation of its nature."

36. Ibid., 40.

37. Siqueiros, "Los vehículos de la pintura dialéctico-subversiva," in Tibol, *Palabras de Siqueiros*, 71: "Hasta ahora la pistola o brocha de aire ha sido usada exclusivamente en trabajos comerciales."

38. Ibid., 72: "Lo repetimos: a nuevos instrumentos, nueva estética. Cada instrumento genera su propia expresión plástica."

39. Siqueiros, "Folio 9.1.15," 254–255: "Es evidente que un arte destinado a esas nuevas realidades humanas, de carácter físicamente superior, e infinitamente superior al de la demanda anterior, no puede ser más que un arte mecánico, o bien, para no producir escalofríos, un arte mecánicamente producido. Es claro que no es lo mismo producir para una élite circunscrita y reducida que producir para millones de hombres, en una acción dinámica necesariamente de combate. Es incuestionable que no es lo mismo producir para la contemplación estática que para fines de educación y de agitación política."

40. Ibid., 257.

41. Siqueiros, "Los vehículos de la pintura," 63: "Nuestra obra fue terminada en dos semanas (primera y segunda de julio de 1932), no obstante las dimensiones del espacio elegido (24 × 19 pies). Esto pudimos hacerlos debido al uso exclusivo de instrumentos mecánicos."

42. Siqueiros, "Folio 9.1.15," 265.

43. Siqueiros, "Los vehículos de la pintura dialéctico-subversiva," 74: "*La pintura matriz fotogénica*, de precisa e infinita reproductividad por los sistemas fotostáticos, tiene un valor enorme como elemento plástico atrayente de agitación y propaganda." Emphasis in the original.

44. Ibid.: "La obra pictórica hecha para tal fin debe tener las condiciones que exige la física fotográfica; es decir, las condiciones objetivas que permitan reproducirla de la manera más precisa y clara."

45. A number of similarities exist between the ideas contained in "Los vehículos de la pintura" and those articulated by Walter Benjamin in his 1934 article on art in the age of mechanical reproduction. Mari Carmen Ramírez grapples with these similarities and points out Siqueiros's earlier articulation of ideas later developed independently and more fully by Benjamin. See Ramírez, "Masses Are the Matrix," in Siqueiros, *Portrait of a Decade*, 70: "it is very significant that, almost two years prior to the publication of Benjamin's essay in 1934, the Mexican artist David Alfaro Siqueiros,

from his civil imprisonment in Taxco, state of Guerrero, was also reflecting on the future of painting and its function within the new mass culture."

46. See Rochfort, *Mexican Muralists*, 147: "Also, in May 1932, when Siqueiros arrived in Los Angeles, a large exhibition at the Museum of Modern Art in New York entitled 'Murals by American Painters and Photographers' was claimed by the author of the exhibition catalogue, Julian Levey, to be the first recognition of the photo-mural as a valid form and in which recognized artists in the medium were invited to exhibit."

47. Ibid.

48. Siqueiros, "Folio 9.1.15," 272: "Este muchacho nos perseguía implacablemente con su aparato, siguiendo implacablemente con el proceso de nuestra obra. Cada trazo le proporcionaba un motivo para emplear una de sus placas. Cada una de las correcciones de nuestros trazos, igualmente. Metódicamente nos seguía, a través del tráfico espectacular de nuestra obra, fotografiando nuestro muro desde todos los ángulos que nosotros escogíamos para la organización de su ejecución. De muy cerca, de muy lejos, desde la derecha, desde la izquierda."

49. Ibid.: "Pero un día, de un golpe, nos puso delante de los ojos más de trescientos documentos fotográficos, que constituían la biografía gráfica de nuestra obra en todo su proceso."

50. Ibid.: "Los documentos fotográficos nos revelaban con exactitud matemática las varias depresiones de las formas, vistas desde diversos ángulos."

51. Jonathan Crary, "Spectacle, Attention, Counter-Memory," in *Guy Debord and the Situationist International: Texts and Documents*, ed. Tom McDonough (Cambridge, Mass.: MIT Press, 2002), 458.

52. Ibid., 455.

53. Siqueiros, "Qué es 'Ejercicio plástico' y cómo fue realizado," in Tibol, *Palabras de Siqueiros*, 106: "Hicimos de la cámara un aparato visual correspondiente a la realidad óptica activa del espectador normal."

54. Siqueiros, "Los vehículos de la pintura," 73: "Sin el documento vivo, sin el documento irrefutable que es el documento fotográfico, el pintor moderno no conseguirá sacar una sola gota de la verdad plástica nueva que vive intensamente en el relámpago mecánico y en el torrente de las grandes masas agitadas por la lucha final de clases. Sin el documento fotográfico nada sabrá plásticamente sobre la diaria represión sangrienta de la clase explotadora. Nada sabrá plásticamente sobre las luchas heroicas que sin descanso están librando en el mundo entero los pueblos coloniales saqueados y torturados por los imperialistas en pugna frenética. Nada sabrá plásticamente sobre las guerras interimperialistas que de periodo en periodo ahogan en sangre al mundo. Las caras de las decenas de millones de muertos proletarios le serán completamente desconocidas. La vida miserable y brutalizada que éstos viven será para él una cosa plásticamente vaga. Sin el boceto fotográfico seguirá tambaleándose como ciego romántico en medio de las férreas anatomías dinámicas de las máquinas y frente a sus formas abstractas en movimiento. Ciego para la intensa verdad social y ciego también para la intensa verdad plástica de la mecánica moderna, como acontece actualmente a los llamados pintores modernos de Francia y del mundo entero. Como ellos, será simplemente snob y su emoción se retorcerá en lucubraciones estériles. En una palabra, sin

el boceto fotográfico el pintor seguirá siendo un estático místico; es decir, un parásito de la belleza."

55. Benjamin, "Work of Art," in *Work of Art*, 23. Emphasis in the original.

56. In reference to Diego Rivera's mural on the Palacio Nacional staircase in Mexico City, Leonard Folgarait writes: "Upon crossing into a mural's field of engagement, the status of the viewer changes from spectator to participant and her or his action within this spatial envelope is then seen in terms of that state of envelopment" (Folgarait, *Mural Painting and Social Revolution in Mexico, 1920–1940: Art of the New Order* [New York: Cambridge University Press, 1998], 28). While the distinction between a mere mural painting and a spatial envelope is of great value, it loses, in my perspective, some of its explanatory value when extended to all the murals. Siqueiros is far from being the only one of the muralists who created spatial envelopes rather than large-scale paintings on walls. Some of Orozco's murals in Guadalajara envelop their viewers in much the same way as Siqueiros's *Ejercicio plástico* and his later *Retrato de la burguesía*. But I would hesitate to include Rivera's mural at the Palacio Nacional, which does not envelop so much as it presents the spectator with a visual plane too large to be taken in from a single point of view. Its composition, as Folgarait writes, is too fragmentary to elicit a fluid, enveloping visual atmosphere.

57. The use of photographs to sketch the nude figures in *Ejercicio plástico* is corroborated by Hurlburt, *Mexican Muralists*, 219: "one receives the impression that rather than passively viewing the paintings, the gigantic female nudes and strange monster-types in severely distorted postures confronted, even challenged, the spectator passing through the mural environment. Siqueiros achieved this effect by having nudes pose on top of plate glass mounted off the floor, photographing them from different angles and positions through the glass, and then projecting the results onto the walls of the room."

58. Siqueiros, "Folio 9.1.15," 269: "La geometría de nuestro muro no era absoluta ni estática, sino profundamente múltiple y móvil. [. . .] En la pintura mural, el carácter móvil del espectador, moviliza la geometría orgánica del muro, la 'distorsiona,' la transforma."

59. As Rochfort notes, Siqueiros's adoption of synthetic paint from the automobile industry was, like his relocation of mural painting to exterior walls, another one of his "chance discoveries." See Rochfort, *Mexican Muralists*, 148.

60. Folgarait writes that in agreeing to paint the mural at the Union's headquarters, Siqueiros's "sole condition was that he would have the choice of walls to paint." See Folgarait, *Mural Painting*, 141. Siqueiros's conditions were significantly more demanding. He was particularly insistent on the need to have complete control of the mural's execution. A letter dated August 18, 1939, signed by Siqueiros and entitled "Criterio del suscrito sobre la pintura mural del edificio nuevo del Sindicato Mexicano de Electricistas" (typescript, Sala de Arte Público Siqueiros, Mexico City), provides a detailed list of these conditions.

61. Hurlburt, *Mexican Muralists*, 240: "the team studied more than one hundred people in the act of climbing the stairway to determine the movement of an 'average' spectator."

62. This is the point made by Jennifer Jolly when she writes: "En un empeño de

crear un estilo de arte popular para una audiencia de trabajadores electricistas, los artistas elaboraron los temas de los murales utilizando fuentes desde periódicos y revistas mexicanas e internacionales hasta fotografías tomadas en plantas eléctricas cerca de la Ciudad de México, así como películas de tendencia socialista y antiguas obras de arte." See Jolly, "David Alfaro Siqueiros, Antonio Pujol, Luis Arenal, Josep Renau y Miguel Prieto: *Retrato de la burguesía*," in *Muralismo mexicano, 1920–1940*, ed. Ida Rodríguez Prampolini (Mexico City: Fondo de Cultura Económica, 2012): 350.

63. Hurlburt sees the photomontages of German artist John Heartfield as a "specific twentieth-century precedent for the painterly experimentation and revolutionary political commentary of the Electricians murals," whose "depiction of Communist subject matter anticipated the basic political thrust of the Electricians Union mural, as well as much of its actual imagery." See Hurlburt, *Mexican Muralists*, 241. Olivier Debroise sees the influence of Heartfield in other works besides *Retrato de la burguesía*. In reference to *Víctima proletaria*, a pyroxylin on canvas easel painting from 1933, Debroise writes: "La imagen es un montaje, y lleva en sí una consigna literal, a la manera de la caricatura periodística, a la manera también de los fotomontajes de John Heartfield." See Debroise, "Arte acción: David Alfaro Siqueiros en las estrategias artísticas e ideológicas de los años treinta," in *Retrato de una década: David Alfaro Siqueiros, 1930–1940* (Mexico City: Instituto Nacional de Bellas Artes, 1996), 54. Heartfield photomontages appeared in *Frente a frente*, an agitational magazine published from 1933 to 1938 under the guidance of Siqueiros. European and Soviet photomontage featured prominently in this publication, together with explicit photographic documents from the Spanish Civil War, documents verging—in their presentation of violence—on the sensationalist. *Frente a frente* featured photomontages by Gustav Klutsis. Most, if not all, of the works reproduced in the magazine are published without attribution.

64. The typescript where this manuscript is filed includes excerpts from several different documents with different titles.

65. Siqueiros, "Folio 9.1.15," 248: "no puede haber obra de arte trascendente en una situación de anacronismo técnico. La obra de arte verdadera no puede florecer mas que en marcha paralela con la técnica de su tiempo en su conjunto. Más aún: la obra de arte verdadera es siempre anticipo técnico al conjunto de la producción técnica industrial de su tiempo."

66. Ibid., 252: "En la antigüedad, la pintura, la escultura y la arquitectura eran un cuerpo indivisible. Era la época de la plástica integral."

67. Ibid., 253: "Más tarde, cuando se modificó la naturaleza económica de la sociedad cristiana surgieron los señores aristócratas del feudalismo."

68. Ibid.: "La pintura mural dejó de hacerse en los grandes centros públicos de concentración de masas para penetrar en las capillas privadas de los Papas y en los palacios 'paganos' de la aristocracia."

69. Ibid.: "La pintura se redujo en sus proporciones materiales paralelamente a la reducción que había sufrido el espectador correspondiente."

70. Ibid., 254: "el mercado de productos de artes plásticas sufre una crisis profunda [. . .] aparece la economía burguesa y con ella otro tipo de mercado, esto es, un mercado más amplio, tan amplio como la nueva clase rica y el cuadro transportable se reduce en proporciones." The point made by Siqueiros is similar to one made by Benjamin when

he states: "It is easier to exhibit a portrait bust that can be sent here and there than to exhibit the statue of a divinity that has a fixed place in the interior of a temple. A panel painting can be exhibited more easily than the mosaic or fresco which preceded it" (Benjamin, "Work of Art," in *Work of Art*, 25).

71. Siqueiros, "Folio 9.1.15," 254: "En el momento actual, el mercado de productos de artes plásticas sufre una crisis profunda, que no es más que la transcripción en el campo de la cultura de la crisis que sufre la sociedad como estructura económica en su conjunto. Y paralelamente aparecen manifestaciones de un nuevo tipo social, es decir, de un nuevo mercado. El mundo se orienta según todas las manifestaciones de la economía base vital de los pueblos, hacia formas colectivas, masas imponentes de hombres, concentraciones de decenas y miles de personas aparecen en la vida diaria de todos los pueblos . . . y con ellas la necesidad de nuevas formas de publicidad y de arte."

72. José Clemente Orozco, *Alegoría nacional* (1947).

73. Luis Cardoza y Aragón, *México: pintura de hoy* (Mexico City: Fondo de Cultura Económica, 1964), 101: "Los nuevos materiales lo condujeron [a Siqueiros] a problemas nuevos que no alteraron las bases principales de su estética: el rechazo del cuadro de caballete, la preocupación didáctica por la utilidad política inmediata de la pintura pública, etc."

74. See Siqueiros, *No hay más ruta*, 71: "Esa enfermedad que hemos denominado 'mexican curios' inició manifiestamente el debilitamiento de la pintura mexicana en su conjunto y hoy infesta gravemente a casi toda la producción literaria, cinematográfica, teatral, escultórica, popular, etc., de nuestro país. La más superlativa de las cursilerías seudo-nacionalista [*sic*] está degradando el arte de México en sus más diversas manifestaciones, y amenaza con hundirlo en la superficialidad, la mediocridad y el desprestigio total."

75. The increasing urbanization and modernization of Mexico from the 1940s onward is documented in Salvador Novo's *Nueva grandeza mexicana*, a 1946 chronicle of the burgeoning city (Mexico City: Cien de México, 2001). Novo, a celebrated poet and author of a great number of articles on film and urban life, was one of the earliest Mexican intellectuals to document the arrival of cars, telephones, radio, and cinema to Mexico City, and he is well known for his candid descriptions of postrevolutionary urban Mexico. Structured as a week-long exploration of the capital that begins with a bus journey through the city and ends at the newly built airport, *Nueva grandeza mexicana* captures the highlights and growing pains of midcentury Mexico City.

76. Robin Greeley, "Muralism and the State in Post-Revolution Mexico, 1920–1970," in *Mexican Muralism: A Critical History,* ed. Alejandro Anreus, Leonard Folgarait, and Robin A. Greeley (Berkeley: University of California Press, 2012), 15.

77. *Arte público: tribuna de pintores muralistas, escultores, grabadores y artistas de la estampa en general*, Ed. Sociedad de Amigos de la Pintura Mexicana Moderna. The first bulletin was published in Mexico City in February 1953.

78. Siqueiros, "Un problema técnico," in Tibol, *Palabras de Siqueiros*, 343: "No existe más que una sola experiencia válida anterior a nuestro actual esfuerzo muralista de intención figurativa y realista hacia la calle: el de la *propaganda comercial*, el *affiche* que cubre los grandes muros descubiertos de las ciudades, financiera, industrial y comer-

cialmente importantes de nuestro tiempo. Y esto, únicamente, por tratarse de obras precisamente figurativas y de intención ultrarrealista, destinadas al exterior."

79. Ibid.: "muralismo de propaganda comercial."

80. Ibid., 348: "¡No asombrarse! La experiencia viva, aún en intensa evolución técnica, por razón del progreso técnico general, del *muralismo comercial*, del gran *affiche* comercial, que cubre las grandes superficies libres de las ciudades modernas, de las grandes urbes en el mundo capitalista: un muralismo comercial que yo llamo [. . .] 'el verdadero muralismo de la clase burguesa,' su única expresión plástica hacia el exterior. Una experiencia, como es obvio, que, independientemente de la superficialidad y lo transitorio, como de lo mercenario, de su mensaje, nos aporta enseñanzas de indiscutible utilidad para lo que nosotros queremos hacer." Emphasis in the original.

81. Diana Sorensen, *A Turbulent Decade Remembered: Scenes from the Latin American Sixties* (Palo Alto, CA: Stanford University Press, 2007), 108–109: "What was truly exceptional in the sixties was that the authors were met by a reading public ready to buy their books. . . . Urban development went hand in hand with the surge of university enrollments, which reached stunning growth in the major cities: in the Universidad de Buenos Aires, for example, the Facultad de Filosofía y Letras saw a 146 percent increase in students and the creation of two new *carreras* (fields of specialization): Sociology and Psychology. The Universidad Nacional Autónoma de Mexico, having inaugurated its ambitious Ciudad Universitaria in 1954, increased its student body from 36,000 in 1955 to almost 67,000 in 1961. Lima, Bogotá, Buenos Aires, and Caracas witnessed the erection of their own Ciudades Universitarias in the fifties; the Universidad de Chile and the Universidad de la República in Montevideo expanded their facilities around that time so as to accommodate new *facultades* and increased enrollments. The new professionals found employment in the developing economy of transnational corporations and state-sponsored institutions; they became part of a middle-class, educated reading public that differed from the elites that had previously validated literary value." Maria Arminda do Nascimento Arruda makes a comparable point in relation to Brazil and to the city of São Paulo in particular. See Arruda, *Metrópole e cultura: São Paulo no meio século XX* (Bauru, São Paulo: Editora da Universidade do Sagrado Coração, 2001), 44: "É marca distintiva deste momento a aproximação entre a antiga elite ilustrada e esses novos intelectuais de classe média, principalmente aqueles formados pela Faculdade de Filosofia da USP."

82. For more details on the commission, see Antonio Rodríguez, *David Alfaro Siqueiros: Mural Painting* (Mexico City: Fondo Editorial de la Plástica Mexicana, 1993), 83–84: "After 1932, when he painted his first two open-air murals on the exterior walls of buildings in Los Angeles, Siqueiros always kept alive the hope that he would be able to repeat the experience. This hope became a reality thanks to architects Guillermo Rossel de la Lama and Lorenzo Carrasco, active promoters and editors of the architecture and visual arts magazine *Espacios*. They invited him to paint a mural on the façade of the Automex (Chrysler) Factory in Mexico City. . . . Siqueiros envisioned an elongated oval within which a woman moves, running at high speed."

83. Siqueiros, "Vigencia del movimiento plástico mexicano contemporáneo," in Tibol, *Palabras de Siqueiros*, 471: "Fue el público, fueron los transeúntes quienes nos dijeron con su sola actuación, con su sola presencia dinámica, cómo debíamos compo-

ner nuestras obras de nuevo tipo, una obra para ser vista desde cientos de ventanas, desde muchos niveles, todos cuantos pueden tener los edificios modernos; para ser vista desde automóviles y camiones; para ser vista desde arriba y desde abajo y desde los ángulos más extremos."

84. For a discussion of *Caminos de Anáhuac* and artists who worked on projects related to the automobile industry, see Cristobal Andrés Jácome, "Journeys and Assemblages," in Eder, *Defying Stability*, 285–295.

85. Siqueiros, "Mi experiencia en el muralismo exterior," in Tibol, *Palabras de Siqueiros*, 410–411: "Hacia afuera las formas objetivamente planas carecen de beligerancia frente a las tridimensionales que las circundan: casas, árboles, vehículos, etcétera. Así lo entendieron los artistas de todos los grandes periodos de la historia. Consideraciones éstas que me condujeron, como aconteció con Rivera, a la aplicación de una técnica que denominamos escultopintura."

86. Siqueiros, "Un problema técnico," in Tibol, *Palabras de Siqueiros*, 353: "Si a mayor magnitud física de una obra, particularmente en la pintura mural exterior, corresponde una mayor violencia en el trazo del dibujo como una mayor violencia en la policromía y coloración en general, me parece de la lógica elemental que la textura o las texturas no pueden permanecer en el grado potencial de aquellas que corresponden al cuadro de caballete y la propia pintura mural interior."

87. Benjamin, "Work of Art," in *Work of Art*, 40.

88. Kiaer, *Imagine No Possessions*, 225.

89. Paz, *El arco y la lira*, in *Obras completas*, vol. 1, 64: "Todos sabemos hasta qué punto es difícil rozar las orillas de la distracción. Esta experiencia se enfrenta a las tendencias predominantes de nuestra civilización, que propone como arquetipos humanos al abstraído, al retraído y hasta al contraído. Un hombre que se distrae, niega al mundo moderno. Al hacerlo, se juega el todo por el todo. Intelectualmente, su decisión no es diversa a la del suicida por sed de saber qué hay del otro lado de la vida. El distraído se pregunta: ¿qué hay del otro lado de la vigilia y de la razón? La distracción quiere decir: atracción por el reverso de este mundo."

90. Benjamin, "Theory of Distraction," in *Work of Art*, 56.

91. Ibid., 57.

92. Siqueiros, "Afirmaciones de Siqueiros," in *Arte público* (February 1953), 17: "La diferencia entre la pintura mural en el exterior de los edificios y en el interior de los mismos, es infinitamente mayor que la que existe entre la pintura mural, en general, y la pintura llamada de caballete. En primer lugar considero que entre la una y la otra hay diferencias ópticas fundamentales: algo para ser visto desde 20, 30, 40 y quizás 50 metros y algo para ser visto desde centenares de metros y quizás kilómetros, que plantean diferencias fundamentales de composición. Si es verdad que el espectador del mural interior, en su tránsito normal, establece las leyes de la composición pictórica, tendremos que admitir que la base del 'gran espectáculo' de la pintura en el exterior, presupone soluciones radicalmente diferentes."

93. Valerie Fraser, *Building the New World: Studies in the Modern Architecture of Latin America 1930–1960* (New York: Verso: 2000), 79.

94. Siqueiros, "Cuatro tendencias intervienen en la ejecución de los murales en el exterior de los edificios de la Ciudad Universitaria," in *Arte público* (February 1953): 9.

"El estilo, en cierta proporción, por manifiesta y declarada voluntad del pintor, muestra elementos del gran 'affiche' o muralismo comercial, aunque sin perder los elementos de síntesis escultórica tradicional, que son comunes a su obra general."

95. Siqueiros, "El 'affiche' como antecedente y experiencia para nuestra pintura mural exterior," in Tibol, *Palabras de Siqueiros*, 363: "'un muralismo en el que la conjunción del neón y los motores mecánicos había llegado a realizar la expresión gráfica del movimiento.'"

96. Folgarait, *So Far from Heaven: David Alfaro Siqueiros' The March of Humanity and Mexican Revolutionary Politics* (New York: Cambridge University Press, 1987), 51.

97. Manuel Suárez, cited in Folgarait, *So Far from Heaven*, 83.

98. Folgarait, *So Far from Heaven*, 23.

99. Ibid.: "most writers on the Mexican economy of the 1960s agree that the tourist trade has been most instrumental in keeping it afloat."

100. Ibid., 51.

101. Siqueiros, cited in Folgarait, *So Far from Heaven*, 27.

Chapter 2: Fascination

1. Reproduced in Augusto de Campos, *Viva vaia: poesia, 1949–1979* (Cotia, São Paulo: Ateliê Editorial, 2000). All poems by Augusto de Campos here cited are included in this volume unless otherwise noted. Note that *Poetamenos* appeared two years before the movement as such received its name: two years before the publication of an article by Augusto de Campos titled "poesia concreta," originally published in *Forum*, the journal of the Faculdade Paulista de Direito, in October 1955. See Augusto de Campos, "poesia concreta," in Campos, Pignatari, and Campos, *Teoria da poesia concreta*, 55–57. The name of the movement derives from the 1930 "Concrete Art Manifesto" by Theo van Doesburg. See Doesburg, "Concrete Art Manifesto," in Saitta and Zucker, *Abstraction in Artificial Intelligence*, 413. For a critical overview of the poems in *Poetamenos* and for a discussion of the place of these poems in Augusto de Campos's work, see Bruce Williams, "'poetamenos': Campo(s) de expressão em cores," *Mester* 14.1 (Spring 1985): 55–65. See also K. David Jackson, "Augusto Fingers: dacto, grypho, grama, clip. Avec une chronologie des oeuvres (art technologique) d'Augusto de Campos," *Brésil(s)* 6 (2014): 165–180.

2. Augusto de Campos showed poems from *Poetamenos* hanging from a wall in the *I Exposição Nacional de Arte Concreta*, the art exhibition that brought together concrete artists from São Paulo and Rio de Janeiro, making the differences between the two groups manifest and marking the split that gives rise to neoconcretism in Rio de Janeiro as a stand-alone movement. The critic, poet, and one-time subscriber to the concrete poetry movement Ferreira Gullar attributed the "great repercussion" of this exhibition to the inaugural presentation of concrete poems. See Gullar, "Arte concreta no Brasil": "A I Exposição Nacional de Arte Concreta deveu sua grande repercussão à presença, nela, das primeiras manifestações da poesia concreta que eram assim trazidas a público pela primeira vez."

3. Augusto de Campos, cited in Mary Ellen Solt, "Introduction," in *Concrete Poetry: A World View* (Bloomington: Indiana University Press, 1968), 12.

4. Haroldo de Campos and Augusto de Campos, "Brazilian Concrete Poetry: How It Looks Today," interviewed by Marjorie Perloff in *Arshile: A Magazine of the Arts* 3 (1994): 63.

5. See, for instance, Claus Clüver's "Klangfarbenmelodie in Polychromatic Poems: A. von Webern and A. de Campos," in *Comparative Literature Studies* 18.3 (Sept. 1981): 386–398. See also Antonio Sergio Bessa, "The 'image of the voice' in Augusto de Campos' *Poetamenos*," *Ciberletras: Revista de Crítica Literaria y de Cultura* 17 (20017), n.p., http://www.lehman.cuny.edu/ciberletras/v17/bessa.htm. The visual arts, painting in particular, provide another important intertext for *Poetamenos* and concrete poetry in general. See João Bandeira, "Words in Space," in *Concreta '56: a raiz da forma = Concret '56: the root of form*, ed. Mammì et al. (São Paulo: Museu de Arte Moderna de São Paulo, 2006), 120: "Augusto de Campos particularly remembers a painting by Luiz Sacilotto (*Concreção*, 1952) which gave him some suggestions on how to graphically organize his poems of the series *poetamenos*; and Haroldo de Campos quotes Sacilotto, [Maurício] Nogueira Lima and [Hermelindo] Fiaminghi to say that 'the way with which . . . they structured their paintings oriented the structuring of some of our poems.'" See also Clüver, "The Noigandres Poets," which studies, in depth and in detail, the link between concrete art and poetry.

6. Taussig, *Nervous System*, 143.

7. Ibid., 147.

8. Ibid., 148.

9. Theodor W. Adorno, "On Lyric Poetry and Society" in *Notes to Literature* (New York: Columbia University Press, 1991), 40.

10. Taussig, *Nervous System*, 145.

11. Benjamin, *One-Way Street*, 77.

12. Taussig, *Nervous System*, 147.

13. Ibid., 146.

14. Certeau, *Practice of Everyday Life*, xi.

15. Rachel C. Lee reads this step in Taussig's theory of vision and mimesis as part of "a broader theoretical movement to shift the question for academic criticism away from vision and semiotics . . . to tactility and affect." Lee, "Haptics, Mobile Handhelds, and Other 'Novel' Devices: The Tactile Unconscious of Reading across Old and New Media," in *Critical Digital Studies: A Reader*, 2nd ed., ed. Arthur Kroker and Marilouise Kroker (Toronto: University of Toronto Press, 2013): 358. Emphasis in the original. For a discussion of the importance of the materiality of language in Brazilian concrete poetry, See Pedro Erber, "The Word as Object: Concrete Poetry, Ideogram, and the Modernization of Language," *Luso-Brazilian Review* 49.2 (2012): 72–101.

16. Price, *Object of the Atlantic*, 171.

17. Daniela Name, "'Eu me lembro,'" in *Diálogo concreto*, 9: "Apesar das inúmeras contradições sociais, [Getúlio] Vargas começou a abrir o país para a urbanização e a industrialização. Nos quatro anos em que comandou o país do Palácio do Catete, as grandes cidades, especialmente o Rio e São Paulo, passaram a roubar do campo o poder de decidir os destinos da nação."

18. Ibid.: "As vanguardas artísticas que se organizam no Brasil neste período precisam ser compreendidas no contexto desenvolvimentista. Levando-o em considera-

ção, fica mais fácil entender por que os artistas ligados aos movimentos Concreto, em São Paulo, e Neoconcreto, no Rio, acabam se aproximando da comunicação visual e do design. . . . Quanto mais desenvolvida é a indústria, mais produtos há para se vender; quanto mais urbano é o país, maior é o raio de ação dos meios de comunicação para divulgar aquilo que é vendido, assim como a quantidade de assalariados para consumir aqueles produtos."

19. Décio Pignatari, "nova poesia: concreta (manifesto)" (1956), in Campos, Pignatari, and Campos, *Teoria da poesia concreta*, 67: "o verso: crise. obriga o leitor de manchetes (simultaneidade) a uma atitude postiça."

20. Süssekind, *Vidrieras astilladas*, 178: "Fue también a fines de los años 50, en pleno optimismo desarrollista, que se inició uno de los diálogos más provechosos entre poesía, tecnología y espectáculo en Brasil. Porque, sin temor a mirar de frente a la publicidad, los carteles luminosos y la televisión fueron los poetas concretos paulistas quienes, en el cambio de la década, redefinieron el libro en cuanto objeto, procuraron modificar la mirada del lector de poesía, ahora también espectador del poema."

21. Ibid.

22. Pignatari, "nova poesia," in Campos, Pignatari, and Campos, *Teoria da poesia concreta*, 67: "uma arte geral da linguagem. propaganda, imprensa, rádio, televisão, cinema. uma arte popular."

23. A. de Campos, *Balanço da bossa*, 59–60: "Os novos meios de comunicação de massa, jornais e revistas, rádio e televisão, têm suas grandes matrizes nas metrópoles, de cujas 'centrais' se irradiam as informações para milhares de pessoas de regiões cada vez mais numerosas. A intercomunicabilidade universal é cada vez mais intensa e mais difícil de conter, de tal sorte que é literalmente impossível a um cidadão qualquer viver a sua vida diária sem se defrontar a cada passo com o Vietnã, os Beatles, as greves, 007, a Lua, Mao ou o Papa. Por isso mesmo é inútil preconizar uma impermeabilidade nacionalística aos movimentos, modas e manias de massa que fluem e refluem de todas as partes para todas as partes. Marx e Engels já o anteviam: 'Em lugar do antigo isolamento de regiões e nações que se bastavam a si próprias, desenvolve-se um intercâmbio universal, uma universal interdependência das nações. E isto se refere tanto à produção material como à produção intelectual. As criações intelectuais de uma nação tornam-se propriedade comum de todas. A estreiteza e o exclusivismo nacionais tornam-se cada vez mais impossíveis; das inúmeras literaturas nacionais e locais, nasce uma literatura universal.'"

24. Haroldo de Campos, "Comunicação na poesia de vanguarda," in *A arte no horizonte do provável e outros ensaios* (São Paulo: Editora Perspectiva, 1969), 151: "Para ambos [Hegel and Marx] a emergência da grande imprensa foi objeto de meditação: Hegel referia que a leitura do jornal passava a ser, para nossa época, uma espécie de oração filosófica matinal; Marx, refletindo sobre a impossibilidade da épica em nosso tempo, usa de uma bela paronomásia para exprimir que, diante da imprensa, a fala e a fábula, o conto e o canto ('das Singen und Sagen'), a Musa dos gregos enfim, cessam de se fazer ouvir. Lamartine, por sinal um poeta representativo do Romantismo ortodoxo na sua vertente de poesia-lágrima, escrevia em 1831: 'O pensamento se difundirá no mundo com a velocidade da luz, instantâneamente concebido, instantâneamente escrito e compreendido até às extremidades do globo [. . .] Não terá tempo para amadu-

recer—para se acumular num livro; o livro chegará muito tarde. O único livro possível a partir de hoje é o jornal'. E Mallarmé, para o seu *Un Coup de Dés* (1897), inspira-se nas técnicas de espacialização visual da imprensa cotidiana, tal como cerca de vinte anos antes um brasileiro genial, o poeta Sousândrade, se voltara para os recursos de montagem de fragmentos do jornal (notícias, eventos, pessoas) na criação do seu 'Inferno de Wall Street', localizado no cenário da Bolsa de Nova Iorque. Mallarmé via na imprensa o 'moderno poema popular', uma forma rudimentar do Livro enciclopédico e último de seus sonhos."

25. Haroldo de Campos, "Concrete Poetry-Language-Communication" (1957), in his *Novas: Selected Writings*, ed. Antonio Sergio Bessa and Odile Cisneros (Evanston, IL: Northwestern University Press, 2007): 235.

26. Ibid., 245: "Another constant source will be Mallarmé's theory of the book and his interest in journalistic techniques."

27. Haroldo de Campos, Augusto de Campos, and Décio Pignatari contributed regularly to the *suplemento dominical* with their own writings and with translations. Most of the manifestos and programmatic texts they published in 1957 (their most prolific year for this kind of writing) appeared first in the *suplemento dominical*, which also reprinted that year some of the writings they had previously published elsewhere.

28. See Wilson Figuereido, "Da crise política fez-se o 'JB': ascensão e queda do 'Jornal do Brasil,'" in *Folha de São Paulo* (July 25 2010), http://www1.folha.uol.com.br/fsp/ilustrissima/il2507201006.htm.

29. See Name, "'Eu me lembro,'" in *Diálogo concreto*, 31–32.

30. Figuereido, "Da crise política": "O 'JB' se destacava pelo modo de fazer jornal e representar a classe média, que veio inaugurar a sociedade de consumo, cujo símbolo seria o automóvel de fabricação nacional."

31. Diana Sorensen, *Turbulent Decade Remembered*, 5.

32. Benjamin, *One-Way Street*, 42.

33. H. de Campos, "Concrete Poetry-Language-Communication" (1957), in *Novas*, 245.

34. Décio Pignatari, "Arte gráfica e a outra," in *Estado de São Paulo: suplemento literário* (May 30, 1964): 6.

35. See H. de Campos, "Miramar na mira," the essay included in the 1990 edition of Andrade's *Memórias sentimentais*. The reissue of Andrade's work was promoted by the concrete poets, who sought out, studied, and republished forgotten and understudied works of Brazilian experimental poetry as part of their work.

36. See H. de Campos, "Da razão antropofágica," in *Metalinguagem & outras metas*, 231–255.

37. Oswald de Andrade, "O caminho percorrido" (1944), in *Ponta de lança* (Editora Civilização Brasileira: Rio de Janeiro, 1971), 93: "Indagar por que se processou na nossa capital a renovação literária é o mesmo que indagar por que se produziu em Minas Gerais a Inconfidência. Como houve as revoluções do ouro, houve as do café."

38. Ibid., 95: "É preciso compreender o modernismo com suas causas materiais e fecundantes, hauridas no parque industrial de São Paulo, com seus compromissos de classe no período áureo-burguês do primeiro café valorizado, enfim com o seu lancinante divisor das águas que foi a Antropofagia nos prenúncios do abalo mundial de

Wall-Street. O modernismo é um diagrama da alta do café, da quebra e da revolução brasileira."

39. See Mark Francis, "Preface," in *Pop*, 12: "In different ways, the graphics of El Lissitzky and the collages of John Heartfield and Kurt Schwitters were Pop *avant la lettre* and were important for the cumulative 'pinboard' aesthetic used by Nigel Henderson, Bruce Connor, Richard Hamilton, and later in Gerhard Richter's *Atlas*." These same references would pop up again, and forcefully, in Chile in the 1970s, particularly in the work of Catalina Parra, who returns to Santiago from Germany soon after the military coup and begins working earnestly as "visualizer" and photomontage artist.

40. Haroldo de Campos, "Maiakovski e o construtivismo," in "*O Estado de São Paulo: suplemento literário* (Sept. 29, 1962), 4: "Lissítski resolve o problema da titulagem dos poemas, criando como que logotipos."

41. Mike Gonzalez and David Treece, *The Gathering of the Voices: The Twentieth-Century Poetry of Latin America* (Verso: London, 1992): 229. Charles Perrone argues against Brazilian concrete poetry's presumed "uncritical identification with nationalist capitalist development" and stresses the movement's *conscious* insertion into its social context: "Brazilian concrete poetry . . . emerged in a conscious context of developmentalism and nationalist sentiment." Perrone, *Seven Faces: Brazilian Poetry since Modernism* (Durham, NC: Duke University Press, 1996), 70.

42. Ibid.

43. Ibid., 230.

44. Ibid., 245.

45. Antonio Candido, "Literatura e subdesenvolvimento" (1970), in *A educação pela noite e outros ensaios*, ed. Marta de Mello e Souza (São Paulo: Editora Ática, 1989), 146: "Certas experiências modernas são fecundas sob o ponto de vista do espírito de vanguarda e da inserção da arte e da literatura no ritmo do tempo, como é o caso do Concretismo e outras correntes. Mas não custa lembrar o que pode ocorrer quando manipuladas politicamente do lado errado, numa sociedade de massas."

46. Benjamin, *One-Way Street*, 43.

47. Ibid., 42.

48. Augusto de Campos, "poesia concreta (manifesto)" (1956), in Campos, Pignatari, and Campos, *Teoria da poesia concreta*, 72: "POESIA CONCRETA: TENSÃO DE PALAVRAS-COISAS NO ESPAÇO-TEMPO."

49. For a more detailed discussion of the movement toward sculpture and the objectual from within concrete poetry, see João Bandeira, "Words in Space," 132–138. See also Pedro Erber, "The Word as Object."

50. Ibid., 231.

51. Mark Hansen, *Embodying Technesis: Technology beyond Writing* (Ann Arbor: University of Michigan Press, 2000), 232. This step in Benjamin's thought should be considered along with the historicization of perception he performs in his seminal essay on reproducibility. See Benjamin, "Work of Art," in *Work of Art*, 23. The way in which human perception is organized—the medium in which it occurs—is conditioned not only by nature but by history." Emphasis in the original. A concise series of substantial claims is made here, in the assertion that perception is not so much given as it is *organized*, and that it is something to be carried out in a platform, a "medium" subject

to historical contingence in a way that the "natural" body—as site and guarantor of a stable, unchanging, and congenitally determined sense perception—is not. In "Paris, The Capital of the Nineteenth Century," Benjamin links the historicity of perception to communication technologies and urban commodity capitalism, noting the imbrication of mass media in the expansion of consumer culture. See Benjamin, "Paris, the Capital of the Nineteenth Century," in *Work of Art*, 100: "For its part, photography greatly extends the sphere of commodity exchange, from mid-century onward, by flooding the market with countless images of figures, landscapes, and events which had previously been available either not at all or only as pictures for individual consumers."

52. Hansen, *Embodying Technesis*, 233.

53. H. de Campos, "Concrete Poetry-Language-Communication," in *Novas*, 245.

54. Ibid.

55. Ibid.

56. Pedrosa, "Science and Art: Communicating Vessels" (1960), in Ferreira and Herkenhoff, *Mário Pedrosa*, 115.

57. See Pedrosa, "World in Crisis, Man in Crisis, Art in Crisis," in Ferreira and Herkenhoff, *Mário Pedrosa*, 135–138.

58. Ronaldo Brito, "Neoconcretismo," in *Malasartes* 3 (April–June 1976): 9–13.

59. Ronaldo Brito, *Neoconcretismo: vértice e ruptura do projeto construtivo brasileiro* (São Paulo: Cosac & Naify Edicões, 1999).

60. Brito, "Neoconcretismo," 9.

61. Ibid., 10: "Para os artistas construtivos ocidentais—de Mondrian e Van Doesburg até Max Bill e os concretistas—o trabalho de arte só podia ser pensado como inserção social sob duas formas: de um modo especulativo e sublimante (é o caso dos delírios vagamente platônicos de Mondrian) e/ou visando uma integração quase necessariamente acrítica no processo de produção vigente (Bauhaus em parte, Escola de Ulm)."

62. See Lorenzo Mammì, "Concret '56: The Root of Form (A Reconstruction of the I National Exhibition of Concrete Art)," in Mammì et al., *Concreta '56*, 26: "Thirty years away, this thesis is still valid, but, as any historical hypothesis, it needs verification and depth. It cannot be reduced just to a mechanical simplification, according to which the concretism of the first half of the 50's would only be a preparatory and scholarly phase (*Bauhausexercise*, according to a statement by A. Barr that quite irritated Mário Pedrosa), followed by a really original and creative production only towards the end of that decade. Besides being unfair with a consistent part of the concrete production of the first phase (that which made possible the national exhibition of 1956), the formula is too schematic to cover the complexity of the issues being discussed."

63. Price, *Object of the Atlantic*, 165: "even as concrete poetry coincided with a postwar explosion of consumer culture, it demonstrated a simultaneous interest in nonobjects, reflecting the split nature of concretude that earlier vanguards had observed."

64. Robert Kaufman, "Adorno's Social Lyric, and Literary Criticism Today: Poetics, Aesthetics, Modernity," in *The Cambridge Companion to Adorno* (Cambridge: Cambridge University Press, 2004), 362.

65. Adorno, *Aesthetic Theory*, 58.

66. See José Gómez Sicre, "Introduction," in *Esso Salon of Young Artists* (n.p.), ex-

hibition catalog. See also Alejandro Obregón, *Primer Salón Intercol de artistas jóvenes* (Bogotá, Colombia: Museo de Arte Moderno de Bogotá, 1964).

67. Pignatari, "Publicidade o texto vivo," in *O Estado de São Paulo* (Nov. 16, 1958): "Dada a necessidade de comunicação rápida e precisa, nos tempos modernos é notável em todos os setores a importância que adquiriu o setor não verbal. Ver é muito mais fácil do que ler. As próprias palavras não escaparam a essa influencia e o seu aspecto visual é valorizado cada vez mais. Essa preocupação é evidente, por exemplo, nas marcas e logotipos: 'Esso', todo curvas no oval característico é muito mais 'vista' do que 'lida.'"

68. Pignatari, "nova poesia," in Campos, Pignatari, and Campos, *Teoria da poesia concreta*, 67: "antieconômico, não se concentra, não se comunica rapidamente."

69. Pignatari, *Poesia pois é poesia, 1950–1975; Poetc, 1976–1986* (São Paulo: Brasiliense, 1986). All poems by Pignatari here cited are included in this volume, unless otherwise noted.

70. The name of this publication also designates the smaller, more prominent group of concrete poets, all of them based in São Paulo: Haroldo de Campos, Augusto de Campos, and Décio Pignatari.

71. Augusto de Campos, "From Dante to the Post-Concrete: An Interview with Augusto de Campos," interview with Roland Greene, in *Harvard Library Bulletin* 3.2 (Summer 1992): n.p.

72. See Solt, "Introduction," in *Concrete Poetry*, 7.

73. Alfonso Reyes, *La experiencia literaria* (Buenos Aires, Editorial Losada: 1961), 160: "Ciertamente que este poema no se dirige a la razón, sino más bien a la sensación y a la fantasía. Las palabras no buscan aquí un fin útil. Juegan solas, casi."

74. Roman Jakobson, "Linguistics and Poetics," in *The Structuralists: From Marx to Lévi-Strauss*, ed. Richard T. De George and Fernande M. De George (Garden City, NY: Anchor, 1972): 107.

75. Price argues against the idea "that concrete poetry was *mimetic* of developmentalism. Explicitly, anyway, it opposed linearity" (Price, *Object of the Atlantic*, 168; emphasis in the original). By being mimetic I take it that what Price refers to is a form of "aping," an uncritical imitation and adaptation to commodity capitalism, rather than the more complex, dialogical form of mimesis Taussig has in mind when he coins the term "capitalist mimetics."

76. Klaus Müller-Bergh stresses that the poem "is more than a clever manipulation of sounds, meanings and word arrangements. It is a powerful indictment of a society ruled by imported Madison Avenue publicity techniques." See Müller-Bergh, "Feijoada, Coke & the Urbanoid: Brazilian Poetry since 1945," *World Literature Today* 53.1 (Winter 1979): 25. Roland Greene locates the poem's critical thrust in the way it "begins to spew filth at us, like cuss words from a baby's mouth, until we literally see that the filth was there all along." See Greene, "From Dante to the Post-Concrete: An Interview with Augusto de Campos," *Harvard Library Bulletin* 3.2 (Summer 1992): n.p. Jon M. Tolman, on his part, interprets the last line of Pignatari's "beba coca cola" as "an explosion of rage/ nausea/ expulsion (as in excretion)." See Tolman, "The Context of a Vanguard: Toward a Definition of Concrete Poetry," *Poetics of the Avant-Garde*, special issue, *Poetics Today* 3.3 (Summer 1982): 160).

77. See the facsimile edition of the magazine *Klaxon* (São Paulo: Cosac Naify, 2013). Ledesma notes the traits shared between Pignatari's "bebe coca cola" and advertisement poems published in *Klaxon*. See Ledesma, *Radical Poetry*, 238.

78. Pignatari, *Semiótica da arte e da arquitetura* (São Paulo: Ateliê Editorial, 2004), 46: "A arte não se pôs simplesmente a 'macaquear' a ciência, e sim a traduzir os métodos e processos tecnológicos e científicos, numa operação, digamos, de tipo homeopático, na base do *similia similibus curantur*, a fim de desafiá-los e neutralizá-los tanto crítica quanto criativamente."

79. José Lino Grünewald, *Escreviver* (São Paulo: Perspectiva, 2008): 90.

80. Pignatari traveled to the Ulm School of Design in Germany in 1955, where he met the Bolivian-born Swiss poet Eugen Gomringer. At the time, Gomringer was working at the Ulm School as Max Bill's secretary, and the meeting with Pignatari, though unplanned, proved providential for the concrete poetry movements incipient in Brazil as in Switzerland.

81. Décio Pignatari, "forma, função e projeto geral" (1957), in Campos, Pignatari, and Campos, *Teoria da poesia concreta*, 154: "As artes visuais encontraram na arquitetura e no urbanismo, bem como no desenho industrial, no cinema, na propaganda, um vasto campo possível de aplicações, enquanto, por urgência de uma comunicação mais rápida e incisiva—mais econômica—a nossa época se colocava sob o signo da comunicação não verbal. A música nova, eletrônica, já começa a ser introduzida no cinema, na televisão e no rádio, para efeitos de sonoplastia. A poesia concreta, por recente, apenas principia a entrever possibilidades utilitárias na propaganda, nas artes gráficas, no jornalismo. Contudo, o objeto útil ou utilitário, em que a *forma*, sem deixar de ser criativa, apenas busca a justa paráfrase de uma *função* (que em outras condições, como na arquitetura, é sinônimo de *conteúdo*) não pode absorver toda a capacidade de criação das artes, que ainda encontram na idéia-objeto autônoma a mais consequente e profunda de suas manifestações."

82. A recent exhibit at the Tate Gallery in London, *The World Goes Pop* (2015), shed some light on the extensive, expansive corpus of pop art in Latin America. *Pop America: Contesting Freedom, 1965–1975*, a forthcoming exhibition (opening 2018) organized by the Nasher Museum of Art at Duke University and curated by Esther Gabara, promises to paint a fuller picture of this understudied moment in the history of art in Latin America.

83. Charles Perrone describes this work as "an actual ad for a pharmaceutical product whose textual effect of collapsing letters merited publication of the piece as creative writing." See Perrone, *Seven Faces*, 54.

84. See Pignatari, *Poesia pois é poesia*, 209.

85. In Jon M. Tolman's interpretation of "Disenfórmio" "the letters of the product invade and consume the 'intestinal disturbance'" (Tolman, "Context of a Vanguard," 161). But it seems to me that the image of digestion put forth by the movement of the letters is one of fecal formation rather than one of invasion and consumption.

86. On the link between Rodchenko's scatological remarks, their attendant anal-eroticism, and his impressions of commodity culture, see Kiaer, *Imagine No Possessions*, 219: "Ideally, the system of modern production and consumption in the West should function as transparently and effectively as its vast systemic technology of sewage and

plumbing (the bidets and hot water), resulting in regulated consumption and clean bodies and streets. But Rodchenko phantasmatically identifies the excessive, irrational desire for the commodity that he witnesses in Paris with excess shit that cannot be contained by the best plumbing in the world."

87. In a review of Joyce's *Portrait*, H. G. Wells writes: "It is no good trying to minimize a characteristic that seems to be deliberately obtruded. Like Swift and another living Irish writer, Mr. Joyce has a cloacal obsession. He would bring back into the general picture of life aspects which modern drainage and modern decorum have taken out of ordinary intercourse and conversation. Coarse, unfamiliar words are scattered about the book unpleasantly, and it may seem to many, needlessly" (Wells, "James Joyce," *New Republic*, March 10, 1917, 158).

88. Pignatari, "Interview," in *Abstracionismo geométrico e informal: a vanguarda brasileira nos anos cinqüenta* (Rio de Janeiro: FUNARTE, 1987), 79: "Quem escreveu primeiro poema sobre Coca-Cola no mundo, em 57, fui eu! Há um quarto de século. Não preciso fazer discurso contra as multinacionais."

89. Pignatari, "Interview," in *Abstracionismo geométrico*, 80: "Os anos 60 deram uma grande lição. Eu já era bem maduro mas remocei, porque a revolução contracultural veio contradizer a visão estritamente industrializada."

90. Pignatari was quick to point out that "os Vargas Llosa, os Cortázar e todos eles não esqueceram que era preciso experimentar e junto com a experimentação de vanguarda tratar de seus problemas nacionais." See Pignatari, "Interview," in *Abstracionismo geométrico*, 79.

91. Ibid., 80: "Eu vou para os meios de massa e quando tiver que lutar você não me ve outra vez praticando pequenos poemas à la Neruda."

92. Gonzalo Aguilar, *Poesia concreta brasileira: as vanguardas na encruzilhada modernista*, trans. Regina Aida Crespo, Rodolfo Mata, and Gênese Andrade (São Paulo: Editora da Universidade de São Paulo, 2005), 119: "a poética de vanguarda e de alto repertório dos poetas concretos dificilmente se adequava à *lógica espetacular* dos meios." Emphasis in the original.

93. Benjamin, *One-Way Street*, 21.

94. Ibid.

95. Marjorie Perloff, "Writing as Re-Writing: Concrete Poetry as Arrière-Garde," in *Ciberletras: revista de crítica literaria y de cultura* 17, n.p.

96. Marjorie Perloff, *Radical Artifice: Writing Poetry in the Age of Media* (Chicago: University of Chicago Press, 1991), 119.

97. Aguilar, *Poesia concreta brasileira*, 79: "Esses objetos dão como resultado muito mais uma dissolução da poesia do que sua integração à vida cotidiana."

98. See Haroldo de Campos, "Comunicação na poesia," in *A arte no horizonte*, 146.

99. For a reading of "stèle pour vivre 3" as a "powerful mapping" of the Cuban missile crisis, see Shellhorse, "Subversions of the Sensible," 183–185. Perrone reads this poem as part of Pignatari's "claims on the technocultural relevance of advertising," describing it as a "verbal montage implementing commercial layout." See Perrone, *Seven Faces*, 53–54.

100. Perrone, *Seven Faces*, 39–40. The impact of this "intentional relativization" is made clear by Teresa Cabañas. See Cabañas, *A poética da inversão: representação e simu-*

lacro na poesia concreta (Goiânia, Brazil: Ed. UFG, 2000), 81: "ativar uma percepção que consiga superar a clássica distância entre figura e fundo implica a reorganização estrutural de ambos os elementos."

101. Augusto de Campos, "poesia concreta (manifesto)," in Campos, Pignatari, and Campos, *Teoria da poesia concreta*, 72: "funções-relações gráfico-fonéticas ('fatores de proximidade e semelhança') e o uso substantivo do espaço como elemento de composição entretêm uma dialética simultânea de olho e fôlego."

Chapter 3: Poetry, Replication, Late Capitalism

1. Extant criticism on Octavio Paz makes him out to be a staunch Luddite. See, for instance, Francisco Álvarez, "Octavio Paz: hacia una poética de la modernidad," in *Hispania* 81.1 (Mar. 1998), 20. José Quiroga's approach is brief but more nuanced. See Quiroga, *Understanding Octavio Paz* (Columbia: University of South Carolina Press, 1999), 138–139.

2. "Los signos en rotación" was first published on its own in Argentina (Editorial Sur, 1965) as a "poetic manifesto." It was later included as the epilogue to the second edition of Paz, *El arco y la lira: el poema, la revelación poética, poesía e historia* (Mexico City: Fondo de Cultura Económica, 1970).

3. In Paz, *El signo y el garabato* (1973). The first version dates to a lecture delivered by Paz on the occasion of his admittance to El Colegio Nacional in 1967.

4. Like many critics after him, Emir Rodríguez Monegal argues that the decade leading up to 1968 was transformative for the work of Paz. Rodríguez Monegal credits the growth evident in Paz's poetry and essays of the late 1960s to extended stays in France and particularly in India. See Rodríguez Monegal, "Relectura de *El arco y la lira*," *Revista Iberoamericana* 37.74 (Jan.–March 1971): 37: "En los once años que corren entre la primera y la segunda edición [de *El arco y la lira*], Paz vive principalmente fuera de México: en Francia y en la India, en particular. [. . .] Pero es, indudablemente, la estancia de unos seis años en Nueva Delhi (1962–1968), como Embajador de su patria, lo que permite a Paz esa fabulosa maduración del pensamiento poético y de la misma poesía."

5. Álvarez, "Octavio Paz"; Yvon Grenier, "A Critique of Modernity," in *From Art to Politics: Octavio Paz and the Pursuit of Freedom* (Lanham, MD: Rowman and Littlefield, 2001); Clara Román-Odio, *Octavio Paz en los debates críticos y estéticos del siglo XX* (La Coruña: TresCTres, 2006).

6. See, for instance, Diana Sorensen's chapter titled "Tlatelolco 1968: Paz and Poniatowska on Law and Violence," in *Turbulent Decade Remembered*, 54–77; David A. Brading, *Octavio Paz y la poética de la historia mexicana* (Mexico City: Fondo de Cultura Económica, 2002); Enrico Mario Santí, *El acto de las palabras* (Mexico City: Fondo de Cultura Económica, 1997).

7. Rolando Vázquez is among the few critics of Octavio Paz to broach the place of technology in the poet's work and his writings on poetics. See Vázquez, "On Visual Modernity and Poetic Critique," in *Octavio Paz: Humanism and Critique*, ed. Oliver Kozlarek (Bielefeld, Germany: Transcript, 2009), 99–100.

8. Paz, *La otra voz* (1990), in *Obras completas*, vol. 1, 590: "La poesía ha resistido a la modernidad y al negarla, la ha vivificado. Ha sido su réplica y su antídoto."

9. Citing abundantly from Paz's Nobel lecture as well as from his 1963 essay "El precio y la significación," Yvon Grenier points to the romanticist origins of the ambivalence in Paz's stance vis-à-vis market capitalism. See Grenier, *From Art to Politics*, 87: "This kind of discrepancy between violent moral outrage and lenient practical appraisal is typical of romanticism in its classic or contemporary (communitarianism, for instance) forms."

10. Paz, *La otra voz* (1990), in *Obras completas*, vol. 1, 589: "La discordia entre poesía y modernidad no es accidental sino consubstancial."

11. For more on the "Mexican miracle," see the chapters "El cardenismo," "El 'milagro' mexicano," and "La crisis del 'milagro' mexicano," in Francisco González Gómez, *Del porfirismo al neoliberalismo* (Mexico City: Ediciones Quinto Sol, 2007). See also John W. Sherman, "The Mexican 'Miracle' and Its Collapse," in *The Oxford History of Mexico*, ed. William H. Beezley and Michael C. Meyer (New York: Oxford University Press, 2010), 537–568.

12. A brief description of the Mixcoac house and household where Paz grew up can be found in Enrique Krauze, *Redeemers: Ideas and Power in Latin America*, trans. Hank Heifetz and Natasha Wimmer (New York: Harper, 2011), 129–132.

13. Paz, *Itinerario poético: seis conferencias inéditas, Colegio Nacional de México, 1975* (Girona: Atalanta, 2014), 88: "En 1953, tras nueve años de ausencia, regresé a México. Era otra ciudad. Una ciudad todavía agradable aunque ya comenzaba a convertirse en el monstruo de ahora."

14. Paz, *Jardines errantes: cartas a J. C. Lambert, 1952–1992* (Barcelona: Seix Barral, 2008), 63: "La atmósfera aquí es atroz: el mundo de *The Waste Land* asociado a aquella región—Malpaís—que describe Huxley en *Brave New World*. Y no queda el recuerdo del campo, el verdadero, aunque petrificado, México, porque estoy anclado en la ciudad."

15. Paz, *Itinerario poético*, 90: "En el México de 1955 la satisfacción era generalizada entre políticos, banqueros, líderes obreros y campesinos. Incluso muchos intelectuales se habían contagiado de ese optimismo."

16. Pere Gimferrer, *Lecturas de Octavio Paz* (Barcelona: Editorial Anagrama, 1980), 93: "Esta noche es, además, una metáfora del lenguaje, pues, ciertamente, los anuncios son, aunque vano, un intercambio de signos."

17. José Emilio Pacheco also yearns for the countryside in *Las batallas en el desierto*, his 1981 fictionalized account of postwar Mexico. See Pacheco, *Las batallas en el desierto* (Mexico City: Biblioteca Era, 2013), 10: "los ríos (aún quedaban ríos), las montañas (se veían las montañas). Era el mundo antiguo."

18. For an overview of the figure of the city in Paz's poetry, see Marta Piña Zentella, *¿Ausencia/presencia? Ciudad en Octavio Paz* (Mexico City: Editorial Praxis, 2014).

19. Paz, *Libertad bajo palabra*, in *Obras completas*, vol. 11, 119.

20. Ibid., 69.

21. A note added by Paz to this identifies the setting as a precise location in Mexico City, where the juxtaposition of life and death, of lust and death, is particularly striking. See Paz, *Obras completas*, vol. 11, 525: "Hasta hace unos pocos años las agencias

funerarias de la ciudad de México tenían sus negocios en la avenida Hidalgo, al lado del parque de la Alameda, en el tramo que va del Correo a la iglesia y plazuela de San Juan de Dios. Frente a la iglesia había un pequeño mercado de flores, especializado en coronas y ofrendas fúnebres. El barrio era céntrico y aislado a un tiempo. Desde el anochecer las prostitutas recorrían la avenida Hidalgo y las callejas contiguas. Uno de sus lugares favoritos era el espacio ocupado por las funerarias, iluminado por la luz eléctrica de los escaparates donde se exhibían los ataúdes."

22. Cecilia Enjuto-Rangel analyzes the link between Paz, Luis Cernuda, and Charles Baudelaire, especially the links between Paz's "Crepúsculos de la ciudad" and Baudelaire's "Crépuscule de soir" and "Crépuscule de matin." See Enjuto-Rangel, "Broken Presents: The Modern City in Ruins in Baudelaire, Cernuda, and Paz," in *Comparative Literature* 59.2 (Spring 2007).

23. Paz, *Libertad bajo palabra*, in *Obras completas*, vol. 11, 71–72.

24. Ibid., 109–111.

25. The city of Paris.

26. Paz, *Salamandra* (1958–1961), in *Obras completas*, vol. 11, 299.

27. So patent is the presence of machines and mechanical devices in *Salamandra* that Roberta Seabrook goes as far as arguing that "[el] latido del motor es el *leitmotiv* de toda la primera parte de *Salamandra*." See Seabrook, "La poesía en movimiento: Octavio Paz," in *Revista Iberoamericana* 37.74 (Jan.–March 1971): 165.

28. Paz, *Salamandra*, 323–328.

29. Ibid., 323.

30. Paz, *Días hábiles* (1958–1961), in *Obras completas*, vol. 11, 263.

31. Paz, *Salamandra*, 308–309.

32. Paz, *Ladera este* (1962–1968), in *Obras completas*, vol. 11, 351–353.

33. Ibid., 367–371.

34. Ibid., 379.

35. Paz, *Hacia el comienzo* (1964–1968), in *Obras completas*, vol. 11, 395–400.

36. Paz, *Vuelta* (1969–1975), in *Obras completas*, vol. 12, 54–56. Composed by Paz for a major surrealist exhibition in Mexico and printed onsite, on the walls of a spiral staircase.

37. Ibid., 38–42.

38. Paz, "Los signos en rotación," in *Obras completas*, vol. 1, 249: "la dócil adopción de formas de pensamiento y conducta erigidas en canon universal por la propaganda comercial y política; la elevación del nivel de vida y la degradación del *nivel* de vida; la soberanía del objetos y la deshumanización de aquellos que lo producen y lo usan [. . .] la vida personal, exaltada por la publicidad, se disuelve en vida anónima."

39. Ibid., 252: "Pero desde el exterior quizá no sea del todo temerario describir algunas de las circunstancias a que se enfrentan los nuevos poetas. Una es la pérdida de la imagen del mundo; otra, la aparición de un vocabulario universal, compuesto de signos activos: la técnica; otra más, la crisis de los significados."

40. Paz, *El arco y la lira* (1967), in *Obras completas*, vol. 1, 114: "Conviene advertir, pues, que designamos con la palabra imagen toda forma verbal, frase o conjunto de frases, que el poeta dice y que unidas componen un poema."

41. Ibid.: "Épica, dramática o lírica, condensada en una frase o desenvuelta en mil páginas, toda imagen acerca o acopla realidades opuestas, indiferentes o alejadas entre sí. Esto es, somete a unidad la pluralidad de lo real."

42. Ibid., 115: "El poeta nombra las cosas: éstas son plumas, aquellas son piedras. Y de pronto afirma: las piedras son plumas, esto es aquello."

43. Paz draws many of his insights on language, capitalism, and the promising uselessness of poetry from Alfonso Reyes, whose writings on literature and poetics were fundamental in shaping Paz's thought. See Reyes, *La experiencia literaria*, 90–91: "Aunque nos llevaría muy lejos, conviene recordar que hay todavía otro uso del habla que ni es poesía ni es coloquio. Tal es el lenguaje científico. [. . .] El camino hacia la ciencia es el camino de las denominaciones unívocas. [. . .] El lenguaje científico procura abolir el halo de indeterminación subjetiva que irradia la palabra, para poder mentar fijamente lo que conoce. [. . .] Pero mientras el lenguaje lírico queda prendido a la forma, el científico la neutraliza en parte, en toda aquella parte que queda fuera del tecnicismo. La parte no técnica del lenguaje científico admite equivalencias múltiples, recortes, extensiones, traducciones, traslados, como el mismo coloquio. No sucede así en la parte técnica del lenguaje científico. La ciencia tiene carácter tautológico. De aquí—observa Pius Servin—que su lenguaje, a través del tecnicismo, camine hacia la tipología simbólica, hacia el álgebra. Ni el lírico ni el técnico dejan nada a la casualidad: en lo cual se parecen. Pero aquél encarna en la lengua, y éste se desencarna hacia el algoritmo. Y entre los dos polos, crece y retumba la casualidad del coloquio, ahogando en sus marejadas a la pobre gramática preceptiva, esfuerzo por jardinear el mar."

44. To add nuance, Paz elaborates his notion of the image in poetry in reference to Hegelian dialectics. The image in poetry, Paz writes, does not communicate concepts; it does not work on a realm of ideas that exists beyond history: "the proper mode of the image," Paz argues, "is not conceptual transmission" (Paz, *El arco y la lira*, 126). The poetic image mediates, but it mediates by transformation and transmutation. There is something revealing about Paz's insistence on the difference between contradiction in poetry and contradiction in the dialectic. In *El arco y la lira* and later in "La nueva analogía," analogy serves as a figure of constitutive resistance against forms of language more closely aligned with analysis and conceptual thought. Like rhythm, like the beat and tune of verse, analogy works not on the basis of rational association but on the basis of correspondence, of cosmic, mythical correspondence.

45. Martin Heidegger, "The Age of the World Picture," in *The Question Concerning Technology and Other Essays* (New York: Harper, 1977): 130.

46. Ibid., 132. At the same time he was writing "Los signos en rotación" Paz was immersed in a study of structuralism leading up to his book *Claude Lévi-Strauss o el nuevo festín de Esopo* (1967). Emir Rodríguez Monegal compared the first edition of *El arco y la lira* and the second, where "Los signos en rotación" was included, and he found that the greatest difference between them is a transformation of Paz's thought following his reading of structuralism. This explains why his idea of a world image often seems more structuralist than phenomenological. But he stays closer to Heidegger's writings on technology, as is clear in a passage from "Los signos en rotación" where Paz, following Heidegger, defines technology as outlook. See Rodríguez Monegal, "Relectura

de *El arco y la lira*," 39. For a critical reading of Paz's appropriation of structuralism, see William Rowe, "Paz, Fuentes and Lévi-Strauss: The Creation of a Structuralist Orthodoxy," *Bulletin of Latin American Research* 3.2 (1984): 77–82. Santí insists on surrealism as another important axis for the discursive scaffolding of the first edition of *El arco y la lira*. See Santí, *El acto de las palabras*, 238: "En su primera edición de 1956 al menos representó un cruce entre los atisbos filosóficos del surrealismo y la fenomenología existencialista."

47. Paz, *Itinerario poético*, 186: "Entre todas las artes, a mi juicio, la arquitectura es la más dependiente de la historia. La que expresa con mayor fidelidad la situación de una sociedad."

48. Paz, "Los signos en rotación," in *Obras completas*, vol. 1, 254: "Un templo maya, una catedral medieval o un palacio barroco eran algo más que monumentos: puntos sensibles del espacio y el tiempo, observatorios privilegiados desde los cuales el hombre podía contemplar el mundo y el trasmundo como un todo. Su orientación correspondía a una visión simbólica del universo."

49. Mário Pedrosa writes of the disconnect between modernity and a cosmological vision of the world in relation to science. In an article where he defends the need for more communication among science and the arts, he writes: "Highly technical, mathematized Science becomes socially and philosophically isolationist. . . . When Science rejects an intuitive—or truly sensitive—total image of the world . . . humanity finds itself for the first time in its developmental curve without an intuitive cosmogonic or even cosmological concept of the universe." See Pedrosa, "Science and Art," in Ferreira and Herkenhoff, *Mário Pedrosa*, 113.

50. Paz, "Los signos en rotación," in *Obras completas*, vol. 1, 255: "Las obras del pasado eran réplicas del arquetipo cósmico en el doble sentido de la palabra: copias del modelo universal y respuesta humana al mundo, rimas o estrofas del poema que el cosmos se dice a sí mismo."

51. Ibid.: "Las construcciones de la técnica [. . .] no representan: son signos de la acción y no imágenes del mundo."

52. Paz, "La nueva analogía," 303: "¿Qué dicen nuestros hangares, estaciones de ferrocarril, edificios de oficinas, fábricas y monumentos públicos? No dicen: son funciones, no significaciones. Son centros de energía, monumentos de la voluntad, signos que irradian poder, no sentido. Las obras antiguas eran una representación de la realidad, la real y la imaginaria; las de la técnica son una operación sobre la realidad."

53. See chapter 1 of this book.

54. See Enrique Metinides, *101 Tragedies of Enrique Metinides*, edited by Trisha Ziff (New York: Aperture, 2012).

55. Paz, "Los signos en rotación," 254: "La técnica es una realidad tan poderosamente real—visible, palpable, audible, ubicua—que la verdadera realidad ha dejado de ser natural o sobrenatural: la industria es nuestro paisaje, nuestro cielo y nuestro infierno."

56. Ibid.: "La técnica se interpone entre nosotros y el mundo, cierra toda perspectiva a la mirada: más allá de sus geometrías de hierro, vidrio o aluminio no hay rigurosamente nada, excepto lo desconocido, la región de lo informe todavía no transformada por el hombre."

57. Paz, "La nueva analogía," 303: "Para la técnica el mundo no es ni una imagen sensible de la idea ni un modelo cósmico: es un obstáculo que debemos vencer y modificar."

58. Ibid., 311: "Doble imperfección: las palabras han dejado de representar a la verdadera realidad de las cosas; y las cosas se han vuelto opacas, mudas."

59. J. L. Austin's *How to Do Things with Words* (1962) was published around the time Paz was writing about a historical shift in the concept of language and of the world, wherein language is understood as something that can act upon the world. There is little to suggest that Paz was reading Austin as he revised the second edition of *El arco y la lira*, but there is something intriguing about the generational resonance between the two.

60. Paz, *El arco y la lira*, 67–68: "Y en cuanto al habla desgarrada de las urbes: no es un lenguaje, sino el jirón de algo que fue un todo coherente y armónico. El habla de la ciudad tiende a petrificarse en formulas y *slogans* y sufre así la misma suerte del arte popular, convertido en artefacto industrial, y la del hombre mismo, que de persona se transforma en masa."

61. Ibid., 96: "No el estilizado lenguaje 'popular', a la manera de Juan Ramón Jiménez, Antonio Machado, García Lorca o Alberti, al fin de cuentas no menos artificial que el idioma de la poesía 'culta', sino el habla de la ciudad."

62. Paz, *La otra voz* (1990), in *Obras completas*, vol. 1, 574: "Los poetas se refugian en las universidades, como en la Edad Media, pero sería funesto que abandonasen la ciudad." Paz himself spent time in US universities.

63. Ibid., 575: "Los poetas deben buscar formas y ritmos más en consonancia con el lenguaje y la vida de nuestras ciudades."

64. Octavio Paz and Haroldo de Campos, *Transblanco: em torno a* Blanco *de Octavio Paz* (Rio de Janeiro: Editora Guanabara, 1986). For more on the collaboration between Paz and Campos, see Mata, "Haroldo de Campos y Octavio Paz."

65. See Josten, "Concrete Poetry," in Eder, *Defying Stability*, 107.

66. Paz, "Los signos en rotación," 269: "El periodismo, la publicidad, el cine y otros medios de reproducción visual han transformado la escritura, que había sido casi totalmente estereotipada por la tipografía."

67. Paz, "La nueva analogía," 307: "Texto visual o texto hablado, el poema se separa del libro y se transforma en un objeto sonoro y/o plástico independiente."

68. Ibid., 306: "Así, lo que distingue a la actitud contemporánea de la que privaba todavía hace unos quince o veinte años no es la primacía de la palabra hablada sobre el signo escrito sino que la experiencia vuelve a ser física, corporal: hoy la palabra nos entra por los oídos, toma cuerpo, encarna. No es menos revelador que la recepción de poemas tienda a convertirse en un acto colectivo: al desplazamiento del libro por los otros medios de comunicación y del signo escrito por la voz corresponden la corporeización de la palabra y su encarnación colectiva."

69. Paz, in Octavio Paz and Haroldo de Campos, *Transblanco: em torno a Blanco de Octavio Paz* (São Paulo, Brasil: Editora Siciliano, 1994), 98: "a relação peculiar entre poesia e crítica que define a poesia concreta não a separa da tradição da poesia ocidental: converte-a em sua contradição complementar. E isso por duas razões: primeiro, o poema concreto se sustenta ou se prolonga em um discurso (explicação do poema, tradução do ideograma); e segundo, por seu caráter imediato e total, o poema con-

creto é uma critica do pensamento discursivo. Negação do curso—do transcurso e do discurso."

70. Paz, *El arco y la lira*, 48: "La piedra triunfa en la escultura, se humilla en la escalera. El color resplandece en el cuadro; el movimiento del cuerpo, en la danza. La materia, vencida o deformada en el utensilio, recobra su esplendor en la obra de arte."

71. Ibid.: "En el poema el lenguaje recobra su originalidad primera, mutilada por la reducción que le imponen prosa y habla cotidiana. La reconquista de su naturaleza es total y afecta a los valores sonoros y plásticos tanto como a los significativos. La palabra, al fin en libertad, muestra todas sus entrañas, todos sus sentidos y alusiones, como un fruto maduro o como un cohete en el momento de estallar en el cielo. El poeta pone en libertad su materia. El prosista la aprisiona."

72. Ibid., 89: "La prosa es un género tardío, hijo de la desconfianza del pensamiento ante las tendencias naturales del idioma."

73. Ibid., 89–90: "La prosa, que es primordialmente un instrumento de crítica y análisis, exige una lenta maduración y sólo se produce tras una larga serie de esfuerzos tendientes a domar al habla. Su avance se mide por el grado de dominio del pensamiento sobre las palabras. La prosa crece en batalla permanente contra las inclinaciones naturales del idioma y sus géneros más perfectos son el discurso y la demostración, en los que el ritmo y su incesante ir y venir ceden el sitio a la marcha del pensamiento."

74. Ibid., 105: "La rebelión poética más profunda del siglo se operó ahí donde el espíritu discursivo se había apoderado casi totalmente de la lengua, al grado que parecía desprovista de poderes rítmicos. En el centro de un pueblo razonador brotó un bosque de imágenes, una nueva orden de caballería, armada de punta en blanco con armas envenenadas."

75. Aristotle, cited in Paz, *El arco y la lira*, 85–86: "'En total, dos parecen haber sido las causas especiales del origen de la poesía, y ambas naturales: primero, ya desde niños es connatural a los hombres reproducir imitativamente; [. . .] segundo, en que todos se complacen en las reproducciones imitativas.'"

76. Paz, "La nueva analogía," 304: "Las relaciones entre la técnica y la poesía son de un orden particular: por una parte la poesía tiende a utilizar, como todas las otras artes, los recursos de la técnica, especialmente en la esfera de los medios de comunicación: radio, televisión, discos, cinematografía, etc.; por la otra, debe enfrentarse a la negación de la imagen del mundo. En el primer caso, la poesía se apoya en la técnica; en el segundo, se opone a ella. Esa oposición es complementaria."

77. Paz, "Los signos en rotación," 268: "Por la eliminación de la música, la caligrafía y la iluminación, la poesía se redujo hasta convertirse casi exclusivamente en un arte del entendimiento."

78. Paz and Rojo, "La fragua de dos libros," 161: "es inadmisible que el radio y la televisión estén en manos de empresas privadas pero también sería deplorable que fuesen un monopolio estatal. Por tanto, habría que buscar una solución mixta, en la que los productores (técnicos, trabajadores, artistas, pedagogos e intelectuales) y los consumidores participasen de un modo decisivo en la dirección y empleo de esos medios de comunicación."

79. Paz, *Discos visuales* (Mexico City: Ediciones Era, 1968), n.p.

80. For more on Paz's work in typography and graphic design, see Fernando Rodríguez, "Transdisciplinas: Octavio Paz, editor tipógrafo," *Encuadre: Revista de la Enseñanza del Diseño* 2.12 (2008).

81. Rita Guibert, *Siete voces: los más grandes escritores latinoamericanos se confiesan con Rita Guibert* (Mexico City: Organización Editorial Novaro), 241: "primero, dotar de movilidad al texto por medio de un ritmo visual; en seguida, hacer más lenta la lectura. Ahora está de moda leer de prisa y hasta hay institutos que se dedican a eso. Una abominación. [. . .] Yo creo que hay que aprender a leer despacio, sobre todo la poesía."

82. See Enrico Mario Santí, "Salida 'Esto no es un poema,'" in *Archivo Blanco*, ed. Enrico Mario Santí (Madrid: Ediciones Turner, 1995), 241: "el otro aspecto importante de la carta a [Emir] Rodríguez Monegal es que Paz vincula el poema explícitamente con otro texto suyo de la misma época. Al decir que 'el poema entero obedece a la misma lógica: son los signos en rotación', alude al célebre ensayo del mismo nombre."

83. See Miguel León Portilla, *La filosofía nahuatl, estudiada en sus fuentes* (Mexico City: Ediciones Especiales del Instituto Indigenista Interamericano, 1956).

84. Fernando Rodríguez is among the more recent scholars to look for an alternative to the term "pages" when writing about the first edition of *Blanco*. He prefers the term "panels," which captures more aptly than "page" the idea of the space of *Blanco* as the space where language takes place, where linguistic phenomena happen. See Rodríguez, "Transdisciplinas," 14–43.

85. See Haroldo de Campos, "To Octavio Paz," in Paz and Campos, *Transblanco*, 109: "Tenho também em mãos, recebida com dificuldade de Cuba, uma *Órbita* de Lezama Lima. E, não é preciso dizer, o último Cortázar—excelente!—, *La vuelta al día en ochenta mundos*."

86. For more on Mallarmé and the newspaper, in relation to Brazilian concrete poetry, see chapter 2 of this book.

87. Paz, *Blanco* (Mexico City: J. Mortiz, 1967), n.p.

88. Ibid.

89. For the most thorough discussion of the reading orders afforded in *Blanco* according to the possibilities listed by Paz, see Santí, "Salida," in *Archivo Blanco*, 276–286.

90. See Nicanor Vélez, "El poema extenso: arquitectura de palabras y silencios en *Piedra de sol* y *Blanco* de Octavio Paz," in *La suma que es el todo y que no cesa: el poema largo en la modernidad hispanoamericana*, edited by María Cecilia Graña (Rosario, Argentina: B. Viterbo Editora, 2006), 59–79.

91. See Richard J. Callan, *The Philosophy of Yoga in Octavio Paz's Poem "Blanco"* (Lewiston, NY: Edwin Mellen, 2005).

92. Román-Odio and Rodney Williamson both discuss at length the mandala as an organizational structure for *Blanco*. See Román-Odio, *Octavio Paz*, 179–189; and Williamson, *The Writing in the Stars: A Jungian Reading of the Poetry of Octavio Paz* (Toronto: University of Toronto Press, 2007).

93. See Hugo J. Verani, "Octavio Paz and the Language of Space," in *World Literature Today* 56.4 (Autumn 1982).

94. Written between 1963 and 1976; published in 1984.

95. Paz, *Blanco*, n.p.

96. Jean Franco, "¡Oh mundo por poblar, hoja en blanco! El espacio y los espacios en la obra de Octavio Paz," *Revista Iberoamericana* 37.74 (Jan.–March 1971); Julio Ortega and David Draper Clark, "*Blanco*: Space of Change," *World Literature Today* 56.4 (Autumn 1982). The latter text is a firsthand account of Haroldo de Campos's translation of *Blanco* in Austin, Texas.

97. Franco notes that the semantic register of incipiency evoked by the meaning of these words ("unheard of," "inaudible," "odd," "pregnant," "void") is echoed in their disposition on the page. As they stand, they seem to gush out onto the surface of the page, visually enacting a burst of words and thus suggesting, as Franco puts it, "un borboteo de imágenes insubstanciales" that, in turn, evokes the stammering or babbling of incipient language. See Franco, "¡Oh mundo por poblar," 159.

98. Paz, "To Haroldo de Campos, March 14, 1968," in Octavio Paz and Haroldo de Campos, *Transblanco*, 98: "a relação peculiar entre poesía e crítica que define a poesia concreta não a separa da tradição da poesia ocidental: converte-a em sua contradição complementar. E isso por duas razões: primeiro, o poema concreto se sustenta ou se prolonga em um discurso (explicação do poema, tradução do ideograma); e segundo, por seu caráter imediato e total, o poema concreto é uma crítica do pensamento discursivo. Negação do curso—do transcurso e do discurso."

99. Paz, *Blanco*, n.p.

100. Paz, "'Blanco' indicaciones escénicas (1971)," in Santí, *Archivo Blanco*, 125–129.

101. Paz, *Blanco*, n.p.

102. Santí, "Salida," in *Archivo Blanco*, 293: "El fuego que se invoca al principio de la sección II se nota en el reflejo de las sombras de una pareja durante el inicio de una sesión erótica."

103. Paz, *Blanco*, n.p.

104. Paz, *Los hijos del limo* (1974), in *Obras completas*, vol. 1, 437: "Apenas si vale la pena recordar otra analogía, destacada muchas veces, entre el 'simultaneísmo' y el montaje cinematográfico, sobre todo tal como fue practicado y expuesto por Sergei Eisenstein."

105. Ibid., 439: "Cendrars se sirve de un método de composición que no es otro que el del relato. Un relato entrecortado, con idas y venidas, anticipaciones, irrupciones, digresiones y enlaces imprevistos. Los poemas de Cendrars están más cerca del cine que de la pintura, más cerca del montaje que del *collage*."

106. Paz, "Cuarenta años de escribir poesía," in Santí, *Archivo Blanco*, 119: "una especie de correspondencia entre lo temporal y lo espacial."

107. Ibid.: "yo quise combinar esto pensando sobre todo en aquellos experimentos simultaneístas que había hecho años antes."

108. Paz, *Los hijos del limo*, in *Obras completas* 440: "Cendrars no canta: cuenta. El habla de todos los días, el lenguaje cotidiano que fluye y transcurre y no el instante y sus onomatopeyas e interjecciones, fue el canal por el que penetró en la poesía de nuestro siglo el tiempo real, el tiempo simultáneo y discontinuo."

109. *Las dos Elenas* (1965), an adaptation of the Fuentes short story by the same name.

110. Paz and Rojo, "La fragua de dos libros," 127: "Desde hace mucho tiempo me

preocupan las relaciones entre sonido, plástica y palabra. A esta preocupación, que no es únicamente estética, responde, entre otras cosas mías, *Blanco*. De ahí mi interés en la versión fílmica, que concibo como una proyección del libro (y del acto de leerlo) en la pantalla. Esa película combinaría en forma dinámica las letras, la palabra hablada, las sensaciones visuales y auditivas y los diferentes sentidos. O sea: traslado del movimiento interior subjetivo (lectura) al movimiento exterior objetivo (proyección de la cámara)."

111. Ibid., 164: "En verdad lo que te propongo es la proyección cinematográfica del libro o, mejor dicho, *la proyección de su lectura* (lectura a veces silenciosa, otras en voz alta)." Emphasis in the original.

112. Gimferrer, *Lecturas de Octavio Paz*, 62: "lo que *Blanco* narra [es] la pura suspensión fenomenológica."

113. Haroldo de Campos, "The Open Work of Art" (1955), trans. Jon Tolman, in *Novas*, 221.

114. Susan Buck-Morss, "The Cinema Screen as Prosthesis of Perception: A Historical Account," in *The Senses Still: Perception and Memory as Material Culture in Modernity*, ed. C. Nadia Seremetakis (Boulder, CO: Westview, 1994), 46.

115. Ibid.

116. Ibid., 46–47.

117. Paz, *La otra voz*: "En el caso de *Blanco* me propuse diseñar un libro cuyas páginas y tipografía fuesen la proyección física de una experiencia mental: la lectura de un poema que se despliega, simultáneamente, en el espacio y en el tiempo. Estas búsquedas desembocaron en el obvio reconocimiento de las insospechadas e inexploradas posibilidades de la cinta cinematográfica y de la pantalla de televisión. Ambas son el equivalente de la página del libro. Páginas sueltas, como quería Mallarmé pero, asimismo, dotadas de un atributo que nunca soñó: el movimiento."

118. Ibid.: "Puede ahora entenderse el verdadero significado de la lectura en público de poemas. Es uno de los signos favorables que mencioné antes. Es un regreso al origen de la poesía, un volver a la fuente. Y por esto mismo las posibilidades de la pantalla de televisión son inmensas."

119. Ibid.: "Tengo la certeza de que los poemas proyectados en la pantalla de televisión están destinados a convertirse en una nueva forma poética. Este género afectará a la emisión y recepción de poemas de una manera no menos profunda que la del libro y la antigua tipografía."

120. See Néstor García Canclini, *Culturas híbridas: estrategias para entrar y salir de la modernidad* (Mexico City: Grijalbo: 1998), 96–106.

121. Paz, *La otra voz* (1990), in *Obras completas*, vol. 1, 589: "En un mundo regido por la lógica del mercado y, en los países comunistas, por la eficacia, la poesía es una actividad de rendimiento nulo [. . .] Poesía: gasto, dispendio, desperdicio."

Chapter 4: Lygia Clark, at Home with Objects

1. Clarice Lispector is another example of an artist or writer interested in the idea of home as something to be surveyed, analyzed, defamiliarized. Lispector is one of

three writers, along with João Cabral de Melo Neto and Guimarães Rosa, whom Paulo Herkenhoff lists as part of the "literary wave" that appeared around the same time that Clark began her work. See Herkenhoff, "Lygia Clark," in Clark, *Lygia Clark*, 36.

2. Lygia Clark and Yve-Alain Bois, "Nostalgia of the Body," *October* 69 (Summer 1994).

3. Suely Rolnik, "Uma terapêutica para tempos desprovidos de poesia," in *Lygia Clark da obra ao acontecimento: somos o molde. A você cabe o sopro* (São Paulo: Pinacoteca do Estado de São Paulo, 2006), n.p.: "Estamos num quarto do apartamento de Lygia Clark no Rio de Janeiro. Um ambiente insólito, por donde se espalha uma infinidade de objetos de toda espécie, que a artista chama de 'Relacionais.'" The dossier was published in conjunction with the exhibition by the same name, on view at the Musée dês Beaux-Arts de Nantes in France in 2005, and at the Pinacoteca do Estado de São Paulo in 2006.

4. See Rolnik, "Molding a Contemporary Soul," in *The Experimental Exercise of Freedom: Lygia Clark, Gego, Mathias Goeritz, Hélio Oiticica, Mira Schendel*, ed. Susan Martin and Alma Ruiz (Los Angeles: Museum of Contemporary Art, 1999), 67: "Clark's artistic life began in 1947, in her own words, 'to survive the crisis' after the birth of her third child."

5. Nicolas Bourriaud cites Carol Bove as one such artist. See Bourriaud, *The Radicant* (New York: Lukas and Sternberg, 2009), 172: "Carol Bove's installations explore the same historical period, 1965–1975, when artistic experiments and experiments in daily life went hand in hand and attenuated the difference between high culture and popular culture through hippie utopias." In her unpublished diaries, Clark herself points to affinities between her work and hippie culture, affinities she felt stronger after visiting California, where her work was warmly received by a younger audience.

6. Ulrike Müller notes that women artists associated with the Bauhaus had begun to rethink and revise, often quite disruptively, the notion of homemaking years before the term acquired the conservative connotations with which it is now loaded. See Müller, *Bauhaus Women*: 104.

7. Sophie Taeuber was the subject of a large exhibition at the third São Paulo Biennial in 1955, where more than forty of her works were on view. As Ferreira Gullar suggests in a 1960 article, Taeuber's exhibition and the Swiss delegation at large consolidated the language of abstraction and of concrete aesthetics in Brazil since 1951, after the prizes awarded to Max Bill and Walter Gropius during the first and second São Paulo Biennials, respectively. See Gullar, "Arte concreta no Brasil." On the relationship between abstraction, decoration, and the arts and crafts in Taeuber's work, see Leah Dickerman, "Zurich," in *Dada*, 36, where Dickerman cites Hans Arp, Taeuber's partner, to define the objective pursued by the couple during their years in Zurich Dada: "Arp described their common goal as that of breaking with 'aesthetics' to produce work that would have more the status of ordinary objects. As part of this pursuit," Dickerman argues, "Taeuber and Arp challenged the hierarchy between 'applied' and 'fine' art, often mobilizing the techniques and media of decorative arts in a deliberate shift toward a 'minor' key."

8. In reference to Clark, Gego, Schendel, and Hesse, Lucy R. Lippard writes: "Women

artists, especially those who were feminists, were busily rehabilitating materials associated with women's work—from traditional arts and domestic labor to assembly-line factory work." See Lippard, "The Materials at Hand: Art, Work, and Life," in *Versions and Inversions: Perspectives on Avant-Garde in Latin America*, ed. Hector Olea and Mari Carmen Ramírez (New Haven, CT: Yale University Press, 2006), 183.

9. Lygia Clark, cited in Lula Wanderley, *O dragão pousou no espaço: arte contemporânea, sofrimento psíquico e o Objeto Relacional de Lygia Clark* (Rio de Janeiro: Rocco, 2002), 9: "Eu comecei com a geometria, mas buscava um espaço orgânico em que fosse possível para alguém entrar na pintura."

10. Luis Pérez-Oramas, "Lygia Clark: If You Hold a Stone," in *Lygia Clark: The Abandonment of Art, 1948–1988*, ed. Cornelia Butler and Luis Pérez-Oramas (New York: Museum of Modern Art, 2014), 37.

11. In 1976, eight years after Clark exhibited *A casa é o corpo* at the Venice Biennale, the US artist Dan Graham installed his *Public Space/Two Audiences*, another intelligent, conceptual take on the role of publics in the reception of art, as well as a commentary on the complex and difficult dynamics of objectification and subjectification at work in art. Graham is best known for his *Homes for America* (1966–1967), intended as an intervention for a magazine and constructed as deeply ironic juxtapositions of images of nondescript, cookie-cutter houses, the kind that bourgeoned in the suburban boom of post-WWII America. In the United States, the expansion of suburbia went hand in hand with growth in the availability of durable consumer goods, markers of social status in an era of prosperity. In Latin America, increases in the acquisition rates of durable goods took place mostly against a background of increasing urbanization.

12. Oscar Niemeyer, cited in Clark, *Lygia Clark*, 352. The biographical sketch where this statement is cited notes the impact that Clark's *Superfícies moduladas* had on architects like Oscar Niemeyer. Clark and Niemeyer would go on to collaborate on a house in Clark's birth city, Belo Horizonte. Niemeyer's impressions of Clark are notable for the social nature that the architect reads in Clark's work, against the usual characterization of her work as being detached from the social and the political on account of its abstraction.

13. *Querida* belongs to the assortment of "dynamic new magazines" that, Diana Sorensen notes, "celebrated modernization while pointing to desirable cultural goods," thereby helping an emergent urban middle class join "the ranks of consumer society" (Sorensen, *Turbulent Decade Remembered*, 108). Within this audience, *Querida* sought out a specific segment, perhaps the most dynamic in terms of consumption practices: educated, middle-class women. See Laura Peretto Salerno and Maria Teresa Santos Cunha, "Discursos para o feminino em páginas da revista *Querida* (1958–1968): aproximações," in *Educar em Revista* 40 (Apr.-June 2011), 129: "*Querida* tinha seu público bem definido [. . .] Mulheres letradas de classe média das principais capitais brasileiras compunham a maioria de seu público leitor." Clark's appearance in *Querida* is striking. Her photo occupies a full page in the magazine. She's profiled as "the modern woman" and interviewed after receiving an award from the São Paulo Biennial.

14. Clark, "Conference Given in the Belo Horizonte National School of Architecture in 1956," in *Lygia Clark*, 71.

15. Ibid., 72: "Thus, in my view, the need for team-work, in which the Concrete artist may fully work in creating with the architect an environment which is 'in itself expressive.'"

16. Daniela Name describes the sense of optimism prevalent in Brazil in the 1950s. See Name, "'Eu me lembro,'" in *Diálogo concreto*, 8: "Em 1954, Juscelino Kubitschek foi eleito presidente do Brasil, prometendo que o país seria levado ao desenvolvimento em tempo recorde. O 'presidente bossa nova' se apresentava como o porta-voz da esperança e do otimismo, depois da comoção nacional causada pelo suicídio de seu antecessor, Getúlio Vargas, naquele mesmo ano. Para tentar cumprir o que prometeu, JK abriu o Brasil para o capital e os produtos estrangeiros; estimulou a criação de novos cursos universitários; deu bolsas para que intelectuais de diversas áreas fossem estudar na Europa e nos Estados Unidos; e, sobretudo, concretizou o sonho de construir uma nova capital em meio ao descampado do Planalto Central." The characterization of Kubitschek as the "*bossa nova* president" is particularly revealing.

17. See Baer and Paiva, "Brazil," in Randall, *Political Economy of Latin America*, 73–74: "Besides the rapid increase in the national product, one should also note the structural changes that occurred in the economy during the growth process. Industry was the motor of growth and the centerpiece of all development strategies implemented throughout the period. Industrial production grew at a yearly average rate of 6.89% during the four decades [1950–1990] but 8.5% if the lost decade [the 1980s] is excluded. For the period as a whole, the yearly average growth rates of agriculture and services were 4.27% and 6.83% respectively. As a result, the share of industry in GDP rose from about 24.14% in 1950 to 34.2% in 1990, after having reached 40.85% in 1980. . . . Industry's share in total employment rose to a much smaller extent than its share in GDP; in 1950 it amounted to 13%, rising to 23% in 1990."

18. Martins, *Constructing an Avant-Garde*, 18: "the historical assertion of the non-object involved not only its legitimation *within* modernism, but also a dispute over the meaning (or rather the *telos*) *of* modernism." Emphasis in the original.

19. See, for instance, Gonzalez and Treece, *Gathering of the Voices*, 229: "For the Concretists, modernization was not problematic or ambiguous. On the contrary, the perspective which overshadowed this period was one of uncritical identification with national capitalist development."

20. Monica Amor, *Theories of the Nonobject: Argentina, Brazil, Venezuela, 1944–1969* (Oakland, California: University of California Press, 2016): 1.

21. Clark, "1963–3": "Os meus planos iniciais para os bichos não incluíam Museus nem 'Marchands.' O que eu queria era fazer montes deles e pôr a venda até nas esquinas por camelô. Mário Pedrosa disse ser um suicídio mas bem que estou arrependida pois acho que era o que deveria ter feito mesmo."

22. Adolpho Leirner, foremost collector of Brazilian constructivist art, recounts a story of the influence Sacilotto's *Concreção 5730* had in the development of the *Bichos*. See Leirner, "Colecionar é uma Busca," in *Arte construtiva no Brasil: coleção Adolpho Leirner*, edited by Aracy Amaral (São Paulo: Melhoramentos, 1998), 11: "I remember discussing music with Sacilotto, at his home in Santo André; and drinking beer with [Hermelindo] Fiaminghi, whose instigating, ironic wit I greatly enjoyed. And Maurício Nogueira Lima's accounts of meetings with Lygia Clark and Sacilotto, at which

Lygia claimed herself capable of making a sculpture like Sacilotto's (*Concreção* 5730), though hers was to be a moving sculpture. Her famous 'bichos' were conceived in those meetings."

23. Clark, "1963" (typescript, Archives of the Clark Art Center, Rio de Janeiro): "Tenho certeza de que a gente do povo vai gostar deles pois aqui se dá a mesma coisa como o Português bosalíssimo que aqui veio para comprar a máquina de funileiro."

24. Ibid.: "Perguntado-me o que fazia com esta máquina, mostrei o bichinho sem dizer nada. Ele olhou e pegando nas mãos virando-o de todos os lados disse: 'Que interessante, não tem avesso.'"

25. Clark, "Bichos," in *Lygia Clark*, 121. Later, in an unpublished journal entry, Clark tells a more candid story about the origin of the name of the *Bichos*. See Clark, "17 de março de 1969" (typescript, Archives of the Clark Art Center, Rio de Janeiro): "Já sonhei duas vezes que havia perdido mesmo minha identidade. A primeira vez durante a minha estadia no Brasil no dia seguinte que tirei a pinta da boca. A pinta sempre foi a minha diferenciação. Por causa dela chamei de 'bichos' os meus trabalhos de 1959 pois ela era apontada pelos garotos quando criança que diziam: — Bicho!"

26. Clark, "Bichos," 121.

27. Lygia Clark and Hélio Oiticica, *Cartas: 1964–1974* (Rio de Janeiro: Editora UFRJ, 1996), 235.

28. Alexandre Wollner, cited in Name, "'Eu me lembro,'" in *Diálogo concreto*, 9: "Se deixei a pintura foi porque desejava um diálogo não com dez, mas com mil ou um milhão de pessoas, entre outras razões."

29. Oiticica, "Esquema geral da nova objetividade," in *Nova objetividade brasileira* (Rio de Janeiro: Museu de Arte Moderna, 1967), n.p. Excerpts of this text appear in English translation in Mari Carmen Ramírez and Héctor Olea, *Inverted Utopias: Avant-Garde in Latin America* (New Haven, CT: Yale University Press, 2004), 523–524. The text cited, though, is my own translation.

30. Haroldo de Campos theorizes the notion of an open work of art in 1955, seven years before the publication of Umberto Eco's monograph on the subject. See Haroldo de Campos, "a obra de arte aberta," in Campos, Pignatari, and Campos, *Teoria da poesia concreta*, 49–53.

31. Oiticica, "Esquema geral da nova objetividade," in *Nova objetividade brasileira*, n.p.: "Vê-se pois que sente esse artista uma necessidade maior, não só de criar simplesmente, mas de comunicar algo que para ele é fundamental, mas essa comunicação teria que se dar em grande escala, não numa elite reduzida a 'experts' mas até contra essa elite, com a proposição de obras não acabadas, 'abertas'. É essa a tecla fundamental do novo conceito de antiarte: não apenas martelar contra a arte do passado ou contra os conceitos antigos [. . .] mas criar novas condições experimentais, em que o artista assume o papel de 'proposicionista', ou 'empresário' ou mesmo 'educador.'"

32. See Pedrosa, cited in Gullar, "Arte concreta no Brasil": "A arte para éles não é atividade de parasitas nem está a serviço de ociosos ricos ou de causas políticas ou do Estado paternalista. Atividade autónoma e vital, ela visa a uma altíssima missão social, qual a de dar estilo à época e transformar os homens, educando-os a exercer os sentidos com plenitude e a modelar as próprias emoções." László Moholy-Nagy, an artist and instructor at the Bauhaus and director of the School of Design in Chicago, also

envisaged the role of the artist as educator of the senses. See Moholy-Nagy, *Vision in Motion* (Chicago, P. Theobald: 1947), 5: "This emotional prejudice—or inertia—is the great hindrance to necessary adjustments and social reforms. The remedy is to add to our intellectual literacy an emotional literacy, an education of the senses, the ability to articulate feeling through means of expression."

33. Irene V. Small reads the design changes by Amilcar de Castro to *Jornal de Brasil* in the late 1950s as evidence of just such interest. See "The Folded and the Flat," in Small, *Hélio Oiticica*, 18–69.

34. See Gullar, "Arte concreta no Brasil": "A posição dêsses dois artistas [Franz Weissmann and Clark]—e principalmente a experiência radical e continuada de Lygia Clark já definiam o caminho que iria tomar a arte no Brasil com a formação, em 1959, do Grupo Neoconcreto."

35. Martins, *Constructing an Avant-Garde*, 23. Martins provides this information to make a point about Pedrosa's early role in the dissemination of Gestalt theory among Brazilian artists and critics.

36. Ibid., 25.

37. Ibid., 27.

38. Jean Baudrillard, *For a Critique of the Political Economy of the Sign*, trans. Charles Levin (St. Louis, MO: Telos, 1981), 185.

39. Ibid., 186.

40. Ibid., 192.

41. Ibid., 187.

42. Ibid., 185.

43. A split that, Baudrillard, argues, is "as profoundly political, as the division of labor." See Baudrillard, *For a Critique*, 191.

44. Ibid., 189: "All possible valences of an object, all its ambivalence, which cannot be reduced to any model, are reduced by design to two rational components, two general models—utility and the aesthetic—which design isolates and artificially opposes to one another."

45. Ibid., 192. Emphasis in the original.

46. Name, "'Eu me lembro,'" in *Diálogo concreto*, 8: "Cada 'Eu me lembro' funcionou, ao longo destes últimos meses, como um tijolo a mais na construção conceitual para *Diálogo concreto*: o entendimento de que o objetivo primordial destes trabalhos em design parece ser justamente sequestrar e seduzir o espectador por meio de sua própria memória [. . .] Memória como elo e cumplicidade. Memória como sedução."

47. A review of the *Ballet Neoconcreto II* appeared in the *Jornal do Brasil: suplemento dominical* on April 18 and 19, 1959.

48. Lygia Pape, cited in Name, "Eu me lembro," in *Diálogo concreto*, 34: "Aquele era um momento em que experimentávamos muito em todas as áreas. Eu, particularmente, nunca gostei de ficar restrita a um suporte. Gostava de fazer com que eles conversassem e acabei levando a escultura para o trabalho como programadora visual. Sempre me diverti muito fazendo as embalagens para a Piraquê. Adorava ir à gráfica, me despencava para Madureira para ver como estavam as provas de impressão [. . .] Aquele vermelho aparecia para valer nas gôndolas do supermercado. Dava para achar os produtos de longe."

49. See Dickerman, "Zurich," in *Dada*, 37: "A long tradition of abstraction existed within the category of the decorative, but it was precisely this transposition of strategies from one sphere to another that had far-reaching implications. Nowhere is this more in evidence than in the couple's [Taeuber and Arp's] preoccupation with the form of the grid during the Dada years from 1916 to 1918."

50. See the chapter titled "Non-Utilitarian Constructions: The Evolution of a Formal Language," in Lodder, *Russian Constructivism*.

51. In her reading of Taeuber's work, Dickerman argues for the arts and crafts as the point of origin for Taeuber's interest in the grid as structure, suggesting a looser, much more playful origin for what would eventually become, in the work of artists like Mondrian, a more rigid and geometrically precise grid structure. See Dickerman, "Zurich," in *Dada*, 37.

52. Name, "'Eu me lembro,'" in *Diálogo concreto*, 34: "Além do desenho de embalagens que se tornaram clássicas, como as dos biscoitos Cream Crackers, Maria e Maisena, Lygia inventou um novo conceito para a embalagem, depois copiado por outras indústrias do Brasil e do exterior. Até então, os biscoitos eram guardados em caixas ou latas padronizadas, fosse qual fosse o seu formato. A artista desenvolveu, no entanto, um método próprio de cortar e colar o papel de embalo, de modo que ele passou a envolver os biscoitos sem gerar sobras dos lados, acima ou abaixo. Os biscoitos passaram a ser empilhados verticalmente e o papel plástico apenas se sobrepunha a esta pilha, criando a forma que as embalagens de Maria, Maisena e Cream Crackers têm até hoje, ou seja, a de sólidos espaciais (cilindros, nos dois primeiros casos, e paralelepípedo, no segundo)."

53. See Lodder, *Russian Constructivism* (7), for a succinct definition of what "laboratory" work meant for Soviet constructivist artists and where this work fits within the larger industrial and design process that they sought to intervene by means of their artwork: "The Constructivists used the term 'laboratory work' to describe formal investigation—usually in three dimensions but sometimes in two—which was undertaken not as an end in itself, nor for any immediately utilitarian purpose, but with the idea that such experimentation would eventually contribute to the solution of some utilitarian task. Theoretically, therefore, 'laboratory work' consisted of artistic explorations into the component elements of form, material, colour, space and construction, which were initiated not for their own sake." For more on the research-like quality of concrete art in Brazil, as well as the link between concrete poets and artists, see Clüver, "The Noigandres Poets."

54. Clark, "To Rediscover the Meaning of Our Routine Gestures," in *Lygia Clark*, 188.

55. Clark and Oiticica, *Cartas*, 36: "Comecei já a trabalhar catando pedras nas ruas, pois dinheiro não há para comprar material! Uso todo que me cai nas mãos, como sacos vazias de batatas, cebolas, plásticos que envolvem roupas que vêm do tintureiro, e ainda luvas de plástico que uso para pintar os cabelos!"

56. Conceived in 1971 by Waly Salomão and Torquato Neto, *Navilouca* was published in 1974 with contributions by some of the most prominent figures of the Brazilian avant-garde: Augusto de Campos, Rogério Duarte, Décio Pignatari, Duda Machado, Hélio Oiticica, Jorge Salomão, Lygia Clark, Stephen Berg, Luiz Otávio Pimentel, Cha-

cal, Luciano Figueiredo, Óscar Ramos, Ivan Cardoso, Caetano Veloso, and Haroldo de Campos.

57. Clark, "On the Suppression of the Object" (1974), in *Lygia Clark*, 264: "o objeto perdeu o seu sentido como meio de comunicação."

58. Ibid., 266.

59. Sut Jhally, *The Codes of Advertising: Fetishism and the Political Economy of Meaning in the Consumer Society* (New York: St. Martin's, 1987), 4.

60. Ibid., 5.

61. Ibid., 4.

62. Clark, "To Rediscover the Meaning of Our Routine Gestures," in *Lygia Clark*, 188.

63. Clark, "Man is the Centre" (1968), in *Lygia Clark*, 227.

64. Haroldo de Campos, "A arte no horizonte do provável," in *A arte no horizonte*, 15: "Enquanto que, numa estética clássica, a tendência seria considerar o objeto artístico *sub specie aeternitatis*, a arte contemporânea [. . .] parece ter incorporado o relativo e o transitório como dimensão mesma de seu ser."

65. Ibid., 16: "De outro lado, explicariam, por exemplo, no âmbito da arte de nosso tempo, a derrocada do primado incontrastável dos materiais nobres—o mármore, o bronze perene—em escultura (lembre-se, para citar apenas um caso, a coluna MERZ de Kurt Schwitters, construída dos fragmentos mais diversos apanhados no despejo do cotidiano)."

66. Ferreira Gullar, "Teoria do não-objeto" (1960), in *Projeto construtivo brasileiro na arte: 1950–1962*, ed. Aracy Amaral (São Paulo: Pinacoteca do Estado de São Paulo, 1977), 86: "Quando mais tarde o dadaísta Kurt Schwitters constrói o seu Merzbau—feito com objetos ou fragmentos de objetos achados na rua—, ainda é a mesma intenção que se amplia, já agora livre da moldura, no espaço real."

67. Clark, "To Rediscover the Meaning of Our Routine Gestures," in *Lygia Clark*, 188–189.

68. Guy Brett, "Lygia Clark: Six Cells," in *Lygia Clark*, 22.

69. Clark, cited in Guy Brett, "Lygia Clark: Six Cells," in *Lygia Clark*, 23.

70. Herkenhoff, "Lygia Clark," in Clark, *Lygia Clark*, 45.

71. Ibid.

72. Taussig, *Devil and Commodity Fetishism*, 35.

73. Suely Rolnik, "Molding a Contemporary Soul," in Martin and Ruiz, *Experimental Exercise of Freedom*, 63.

74. Small, *Hélio Oiticica*, 7.

75. Gestalt theory was received, appropriated, and reinterpreted early on in Brazil by Mário Pedrosa in his thesis on Gestalt titled *Da natureza afetiva da forma na obra de arte*, defended in 1949 at the Faculdade Nacional de Arquitetura do Rio de Janeiro. As Sérgio B. Martins notes, it was thanks to Pedrosa that Gestalt theory came to shape the discursive apparatus of neoconcretism, and it was largely thanks to the younger Ferreira Gullar that Merleau-Ponty's critical stance on Gestalt psychology began to circulate in the theoretical writings of neoconcretism. See Sérgio B. Martins, "Phenomenological Openness: Historicist Closure; Revisiting the Theory of the Non-Object," *Third Text* 26.1 (2012): 80–81.

76. Christine Macel lists the writers, psychoanalysts, and intellectuals whose work

influenced Clark's proposals and writings. See Macel, "Lygia Clark: At the Border of Art," in Butler and Pérez-Oramas, *Lygia Clark*, 256: "Though she had no academic background in the field, she read Herbert Marcuse—who, she said, was too difficult for her—as well as Félix Guattari, Laing (the pope of antipsychiatry), Groddeck, Melanie Klein, D. W. Winnicott, Nicolas Abraham and Maria Torok, and doubtless Didier Anzieu."

77. Marion Milner, "The Role of Illusion in Symbol Formation" (1952), in *The Suppressed Madness of Sane Men: Forty-Four Years of Exploring Psychoanalysis* (Tavistock: London, 1987).

78. Clark, "The Full-Emptiness" (1960), in *Lygia Clark*, 111.

79. Clark, "A Modern Myth: The Instant as Nostalgia of the Cosmos" (1983), in *Lygia Clark*, 154–155.

80. Clark, cited by Brett, "Lygia Clark: Six Cells," in *Lygia Clark*, 28.

81. Brett, "Lygia Clark: Six Cells," in *Lygia Clark*, 25.

82. Milner, "The Sense in Nonsense (Freud and Blake's *Job*)" (1956), in *Suppressed Madness*, 178.

83. This is not to deny that there is a place for narrow focus and purpose-driven reason in our lives. See Milner, "Sense in Nonsense," in *Suppressed Madness*, 181–182: "we do in fact continually crucify our imagination, kill our capacity for the imaginative understanding of others, and for two reasons. It is partly because such understanding can bring pain and responsibility; but it is also due to our clinging to those principles of logical thought which require a duality, a split between subject and object, between seer and seen."

84. Ibid., 179.

85. Milner, "Role of Illusion in Symbol Formation," in *Suppressed Madness*, 85.

86. Ibid.

87. Ibid.: The fundamental idea here is that symbolism "may be a regression in order to take a step forward."

88. Mário Pedrosa, "The Vital Need for Art," in Ferreira and Herkenhoff, *Mário Pedrosa*, 106.

89. The Ateliê do Engenho de Dentro, as this experiment in art and psychiatry came to be known, operated in the Centro Psiquiátrico Nacional Hospital Dom Pedro II in the Engenho de Dentro district of Rio de Janeiro from 1946 to 1951. It convened rising Brazilian abstract artists like Abraham Palatnik, Ivan Serpa, and Almir Mavignier as well as Pedrosa himself. For an account of the links between the Ateliê and concrete art in Rio de Janeiro, see Glaucia Villas Bôas, "A estética da conversão: o ateliê do Engenho de Dentro e a arte concreta carioca (1946–1951)," in *Tempo social, revista de sociologia da USP* 20.2 (2008): 197–219.

90. Pedrosa, "Vital Need for Art," in Ferreira and Herkenhoff, *Mário Pedrosa*, 105.

91. This is what Macel gestures toward when she writes that Clark's *O dentro é o fora* (1963) is "stamped with a fantasy feel linked to the body through its preverbal stage, where the border between oneself and the outside is inverted and the body becomes externalized, as though turning a glove inside out." See Macel, "Lygia Clark: At the Border of Art," in Butler and Pérez-Oramas, *Lygia Clark*, 254.

92. Ibid., 259: "Clark surely had her finger, so to speak, on major issues involving

pathology and its therapies. Nevertheless, her borderline practice, on the edges of psychoanalysis (a boundary she continually played with in her life and her art), has never been recognized, despite the therapeutic success affirmed by Clark herself and the people she trained, such as Wanderley and Gina Ferreira, and despite her efforts to pass down her work so that it could endure. Psychologists and psychoanalysts have held her practice at arm's length, as has the art world, aside from Brazilian critics Pedrosa and Frederico Morais. The Neo-Concretist theorist Ferreira Gullar was particularly critical of her last period, while most art historians, like Brett and Yve-Alain Bois, maintain that to them, she remained an artist."

93. Clark, "On the Suppression of the Object," in *Lygia Clark*, 264.

94. Bleger, *Symbiosis and Ambiguity*, 4.

95. Ibid., 24–25: "Re-introjection can be done only in small 'doses' and at an appropriate pace, so that when a certain 'threshold' is passed, the re-introjection functions as an abrupt return of the repressed. In this case re-introjection may occur on the bodily level which already involves the possibility of a certain degree of re-introjection but also means using the body as a 'buffer' that tends to prevent alterations of equilibrium on the mental level. I call this function a 'buffer' because this word originally refers to solutions that counter or damp down any change in the acidity or alkalinity of a medium. (The body 'buffers' as a homeostatic mechanism.)"

96. Previously, Clark taught art at the Instituto Nacional de Educação dos Surdos in Brazil.

97. See Clark, "Eu, Lygia Clark," n.d. (typescript, Archives of the Clark Art Center, Rio de Janeiro): "Aqui ao chegar estava ainda no arcaico, estado em que o Fedida me largou, depois de um belo tratamento fui por indicação do mesmo procurei o Sapir que me indicou três nomes para escolher em que fizesse a aplicação do seu método em mim. Depois de uma relação tão conturbada com o Fedida, francamente não queria fazer com um homem. Escolhi a Madame Karlikof e passei pela relaxação durante o tempo que me restava, antes da minha volta."

98. Ibid. "Quando recebo pela primeira vez um cliente, ele quer me contar seus problemas, eu o Interrompo para lhe dizer—'Se você conhecesse a sua verdadeira história, você não estaria aqui. Você vai começar a conhecê-la no 'aqui e agora' no 'pré-verbal.'"

99. Ibid.: "Nesta época tratava o cliente com a relaxação do Sapir e com alguns objetos meus. Aos poucos fui retirando a indução verbal do Sapir e passei a trabalhar exclusivamente com os meus objetos—relacionais e no pré-verbal."

100. Clark, "O objeto, o método e a prática," n.d. (typescript, Archives of the Clark Art Center, Rio de Janeiro).

101. Ibid.: "Mando que eles se espreguicem como bichos."

102. The relational object consisting of a dropper and honey, the only one that engaged the sense of taste, was Gina Ferreira's innovation, gladly adopted by Lygia Clark.

103. See Rolnik, "Uma terapêutica": "Com a ajuda de seus objetos, Lygia ia preenchendo buracos, fechando fissuras, repondo partes ausentes, soldando articulações desconcertadas, escorando pontos sem sustentação, abrindo espaço corporal em pontos de encolhimento—fazendo enfim o que pedisse o corpo de seu cliente, a cada instante do processo."

104. Ibid.

105. Taussig, *Devil and Commodity Fetishism*, 26.

106. See Virilio, *Vision Machine*, 59: "'Now objects perceive me,' the painter Paul Klee wrote in his *Notebooks*." Reading Mallarmé, Paz picks up on this uncanny dynamic of objects animated, except in reference to words. See Paz, "Los signos en rotación," *Obras completas*, vol. 1, 273: "la noción del *poema crítico* entraña la de una lectura y Mallarmé se refirió varias veces a una escritura ideal en la que las frases y palabras se reflejarían unas a otras y, en cierto modo, se contemplarían o leerían."

Conclusion

1. Randall, "Introduction," in *Political Economy of Latin America*, 7–8.

2. Roberto Jacoby formulates the puritan limits of the progressive imagination in his theorization of what he calls "the strategy of joy" ("la estrategia de la alegría"). See Roberto Jacoby, *El deseo nace del derrumbe: acciones, conceptos, escritos* (Barcelona: Ediciones de la Central, 2011), 411: "La piel era considerada como territorio de placer y no de tormento. La 'superficie' también era lo opuesto al calabozo y la clandestinidad. Es fácil de ver que en el tono moralizante de esas críticas se vertía el puritanismo revolucionario tradicional, mezcla del estalinismo con el ascetismo cristiano y militar, hegemónico tanto dentro de las fuerzas progresistas como de las reaccionarias."

Bibliography

Adorno, Theodor W. *Aesthetic Theory*. 1970. Translated by Robert Hullot-Kentor. New York: Continuum, 2002.

———. *The Culture Industry: Selected Essays on Mass Culture*. London: Routledge, 2001.

———. "On Lyric Poetry and Society." 1958. Translated by Shierry Weber Nicholsen. In *Notes to Literature*, 37–54. New York: Columbia University Press, 1991.

———. *Prisms*. 1967. Translated by Samuel and Shierry Weber. Cambridge, MA: MIT Press, 1997.

———. "Theodor Adorno: Letters to Walter Benjamin." In *Aesthetics and Politics*. New York: Verso, 2007.

Aguilar, Gonzalo. "Hélio Oiticica, Haroldo y Augusto de Campos: el diálogo velado—la aspiración a lo blanco." *O Eixo e a Roda: Revista de Literatura Brasileira* 13 (Dec 31, 2006): 55–84.

———. *Poesia concreta brasileira: as vanguardas na encruzilhada modernista*. Translated by Regina Aida Crespo, Rodolfo Mata, and Gênese Andrade. São Paulo: Editora da Universidade de São Paulo, 2005.

Álvarez, Francisco. "Octavio Paz: hacia una poética de la modernidad." *Hispania* 81.1 (Mar. 1998): 20–30.

Álvarez, Gabriela, and María García Holley. "Museums for Modernization." In Eder, *Defying Stability*, 340–355.

Amor, Mónica. *Theories of the Nonobject: Argentina, Brazil, Venezuela, 1944–1969*. Berkeley: University of California Press, 2016.

Andrade, Oswald de. *Memórias sentimentais de João Miramar*. 1924. São Paulo: Editora Globo, 1990.

———. "O Caminho Percorrido." 1944. In *Ponta de lança*, 93–102. Rio de Janeiro: Editora Civilização Brasileira, 1971.

Anjos, Moacir dos. "As ruas e as bobagens: anotações sobre o *delirium ambulatorium* de Hélio Oiticica," in *Ars* 10.20 (2012): 22–44.

Arruda, Maria Arminda do Nascimento. *Metrópole e cultura: São Paulo no meio século XX*. Bauru, São Paulo: Editora da Universidade do Sagrado Coração, 2001.

Arte construtiva no Brasil: coleção Adolpho Leirner. São Paulo: Melhoramentos, 1998.

Baer, Werner, and Claudio Paiva. "Brazil." In Randall, *Political Economy of Latin America*, 70–100.

Banash, David. "From Advertising to the Avant-Garde: Rethinking the Invention of Collage." *Postmodern Culture: An Electronic Journal of Interdisciplinary Criticism* 14.2 (Jan. 2004). https://muse.jhu.edu/article/55199.

Bandeira, João. "Words in Space: Poetry at the National Exhibition of Concrete Art." In Mammì et al., *Concreta '56*, 120–140.
Banham, Reyner. "Introduction." *Man, Machine, & Motion*. Durham, UK: King's College, 1955.
Barbosa, Marialva, and Ana Paula Goulart Ribeiro. "Telejornalismo na Globo: vestigios, narrativa e temporalidade." In *Rede Globo—40 anos de poder e hegemonia*, organized by Valério Cruz Brittos and César Ricardo Siqueira Bolaño, 205–223. São Paulo: Paulus, 2005.
Bataille, Georges. *The Accursed Share: An Essay on General Economy*. Translated by Robert Hurley. New York: Zone Books, 1991.
Baudrillard, Jean. *For a Critique of the Political Economy of the Sign*. Translated by Charles Levin. St. Louis, MO: Telos, 1981.
———. *Seduction*. New York: St. Martin's, 1990.
Benjamin, Walter. *One-Way Street*. Translated by Edmund Jephcott. Cambridge, MA: Harvard University Press, 2016.
———. "Paris, the Capital of the Nineteenth Century." In Benjamin, *Work of Art*, 96–115.
———. *Reflections: Essays, Aphorisms, Autobiographical Writings*. Edited by Peter Demetz; translated by Edmund Jephcott. New York: Harcourt Brace Jovanovich, 1978.
———. "Theory of Distraction." In Benjamin, *Work of Art*, 56–57.
——— "The Work of Art in the Age of its Technological Reproducibility." In Benjamin, *Work of Art*, 19–55.
———. *The Work of Art in the Age of Its Technological Reproducibility, and Other Writings on Media*, edited by Michael W. Jennings, Brigid Doherty, and Thomas Levin. Cambridge, MA: Harvard University Press, 2008.
Berghaus, Günter. *Italian Futurist Theatre, 1909–1944*. Oxford: Clarendon, 1998.
Bessa, Antonio Sergio. "The 'image of the voice' in Augusto de Campos' *Poetamenos*." *Ciberletras: Revista de Crítica Literaria y de Cultura* 17 (20017), n.p., http://www.lehman.cuny.edu/ciberletras/v17/bessa.htm.
Bleger, José. *Symbiosis and Ambiguity: A Psychoanalytic Study*. 1967. New York: Routledge, 2013.
Bourriaud, Nicolas. *The Radicant*. New York: Lukas and Sternberg, 2009.
Bowallius, Marie-Louise, and Michael Toivio. "Powerful Marks: On Trademarks and Ethics from the Perspective of Design History." In *Identity: Trademarks, Logotypes and Symbols*, edited by Lena Holger and Ingalill Holmberg, 13–27. Stockholm: Nationalmuseum and Raster Förlag, 2002.
Brading, David A. *Octavio Paz y la poética de la historia mexicana*. Mexico City: Fondo de Cultura Económica, 2002.
Brett, Guy. "Lygia Clark: Six Cells." In Clark, *Lygia Clark*, 17–35.
Brito, Ronaldo. "Neoconcretismo." *Malasartes* 3 (April–June 1976). Rio de Janeiro: 9–13.
———. *Neoconcretismo: vértice e ruptura do projeto construtivo brasileiro*. São Paulo: Cosac & Naify Edicões, 1999.
Brodsky, Claudia. "Framing the Sensuous: Objecthood and 'Objectivity,'" in *Art and*

Aesthetics after Adorno, by J. M. Bernstein et al., 69–115. Berkeley: Townsend Center for the Humanities, University of California, 2010.
Buchloh, Benjamin. "From Faktura to Factography," *October* 30 (Autumn 1984): 82–119.
Buck-Morss, Susan. "The Cinema Screen as Prosthesis of Perception: A Historical Account." In *The Senses Still: Perception and Memory as Material Culture in Modernity*, edited by C. Nadia Seremetakis, 45–62. Boulder, CO: Westview, 1994.
———. *Dreamworld and Catastrophe: The Passing of Mass Utopia in East and West*. Cambridge, MA: MIT Press, 2000.
———. *The Origin of Negative Dialectics: Theodor W. Adorno, Walter Benjamin, and the Frankfurt Institute*. New York: Free Press, 1977.
Bunker, Steven B. *Creating Mexican Consumer Culture in the Age of Porfirio Díaz*. Albuquerque: University of New Mexico Press, 2012.
Bürger, Peter. *Theory of the Avant-Garde*. Translated by Michael Shaw. Minneapolis: University of Minnesota Press, 1984.
Cabañas, Teresa. *A poética da inversão: representação e simulacro na poesia concreta*. Goiânia, Brazil: Ed. UFG, 2000.
Callan, Richard J. *The Philosophy of Yoga in Octavio Paz's Poem* Blanco. Lewiston, NY: Edwin Mellen Press, 2005.
Campos, Augusto de. "a moeda concreta da fala." 1957. In Campos, Pignatari, and Campos, *Teoria da poesia concreta*, 157–174.
———. *Balanço da bossa e outras bossas*. São Paulo: Editora Perspectiva, 1974.
———. "From Dante to the Post-Concrete: An Interview with Augusto de Campos." Interview with Roland Greene. *The Harvard Library Bulletin* 3.2 (Summer 1992). http://www.ubu.com/papers/decampos.html.
———. "poesia concreta (manifesto)." 1956. In Campos, Pignatari, and Campos, *Teoria da poesia concreta*, 71–72.
———. "pontos-periferia-poesia concreta." 1956. In Campos, Pignatari, and Campos, *Teoria da poesia concreta*, 31–42.
———. *Viva vaia: poesia, 1949–1979*. Cotia, São Paulo: Ateliê Editorial, 2000.
Campos, Augusto de, Décio Pignatari, and Haroldo de Campos. *Teoria da poesia concreta: textos críticos e manifestos, 1950–1960*. Cotia, São Paulo: Ateliê Editorial, 2006.
Campos, Haroldo de. "A arte no horizonte do provável." In *A arte no horizonte do provável e outros ensaios*, 15–34. São Paulo: Editora Perspectiva, 1969.
———. "Comunicação na poesia de vanguarda." In *A arte no horizonte do provável e outros ensaios*, 131–154. São Paulo: Editora Perspectiva, 1969.
———. "Concrete Poetry-Language-Communication." 1957. Translated by A. S. Bessa. In *Novas: Selected Writings*, 235–245.
———. "Da razão antropofágica: diálogo e diferença na cultura brasileira" (1981). In *Metalinguagem & outras metas*, 231–255. São Paulo: Perspectiva, 2006.
———. "evolução de formas: poesia concreta." 1957. In Campos, Pignatari, and Campos, *Teoria da poesia concreta*, 77–87.
———. "Maiakovski e o construtivismo." *O Estado de São Paulo: suplemento literário* (Sept. 29, 1962): 4.
———. *Metalinguagem & outras metas*. São Paulo: Perspectiva, 1992.

———. "Miramar na mira." In Andrade, *Memórias sentimentais*, 5–33.
———. *Novas: Selected Writings*. Edited by Antonio Sergio Bessa and Odile Cisneros. Evanston, IL: Northwestern University Press, 2007.
———. "a obra de arte aberta." In Campos, Pignatari, and Campos, *Teoria da poesia concreta*, 49–53.
———. "olho por olho a olho nu (manifesto)." *ad—arquitetura e decoração* 20 (Nov.-Dec. 1956). Reprinted in Campos, Pignatari, and Campos, *Teoria da poesia concreta*, 73–76.
———. "The Open Work of Art" (1955). In *Novas: Selected Writings*, 220–222.
———. "To Octavio Paz." Feb. 24, 1968. In Paz and Campos, *Transblanco*, 96–97.
———. "To Octavio Paz." Undated. In Paz and Campos, *Transblanco*, 109–111.
Campos, Haroldo, and Augusto de Campos. "Brazilian Concrete Poetry: How It Looks Today." Interview by Marjorie Perloff. *Arshile: A Magazine of the Arts* 3 (1994): 61–78.
———. "Poesía concreta: configuración/textos." Trans. Antonio Alatorre. "Suplemento." *Plural* 8 (May 1972): 21–22.
Candido, Antonio. "Literatura e subdesenvolvimento." 1970. In *A educação pela noite e outros ensaios*, edited by Marta de Mello e Souza, 141–162. São Paulo: Editora Ática, 1989.
Cardoza y Aragón, Luis. *México: pintura de hoy*. Mexico City: Fondo de Cultura Económica, 1964.
———. *Pintura mexicana contemporánea*. Mexico City: Imprenta Universitaria, 1953.
Cendrars, Blaise. *La prose du Transsibérien et de la petite Jehanne de France* (Paris: Editions des Hommes Nouveaux), 1913.
Certeau, Michel de. *The Practice of Everyday Life*. Translated by Steven Rendall. Berkeley: University of California Press, 1984.
Charlot, Jean. *The Mexican Mural Renaissance, 1920–1925*. New Haven, CT: Yale University Press, 1963.
Clark, Lygia. "17 de março de 1969." 1969. Typescript held at the Archives of the Clark Art Center, Rio de Janeiro.
———. "1963–3." 1963. Typescript held at the Archives of the Clark Art Center, Rio de Janeiro.
———. "Bichos." 1983. In *Lygia Clark*, 121.
———. "Conference Given in the Belo Horizonte National School of Architecture in 1956." In *Lygia Clark*, 71–73.
———. "Eu, Lygia Clark." N.d. Typescript held at the Archives of the Clark Art Center, Rio de Janeiro.
———. "The Full-Emptiness." In *Lygia Clark*, 111–113.
———. *Lygia Clark*. Barcelona: Fundació Antoni Tàpies, 1998.
———. "Man is the Centre." In *Lygia Clark*, 227–228.
———. "A Modern Myth: The Instant as Nostalgia of the Cosmos." In *Lygia Clark*, 154–155.
———. "O objeto, o método e a prática." N.d. Typescript held at the Archives of the Clark Art Center, Rio de Janeiro.
———. "On the Suppression of the Object." 1974. In *Lygia Clark*, 264–269.

———. "To Rediscover the Meaning of Our Routine Gestures." Extract from "L'art c'est le corps." (1973). In *Lygia Clark*, 188–189.

Clark, Lygia, and Yve-Alain Bois. "Nostalgia of the Body." *October* 69 (Summer 1994): 85–109.

Clark, Lygia, and Hélio Oiticica. *Cartas: 1964–1974*. Edited by Luciano Figueiredo. Rio de Janeiro: Editora UFRJ, 1996.

Clüver, Claus. "Klangfarbenmelodie in Polychromatic Poems: A. von Webern and A. de Campos." *Comparative Literature Studies* 18.3 (Sept. 1981): 386–398.

———. "The Noigandres Poets and Concrete Art." *Ciberletras: Revista de Crítica Literaria y de Cultura* 17 (2007), n.p., http://www.lehman.cuny.edu/ciberletras/v17/cluver.htm.

Cordeiro, Waldemar. "Ainda o abstracionismo." In *Arte concreta paulista: documentos*, edited by João Bandeira, 17. São Paulo: Cosac & Naify, 2002.

Cosío Villegas, Daniel. "Mexico's Crisis." 1947. In *The Mexico Reader: History, Culture, Politics*, edited by Gilbert M. Joseph and Timothy J. Henderson, 470–481. Durham, NC: Duke University Press, 2002.

Costa, Horácio. "Acerca de la poesía visual brasileña." In *Mar abierto: Ensayos sobre literatura brasileña, portuguesa e hispanoamericana*, 45–75. Mexico City: Fondo de Cultura Económica, 1998.

Crary, Jonathan. "Spectacle, Attention, Counter-Memory." In *Guy Debord and the Situationist International: Texts and Documents*, edited by Tom McDonough, 455–466. Cambridge, MA: MIT Press, 2002.

———. *Suspensions of Perception: Attention, Spectacle, and Modern Culture*. Cambridge, MA: MIT Press, 1999.

Cuevas, José Luis. "El mural efímero." *Letras Libres* (February 1999): 69–71.

Darnton, Robert. *Mesmerism and the End of Enlightenment in France*. Cambridge, MA: Harvard University Press, 1968.

Debroise, Olivier. "Arte acción: David Alfaro Siqueiros en las estrategias artísticas e ideológicas de los años treinta." In *Retrato de una década: David Alfaro Siqueiros, 1930–1940*, 18–67. Mexico City: Instituto Nacional de Bellas Artes, 1996.

———, ed. *Otras rutas hacia Siqueiros*. Mexico City: MUNAL/CURARE, 1996.

Deleuze, Gilles. *The Movement-Image*. Translated by Hugh Tomlinson and Barbara Habberjam. New York: Continuum, 2005.

Deleuze, Gilles, and Félix Guattari. *Anti-Oedipus: Capitalism and Schizophrenia*. Translated by Robert Hurley, Mark Seem, and Helen R. Lane. Minneapolis: University of Minnesota Press, 1983.

Dettman, Jonathan. "Consumption and the Culture Industry." In Durão, *Culture Industry Today*, 141–154.

Dickerman, Leah. "Zurich." In *Dada: Zurich, Berlin, Hannover, Cologne, New York, Paris*, 16–44. Washington, DC: National Gallery of Art, 2005.

Doesburg, Theo van. "Concrete Art Manifesto." In Lorenza Saitta and Jean-Daniel Zucker, *Abstraction in Artificial Intelligence and Complex Systems*, 413–414. New York: Springer, 2013.

Downs, Linda. "Octavio Paz y el muralismo mexicano." In *Homenaje a Octavio Paz*, edited by Juan Valencia, 131–144. New York: Instituto Cultural Mexicano de Nueva York, 2001.

Dreyfus, Hubert. “Heidegger on the Connection between Nihilism, Art, Technology and Politics.” In *The Cambridge Companion to Heidegger*, edited by Charles Guignon, 345–372. New York: Cambridge University Press, 1993.

Duarte, Rogério. “The Culture Industry in Brazil.” In Durão, *Culture Industry Today*, 93–112.

Durão, Fabio Akcelrud, ed. *Culture Industry Today*. Newcastle upon Tyne: Cambridge Scholars Publishing, 2010.

Eder, Rita, ed. *Defying Stability: Artistic Processes in Mexico 1952–1967*. Mexico City: Turner, 2014.

Eisenstein, Sergei. 1932. “Síntesis de las opiniones emitidas sobre la obra de Siqueiros.” Catalog. Sala de Arte Público Siqueiros. Mexico City.

Enjuto-Rangel, Cecilia. “Broken Presents: The Modern City in Ruins in Baudelaire, Cernuda, and Paz.” *Comparative Literature* 59.2 (Spring 2007): 140–157.

Erber, Pedro. “The Word as Object: Concrete Poetry, Ideogram, and the Modernization of Language.” *Luso-Brazilian Review* 49.2 (2012): 72–101.

Ferreira, Glória. “The Permanent Revolution of the Critic.” In Ferreira and Herkenhoff, *Mário Pedrosa*, 14–23.

Ferreira, Glória, and Paulo Herkenhoff, eds. *Mário Pedrosa: Primary Documents*. New York: Museum of Modern Art, 2015.

Figuereido, Wilson. “Da crise política fez-se o ‘JB’: ascensão e queda do ‘Jornal do Brasil.’ ” In *Folha de São Paulo* (July 25, 2010). http://www1.folha.uol.com.br/fsp/ilustrissima/il2507201006.htm.

Flaherty, George F. “Uncanny Tlatelolco, Uncomfortable Juxtapositions.” In Eder, *Defying Stability*, 401–417.

Folgarait, Leonard. *Mural Painting and Social Revolution in Mexico, 1920–1940: Art of the New Order*. New York: Cambridge University Press, 1998.

———. *So Far from Heaven: David Alfaro Siqueiros'* The March of Humanity *and Mexican Revolutionary Politics*. New York: Cambridge University Press, 1987.

Foster, Hal. *Prosthetic Gods*. Cambridge, MA: MIT Press, 2004.

———. *The Return of the Real*. Cambridge, MA: MIT Press, 1996.

———. “Survey.” In *Pop*, edited by Mark Francis, 18. New York: Phaidon, 2005.

Francis, Mark. “Preface.” In *Pop*, 10-13. New York: Phaidon, 2005.

Franco, Jean. “¡Oh mundo por poblar, hoja en blanco! El espacio y los espacios en la obra de Octavio Paz.” *Revista Iberoamericana* 37.74 (Jan.–Mar. 1971): 147–160.

Fraser, Valerie. *Building the New World: Studies in the Modern Architecture of Latin America 1930–1960*. New York: Verso, 2000.

Freyre, Gilberto. *O escravo nos anúncios de jornais brasileiros do século XIX; tentativa de interpretação antropológica, através de anúncios de jornais, de características de personalidade e de deformações de corpo de negros ou mestiços, fugidos ou expostos à venda, como escravos, no Brasil do século passado*. Recife: Imprênsa Universitária, 1963.

Gabara, Esther. *Errant Modernism: The Ethos of Photography in Mexico and Brazil*. Durham, NC: Duke University Press, 2008.

Gago, Verónica. *La razón neoliberal: economías barrocas y pragmática popular*. Buenos Aires: Tinta Limón Ediciones, 2014.
Gallo, Rubén. *Mexican Modernity: The Avant-Garde and the Technological Revolution*. Cambridge, MA: MIT Press, 2005.
———. "Wireless Modernity: Mexican Estridentistas, Italian and Russian Futurism." *International Yearbook of Futurism Studies* 2.1 (2012): 141–170.
García Canclini, Néstor. 1995. *Consumers and Citizens: Globalization and Multicultural Conflicts*. Translated by George Yúdice. Minneapolis: University of Minnesota Press, 2001.
———. *Culturas híbridas: estrategias para entrar y salir de la modernidad*. 1989. Mexico City: Grijalbo, 1998.
Gillet, Louis. "Joyce's Way." 1925. *Claybook for James Joyce 1876–1943*. London: Abelard-Schuman, 1958.
Gimferrer, Pere. *Lecturas de Octavio Paz*. Barcelona: Editorial Anagrama, 1980.
Goldman, Shifra M. "Siqueiros and Three Early Murals in Los Angeles." *Art Journal* 33.4 (Summer 1974): 321–327.
Gómez Sicre, José. "Introduction." In *Esso Salon of Young Artists*, n.p. Sponsored by Pan American Union and Esso. Catalog of an exhibition that opened on April 21, 1965, at the Pan American Union, Washington, D.C.
Gonzalez, Mike, and David Treece. *The Gathering of the Voices: The Twentieth-Century Poetry of Latin America*. London: Verso, 1992.
González Gómez, Francisco. *Del porfirismo al neoliberalismo*. Mexico City: Ediciones Quinto Sol, 2007.
Greeley, Robin A. "Muralism and the State in Post-Revolution Mexico, 1920–1970." In *Mexican Muralism: A Critical History*, edited by Alejandro Anreus, Leonard Folgarait, and Robin A. Greeley, 13–36. Berkeley: University of California Press, 2012.
Greene, Roland. "From Dante to the Post-Concrete: An Interview with Augusto de Campos." *Harvard Library Bulletin* 3.2 (Summer 1992). http://www.ubu.com/papers/decampos.html.
Grenier, Yvon. *From Art to Politics: Octavio Paz and the Pursuit of Freedom*. Lanham, MA: Rowman and Littlefield, 2001.
Grünewald, José Lino. *Escreviver*. São Paulo: Perspectiva, 2008.
Grünfeld, Mihai G. *Antología de la poesía latinoamericana de vanguardia 1916–1935*. Madrid: Hiperión, 1995.
Guibert, Rita. "Interview with Octavio Paz." In *Siete voces: los más grandes escritores latinoamericanos se confiesan con Rita Guibert*, 198–293. Mexico City: Organización Editorial Novaro, 1974.
Gullar, Ferreira. "Arte concreta no Brasil: etapas da pintura contemporânea XXXIX—arte concreta V." *Jornal do Brasil: suplemento dominical* (Aug. 6, 1960): 3.
———. "Teoria do não-objeto." (1960). In *Projeto construtivo brasileiro na arte: 1950–1962*, edited by Aracy Amaral, 85–94. São Paulo: Pinacoteca do Estado de São Paulo, 1977.
Hansen, Mark. *Embodying Technesis: Technology beyond Writing*. Ann Arbor: University of Michigan Press, 2000.

Heidegger, Martin. "The Age of the World Picture." 1938. In *The Question Concerning Technology and Other Essays*, 115–154. Translated and with an introduction by William Lovitt. New York: Harper, 1977.

———. "The Origin of the Work of Art." 1950. In *Poetry Language Thought*, by Heidegger, 15–86. Translated by Albert Hofstadter. New York: Harper Collins, 2001.

Herkenhoff, Paulo. "Lygia Clark." In Clark, *Lygia Clark*, 36–53.

Hirschman, Alberto O. "The Political Economy of Import-Substituting Industrialization in Latin America." In *The Essential Hirschman*, edited by Jeremy Adelman, 102–136. Princeton, NJ: Princeton University Press, 2013.

Horkheimer, Max, and Theodor W. Adorno. "The Culture Industry: Enlightenment as Mass Deception." In *Dialectic of Enlightenment: Philosophical Fragments*, edited by Gunzelin Schmid Noerr, 95–136. Translated by Edmund Jephcott. Palo Alto, CA: Stanford University Press, 2002.

Hullot-Kentor, Robert. "The Exact Sense in Which the Culture Industry No Longer Exists." In Durão, *Culture Industry Today*, 5–22.

———. "A New Type of Human Being and Who We Really Are." *The Brooklyn Rail: Critical Perspectives on Art, Politics, and Culture*. Nov. 10, 2008. http://brooklynrail.org/2008/11/art/a-new-type-of-human-being-and-who-we-really-are.

———. *Things beyond Resemblance: Collected Essays on Theodor W. Adorno*. New York: Columbia University Press, 2006.

Hulten, Pontus. *The Machine: As Seen at the End of the Mechanical Age*. New York: The Museum of Modern Art, 1968.

Hurlburt, Laurance P. *The Mexican Muralists in the United States*. Albuquerque: University of New Mexico Press, 1989.

Indych-López, Anna. *Muralism without Walls: Rivera, Orozco, and Siqueiros in the United States, 1927–1940*. Pittsburgh: University of Pittsburgh Press, 2009.

Jackson, K. David. "Music of the Spheres in Galáxias." In *Haroldo de Campos: A Dialogue with the Brazilian Concrete Poet*, edited by K. David Jackson, 119–128. Oxford: Centre of Brazilian Studies, Oxford University, 2005.

Jacoby, Roberto. *El deseo nace del derrumbe: acciones, conceptos, escritos*. Barcelona: Ediciones de la Central, 2011.

Jácome, Cristobal Andrés. "Journeys and Assemblages." In Eder, *Defying Stability*, 284–295.

Jaimes, Héctor. *Filosofía del muralismo mexicano: Orozco, Rivera y Siqueiros*. Mexico City: Plaza y Valdés, 2012.

———. *Fundación del muralismo mexicano: textos inéditos de David Alfaro Siqueiros*. Mexico City: Siglo Veintiuno Editores, 2012.

Jakobson, Roman. "Linguistics and Poetics." 1958. In *The Structuralists: From Marx to Lévi-Strauss*, edited by Richard T. De George and Fernande M. De George, 85–122. Garden City, NY: Anchor, 1972.

Jameson, Fredric. *Late Marxism: Adorno, or, The Persistence of the Dialectic*. New York: Verso, 1990.

Jennings, Michael W., Brigid Doherty, and Thomas Y. Levin. "Editors' Introduction." In Benjamin, *Work of Art*, 1–18.

Jhally, Sut. *The Codes of Advertising: Fetishism and the Political Economy of Meaning in the Consumer Society*. New York: St. Martin's, 1987.

Jolly, Jennifer. "David Alfaro Siqueiros, Antonio Pujol, Luis Arenal, Josep Renau y Miguel Prieto: *Retrato de la burguesía*." In *Muralismo mexicano, 1920–1940*, edited by Ida Rodríguez Prampolini, 349–358. Mexico City: Fondo de Cultura Económica, 2012.

Josten, Jennifer. "Concrete Poetry." In Eder, *Defying Stability*, 107.

Juárez Reyes, América. "Siqueiros el devorador de imágenes." Discurso Visual. CONACULTUA-INBA-CENART, n.d. Accessed July 9, 2010. http://discursovisual.net/1aepoca/dvweb10/art02/art02.html.

Karatani, Kojin. *The Structure of World History: From Modes of Production to Modes of Exchange*. Translated by Michael K. Bourdaghs. Durham, NC: Duke University Press, 2014.

Kaufman, Robert. "Adorno's Social Lyric, and Literary Criticism Today: Poetics, Aesthetics, Modernity." In *The Cambridge Companion to Adorno*, edited by Thomas Huhn, 354–375. Cambridge: Cambridge University Press, 2004.

Kiaer, Christina. *Imagine No Possessions: The Socialist Objects of Russian Constructivism*. Cambridge, MA: MIT Press, 2005.

Klaxon. São Paulo: Cosac Naify, 2013.

Krauze, Enrique. *Redeemers: Ideas and Power in Latin America*. Translated by Hank Heifetz and Natasha Wimmer. New York: Harper, 2011.

Le Blanc, Aleca. "Under Construction: Calder at Rio de Janeiro's Museu de Arte Moderna in 1959." In *Modernidad y vanguardia: rutas de intercambio entre España y Latinoamérica (1920–1970)*, edited by Paula Barreiro López, Fabiola Martínez Rodríguez, Jesús Carrillo, Olga Fernández López, Eamon McCarthy, Rodrigo Gutiérrez Viñuales, Irene Herner, Idoia Murga Castro, Miguel Cabañas Bravo, and Ana María León, 207–218. Madrid: Museo Nacional Centro de Arte Reina Sofía, 2015.

Ledesma, Eduardo. *Radical Poetry: Aesthetics, Politics, Technology, and the Ibero-American Avant-Gardes, 1900–2015*. Albany, NY: SUNY Press, 2016.

Lee, Rachel C. "Haptics, Mobile Handhelds, and Other 'Novel' Devices: The Tactile Unconscious of Reading across Old and New Media." In *Critical Digital Studies: A Reader*, 2nd ed., edited by Arthur Kroker and Marilouise Kroker, 358–372. Toronto: University of Toronto Press, 2013.

Lehman, Harold. Oral history interview with Harold Lehman. 1997. Typescript held at the Archives of American Art, Smithsonian Institution, New York City.

Leirner, Adolpho. "Colecionar é uma Busca." In *Arte construtiva no Brasil: coleção Adolpho Leirner*, edited by Aracy Amaral, 7–17. São Paulo: Melhoramentos, 1998.

León Portilla, Miguel. *La filosofía nahuatl, estudiada en sus fuentes*. Mexico City: Ediciones Especiales del Instituto Indigenista Interamericano, 1956.

Lippard, Lucy R. "The Materials at Hand: Art, Work, and Life." In *Versions and Inversions: Perspectives on Avant-Garde in Latin America*, edited by Héctor Olea and Mari Carmen Ramírez, 159–193. New Haven, CT: Yale University Press, 2006.

Lodder, Christina. *Russian Constructivism*. New Haven, CT: Yale University Press, 1983.

Lupton, Ellen. "Thoughts on Identity at the Century's End." *Communication Arts* 38.7 (Dec. 1996): 248–252.

Macel, Christine. "Lygia Clark: At the Border of Art." In *Lygia Clark: The Abandonment of Art, 1948–1988*, edited by Cornelia Butler and Luis Pérez-Oramas, 253–261. New York: Museum of Modern Art, 2014.

Mahan, Elizabeth. "Mass Media and Society in Twentieth-Century Mexico." *Journal of the West* (Oct 1988): 41–49.

Mammì, Lorenzo. "Concret '56: The Root of Form (A Reconstruction of the I National Exhibition of Concrete Art)." In Mammì et al., *Concreta '56*, 22–50.

Mammì, Lorenzo, João Bandeira, André Stolarski, and Carolina Soares. *Concreta '56: a raiz da forma = Concret '56: The Root of Form*. São Paulo: Museu de Arte Moderna de São Paulo, 2006.

Maples Arce, Manuel. "*Actual* no. 1: hoja de vanguardia; comprimido estridentista." December 1921. Museo Nacional de Arte, Mexico City.

Marcondes, Pyr. *Uma história da propaganda brasileira: as melhores campanhas, gênios da criação, personagens*. Rio de Janeiro: Ediouro, 2001.

Marinetti, F. T. *Critical Writings*. Edited by Günter Berghaus. New York: Farrar, Straus, and Giroux, 2006.

———. "Gli avvisi luminosi. Lettera aperta a S. E. Mussolini." L'Impero, February 12, 1927, reissued as "Estetica degli avvisi luminosi." *La fiera letteraria* 3.19 (Mar. 6, 1927): 3.

Martín-Barbero, Jesús. *Oficio de cartógrafo: Travesías latinoamericanas de la comunicación en la cultura*. Santiago: Fondo de Cultura Económica, 2002.

Martins, Sérgio B. *Constructing an Avant-Garde: Art in Brazil, 1949–1979*. Cambridge, MA: MIT Press, 2013.

———. "Phenomenological Openness: Historicist Closure; Revisiting the Theory of the Non-Object." *Third Text* 26.1 (2012): 79–90.

Marx, Karl. *Economic and Philosophic Manuscripts of 1844*. Translated by Martin Milligan. Mineola, NY: Dover, 2007.

Masiello, Francine. *The Art of Transition: Latin American Culture and Neoliberal Crisis*. Durham, NC: Duke University Press, 2001.

Mata, Rodolfo. "Haroldo de Campos y Octavio Paz: del diálogo creativo a la mediación institucional." *Anuario Latinoamérica* 32 (2001): 254–270.

Mayakovsky, Vladimir. *For the Voice*. Cambridge, MA: MIT Press, 2000.

McLuhan, Marshall. *The Gutenberg Galaxy: The Making of Typographic Man*. Toronto: University of Toronto Press, 1962.

———. *Understanding Media: The Extensions of Man*. 1964. Cambridge, MA: MIT Press, 1994.

Metinides, Enrique. *101 Tragedies of Enrique Metinides*. Edited by Trisha Ziff. New York: Aperture, 2012.

Miller, Daniel. "Consumption as the Vanguard of History: A Polemic by Way of an Introduction." In *Acknowledging Consumption: A Review of New Studies*, edited by Daniel Miller, 1–57. London: Routledge, 1995.

Milner, Marion. "An Adult Patient Uses Toys." In *Suppressed Madness*, 66–72.

———. "The Role of Illusion in Symbol Formation." 1952. In *Suppressed Madness*, 83–113.

———. “The Sense in Nonsense (Freud and Blake’s *Job*).” 1956. In *Suppressed Madness*, 168–191.

———. *The Suppressed Madness of Sane Men: Forty-Four Years of Exploring Psychoanalysis*. Tavistock: London, 1987.

Moholy-Nagy, László. *Vision in Motion*. Chicago: P. Theobald, 1947.

Montaldo, Graciela. *Museo del consumo: archivos de la cultura de masas en Argentina*. Buenos Aires, Argentina: Fondo de Cultura Económica, 2016.

Morais, Fernando. *Chatô, o rei do Brasil*. São Paulo: Companhia das Letras, 1994.

Moreno, Julio. *Yankee Don’t Go Home: Mexican Nationalism, American Business Culture, and the Shaping of Modern Mexico*. Chapel Hill: University of North Carolina Press, 2003.

Muchnic, Suzanne. “Events Put David Alfaro Siqueiros Back in the Spotlight.” *Los Angeles Times* (Sept. 12, 2010). http://articles.latimes.com/2010/sep/12/entertainment/la-ca-siqueiros-20100912.

Müller, Ulrike. *Bauhaus Women: Art, Handicraft, Design*. Paris: Flammarion, 2009.

Müller-Bergh, Klaus. “Feijoada, Coke & the Urbanoid: Brazilian Poetry since 1945.” *World Literature Today* 53.1 (Winter 1979): 22–30.

Name, Daniela. *Diálogo concreto: design e construtivismo no Brasil*. Rio de Janeiro: Caixa Cultural, 2008.

———. “Eu me lembro.” In *Diálogo concreto*, 6–41.

Ngai, Sianne. *Our Aesthetic Categories: Zany, Cute, Interesting*. Cambridge, MA: Harvard University Press, 2012.

Niemeyer, Lucy. *Design no Brasil: origens e instalação*. Rio de Janeiro: 2AB, 1998.

Novo, Salvador. *Nueva grandeza mexicana*. 1946. Mexico City: Cien de México, 2001.

Obregón, Alejandro. *Primer Salón Intercol de Artistas Jóvenes*. Bogotá, Colombia: Museo de Arte Moderno de Bogotá, 1964.

Oiticica, Hélio. “Esquema geral da nova objetividade.” *Nova objetividade brasileira*. Rio de Janeiro: Museu de Arte Moderna, 1967.

Olea, Héctor. “El prestridentismo: Siqueiros, un antihéroe en el cierne del antisistema manifestario.” In Debroise, *Otras rutas hacia Siqueiros*, 93.

Ortega, Julio, and David Draper Clark. “*Blanco*: Space of Change.” *World Literature Today* 56.4 (Autumn 1982): 635–638.

Pacheco, José Emilio. *Las batallas en el desierto*. Mexico City: Biblioteca Era, 2013.

Paz, Octavio. “El águila, el jaguar y la Virgen.” 1989. In *Obras completas*, vol. 8, 21–70.

———. *Apariencia desnuda: la obra de Marcel Duchamp*. Mexico City: Ediciones Era, 1973.

———. *El arco y la lira*. 1967. In *Obras completas*, vol. 11, 33–287.

———. *El arco y la lira: el poema, la revelación poética, poesía e historia*. Mexico City: Fondo de Cultura Económica, 1970.

———. *Blanco*. Mexico City: J. Mortiz, 1967.

———. “*Blanco* indicaciones escénicas.” In Santí, *Archivo Blanco*, 124–129.

———. “El canal y los signos.” 1967. In *Obras completas*, vol. 1, 600–605.

———. “Comentário de Octavio Paz sobre o Poema ‘Blanco.’” In Paz and Campos, *Transblanco*, 87–90.

———. “Cuarenta años de escribir poesía.” In Santí, *Archivo Blanco*, 119–121.
———. *Días hábiles*. In *Obras completas*, vol. 11, 261–285.
———. *Discos visuales*. Mexico City: Ediciones Era, 1968.
———. *Hacia el comienzo*. 1964–1968. In *Obras completas*, vol. 11, 393–419.
———. *Los hijos del limo*. 1974. In *Obras completas*, vol. 1, 321–484.
———. *Itinerario poético: seis conferencias inéditas, Colegio Nacional de México, 1975*. Girona: Atalanta, 2014.
———. *Jardines errantes: cartas a J. C. Lambert, 1952–1992*. Barcelona: Seix Barral, 2008.
———. *Ladera este*. 1962–1968. In *Obras completas*, vol. 11, 341–390.
———. *Libertad bajo palabra*. 1935–1957. In *Obras completas*, vol. 11, 21–238.
———. “La nueva analogía: poesía y tecnología.” 1973. In *Obras completas*, vol. 1, 299–317.
———, ed. *Obras completas de Octavio Paz*. 15 vols. Mexico City: Fondo de Cultura Económica, 1994.
———. *La otra voz: poesía y fin de siglo*. 1990. In *Obras completas*, vol. 1, 489–592.
———. “El precio y la significación.” 1966. In *Obras completas*, vol. 8, 321–337.
———. “Re/visiones: la pintura mural.” 1986. In *Obras completas*, vol. 7, 188–277.
———. *Salamandra*. 1958–1961. In *Obras completas*, vol. 11, 297–328.
———. *Semillas para un himno*. 1954. In *Obras completas*, vol. 11, 115–144.
———. “Los signos en rotación.” 1965. In *Obras completas*, vol. 1, 247–273.
———. “Tamayo en la pintura mexicana.” 1950. In *Obras completas*, vol. 7, 257–264.
———. *Vuelta*. 1969–1975. In *Obras completas*, vol. 12, 21–71.
Paz, Octavio, and Haroldo de Campos. *Transblanco: em torno a* Blanco *de Octavio Paz*. Rio de Janeiro: Editora Guanabara, 1986.
Paz, Octavio, and Vicente Rojo. “La fragua de dos libros.” *Syntaxis* 25 (1991): 120–165.
Pedrosa, Mário. “Science and Art: Communicating Vessels.” 1960. In Ferreira and Herkenhoff, *Mário Pedrosa*, 113–117.
———. “The Vital Need for Art.” 1947. In Ferreira and Herkenhoff, *Mário Pedrosa*, 103–112.
———. “World in Crisis, Man in Crisis, Art in Crisis.” In Ferreira and Herkenhoff, *Mário Pedrosa*, 135–138.
Pérez-Oramas, Luis. “Lygia Clark: If You Hold a Stone.” In *Lygia Clark: The Abandonment of Art, 1948–1988*, edited by Cornelia Butler and Luis Pérez-Oramas, 30–49. New York: Museum of Modern Art, 2014.
Perloff, Marjorie. *The Futurist Moment: Avant-garde, Avant Guerre, and the Language of Rupture*. Chicago: University of Chicago Press, 2003.
———. *Radical Artifice: Writing Poetry in the Age of Media*. Chicago: University of Chicago Press, 1991.
———. “Writing as Re-Writing: Concrete Poetry as Arrière-Garde.” *Ciberletras: Revista de crítica literaria y de cultura* 17. https://dialnet.unirioja.es/servlet/articulo?codigo=232129.
Perrone, Charles A. *Seven Faces: Brazilian Poetry since Modernism*. Durham, NC: Duke University Press, 1996.

Pignatari, Décio. "arte concreta: objeto e objetivo," 1956. In Campos, Pignatari, and Campos, *Teoria da poesia concreta*, 63–65.

———. "Arte gráfica e a outra." *Estado de São Paulo: suplemento literário*, May 30, 1964, 6.

———. "forma, função e projeto geral." 1957. In Campos, Pignatari, and Campos, *Teoria da poesia concreta*, 153–155.

———. "Interview." In *Abstracionismo geométrico e informal: a vanguarda brasileira nos anos cinqüenta*, edited by Fernando Cocchiarale and Anna Bella Geiger, 70–83. Rio de Janeiro: FUNARTE, 1987.

———. "nova poesia: concreta (manifesto)." 1956. In Campos, Pignatari, and Campos, *Teoria da poesia concreta*, 67–70.

———. *Poesia pois é poesia, 1950–1975; Poetc, 1976–1986*. Cotia, SP: Ateliê Editorial, 2004.

———. "Publicidade o texto vivo." *O Estado de São Paulo* (Nov. 16, 1958), 84.

———. *Semiótica da arte e da arquitetura*. São Paulo: Ateliê Editorial, 2004.

———. *semiótica & literatura*. 1974. São Paulo: Ateliê Editorial, 2004.

Piña Zentella, Marta. *¿Ausencia/presencia? Ciudad en Octavio Paz*. Mexico City: Editorial Praxis, 2014.

Price, Rachel. *The Object of the Atlantic: Concrete Aesthetics in Cuba, Brazil, and Spain, 1868–1968*. Evanston, IL: Northwestern University Press, 2014.

Quiroga, José. *Understanding Octavio Paz*. Columbia: University of South Carolina Press, 1999.

Ramírez, Mari Carmen. "El clasicismo-dinámico de David Alfaro Siqueiros: paradojas de un modelo excéntrico de vanguardia." In Debroise, *Otras rutas hacia Siqueiros*, 125–146.

———. "The Masses Are the Matrix: Theory and Practice of the Cinematographic Mural in Siqueiros." In David Alfaro Siqueiros, *Portrait of a Decade: David Alfaro Siqueiros, 1930–1940*, 68–99. Mexico City: Instituto Nacional de Bellas Artes, 1997.

Ramírez, Mari Carmen, and Héctor Olea. *Inverted Utopias: Avant-Garde in Latin America*. New Haven, CT: Yale University Press, 2004.

Ramírez, Miguel. "Mexico." In Randall, *Political Economy of Latin America*, 111–148.

Randall, Laura. "Introduction." In Randall, *Political Economy of Latin America*, 1–21.

———, ed. *The Political Economy of Latin America in the Postwar Period*. Austin: University of Texas Press, 1997.

Reyes, Alfonso. *La experiencia literaria*. 1952. Buenos Aires: Editorial Losada, 1961.

Richardson, William, "Siqueiros soviético: David Alfaro Siqueiros en el imaginario soviético." In Debroise, *Otras rutas hacia Siqueiros*, 285–298.

Rochfort, Desmond. *Mexican Muralists: Orozco, Rivera and Siqueiros*. London: L. King, 1993.

Rodríguez, Antonio. *David Alfaro Siqueiros: Mural Painting*. Mexico City: Fondo Editorial de la Plástica Mexicana, 1992.

Rodríguez, Fernando. "Transdisciplinas: Octavio Paz, editor tipógrafo." *Encuadre: Revista de la Enseñanza del Diseño* 2.12 (2008): 14–43.

Rodríguez Monegal, Emir. "Relectura de *El arco y la lira*." *Revista Iberoamericana* 37.74 (Jan.–Mar. 1971): 35–46.

Rogo, Elsa. "David Alfaro Siqueiros." *Parnassus* 6.4 (Apr. 1, 1934): 5–7.

Rolnik, Suely. "Molding a Contemporary Soul: The Empty-Full of Lygia Clark." In *The Experimental Exercise of Freedom: Lygia Clark, Gego, Mathias Goeritz, Hélio Oiticica, Mira Schendel*, organized by Rina Carvajal and Alma Ruiz, 59–82. Los Angeles: Museum of Contemporary Art, 1999.

———. "Uma terapêutica para tempos desprovistos de poesia." *Lygia Clark da obra ao acontecimento: somos o molde. A você cabe o sopro*. São Paulo: Pinacoteca do Estado de São Paulo, 2006.

Román-Odio, Clara. *Octavio Paz en los debates críticos y estéticos del siglo XX*. La Coruña: TresCTres, 2006.

Rowe, William. "Paz, Fuentes and Lévi-Strauss: The Creation of a Structuralist Orthodoxy." *Bulletin of Latin American Research* 3.2 (1984): 77–82.

Saldaña-Portillo, María J. *The Revolutionary Imagination in the Americas in the Age of Development*. Durham, NC: Duke University Press, 2003.

Salerno, Laura Peretto, and Maria Teresa Santos Cunha. "Discursos para o feminino em páginas da revista *Querida* (1958–1968): aproximações." *Educar em Revista* 40 (Apr.-June 2011): 127–139.

Sánchez-Mejorada, Alicia. "Poesía concreta." In Mathias Goeritz, *Los ecos de Mathias Goeritz: catálogo de la exposición*, 199–202. Mexico City: Instituto Nacional de Bellas, 1997.

Santí, Enrico Mario. *El acto de las palabras: estudios y diálogos con Octavio Paz*. Mexico City: Fondo de Cultura Económica, 1997.

———, ed. *Archivo Blanco*. Madrid: Ediciones Turner, 1995.

———. "Salida 'Esto no es un poema.'" In Santí, *Archivo Blanco*, 235–321.

———. "Textos y contextos: Heidegger, Paz y la poética."

Schmelz, Itala. "Siqueiros: bocetos fotográficos." *Luná Córnea* 4 (1994): 86–89.

Schor, Juliet B. "In Defense of Consumer Critique: Revisiting the Consumption Debates of the Twentieth Century." *Annals of the American Academy of Political and Social Science* 611 (May 2007): 16–30.

———. "Towards a New Politics of Consumption." In *The Consumer Society Reader*, 446–462. New York: New Press, 2000.

Scovino, Felipe. "Brasileiros em Ulm: vanguarda e ruptura." In Name, *Diálogo concreto*, 43–52.

Seabrook, Roberta. "La poesía en movimiento: Octavio Paz." *Revista Iberoamericana* 37.74 (Jan.–Mar. 1971): 161–175.

Shellhorse, Adam Joseph. "Subversions of the Sensible: The Poetics of Antropofagia in Brazilian Concrete Poetry." *Revista Hispánica Moderna* 68.2 (December 2015): 165–190

Sherman, John W. "The Mexican 'Miracle' and Its Collapse." In *The Oxford History of Mexico*, edited by William H. Beezley and Michael C. Meyer, 537–568. New York: Oxford University Press, 2010.

Shtromberg, Elena. *Art Systems: Brazil and the 1970s*. Austin: University of Texas Press, 2016.

Sinclair, John, and Anna Cristina Pertierra, eds. *Consumer Culture in Latin America*. New York: Palgrave Macmillan, 2012.

Silva, Nelson do Valle. "Brazilian Society: Continuity and Change, 1930–2000." In *The Cambridge History of Latin America*, edited by Leslie Bethell, vol. 9, 455–544. New York: Cambridge University Press, 2008.

Siqueiros, David Alfaro. "Afirmaciones de Siqueiros." *Arte público* (February 1953): 17.

———. "El 'affiche' como antecedente y experiencia para nuestra pintura mural exterior." 1952. In Tibol, *Palabras de Siqueiros*, 362–364.

———. *Art and Revolution*. Translated by Sylvia Calles. London: Lawrence and Wishart, 1975.

———. "L'art dans la bataille sociale contemporaine." 1938. Typescript held at the Sala de Arte Público Siqueiros, Mexico City.

———. "Cartas a María Asúnsolo." 1936. In Tibol, *Palabras de Siqueiros*, 128–139.

———. "Cinematografía mexicana." 1921. In Tibol, *Palabras de Siqueiros*, 21–22.

———. "Conferencia en Argentina." In Jaimes, *Fundación del muralismo mexicano*, 17–35.

———. "Criterio del suscrito sobre la pintura mural del edificio nuevo del Sindicato Mexicano de Electricistas." 1939. Typescript held at the Sala de Arte Público Siqueiros, Mexico City.

———. "Cuatro tendencias intervienen en la ejecución de los murales en el exterior de los edifícios de la Ciudad Universitaria." *Arte Público* (Feb. 1953): 9.

———. "Folio 9.1.15." 1932. Typescript held at the Sala de Arte Público Siqueiros, Mexico City.

———. "La función de la fotografía." 1945. In Tibol, *Palabras de Siqueiros*, 227–231.

———. *Me llamaban el Coronelazo: memorias*. Mexico City: Grijalbo, 1977.

———. "Mi experiencia en el muralismo exterior." 1956. In Tibol, *Palabras de Siqueiros*, 408–414.

———. *Mi respuesta: la historia de una insidia. ¿Quiénes son los traidores a la patria?* Mexico City: Ediciones de Arte Público, 1960.

———. *No hay más ruta que la nuestra*. Mexico City: Talleres gráficos núm. 1 de la Secretaría de Educación Pública, 1945.

———. "Nuestra experiencia en Los Ángeles, California." 1940. Typescript held at the Sala de Arte Público Siqueiros, Mexico City.

———. "Nueva era, plástica fílmica." *Siempre* (Sept. 29, 1954): 24.

———. *Palabras de Siqueiros*. Edited by Raquel Tibol. Mexico City: Fondo de Cultura Económica, 1996.

———. "Por el materialismo marxista sabemos." N.d., typescript held at the Getty Research Institute, Los Angeles, California.

———. "Un problema técnico sin precedente en la historia del arte: el muralismo figurativo y realista en el exterior." 1952. In Tibol, *Palabras de Siqueiros*, 340–359.

———. "Qué es 'Ejercicio plástico' y cómo fue realizado." 1933. In Tibol, *Palabras de Siqueiros*, 103–110.

———. "Rectificaciones sobre las artes plásticas en Mexico." 1932. In Tibol, *Palabras de Siqueiros*, 48–61.

———. *La trácala: mi réplica a un gobierno fiscal-juez*. Mexico City: n.p., 1962.

———. "Tres llamamientos de orientación actual a los pintores y escultores de la nueva generación americana." 1921. In Tibol, *Palabras de Siqueiros*, 17–20.

———. "Los vehículos de la pintura dialéctico-subversiva." 1932. In Tibol, *Palabras de Siqueiros*, 62–78.
———. "Vigencia del movimiento plástico mexicano contemporáneo." 1966. In Tibol, *Palabras de Siqueiros*, 452–476.
Small, Irene V. *Hélio Oiticica: Folding the Frame*. Chicago: University of Chicago Press, 2016.
———. "Permanent Evolution: Hélio Oiticica and the Return to Rio, 1978–80." In *Hélio Oiticica, To Organize Delirium*, edited by Lynn Zelevansky, Elisabeth Sussman, James Rondeau, and Donna De Salvo, 256–267. Pittsburgh: Carnegie Museum of Art, 2016.
Sociedad de Amigos de la Pintura Mexicana Moderna, eds. *Arte público: tribuna de pintores muralistas, escultores, grabadores y artistas de la estampa en general*. Mexico City, 1953–1955.
Solt, Mary Ellen. "Introduction." In *Concrete Poetry: A World View*, edited by Mary Ellen Solt, 6–66. Bloomington: Indiana University Press, 1968.
Sorensen, Diana. *A Turbulent Decade Remembered: Scenes from the Latin American Sixties*. Palo Alto, CA: Stanford University Press, 2007.
Süssekind, Flora. *Cinematograph of Words*. Palo Alto, CA: Stanford University Press, 1997.
———. *Literatura e vida literaria: polêmicas, diários e retratos*. Rio de Janeiro: Jorge Zahar, 1985.
———. *Papéis colados*. Rio de Janeiro: Editora UFRJ, 1993.
———. *Vidrieras astilladas: Ensayos críticos sobre la cultura brasileña de los sesentas a los ochentas*. Translated by María Teresa Villares. Buenos Aires: Ediciones Corregidor, 2003.
Taussig, Michael T. *The Devil and Commodity Fetishism in South America*. Chapel Hill: University of North Carolina Press, 1980.
———. *The Nervous System*. New York: Routledge, 1992.
Tibol, Raquel. *Episodios fotográficos*. Mexico City: Libros de Proceso, 1989.
———, ed. *Palabras de Siqueiros*. Mexico City: Fondo de Cultura Económica, 1996.
Tolman, John M. "The Context of a Vanguard: Toward a Definition of Concrete Poetry." *Poetics of the Avant-Garde*, special issue, *Poetics Today* 3.3 (Summer 1982): 149–166.
Vázquez Mantecón, Álvaro. "The Dissident Image: Discrepancies to the Modernization Project in Cinema and Photography during the Fifties and Sixties." In Eder, *Defying Stability*, 329–339.
Vázquez, Rolando. "On Visual Modernity and Poetic Critique." In *Octavio Paz: Humanism and Critique*, edited by Oliver Kozlarek, 99–100. Bielefeld, Germany: Transcript, 2009.
Veblen, Thorstein. *The Theory of the Leisure Class*. New York: Modern Library, 2001.
Vélez, Nicanor. "El poema extenso: arquitectura de palabras y silencios en *Piedra de sol* y *Blanco* de Octavio Paz." In *La suma que es el todo y que no cesa: el poema largo en la modernidad hispanoamericana*, edited by María Cecilia Graña, 59–79. Rosario, Argentina: B. Viterbo Editora, 2006.
Verani, Hugo J. "Octavio Paz and the Language of Space." *World Literature Today* 56.4 (Autumn 1982): 631–635.

Villas Bôas, Glaucia. "A estética da conversão: o ateliê do Engenho de Dentro e a arte concreta carioca (1946–1951)." *Tempo social, revista de sociologia da USP* 20.2 (2008): 197–219.

Virilio, Paul. *The Vision Machine*. Translated by Julie Rose. Bloomington: Indiana University Press, 1994.

Wanderley, Lula. *O dragão pousou no espaço: arte contemporânea, sofrimento psíquico e o Objeto Relacional de Lygia Clark*. Rio de Janeiro: Rocco, 2002.

Wells, H. G. "James Joyce." *New Republic* (March 10, 1917): 158.

Williams, Bruce. "'poetamenos': Campo(s) de expressão em cores." *Mester* 14.1 (Spring 1985): 55–65.

Williams, Gareth. "From Populism to Neoliberalism: Formalities of Identity, Citizenship, and Consumption in Contemporary Latin Americanism." *Dispositio* 22.49 (Jan. 1, 1997): 13–41.

Williamson, Rodney. *The Writing in the Stars: A Jungian Reading of the Poetry of Octavio Paz*. Toronto: University of Toronto Press, 2007.

Wollen, Peter. "Perhaps . . ." *October* 88 (Apr. 1, 1999): 43–50.

Yúdice, George. *The Expediency of Culture: Uses of Culture in the Global Era*. Durham, NC: Duke University Press, 2003.

Zurián, Tomás. "Arte y significación ideológica en Siqueiros: hallazgo iconográfico de América tropical." *La Jornada* (Sept. 13, 1997): 2.

Index

Page numbers followed by f indicate figures.

1ª Exposição Nacional de Arte Concreta (1956), 93
1965 Salón Esso, 102
Abraham, Nicolas, 246n76
Abrigo poético (Clark 1964), 156
abstraction: and capitalism, 168; and Clark's work, 160, 172, 179, 241n12; and concretism, 36–37, 101, 240n7; and consumer society, 6; and Dada, 244n49; and Pape's work, 169–170; and participation, 166; and Paz's work, 152; versus realism, 100; and São Paulo Biennal, 16; and Taeuber's work, 31
Academy of San Carlos, 210–211n18
A casa do poeta (Clark 1967–1969), 156
A casa é o corpo (Clark 1966), 241n11
A Cigarra magazine, 93
"*Actual* no. 1" (Maples Arce 1921), 31–32, 47
ad—arquitetura e decoração magazine, 90
Adorno, Theodor: on appearances, 8; on attraction, 7; on consumption, 20; on culture industry, 21; on distraction, 4–5, 196–197n12; on enchantment, 101–102; functionalist analyses of, 22; on Hegel, 197n15; Hullot-Kentor on, 198–199n31; on reaction to commodity culture, 84–85; on shock, 197n16
advertisement-poems, 112
advertising: and associative techniques, 107; and avant-gardes, 27; and *Blanco*, 144; and Brazilian concrete poetry, 41; and Brazilian poetry, 32–33; and concrete poetry, 97–98, 105–106; and *Discos visuales*, 137; Freyre's interest in, 34; as industry, 17–18; and *Jornal do Brasil*, 94; and language, 101; in Mexico City, 209n14; and neoconcretism, 162; and *New York Dada* magazine, 31; and Pape, 169–171; Paz's appropriation of, 42; Paz's experiments with, 40; and politicized oppositional art, 46; Siqueiros on, 69, 70–71; and Siqueiros's billboard muralism, 45; and visual structure, 136–137
aesthetics: and consumer capitalism, 2; and distraction, 5–6; and homemaking, 154; and industry, 165; and politics, 178; and rationality, 26; and relational objects, 180; Siqueiros on, 47; and technology, 55
Aesthetic Theory (Adorno 1970), 5
"Age of the World Picture, The" (Heidegger 1938), 128
Aguilar, Gonzalo, 112
Alber, Josef, 159
Alberti, Leon Battista, 132
Alemán, Miguel, 71, 122
alienation, 2–3, 6, 134, 167–168, 192, 196n8
Allied Forces, 14

alliteration, 145
Álvarez, Francisco, 230n1
Álvarez Bravo, Lola, 65
ambiguity, 85, 196n7
América tropical (Siqueiros 1932), 48–49, 51–54, 53f, 213nn29–30, 213n32
Amor, Mónica, 162
Andrade, Oswald de, 22, 95–96, 224n35
anti-art, 164–165
antropofagia: Andrade on, 22, 95; and *Bestiário*, 117; Certeau on, 202n76; and consumption, 118; and *produssumo*, 24
anunciologia, 34
Anzieu, Didier, 181, 246n76
Apariencia desnuda (Paz 1973), 141
Apollinaire, Guillaume, 27
Appadurai, Arjun, 18
architecture: Benjamin on, 55; and Clark's work, 154, 155–156; and concretism, 160; and Goeritz, 39; as Paz influence, 121; and reception in distraction, 76–77; and technology, 128–129
Arenal, Angélica, 78–79
Arenal, Luis, 62
Aristotelian thought, 99
Arp, Hans, 240n7
Arquiteturas biológicas (Clark 1968–1969), 156, 183, 191
Arreola, Juan José, 150
"Arte, necessidade vital" (Pedrosa), 184–185
Arte Concreto-Invención, 157
Arte Madí, 157
Arte público (bulletin), 71, 72f, 78
"Artistic Pre-Requisites for the Standardisation of Furniture" (Lissitzky 1928), 28–29
arts and crafts, 10, 31, 172–173, 240n7, 244–245n51
arts integration movement, 39–40
Arvatov, Boris, 30
"Aspa" (Paz 1968), 141, 142
Asúnsolo, María, 210n17
Ato Institucional Número Cinco (AI-5), 169
authoritarianism, 33
avant-garde aesthetics, 95, 191
Ávila Camacho, Manuel, 71

Baer, Werner, 14
Ball, Hugo, 30
Ballet Neoconcreto (Pape and Jardim 1958), 169
Ballet Neoconcreto II (Pape and Jardim 1959), 169
Bardi, Lina Bo, 17, 161
Barragán, Luis, 130
Barros, Geraldo de, 38, 109, 161
Barsotti, Hércules, 109
Bataille, Georges, 1, 3
Baudelaire, Charles, 184, 232n22
Baudrillard, Jean: on consummativity, 6; on consumption, 3, 20; on culture, 203n80; on functionality, 167–168; on political economy of signs, 174
Bauhaus: and artist as educator, 243n32; Baudrillard on, 167–168; and Brazilian design, 33; as Clark influence, 154; and homemaking, 10; and Pignatari, 109; and women artists, 240n6
Beatles, 24
"beba coca cola" (Pignatari 1957), 105–108, 107f, 111, 227n76
Belo Horizonte National School of Architecture, 159
Benjamin, Walter: on advertising, 27, 28; on art and the market, 217n70; on commodity's dream-power, 209n10; on consumption, 3; on distraction, 4–5, 78, 196–197n12; on language, 152; on literary effectiveness, 112–113; on mimetics, 85, 86, 98–99; on neon light, 101; on Parisian Arcades, 46; on perception, 225–226n51; on reception in distraction, 76–77; on reproducibility, 54–55, 60, 214n35, 214n45; Taussig on, 23, 84; on *Un coup de dés*, 95

Berg, Stephen, 245n56
Berlin Dada, 10
Berni, Antonio, 59
Bessa, Antonio Sergio, 222n5
Bestiário (A. de Campos 1955), 116–118
Bicho-monumento: Monumento a todas as situações (Clark 1960–1966), 163
Bichos (Clark 1960–1966): conception of, 242n22; and geometric space, 159; and industrial production, 163; naming of, 242–243n25; and nonobject theory, 162; as objects, 191; structure of, 164, 172–173, 178
Bilac, Olavo, 33
Bill, Max, 100, 228n80, 240n7
billboard muralism, 44–45, 67–71, 73–81, 166
Blake, William, 183–184
Blanco (Paz 1967), 147f; and H. de Campos, 39, 132–133, 237n96; discussion of, 142–146, 148–151; and Paz's experimental phase, 42, 119; and Rojo, 137–138; and spirals, 126; structure of, 237n84, 237n89, 237n92
Bleger, José, 2, 185–186
Bois, Yve-Alain, 153, 247n92
Bourdieu, Pierre, 18
Bourriaud, Nicolas, 9, 240n5
Bove, Carol, 240n5
Branco, Castelo, 200–201n50
Brasília, 15, 17, 34, 90, 206n120
Brazil at War (1943), 14
Brazilian concrete poetry: and advertising, 41; and Andrade, 96; and architecture, 160; and commercialism, 166; and consumer culture, 85; and fascination, 7, 9; and organized desire, 89; as Paz influence, 39, 120; and *salto participante*, 112; and São Paulo Biennial, 16. *See also specific works*
Brazilian concrete poets: aesthetics of, 38; legacy of, 27; manifestos of, 101; and reading posture, 36, 142; and regression, 23. *See also* concrete poets; *specific poets*
Brazilian economy, 14–15, 90, 199n37
Breton, André, 124
Brett, Guy, 177, 183, 247n92
Brito, Ronaldo, 41, 100, 177
Brull, Mariano, 105
Buck-Morss, Susan, 30, 131, 150–151, 180
Bunker, Steven B., 3, 11–12, 47
Buñuel, Luis, 122
Burle Marx, Roberto, 155, 158

Cabaret Voltaire, 30–31, 205n108
Cage, John, 24
Caminhando (Clark 1963), 172, 173f
Caminos de Anáhuac, 75, 219–220n84
Campos, Augusto de: and advertising, 41; *Bestiário* (1955), 116–118; "Codigo" (1973), 113–115; collaborations of, 38; on "coma Lacta" ad, 106; on concrete poetry, 98; on "hombre hambre hembra" (Pignatari 1957), 103; "Luxo" (1965), 8f; manifesto of, 89; and *Navilouca*, 245n56; and neon light, 7; *Poetamenos* (1953), 83; on *produssumo*, 24; "Psiu!" (1966), 91, 91f; and *suplemento dominical*, 224n27; and tmesis, 118; on universal intercommunicability, 92; on visual arts as inspiration, 221–222n3
Campos, Haroldo de: on art and the market, 37; and *Blanco*, 237n96; on concretism's aesthetics, 207–208n133; on Cortázar, 143; "da fenomenologia da composição a matematica da composição" (1957), 38; on language, 114–115; on Lissitzky, 96; on Mallarmé, 150; manifesto of, 89, 99; and *Navilouca*, 245n56; on open work of art, 243n30; and Paz, 39, 120, 132–133, 133, 208n135; on *produssumo*, 23; on Schwitters, 176; and *suplemento dominical*, 224n27; on *Un coup de dés*, 95; on universal intercommunicability, 92; on visual arts as inspiration, 221–222n3
Candido, Antonio, 97

capitalism: and advertising, 32; and alienation, 168; and Brazilian concrete poets, 7, 97–98, 101; and citizenship, 20; and Clark's work, 43; and concrete poetry, 8–9, 41, 100, 104, 227n75; and consumer culture, 192, 225–226n51; and consumption, 25–26; and creativity, 193–194; homeopathic response to, 112–113; and language, 39, 42, 133, 135, 136, 152; and meaning, 27; and mimesis, 84; and objectivity, 174, 175, 179; and packaging, 171; Paz on, 120–121, 142, 230–231n9; and periphery, 34–35; politics of, 2–3; responses to, 33; Reyes on, 232–233n43; and Russian constructivists, 28–30; and Siqueiros's politics, 45–46, 50, 71, 81; and tools of domination, 33
Cárdenas, Lázaro, 13
Cardoso, Ivan, 245n56
Cardoza y Aragón, Luis, 70, 208n1
Carneiro, Mário de, 188
Carneiro, Pereira, 94
"carne leite pao" (Grunewald 1963), 108–109
Carrasco, Lorenzo, 73, 219n82
Carvalho, Aluísio, 161–162
Casino Español, 50
Castagnino, Juan Carlos, 59
Castro, Amilcar de, 93, 95, 155, 161–162, 243n33
Castro, Willys de, 109
Casulos (Clark 1959–1960), 159
Cendrars, Blaise, 27, 148
Centro Psiquiátrico Nacional, 184–185
Cernuda, Luis, 232n22
Certeau, Michel de, 3, 21–23, 86, 202n76
Charlot, Jean, 57
Chateaubriand, Assis, 15, 201n51
Chouinard School of Arts, 50–51, 58
cinema, 50–51, 55, 59, 145–146, 148, 150–151, 218n75. *See also* film
Cinema Novo, 169
"Cinema Screen as Prosthesis of Perception, The" (Buck-Morss), 151
Cinematograph of Words (Süssekind 1997), 32–33
"Ciudad de México" (Paz tryptich 1968), 126
Ciudad Satélite, Mexico, 13, 39, 130, 133
Ciudad Universitaria: and artists, 161; and collaboration, 159; construction of, 13; and Mexico City's urbanization, 130; and Siqueiros murals, 69–70, 79–80; Siqueiros on, 73; as synthesis of art and urbanization, 17; and UNAM's growth, 219n81
Clark, Lygia, 173f, 175f; aesthetics of, 38, 191; on art and life, 159–160; artistic trajectory of, 37, 153–154; on *Bichos*, 163–164; and biological architectures, 170; early work of, 155–158; *Estruturação do self*, 22; as founding figure, 162; and Grupo Frente, 165; Herkenhoff on, 195–196n6; and hippie culture, 240n5; and homemaking, 10, 42–43; influences of, 181; on introjection, 178; legacy of, 27; and "Manifesto neoconcreto," 94; and *Navilouca*, 245n56; and Niemeyer, 241n12; on nostalgia for the body, 172; Oiticica on, 166; and optimism, 161; and Pape, 169; and participatory aesthetics, 36; in *Querida*, 241n13; and regression, 23, 31; on regression, 185, 186–187; on relational objects, 173–174, 175–176, 177; on spiritual emptiness, 182; as woman artist, 240n8. *See also specific works*
Clüver, Claus, 207n132, 221n5, 245n53
"Codigo" (A. de Campos 1973), 113–115, 114f
commodity capitalism, 43, 97, 98, 179
commodity fetishism, 22
Communist Party, 36, 46, 206n122
Complejo Nonoalco-Tlatelolco (Pani), 130

"Concorde" (Paz 1968), 141–142
Concreção 5730 (Sacilotto 1957), 163, 242n22
"Concrete Art Manifesto" (van Doesburg 1930), 38, 221n1
concrete poetry: and advertising, 105–106; and commercialism, 113; and developmentalism, 227n75; and Goeritz, 39–40, 133; and language, 101, 104–105; and *Noigandres*, 103; and nonobject theory, 226n63; and Pape, 169; and perception, 116; as popular art, 90–91; and typography, 96–97; and Ulm School of Design, 228n80; and visual structure, 105
concrete poets: and aesthetics, 38; and Andrade, 95–96, 224n35; and desire, 89; and developmentalism, 90–91; and environment, 160; and Joyce, 103; and language, 39, 98, 101, 114, 116, 152; and Mallarmé, 150; and *Noigandres*, 227n70; as Paz influence, 133, 136; poetics of, 112; and reading posture, 142; and regression, 23. *See also* Brazilian concrete poets; *specific poets*
concretism: and abstraction, 100–101; aesthetics of, 207n132; and Brazilian modern art, 36–37; constructivist roots of, 100; and historicization, 226n62; and modernization, 97; and neoconcretism, 38–39, 161–162
Conjunto Urbano Nonoalco-Tlatelolco, 13
Conjunto Urbano Presidente Alemán, 13
Connor, Bruce, 224–225n39
Construa você mesmo seu espaço de viver (Clark 1960), 156
constructivism: and avant-gardes in Brazil, 33–34; Brito on, 100; and *Diálogo concreto*, 168–169; and Pape's work, 170–171. *See also* Russian constructivists
constructivist design, 162
consumer culture: and appropriation of colonial order, 202n76; and *Blanco*, 144; and Clark's work, 192; and concrete poetry, 226n63; and distraction, 6; effects of, 1; and environment, 160; and *Jornal do Brasil*, 95; and language, 133; and Latin American development, 34–35; and Pignatari, 109; and prose, 135; and relational objects, 174; replication of, 9; and resistance, 82
Consumer Culture in Latin America (Sinclair and Pertierra 2012), 9–10
Consumers and Citizens (García Canclini 2001), 18–20
consumption: and civil society, 196n8; as colonial force, 193; as cultural paradigm, 11, 198–199n31; dialectical understanding of, 35; dialectics of, 18–26; gendered notions of, 4; Paz's engagement with, 121; and power, 3, 11; and production, 1; as productive force, 36; and resistance, 82
Contreras Torres, Miguel, 50
Cordeiro, Waldemar, 38, 109, 161, 206n122, 207n132
Corpo coletivo (set of propositions, Clark), 183
Cortázar, Julio, 143
Crary, Jonathan, 6, 45–46, 58–59, 177, 197n21
creativity, 182–183, 184–185, 190, 194
"Crepúsculos de la ciudad" (Paz), 123–124
cubism, 148
Cuevas, José Luis, 14
cultural paradigms, 198–199n31
culture industry: in Brazil, 201n53; and Brazilian concrete poets, 7, 41, 85, 112; and colonization of aesthetics, 6; critiques of, 21; Hullot-Kentor on, 197n24; and language, 107–108; preconsumerist attitude to, 34–35; and *Retrato de la burguesía*, 66
cummings, e. e., 39

Dada: and abstraction, 244n49; aesthetics of, 240n7; and appropriation of mass culture, 10; and cabaret, 30–31; and homemaking, 10, 154; and industry, 170; origins of, 205n108; Pignatari on, 226–227n67; and refuse, 176
"da fenomenologia da composição à matemática da composição" (H. de Campos 1957), 38
"Da supressão do objetos (anotações)" (Clark 1974), 173–174
Dávila, Arlene, 4
Debord, Guy, 3
decoration, 154, 240n7
defamiliarization, 166–167
Delaunay-Terk, Sonia, 27, 148
de Menezes, Emílio, 33
design: asceticism of, 168–169; as bridge between beauty and industry, 167; and concretism, 90, 100, 113, 162; and constructivism, 33–34, 245n53; and mass production, 164; and Pape, 170–171; and Pignatari, 109, 228n80; professionalization of, 161; as synthesis of art and profit, 17–18
"Design and Environment" (Baudrillard), 167–168
Dettman, Jonathan, 25
Deus e o Diabo na Terra do Sol (Rocha), 169
developmentalism, 41, 90–91, 97–98, 200n43, 227n75
Diálogo concreto (Name 2008), 33–34, 168–169
Días hábiles (Paz 1958–1961), 125, 126
Dickerman, Leah, 30, 240n7
Díez-Canedo, Joaquín, 144, 149
Dillon, Osmar, 98
Discos visuales (Paz 1968), 139f, 140f, 141f; and Brazilian concrete poetry, 39; and Paz's experimental phase, 42, 119; and Rojo, 133; structure of, 137–142
"disenformio" (Pignatari 1963), 109, 110f, 111, 228n83, 228n85
distraction: and aesthetics, 2; Benjamin and Adorno on, 4–5; and mimetic appropriation, 85; positive and negative sense of, 196–197n12; and Siqueiros's billboard muralism, 44; and tactile reception, 76–77
Divisor (Pape 1968), 169–170
Dlia golosa (*For the Voice*, Mayakovsky 1923), 28, 96–97
Draper, David, 144
Dreamworld and Catastrophe (Buck-Morss 2000), 131
Dreyfus, Hubert, 198–199n31
Duarte, Rogério, 245n56
Duchamp, Marcel, 31, 141
Duco (pyroxylin), 62

Eagleton, Terry, 180
Eco, Umberto, 243n30
Economic and Philosophic Manuscripts of 1844 (Marx), 1, 24–25, 195n1
Ediciones Era, 141
Ehrenburg, Ilya, 28
Eisenstein, Sergei, 50, 51f, 148, 212n23
"eis os amantes" (A. de Campos 1953), 87–89, 88f, 148
Ejercicio plástico (Siqueiros 1933), 59, 60–62, 61f, 73, 215–216n56, 216n57
El arco y la lira (Paz 1970), 127, 134, 135, 136, 230n2, 233n44, 233n46
El caporal (Contreras Torres 1921), 50
"El dia en Udaipur" (Paz), 126
Eliot, T. S., 132
El Machete, 46–47
"El ocaso de la vanguardia" (Paz 1972), 148
El pueblo a la universidad, la universidad al pueblo (Siqueiros 1952–1956), 69, 69f, 70, 72f, 79, 79f
El Quebrantahuesos (Parra et al. 1952), 86–87
El sueño de los pobres II (Álvarez Bravo 1935), 65
Embratel, 205–206n119
enchantment, 85, 101–102, 222n15. *See also* fascination

"En la calzada" (Paz), 124
Enlightenment, 7, 197n23
"Entrada en materia" (Paz 1958–1961), 42, 125–126
environment, 100, 154, 159–160, 167
Erber, Pedro, 222n15, 225n49
Escola Nacional de Arquitetura in Belo Horizonte, 159
Escola Superior de Desenho Industrial, 109, 161
Escola Superior de Propaganda e Marketing, 17, 161
Escuela Nacional de Maestros, 70
Escuela Nacional Preparatoria, 48, 70
esculto-pintura, 76
Espaços modulados (Clark), 158–159
"Esquema geral da nova objetividade" (Oiticica 1967), 164–165
Esso, 102, 103
Estridentismo, 12, 31, 32, 47, 205n112
Estruturação do self (Clark), 189f; and homemaking, 10, 43; origins of, 186; and regression, 31, 185; sessions of, 187–188, 190; and subject-object relations, 22, 181, 191
Ewen, Stuart, 18
Excélsior (newspaper), 78
Experimental Workshop, 53, 213n31
expressionism, 37

fascination, 2, 7–9, 41, 85, 101, 118. *See also* enchantment
Fèdida, Pierre, 181, 186
Ferreira, Gina, 186, 247n92, 248n102
Ferreira, Glória, 16–17
Fiaminghi, Hermelindo, 109, 221–222n3, 242n22
Figueiredo, Luciano, 245n56
Figuereido, Wilson, 93
film: and attraction, 7; Benjamin on, 54; and *Blanco*, 144, 145–146, 148–150; and Clark's work, 188; history of, 201n53; and language, 137; Novo on, 218n75; and Pape's work, 169; Paz on, 37, 120, 133; and Siqueiros's work, 40, 45, 48, 50, 59, 62–63. *See also* cinema
Folgarait, Leonard, 67
Form-Inform, 161
Fósforos de Brazil, 169
Foster, Hal, 195n4
Foundation and Manifesto of Futurism (Marinetti 1909), 27
found objects, 176, 196n10
framing, 43, 154, 157
Frente a frente magazine, 66–67, 217n63
Freyre, Gilberto, 34
Fuentes, Carlos, 149
"Full-Emptiness, The" (Clark 1960), 182
functionalism, 8, 22, 167–168
functionalist architecture, 130
futurism, 27, 31, 148, 203–204n91

Gabara, Esther, 228n82
Gago, Verónica, 25–26
Galáxias (H. de Campos 1984), 144
Galbraith, John Kenneth, 20
Galería Universitaria Aristos, 40
Gaos, José, 42
García, Héctor, 130
García Canclini, Néstor, 3, 18–19, 20–21, 26, 152, 202n65
García Lorca, Federico, 132
García Ponce, Juan, 13
Gassner, Hubertus, 30
Gego, 154, 240n8
Gestalt theory, 181, 246n75
"Gesture of Communication, The" (class, Clark at the Sorbonne), 186
Gimferrer, Pere, 122, 150
Goeritz, Mathias, 39–40, 133, 208n137
Gomringer, Eugen, 228n80
Gonzalez, Mike, 97
gráfica popular, 56–57
Graham, Dan, 241n11
Greeley, Robin, 70–71
Groddeck, 246n76
Gropius, Walter, 240n7
Grünewald, José Lino, 108
Grupo Frente, 156, 165, 169

Grupo Internacional de Artistas Plásticos, 62
Guadalupe Posada, José, 56–57
Guattari, Félix, 246n76
Guibert, Rita, 142
Gullar, Ferreira: and Clark's work, 247n92; and concrete poetry, 98; on concretism/neoconcretism split, 221n2; and Gestalt theory, 246n75; and "Manifesto neoconcreto," 93–94; Martins on, 207n130; on neoconcretism, 100; and nonobject theory, 38, 43, 154, 162, 181; on São Paulo Biennial, 16; on Schwitters, 176; on Taeuber, 240n7

Hamilton, Richard, 224–225n39
Hanover Dada, 176
Hansen, Mark, 99
Heartfield, John, 67, 96, 217n63, 224–225n39
Hegel, Georg Wilhelm Friedrich, 92, 160, 197n15
Hegelian dialectics, 233n44
Heidegger, Martin, 42, 121, 127–129, 130–131, 198–199n31, 233n46
Henderson, Nigel, 224–225n39
Hennings, Emmy, 30
Herkenhoff, Paulo, 178, 195–196n6, 239n1
Herrigel, Eugen, 181
Hesse, Eva, 154, 240n8
Hidalgo y Costilla, Miguel, 31
Hirschman, Albert O., 199n35
"hombre hambre hembra" (Pignatari 1957), 103–104, 104f
homemaking: and aesthetics, 2; and art, 154; and Bauhaus, 240n6; and Clark's legacy, 153; and experimental art, 9–10; and gender, 154; and political readings of Clark's work, 177; and relationship to objects, 43
Homes for America (Graham 1966–1967), 241n11
Horkheimer, Max, 20, 21, 22
"House of Presence, The" (Paz), 128
Huelsenbeck, Richard, 205n108
Hullot-Kentor, Robert, 197n24, 198–199n31
Huneeus, Cristián, 87
Hurlburt, Laurance P., 60–61
Husserl, Edmund, 150–151

Ibáñez, José Luis, 149
import-substitution industrialization, 2, 10–11, 12, 90, 199n35
industrial design, 33–34, 109, 161–162, 164
Instituto de Arte Contemporânea do Museu de Arte de São Paulo (IAC/MASP), 17, 161
instrumentalization, 134–135
interactivity, 172
introjection, 177–178
Invenção magazine, 109, 115
Italian futurism, 27, 31

Jackson, K. David, 207n133, 221n1
Jacoby, Roberto, 194, 249n2
Jakobson, Roman, 101, 105
Jameson, Fredric, 7–8, 41, 203n80
Janco, Marcel, 30
Jardim, Reynaldo, 93, 169
Jardines del Pedregal, 13, 130
Jhally, Sut, 174–175
Jiménez, Juan Ramón, 132
jitanjáforas (Reyes), 105
Jodorowsky, Alejandro, 87
John Reed Club, 55
Jornal do Brasil, 92–96, 224n27, 243n33, 244n47
Joyce, James, 27–28, 89, 111, 132, 204n95, 229n87
"Juventud" (Paz 1968), 141

Karatani, Kojin, 25
Kaufman, Robert, 101
Kay, Ronald, 87
Kiaer, Christina, 28, 29–30, 46, 77
klangfarbenmelodie (Webern), 84

Klaxon magazine, 106
Klee, Paul, 191, 248n106
Klein, Melanie, 246n76
Klimovsky, León, 59
Klutsis, Gustav, 28, 46, 57–58, 67, 217n63
Koch, Gertrude, 86
Kracauer, Siegfried, 4
Kubitschek, Juscelino, 15, 90, 93, 161

"La exclamación" (Paz), 126
Lafer, Celso, 132
La hija de Rapaccini (Paz), 150
"La imagen" (Paz), 127
Laing, R. D., 246n76
La Jornada, 141
La marcha de la humanidad en la tierra y hacia el cosmos (Siqueiros 1964–1971), 67, 80–81
Lamartine, Alphonse de, 92
Lambert, Jean-Clarence, 121
language: of abstraction, 240n7; and advertising, 85; and *antropofagia*, 202n76; and authoritarianism, 33; and *Blanco*, 143–145, 148, 237n84; and Brazilian concrete poetry, 9, 86; and concrete poetry, 39, 89, 90–92, 99, 104, 116–118; and concrete poets, 97–98, 101; and *Discos visuales*, 152; and distraction, 78–79; and Estridentismo, 32; and *Estruturação do self*, 187–188; Jakobson on, 105; Paz on, 37, 42, 120–121, 128–129, 131–136, 233n44; and Paz's work, 234–235n59; Pignatari on, 102–103; and Pignatari's work, 111–115; and regression, 23, 184; Reyes on, 232–233n43; and syntax, 27–28; and technology, 151
"La nueva analogía: poesía y tecnología" (Paz [1967] 1973), 119, 126, 233n44
La otra voz (Paz 1990), 132
La prose du Transsibérien et de la petite Jehanne de France (Cendrars 1913), 27, 148
la ruptura, 13–14
Las batallas en el desierto (Pacheco 2013), 231n17
Las fechas en la historia de México o el derecho a la cultura (Siqueiros 1952–1956), 69, 79
La vuelta al día en ochenta mundos (Cortázar 1967), 143
Lázaro, Enrique, 59
Le Corbusier, 130
Lectures (Husserl), 150
Ledesma, Eduardo, 205n114, 227n77
Léger, Fernand, 155
Lehman, Harold, 52–54
Leirner, Adolpho, 242n22
Libertad bajo palabra (Paz 1935–1957), 123, 124–125
Lihn, Enrique, 87
"Linguistics and Poetics" (Jakobson 1958), 105
Lispector, Clarice, 239n1
Lissitzky, El, 28–29, 46, 57–58, 96–97, 156, 224–225n39
"Literatura e subdesenvolvimento" (Candido), 97
Livro da arquitetura (Pape), 169
Livro da criação (Pape), 169
Livro do tempo (Pape), 169
López, Nacho, 130
López Mateos, Adolfo, 200n42
Los hijos del limo (Paz 1974), 148
Los olvidados (Buñuel 1950), 122
"Los signos en rotación" (Paz 1965): and *Blanco*, 142, 237n82; and consumer culture, 37, 119; publication of, 230n2; and structuralism, 233n46; and technology, 126–127, 131
"Los vehiculos de la pintura dialectico-subversiva" (Siqueiros 1932), 55–56
Lua (Dillon 1959–1960), 98
Lukács, Georg, 134
lyric poetry, 9, 42, 118, 120

Macedo, Walter, 161
Macel, Christine, 181
Machado, Antonio, 132

Machado, Duda, 245n56
Maldonado, Tomás, 206n122
Mallarmé, Stéphane: H. de Campos on, 92, 95, 150, 223–224n24, 224n26; and newspaper form, 237n86; Paz on, 135–136, 239n117, 248n106; *Un coup de dés* (1897), 89, 115, 143; and word diffraction, 88
Mammì, Lorenzo, 100
Manchete magazine, 93
"Manifesto neoconcreto," 93–94, 169. *See also* neoconcretism
Manuscritos (arts magazine), 87
Maples Arce, Manuel: "*Actual* no. 1" (1921), 47; and Estridentismo, 31–32
Maquetes para interior (Clark 1955), 156, 156f
Marcuse, Herbert, 20, 174, 246n76
Maria, Pietro, 17, 161
Marinetti, Filippo, 27, 28, 31, 203–204n91
marketing, 17–18, 32, 90
Martins, Rubem de Freitas, 109, 161
Martins, Sérgio B., 38, 162, 166–167, 207n130, 242n18, 246n75
Marx, Karl: on alienation, 167; on commodity fetishism, 22, 209n10; on humanized object, 24–25; on labor, 195n1; on private property, 195n3; on production, 1
Máscaras sensoriais (Clark), 183
masculinity, 209n5
Masiello, Francine, 19, 202n66
mass media: Benjamin on, 225n51; in Brazil, 15–16, 200–201n50; and Brazilian poetics, 95; Brazilian poetics of, 95–96; and concrete poetry, 90, 118; and distraction, 78; and language, 132–133; and *Noigandres* poets, 112; Paz on, 138; Paz's appropriation of, 42; Paz's interest in, 119, 121, 136, 152; rhythm of, 142; and Siqueiros's work, 80; visual aspects of, 102
mass publics, 48, 50, 54, 55–57, 69
Mata, Rodolfo, 39
materialism, 23, 191
mathematics, 99–100
Mauss, Marcel, 24
Mavignier, Almir, 162, 247n89
Mayakovsky, Vladimir, 28, 46, 96–97
McLuhan, Marshall, 136
Médici, Emílio, 115, 199n37
Mello e Souza, Cláudio, 93
Memória do corpo (Carneiro 1984), 188
Memórias sentimentais de João Miramar (Andrade 1924), 95, 224n35
Merleau-Ponty, Maurice, 160, 181, 246n75
Mesmer, Franz Anton, 7, 197n23
Metinides, Enrique, 130
Mexican Folkways, 56–57
Mexican miracle, 19, 70, 121–122, 130, 199–200n41, 200nn42–43, 231n11
Mexican muralism: and advertising, 45; and economic growth, 12; and education, 70; Paz's interest in, 40; and São Paulo Biennial, 16; and Siqueiros, 36, 80, 210–211n18; Siqueiros on, 81; and social realism, 13–14
Mexican School, 14
Mexico City: and industrialization, 121–122; in Paz's poems, 125–126; and postwar infrastructural changes, 13; and urbanization, 129–130
micropolitics, 177
Miller, Daniel, 3, 174, 198n29
Milliet, Sérgio, 16
Milner, Marion, 182–184, 185
mimetics, 98
Mitin de fábrica (Siqueiros 1932), 50
Mitin en la calle (Siqueiros 1932), 50
Mitin obrero (Siqueiros 1932), 48–49, 51, 213n30
Mixcoac, 122, 231n12
modernismo, 96
modernist grid, 39, 170–171, 244–245n51, 244n49
modernist poetry, 89–90, 95
Moholy-Nagy, László, 243n32
Mondrian, Piet, 100, 244–245n51
montage, 62, 148–149

Montaldo, Graciela, 4
Morais, Frederico, 247n92
Moreno, Julio, 12
"Movimiento" (Paz), 126
Moya, Rodrigo, 130
Müller, Ulrike, 10, 240n6
Multifamiliar Miguel Alemán (housing project, Pani), 129–130
Museo de Arte Moderno, 13, 102
Museo de Arte Moderno de Bogotá, 102
Museo Experimental El Eco, 39; and Goeritz, 133
Museo Nacional de Antropología, 13
Museu de Arte Moderna (MAM), 16, 164
Museu de Arte Moderna de São Paulo (MASP), 15, 16, 17, 161

Nabuco, Joaquim, 93
Name, Daniela, 33–34, 90, 94, 168–169, 171
National Electricians' Union, 62
Navilouca, 245n56
Necker cube, 159
neoconcrete aesthetics, 165, 207–208n133
"Neoconcrete Manifesto" (1957), 169
neoconcretism: and artist as proposer, 165; and Clark's work, 166, 177; and concretism, 38–39, 161–162, 207nn131–133; constructivist roots of, 100; and Gestalt theory, 181, 246n75; and *Jornal do Brasil*, 92–94; and language, 97; and nonobject theory, 180; and object relations theory, 154, 179; and Pape's work, 169, 171; and politics, 178; rise of, 221n2; and Schwitters's work, 176. *See also* "Manifesto neoconcreto"; *specific artists*
neoliberalism, 25–26, 193
neon light: and Brazilian concrete poets, 7; and concrete poetry, 84; and "eis os amantes," 89; function of, 101; in Paz's poems, 125–126; and *Poetamenos*, 86; Siqueiros on, 80
Neto, João Cabral de Melo, 239n1
Neto, Torquato, 245n56
New Economic Policy (1921–c. 1928), 28, 67
new objectivity, 164–166
newspapers: and avant-garde artists, 96; and *Blanco*, 143, 144; and Chateaubriand, 15; and concrete poetry, 90–91, 95, 118; and criticism, 17; and *El Quebrantahuesos*, 87; Freyre's interest in, 34; imitation of, 7; and Mallarmé, 237n86; Pignatari on, 103, 112; and *Retrato de la burguesía*, 66; and Rojo, 141; and "stèle pour vivre 3," 115–116; and universal intercommunicability, 92
New York Dada magazine, 31
Niemeyer, Oscar, 17, 158, 241n12
Niño en vientre de concreto (García 1952), 130
"Noche en claro" (Paz), 124
Nogueira Lima, Maurício, 221–222n3, 242n22
Noigandres magazine, 103, 109
Noigandres poets, 90, 112
nostalgia for the body, 172
Nova figuração, 166
Nova objetividade brasileira (1967), 164
Novo, Salvador, 205n116, 218n75
Nueve pintores mexicanos (Garcia Ponce 1968), 13
Nuevo emblema universitario (Siqueiros 1952–1956), 69, 79

objectification, 174–175, 179, 181
object relations theory, 181, 182
objetos relacionais (Clark). *See* relational objects
"O caminho percorrido" (Andrade 1944), 96
O Cruzeiro, 15
O dentro é o fora (Clark 1963), 247n91
O escravo nos anúncios de jornais brasileiros do século XIX (Freyre 1963), 34
O Estado de São Paulo newspaper, 96

Office of the Coordinator of Inter-American Affairs (OCIAA), 14, 102
O'Gorman, Juan, 70, 72f, 75
Oiticica, Hélio, 245n56; and Clark's correspondence, 173; on Clark's work, 191; and *delírio ambulatório*, 196n10; and *delirium ambulatorium*, 3; as founding figure, 162; as neoconcrete artist, 38; on new objectivity, 164–166
Olvera Street, Los Angeles, 52, 54
One-Way Street (Benjamin 2016), 27, 85
Ong, Walter J., 136
"O objeto, o metodo e a pratica" (Clark), 187
Organization of American States (OAS), 102
"Origin of the Work of Art, The" (Heidegger 1950), 128–129
Orozco, José Clemente, 49, 70, 211n20, 215–216n56
Ortega, Julio, 144
Ovid, 117

Pacheco, José Emilio, 231n17
Paiva, Claudio, 14
Palatnik, Abraham, 161–162, 247n89
Panagia, Davide, 177
Pani, Mario, 13, 130
Pape, Lygia, 94, 109, 155, 168, 169–171
paradox, 127
Parque Ibirapuera, 17
Parra, Catalina, 87, 224–225n39
Parra, Nicanor, 87
"Pasaje" (Paz 1968), 141
Paz, Octavio: on analogy, 233n44; on *Blanco*, 144, 149, 150; on cinema and poetry, 148; on concrete poetry, 133–134; on consumer culture, 42; on distraction, 78; on Duchamp, 141; and experimental poems, 152; and foreign sojourns, 230n4; and H. de Campos, 39, 208n135; influences of, 232n22, 233n43; and language, 234–235n59; on language, 119–120, 131–132; on *la ruptura*, 13; legacy of, 27; and market capitalism, 230–231n9; and mass media, 138; on modernity, 9; as Nobel laureate, 36; on objects animated, 248n106; on prose, 135; on reading speed, 142; and regression, 23; on Siqueiros, 40, 213n31; and structuralism, 233n46; and technology, 230n1, 230n7; on technology, 130–131, 136; on television, 151; on world image, 127–128; on writing and the market, 37
Pedra e ar (Clark 1966), 174, 175f
Pedrosa, Mário: on artist as educator, 165; on artistic genius, 184–185; on *Bichos*, 163; and Brazilian art criticism, 16–17; and Clark, 247n92; on concrete/neoconcrete art, 207n131; and concretism, 226n62; and Gestalt theory, 181, 246n75; on introjection, 178; and political commitment, 166–167; on science and the arts, 99–100, 234n49
Penteado, Yolanda, 16
Pereira dos Santos, Nelson, 169
Péret, Benjamin, 124
Pérez-Oramas, Luis, 155
Perloff, Marjorie, 83, 113
Perrone, Charles, 116, 225n41, 228n83, 229n99
Pertierra, Anna Cristina, 3–4, 9–10
phenomenology, 150–151, 181
photography: Benjamin on, 54–55, 225–226n51; and *Ejercicio plástico* (Siqueiros 1933), 61–62; and Pape's work, 169; and Siqueiros, 40, 45, 57–58; Siqueiros on, 48, 59–60
Pignatari, Décio: and advertising, 41, 109; "beba coca cola" (1957), 105–108; and concrete movement, 161; "disenformio" (1963), 109; "Graphic Arts and the Other Arts," 95; "hombre hambre hembra" (1957), 103–104; on language, 102–103, 104; manifesto of, 89, 90; and *Navilouca*, 245n56; on *produssumo*, 23–24; and rejection of

social realism, 206n122; and *salto participante*, 111–112; *Semiótica da arte e da arquitetura* (2004), 108; “stèle pour vivre 3” (1974), 115–116; and *suplemento dominical*, 224n27; and tmesis, 118; and Ulm School of Design, 228n80
Pimentel, Luiz Otávio Chacal, 245n56
Pinochet, Augusto, 87
Piraquê, 170–171
Plano de Metas, 90
Planos em superfície modulada (Clark), 158–159
plástica fílmica, 63
Plural, 141
“Poema circulatorio (para la desorientacion general)” (Paz), 126
poema/processo, 97
Poemas luz (Pape), 169
Poemas objeto (Pape 1956–1957), 169
“poesia concreta” (A. de Campos 1955), 221n1
Poesía concreta internacional (1966 Goeritz exhibition), 40, 133
Poesía en voz alta (Arreola 1956), 149–150
“Poesia y poema” (Paz), 134
Poetamenos (A. de Campos 1953), 221–222n3, 221nn1–2; bright colors of, 92; and Campos’s intent, 83; form of, 87; and mimetic appropriation, 86; and neon light, 7, 41; and Paz’s poetry, 126; and tmesis, 118
Poetry, Language, Thought (Heidegger), 128–129
politics: and Chateaubriand, 15; and Clark’s work, 177–178, 190–191; and neoconcretism, 162; and neoliberalism, 25–26; of representation, 100; of Siqueiros and Oiticica, 166; Siqueiros on, 47; Siqueiros’s abandonment of, 67, 81; and Siqueiros’s work, 45, 70; Süssekind on, 32–33
Pollock, Jackson, 53
Pop América: Contesting Freedom, 1965–1975 (exhibition, 2018), 228n82
pop artists, 96
Popova, Lyubov, 154
Porfirian society, 11–12
Portilla, Miguel León, 142
Portinari, Cândido, 37, 100
Portrait of the Artist as a Young Man (Joyce 1916), 111
posters, 47
Pound, Ezra, 89, 132
Practice of Everyday Life (Certeau 1984), 21–23, 86
Price, Rachel, 89, 100–101
Prieto, Miguel, 62
Prisms (Adorno 1967), 8
private property, 1, 4, 24–25, 195n1, 195n3
production: of art under capitalism, 45–46; and Clark’s work, 155, 158, 162–164, 172–173; and commodity capitalism, 179; and commodity fetishism, 22; and concrete poets, 90, 97; and concretism, 226n62; and concretism/neoconcretism split, 100; and constructivism, 28–29, 33–34; and consumption, 1, 21, 25, 194, 195n3, 228n86; dialectics of, 23–24, 35–36; in free-market economies, 18; industrial modes of, 50; and neoconcretism, 38; Oiticica on, 165; and reception, 37, 210–211n18; and reproducibility, 55–57; and technology, 68; and war, 199n35
produssumo, 23–24
Programa de Metas, 15
Proun Room (Lissitzky 1923), 156
“Psiu!” (A. de Campos 1966), 91, 91f
psychoanalysis, 181, 186, 247n92
psychology, 155, 181, 246n75
“Publicidade o texto vivo” (Pignatari), 102
Public Space/Two Audiences (Graham 1976), 241n11
Pujol, Antonio, 62
pyroxylin (Duco), 62

Quebra da moldura (Clark 1954), 156, 157f
Querida magazine, 158, 241n13
"Question Concerning Technology, The" (Heidegger), 128
¡Que Viva México! (Eisenstein [1931] 1979), 50, 51f
Quiroga, José, 230n1

Radicant (Bourriaud 2009), 9
Rádio Jornal do Brasil, 93
Ramos, Óscar, 245n56
Randall, Laura, 193, 195n5
Ray, Man, 31
Rayuela (Cortázar 1963), 143
Read, Herbert, 184
regression: and ambiguity, 196n7; and Cabaret Voltaire, 30–31; and Clark's work, 185–186, 187; and fascination, 41; and materialism, 23; and symbolism, 247n87
relational objects, 191; and arts and crafts, 172; and Clark's home, 153; Clark's vision of, 173–174; and *Estruturação do self*, 187–188; and homemaking, 43; inspiration for, 175–176; political dimensions of, 177–178; and regression, 23; and subjects, 22; and thinghood, 179
Renau, Josep, 62, 67
réplica, 9, 42, 120, 193
Representación histórica de la cultura (O'Gorman 1952), 72f
reproducibility: Benjamin on, 5, 41, 54–55, 60, 76, 196–197n12, 225–226n51; Paz on, 37; Siqueiros on, 56–57
Retrato de la burguesía (Siqueiros et al. 1939–1940), 62–63, 64f, 65–67, 65f, 66f, 215–216n56
Reyes, Alfonso, 42, 105, 121, 127, 134, 232–233n43
Richter, Gerhard, 224–225n39
Rivera, Diego: and Ciudad Universitaria, 70; murals of, 52, 75, 76, 215–216n56; on popular graphic arts, 56–57; US sojourn of, 49, 211n20
Rocha, Glauber, 169
Rochfort, Desmond, 58
Rockefeller, Nelson, 14
Rodchenko, Aleksandr, 28, 29–30, 111, 154, 204n100, 205n109, 228n86
Rodríguez, Fernando, 237n84
Rodríguez Luna, Antonio, 62
Rodríguez Monegal, Emir, 230n4, 233n46
Rojo, Vicente: and *Blanco*, 149, 150; and *Discos visuales*, 139–141; and Paz, 39, 151; and *Poesía concreta internacional*, 40, 133
"Role of Illusion in Symbol Formation, The" (Milner 1952), 184
Rolnik, Suely, 153, 177, 180, 190
Rosa, Guimarães, 239n1
Rosenquist, James, 109
Rossel de la Lama, Guillermo, 73, 219n82
Ruiz Cortines, Adolfo, 122
Ruscha, Edward, 109
Russian constructivists, 28, 154, 170–171, 245n53. *See also* constructivism; *specific artists*

Sacilotto, Luiz, 163, 221–222n3, 242n22
Sala de Arte Público Siqueiros, 71
"Salamandra" (Paz), 125
Salamandra (Paz 1958–1961), 124–125, 232n27
Saldana-Portillo, María Josefina, 209n5
Salomão, Jorge, 245n56
Salomão, Waly, 245n56
Salón Intercol de Artistas Jóvenes, 102
salto participante, 7, 112
Santí, Enrico Mario, 142, 146
São Paulo (1944), 14
São Paulo Biennial, 16, 170, 240n7, 241n13
Sapir, Michel, 186–187
Sardinhas Coqueiro, 168
Sartre, Jean-Paul, 174
Schendel, Mira, 154, 240n8
Scherer García, Julio, 78

School of Design in Chicago, 243n32
Schor, Juliet, 3, 20–21
Schwarz, Roberto, 41
Schwitters, Kurt, 96, 176, 224–225n39
sculpto-murals, 76, 77
Sears, Roebuck and Company, 12
Secretaría de Educación Pública, 52, 70
Semana de Arte Moderna, 12, 106
Semiótica da arte e da arquitetura (Pignatari 2004), 108
Serpa, Ivan, 247n89
Shellhorse, Adam Joseph, 202n76, 229n99
Shtromberg, Elena, 201n51
Silva, Nelson do Valle, 15, 16
Silveira, Nise da, 184
simultaneism, 148
Sinclair, John, 3, 9–10
Siqueiros, David Alfaro, 51f; on art and the market, 37, 217n70; and arts integration movement, 39–40; on billboard muralism, 71; Cardoza y Aragón on, 208n1; and Ciudad Universitaria, 70; on collaboration, 159; and commercialism, 44–47; on distraction, 77–78; and Experimental Workshop, 213n31; and Hollywood influence, 48–53, 212n23; legacy of, 27; on muralism's history, 67–69; and outdoor painting, 210–211n18, 213–214n34; and photography, 57, 58, 59–60, 216n57; on public art, 73; and regression, 23; on reproducibility, 55–56, 214n45; and *Retrato de la burguesía*, 62–67; on sculptural painting, 76; and Sindicato de Electricistas, 216n60; and spectatorship, 36, 54; on spectatorship, 74–75; and synthetic paint, 216n59; techniques used by, 210n17; and US sojourn, 211–212n21, 211n20, 213n30, 214–215n46; and *Velocidad* (1953), 219n82; writings of, 166, 210nn15–16. *See also specific works*
Small, Irene V., 180
Sobrinho, Francisco Matarazzo, 16
socialism, 28, 29, 211n20
social realism, 13, 36
Sodré, Niomar Moniz, 16
Solt, Mary Ellen, 83, 104
Sorensen, Diana, 73, 94
Soviet constructivists. *See* Russian constructivists
Spanish Civil War, 62, 140
Spanudis, Theon, 94
spatial envelopes, 215–216n56
spectatorship: and moving publics, 74–76; and *Retrato de la burguesía*, 63; Siqueiros on, 59–60, 61; Siqueiros's interest in, 36, 54, 216n61
Spilimbergo, Lino, 59
spirituality, 182
Spratling, William, 51f
status models, 20
"stèle pour vivre 3" (Pignatari 1962), 115–116, 115f
Stepanova, Varvara, 154
Structural Constellations (Alber), 159
structuralism, 20–21, 233n46
subjectification, 23, 25–26, 180–181, 185, 190–191, 241n11
Superfície modulada (Clark 1955), 158, 159, 241n12
suplemento dominical, 92–96, 224n27, 244n47
surrealism, 233n46
Suspensions of Perception (Crary 1999), 6
Süssekind, Flora, 32–33, 90–91, 200–201n50
symbolism, 176, 178–179, 184, 188, 247n87

Taeuber, Sophie, 10, 31, 154, 240n7, 244–245n51
Taller de Gráfica Popular, 63
Tamayo, Rufino, 13
Tatlin, Vladimir, 154
Taussig, Michael: on alienation, 167; on development, 34; on gift as object of exchange, 24; on identities, 190; on

mimetics, 3, 84, 85–86, 221–222n3, 227n75; reading Benjamin, 23; on thinghood's dominance, 179
technology: and aesthetics, 55; and art, 68; and Brazilian dictatorship, 205–206n119; and concrete poetry, 89–91; and Dada, 205n108; and distraction, 84; and environment, 100; Paz on, 119–120, 127–128, 129, 131, 136, 151, 233n46; in Paz's poems, 126; and Paz's work, 230n7; Rodchenko on, 228n86
Televisa, 138, 151
television: and advertising, 102; and *Ballet Neoconcreto*, 169; in Brazil, 15–16, 200–201n50, 201n51, 205–206n119; and Brazilian concrete poets, 208n140, 223n20; and concrete poetry, 90–91; and fascination, 8; and language, 120, 137; in Mexico, 70, 75; Paz on, 136, 138, 152; and print journalism, 94
Theory of the Leisure Class (Veblen 1899), 3
tmesis, 116, 117–118
Topopoemas (Paz 1967), 39, 42, 119, 140
"To Rediscover the Meaning of Our Routine Gestures" (Clark), 175–176
Torok, Maria, 246n76
Torre Latinoamericana, 130
Transblanco (Paz and H. de Campos 1986), 132–133
Trans World Airlines (TWA), 137, 138f, 139
Treece, David, 97
Tropicália movement, 24, 208n140
TV Globo, 15
TV Tupi, 15, 201n51
typography, 96–97
Tzara, Tristan, 30

Ulm School of Design, 33, 100, 109, 228n80
Último round (Cortázar 1969), 143
Ulysses (Joyce 1922), 27–28
Un coup de dés (Mallarmé 1897), 89, 92, 95, 115, 135–136, 143, 223–224n24
Unidades (Clark), 158–159
Unidad Habitacional Adolfo López Mateos (Pani), 130
United States: and African Americans, 52; and Brazil, 14; interventionist policies of, 12; and Latin American development, 35; and Mexican muralists, 49–50, 211n20; and suburban expansion, 241n11
Universidad Autónoma de México (UNAM), 219n81; and Ciudad Universitaria, 13, 130
urbanism, 39
Urueta, Chano, 51f
US imperialism, 211n20

Valéry, Paul, 105
van Doesburg, Theo, 38, 100, 221n1
Vargas, Getúlio, 15
Vasconcelos, José, 70
Vázquez, Rolando, 230n7
Veblen, Thorstein, 3, 20, 198n27; Adorno's critique of, 8
"Vehicles of Dialectical-Subversive Painting, The" (Siqueiros 1932), 166
Velocidad (Siqueiros 1953), 69, 73–76, 74f, 75f, 79, 219n82
Veloso, Caetano, 245n56
Venice Biennale, 241n11
Venice Biennale (1968), 183
"Verdehalago" (Brull), 105
Veríssimo, José, 93
Veshch'/Gegenstand/Objet, 28
vibratory body, 190
Vida Americana (Siqueiros 1921), 50
Vidas secas (Pereira dos Santos), 169
Vidrieras astilladas (Süssekind 1985), 32
Vieira, Mary, 162
"Viento entero" (Paz), 126
Violão de Rua poets, 97
Virilio, Paul, 6
"Visitas" (Paz), 122–123

"Vrindaban" (Paz), 126
Vrindaban (Paz 1966), 137
Vuelta (Paz-founded literary magazine), 39, 126, 232n36

Wanderley, Lula, 186, 247n92
Warhol, Andy, 109
Webern, Anton, 84
Weissmann, Franz, 94
Wells, H. G., 111, 229n87
Williams, Bruce, 221n1
Williams, Gareth, 19
Winnicott, Donald, 181, 247n76
Wittgenstein, Ludwig, 159
Wollner, Alexandre, 109, 161, 165, 168
World Goes Pop, The (exhibition, 2015), 228n82

Yúdice, George, 3, 19–20, 196n8

Zen and the Art of Archery (Herrigel 1948), 181–182
Zona Rosa, 13, 14
Zurián, Tomás, 213n29
Zurich Dada, 205n108, 240n7